Religious Life
in Poland

Religious Life in Poland

History, Diversity and Modern Issues

CHRISTOPHER GARBOWSKI

McFarland & Company, Inc., Publishers

Jefferson, North Carolina

Library of Congress Cataloguing-in-Publication Data

Garbowski, Christopher.
    Religious life in Poland : history, diversity, and modern
issues / Christopher Garbowski.
        p.   cm.
    Includes bibliographical references and index.

    ISBN 978-0-7864-7589-6 (softcover : acid free paper) ∞
    ISBN 978-1-4766-1245-4 (ebook)

    1. Poland—Religion.   2. Poland—Religious
life and customs.   I. Title.
    BL980.P6G37 2014
    200.9438—dc23   2013050523

British Library cataloguing data are available

Front cover: colorful textiles (iStockphoto/Thinkstock)

Manufactured in the United States of America

*McFarland & Company, Inc., Publishers
    Box 611, Jefferson, North Carolina 28640
    www.mcfarlandpub.com*

To Monika, Marcin and Jacek

Table of Contents

Preface and Acknowledgments

The idea for this book originated from my lectures on religion in Poland for foreign exchange students at Maria Curie-Skłodowska University in Lublin. Among the points I would stress is that religion in Poland, especially from a historical perspective, goes beyond Catholicism—something of which most students had only a vague notion. Preparing for the lecture led to the realization that although a surprising number of books were published on the topic, something was missing, and another book could fill a significant gap.

Earlier books tend to treat specific questions of religion in Poland. Among them is Jerzy Kłoczowski's historical overview *A History of Polish Christianity* (2000), covering the dominant tradition effectively until 1989, the year the Communist regime ended, while a number of books deal with Jews in Poland—their religious life coming to the fore especially in regard to the phenomenon of Hasidism. The history of Protestant groups has also received more extensive attention of late (e.g., Peter J. Klassen's *Mennonites in Early Modern Poland and Prussia*, 2009). Several books look at vital issues of religion in contemporary Poland, such as religion and identity in Genevieve Zubrzycki's *The Crosses of Auschwitz* (2006) or religion and the ethic of solidarity in Gerald Beyer's *Recovering Solidarity* (2010). Quite recently Brian Porter-Szücs published his penetrating study *Faith and Fatherland: Catholicism, Modernity and Poland* (2011) which focuses on Catholic discourse in the country from the late eighteenth century to the present. These books and numerous others add substantially to the knowledge of religion in Poland, with the caveat, however, that the knowledge is scattered and it remains difficult to create an overall picture from them.

Moreover, the topic is hardly exhausted; on the one hand, it is so rich, and on the other, it remains dynamic and in motion. For instance, for a time debates on religion in Poland became quite intense after the Smoleńsk airplane tragedy of April 10, 2010, in which then-president Lech Kaczyński and ninety-five passengers died. The event occurred after the earlier books were published or had gone to print; its impact on religion in the country is worthy of a separate study.

I mention the above books because my aim is not to provide an encyclopedia of religion in the country. Such a work would be static: religion in Poland, a country with more than thirty-five million inhabitants and a tumultuous history, is anything but. And so at least to some extent I wish to convey a degree of the academic discussion on the topic, which in turn gives an indication of its vibrancy. In a related manner, one of the elements in the authorship of this book that gives me no small pleasure is to partially present the alternative perspective of Polish scholarship on the subject of religion in their country. To say that Polish literature has a somewhat different perspective than scholarship on the topic from abroad is a truism. The difference derives by and large from the questions the scholars ask; different issues interest Polish scholars than their colleagues abroad.

Thus the main purpose of the present book is to provide an accessible scholarly overview of religion in Poland, including a substantial historical introduction followed by a discussion of the major contemporary issues which are affected by or else affect religion itself. Within this goal, my book aims to impart to the reader the rich variety of religious life in the country, since I believe this is not the impression many have regarding religion in Poland. Considering the dynamic role that religion, especially Catholicism, has played— a role that has rightly garnered much international attention for its epochal contribution to bringing down the Communist regime—and, albeit in a less dramatic fashion, continues to play in Polish society, the need for this manner of study is largely self-explanatory.

Such a multidisciplinary project would be difficult for a single scholar to complete without assistance. I am grateful to the experts who patiently discussed a number of complex issues with me, among them the Rev. Andrzej Draguła and Zbigniew Nosowski, both from the Catholic think tank "Laboratorium Więź," connected to the Warsaw Club of Catholic Intellectuals. Scholars such as Eugeniusz Sakowicz, a specialist on interfaith dialogue from the Cardinal Stefan Wyszyński University in Warsaw, and sociologist Krzysztof Kosela of the University of Warsaw graciously responded to a number of e-mails. I am also grateful to Dr. Grzegorz Kuprianowicz from Maria Curie-Skłodowska University for answering my queries on the Orthodox Christians in the country, while the Rev. Jan Sikora informed me of the concerns of Lutherans in Cieszyn. Professor Tomasz Schramm from the University of Adam Mickiewicz provided me with valuable information concerning a Polish student contending with antireligious academic prejudices in a Belgian university. Discussing my book with British journalist Jonathan Luxmoore who specializes in religion in Eastern Europe helped me gain an outside view on my project. Conducting a panel on challenges facing religion in Poland during the 2012 annual conference of the Polish Institute of Arts and Sciences of America in Boston also allowed me to discuss numerous issues with experts and other concerned participants. I might add that as someone who has lived and worked in Poland for several decades, I have also had the opportunity to participate in a number of the events discussed in the book, such as the Day of Judaism a number of times, or to listen to members of different faith communities publically speaking, quite often in Catholic churches or institutions, and expressing their concerns.

Several colleagues closer to home have read portions of the manuscript, offering me advice at various stages of its development. My university colleague, historian Robert Bubczyk, read the historical chapters and prevented me from making a number of errors, while political philosopher Jan Hudzik also read a pertinent chapter. The Rev. Alfred Wierzbicki of John Paul II Catholic University of Lublin read the epilogue, while Jacek Dąbała of the same university commented on fragments concerning religion and media. I am especially grateful to Piotr Gutowski, of John Paul II Catholic University of Lublin, and his wife Antonina, a psychologist deeply concerned in Catholic affairs and heir to the best traditions of the Catholic intelligentsia in Poland, for their careful readings of large portions of the manuscript and their subsequent advice. My wife Monika Adamczyk-Garbowska also read the manuscript a number of times and made critical suggestions that were most helpful. Needless to say, while grateful for the invaluable advice from many people, I take responsibility for all opinions expressed in the book. Research has been generously assisted by a grant from the National Science Centre of the Polish Ministry of Higher Education for the years 2010–13. One article written on the basis of this research was published in the fourth issue of the 2011 volume of *The Polish Review*, entitled "The Analogical Imagination and the Past and Present of Popular Religion in Poland." Portions of the material concerning the history of Hasidism were adapted from my article "Ba'al Shem Tov: 'The Holy Epistle,'" published in *Milestone Documents in World Religions: Exploring Traditions of Faith Through Primary Sources*, ed. David M. Fahey (Dallas: Schlager Group, 2011). Both are reprinted with permission. Unless otherwise noted, translations of Polish texts are my own.

Introduction

With the world's most secular continent on one side, and religious revival on a number of other nearby geographical fronts,[1] Poland's location on the religious map straddles radically different camps but carves a space of its own. In a number of the more deeply secularized countries of Europe, such as England, immigrants from religious countries have injected some vigor into the host society's tepid religious life[2]; similarly with Poland's return to the mainstream of the European fold—along with several other religious countries from Eastern Europe—the continent's religious "exceptionalism," as its unique secularism on a global scale has been termed, has become less pronounced. Naturally this "return" has not been without consequences for religion in the country, but in the meantime a number of observers have noted that Europe isn't so devoid of religion as had been claimed.

Perhaps the primary reason religion in Poland attracts interest is because the phenomenon is so closely associated with John Paul II. And because the country is associated so strongly with the former pope, most Europeans or Americans as well as many others connect Poles with Catholicism. Recent events like the crowds in the streets and public squares of Poland coinciding with the beatification mass of John Paul in Rome on May 1, 2011, bear this out. The even more vivid images crossing the globe a number of years back of a country in mourning after the pope's death further bolster the impression. Statistics also confirm the overwhelmingly Catholic nature of the country's population. Survey figures of approximately 90 to 95 percent have often been bandied about. Nonetheless this is hardly the whole story. For instance, at the onset of the millennium there was a year when the sportsman of the year, the recipient of the country's top literary prize and the prime minister were all Lutherans, while the country's minister of foreign affairs was Jewish.[3] Moreover, those who followed the details of the Polish pontiff's visits to his homeland could note that on various occasions he would meet with heads or representatives of the country's remaining religious minorities.

During a meeting with Polish pilgrims before their country's referendum on access to the European Union in 2004, in characteristic fashion John Paul encouraged his countrymen to accept accession with the slogan, "From the Union of Lublin to the European Union." The Union of Lublin the pontiff referred to had established the Polish-Lithuanian Commonwealth in the late sixteenth century: a multinational and ethnic polity with a wealth of religious diversity, initiating a period of relatively harmonious coexistence uncommon in Europe at the time. As the Polish pontiff himself said of that golden era on another occasion, "For five centuries the Polish spirit of the Jagiellonian era prevailed. This made possible the emergence of a Republic embracing many nations, many cultures, and many religions." And he added optimistically, "All Poles bear within themselves a sense of this religious and national diversity."[4]

John Paul's assessment of the Jagiellonian era might be somewhat rosy; nevertheless, he effectively encouraged Poles to see themselves as precursors of European unification, simultaneously indicating that part of the success of their integration relies on a profounder understanding of their own religious past. It is worth noting in this context that an alternative tradition to that of the Commonwealth stems from Poland's role as a bulwark of Western Christianity in the seventeenth century, defending Europe against the Ottoman Empire, or by extension when Catholics largely closed ranks to uphold the threatened national identity in the Partitions—during which the Polish state ceased to exist for over a century—a tradition closer to the nationalistic current, and one that pessimists of the religious scene in Poland claim dominates at present. The Polish pope's highlighting of the so-called Jagiellonian tradition at that juncture was quite telling. Moreover, in encouraging Poles to appreciate their pluralistic past, the Pope was by extension also praising European pluralism, both in its cultural and religious dimensions. He had already made this quite explicit in a speech to the Polish parliament in 1999, where he stated that European unity should be founded upon spiritual values built upon the "wealth and diversity of the cultures and traditions of individual nations. This must be a great European Community of the Spirit."[5]

Taking my cue from John Paul, so to speak, while providing a much-needed overview, my presentation of and reflection upon religion in Poland also underlines its historical pluralism and current variety, as well as its multiple aspects. The historical section, comprising roughly a third of the main body of the book, provides a concise, two-chapter outline of religion in Poland up until the country's entry into the European Union in 2004. Catholicism still plays a major role in the narrative and I have no wish to downplay it. With its central role extending over a millennium, even a discussion of religious diversity in Poland must refer to Catholicism as a matrix from which discussions of other pertinent religions develop. However, the book also presents a perspective only touched upon by serious studies but somewhat less known to the public abroad and which is nonetheless a key for understanding religion in the country. For instance, on account of the Holocaust, many are cognizant that a sizeable Jewish community existed in the lands of the historical Poland, but relatively few have any deeper knowledge of its rich heritage. Besides what is left of a variety of Christian traditions once imbedded in thriving communities, there also remains a minuscule Muslim community with roots going back to the Middle Ages, when it was actually the largest such community in Christian Europe. This community is significant in that while its role lay largely in bolstering the polity's military component, it was loyal to the Polish-Lithuanian Commonwealth despite the wars that were conducted with the Ottomans. Not that the need for any group to fight against coreligionists is praiseworthy, but it does proffer a salient example of a loyal European Muslim group under trying circumstances. Lest we forget, it must also be stressed that Catholicism, too, is far from monolithic. Paradoxically, a religion with a strong core seems to allow more room for experimentation without falling apart. The paradox that Rabbi Jonathan Sacks claims of monotheism in this vein is certainly true of Catholicism in Poland: "Unity leads to diversity."[6]

John Paul's slogan and remarks imply an agenda that remains quite valid in Polish society even after the country has entered the EU. Albeit largely monoethnic and overwhelmingly Catholic since the post–World War II border shifts, as well as from the loss of one of the world's largest Jewish communities to the Holocaust, as suggested above, traces of this diversity remain in the country to date: the historical coat of many colors that religion in Poland metaphorically represents is not solely a thing of the past. Moreover, the course of the modernization of the country upon entry into the European Union is far from over, but some of the current trends with regard to religion and their possible outcomes will be discussed.

More specifically, in the second part of the book a crucial transitional chapter following the comparatively general historical ones and preceding the more focused contemporary problems of the concluding chapters essentially establishes the broad foundations of contemporary religious tradition in the country and probes the trials of earlier traumatic experiences and current confrontations with dynamic political, economic and social transformations and their effect on religion—as well as vice versa—in the context of building civil society. The following chapter surveys the current religious minorities, both Christian and non–Christian, in the country. The second part of the chapter looks at the relationship between the Catholic majority and the religious minorities. Although a nationalist streak exists in Poland which cannot be ignored and affects Catholics, on the positive side many Poles are slowly becoming aware of the wealth of religious traditions that make up their past and that to some extent exist to this day. The last full-length chapter generally deals with the impact of joining the European Union on religion in Poland. Some religious practices are declining due to a variety of factors discussed, while a separate problem is the secularism that a portion of the opinion-making elite are adopting. The Catholic elite, on the other hand—as opposed to the institutional and mass Church as such—is largely divided between a liberal and what might be termed an evangelical Catholic response. The last part of this concluding chapter looks at religion in the country's public sphere. At times the public response to the Church's teaching has been quite divided. However, among the spheres where something approaching common ground has been developed is in what might broadly be called civil religion in Poland.

One of the most vivid images from Poland's post–World War II history is that of heroic striking shipyard workers attending impromptu masses in an officially atheist totalitarian state. Additionally, as Lech Wałęsa relates, "during their memorable strike in 1980, the first thing the Gdansk workers did was to fix a cross, an image of the Virgin Mary, and a portrait of John Paul II to the gates of the shipyards. They became *the symbols of victory*."[7] Although inspired to no small extent by John Paul II and predominantly Catholic, Solidarity united Poles from various ethnic and religious backgrounds. Poland's Solidarity movement of the early 1980s must rank as among the twentieth century's great movements of peaceful resistance, all the more remarkable in that in the Soviet Empire it confronted one of the most inhuman regimes in an era of unfathomable atrocities.[8]

An essential component of solidarity is trust. To some extent implicit in this book will be a nod toward the "history of trust" that Geoffrey Hosking calls for. The historian points out that the virtue of trust "is one of the most pervasive—and perhaps for that reason least noticed—aspects of social life." I agree that it is high time for this neglect to be addressed. More to the point of my study, religion involves trust, as Hosking observes, because it "expresses in symbolic and ritual form the norms and values to which members of the society attribute the highest importance."[9] In other words, if on the one hand many forces in society are centrifugal, for better and worse, religion is largely a force of cohesion, generally for the common good.

Nevertheless, no matter how one evaluates the phenomenon, religion has also been quite divisive throughout the ages. As Sacks sagaciously puts it, faith is akin to fire, "and like fire it warms but it also burns."[10] Others have put it less charitably. Naturally, the Jagiellonian tradition John Paul praises, not without its own flaws, was hardly the only one in Polish history; in this account of religion in Poland, most of the major blights are presented. Even quite recently, as the controversy in 2010 over the cross in front of the presidential palace commemorating the tragically deceased President Lech Kaczyński has demonstrated, there is evidence of divisive strains within Polish Catholicism itself, let alone in relations with other religions. In other words, the tragic lapses are not ignored in the study: the problem of trust includes studying why trust breaks down, which will also be examined in relation to religion in the country.

Finally, in the European context, Polish Catholicism in itself certainly adds to the continent's proverbial coat of many colors. This additional "color" is not necessarily welcome in Europe. As Brian Porter-Szücs puts it, "Just as it was once common to speak of a distinctive (and pathological) 'Eastern' form of nationalism, so today many commentators perceive a unique, atavistic, not quite European form of public religiosity in Poland."[11] Stereotypes similar to the one above often say more about the portion of society that holds them than about the culture they describe, and this one also significantly reflects upon part of the European elites. And at a time when the unification of Europe is experiencing unexpected difficulties, the question arises whether or not the core values behind such an attitude are themselves a hindrance to deeper integration. Moreover, one must also question whether the rights-based individualism that in practice forms the axiological foundation of contemporary European society and concentrates so heavily on diversity can of itself generate a vision fostering a genuine commonwealth. In the largely secularist public square, European elites ignore religious resources for creating a broader cultural vision of the common good to the detriment of the EU itself.

PART I

"From the Union of Lublin to the European Union": A Historical Overview

1

From the Beginnings of Christianity to the Twentieth Century

Religion in Poland Up to the Partitions

Earlier Communist Poland hosted thousands of university students from poorer socialist countries, among them a sizeable contingent of Vietnamese, some of whom ended up staying in the country. Moreover, on account of the foreign debt incurred throughout the former socialist bloc by the Vietnamese communists for "brotherly assistance" during the time of their war with the United States, a small number of Vietnamese citizens participated in contracted labor, and possibly some decided not to return to their "workers' paradise." Along with a sizeable group of more recent immigrants from their country, this community of twenty to thirty thousand forms one of the largest Vietnamese minorities in Europe, and possibly from among them—some are also Christian—come the highest number of non-monotheist citizens in Poland, now possibly augmented by a small but growing influx of Chinese. In other words, although this study will in part look at the diversity of religious traditions in historical and contemporary Poland, the binding thread for the bulk of the narrative is monotheism.

Since the following two chapters concern the historical consequences of religion, at the outset of the overview it is worth discussing briefly how monotheism possibly provides meaning for its followers, which in turn strengthens its hold on the faithful. Sociologist Rodney Stark argues that in contrast to godless religions, such as Buddhism, which place higher stock in wisdom and mystery, monotheistic religions have usually further developed a theology which guides them in principle. This has ramifications, since "theology seeks clarity, and while that is often not achieved, obscurity of expression is seen as the result of human limitations, not virtue."[1] We can add that this dynamic has likewise led to the development of the concept of human dignity of which John Paul II was so eloquent an exponent, and which is quite pertinent to any discussion of religion in Poland.

Our historical account begins not long into the second half of the tenth century when Poland through its political elite took its first steps toward becoming a Christian country. Worth pointing out is that while it is hardly possible to sort out the various historical motives when evidence is bountiful, the task increases exponentially when the sources available are few—precisely the case in that seminal moment for the history of religion in Poland when its ruler accepted Christianity. Following the dynastic politics of the Middle Ages, a mid–tenth-century prince of a fledgling but aspiring pagan nation flanked by comparatively powerful Christian states married the daughter of one of the monarchs of those states, a Bohemian princess, and subsequently accepted the dynamic religion.

Some authors understandably reduce this acceptance of Christianity in 966 to reasons of state. The author of one history of Poland presents a rather typical view: "Mieszko seems to have made a political decision to convert and to be accepted into the Christian faith.... By converting, Mieszko denied the Holy Roman Empire an excuse for conquest, since the right to military subjugation of pagans in order to convert them to Christianity would no longer be valid."[2] No doubt political pragmatism did play a role in the Polish prince's decision; whether it was the only factor, and if he had any genuine feeling for his new faith, we will simply never know; the sources hardly allow for conjecture.

At any rate, even if the above was the primary motivation for the Polish ruler's voluntary acceptance of the new faith, one momentous consequence in the context of the period is that his subjects avoided forceful conversion to Christianity, as happened to—among others—neighboring Slavs to the northwest. By all accounts acceptance of the new religion proceeded slowly and not without backsliding, even among the elite, but it went at the polity's own rate. The importance of freely accepting religion may account for the fact that, within a few centuries, among Poles were eventually found ardent defenders of the free acceptance of the faith by pagans.

What of the religion the Poles finally gave up, though not without a struggle? According to what has been pieced together on the basis of sparse evidence and conjecture from comparative religious studies, it is largely held that, in common with other Slavs, their religion was "complex, based on the worship of a hierarchy of numerous gods and idols, each one performing its own particular function."[3] Archeological remains tell us of a number of details, but not much that distinguishes the religion from numerous nature religions. Aside from some rites that are often carried out in conjunction with Catholic ones in small towns and rural areas, which will be discussed further on, not much remains today.

One contemporary Polish author bemoaning the fact that no Slavic mythology has survived accuses Christianity of destroying what was possibly a rich culture.[4] Such a hypothesis is impossible to either validate or disprove. However, it is true that the Catholicism that came to Poland was different from the one that visited the shores of England in the sixth and seventh centuries. There, Pope Gregory the Great had wisely suggested that "the idol temples of the race should by no means be destroyed, but only the idols in them," and some metaphorical temples were left standing, with works such as *Beowulf* "sprinkled with holy water," but surviving largely intact. In the intervening centuries the Catholic Church had experienced the Carolingian Renaissance and was about to undergo the Gregorian reforms that would eventually lead to the emergence of the modern state with the—remarkable in a global context—separation of religion and state, along with hardly less remarkable cultural developments such as universities and hospitals. The bold spirit of change inspired by Pope Gregory VII is encapsulated in his saying, "God did not say: 'my name is Custom.'"[5] Pagan religions could hardly compete with any of the so-called axial religions; in Poland, quite simply, Christianity was ascending, and less developed religious cultures stood little chance of long-term survival, and at this stage its proponents did not see much to be patient with in what rightly or wrongly seemed to be practices more and more bathed in superstition.

Another related point that must be made concerning Mieszko's acceptance of Christianity is the significance of the fact that he accepted it from Rome and not from Constantinople, a viable option at that time. Kievan Rus accepted Orthodox Christianity in 988, just a couple of decades after Poland accepted Catholicism. On account of the missionary efforts of St. Cyril and St. Methodius, a Slavic liturgy was developed in the ninth century in order to more effectively reach the Slavs. It was this liturgy that Kiev finally received. This might have had the advantage for the eastern Slavs of receiving a version of Christianity that seemed closer, but it meant accepting a substantially different civilization. Effectively, as can be seen by the discussion in the previous paragraph, the Poles were on their way to becoming "westernized," albeit losing a substantial part of their native culture. To some extent this can be traced at the level of popular culture to this day. As one scholar notes in her discussion of Slavonic folk music, "The area dominated by the Roman Catholic religion covers the area of 'de-Slavonisized' music, whereas the oldest strata of Slavonic music are to be found in the territory where the 'eastern' Christian religions were practiced."[6] Whatever the cultural loss may have been, for some centuries the participation in Western Christendom also helped make the kingdom relatively competitive in a dynamic Europe.

At any rate, for several centuries the story of religion in Poland from the juncture of Mieszko's conversion is primarily the slow advancement of the Catholic Church within the fluctuating boundaries of the Polish realm. Initially a missionary country, this meant most of the Church elite came from the outside. Like elsewhere in Europe these churchmen formed the educated elite of the kingdom. Among other things, the earliest historical chronicles of the Polish state were written by them, which perhaps helps explain why relatively few details of Slavic belief were recorded.

The broad story is a familiar one: the establishing of bishoprics, the influx of monastic orders, and the development of the parochial system. All the while the Church was becoming more ingrained in society. As Jerzy Kłoczowski puts it in his sweeping *A History of Polish Christianity*, by the thirteenth century "the clergy were so deeply involved in the life of the society, with its tensions, family or local interests and loyalties, that it is difficult to regard them as isolated."[7] By this time most of the church elites, the canons and bishops, were already drawn from the Polish nobility.

It was especially the introduction of the newly established mendicant orders—the Franciscans and Dominicans—that started the process of deepening the faith of a larger public. Slowly but surely Christianity became rooted in ever-expanding circles of medieval society. The mendicant orders were the primary bearers of the "internal crusade," as philosopher Charles Taylor calls the new demand for auricular confession throughout the Church after the Fourth Lateran Council in the first quarter of the thirteenth century.[8] Within this crucial part of a campaign to deepen believers' spirituality, the requisite act of searching one's own conscience can be seen, centuries before the Reformation, as a milestone in developing the individualism characteristic of Western civilization, and Poles were now included in this incremental but ever-so-profound movement.

For the first several centuries of the Polish state there can be little talk about religious diversity, although it must be admitted, as Stark puts it, that Catholicism had a good deal of diversity built into it structurally: "By basing its parishes on geographic boundaries and by permitting substantial variations as to styles of worship, and levels of intensity across nearby parishes, the Church accommodated a range of preferences, catering especially to niches rooted in class and ethnicity."[9] This general observation certainly pertains to religion in Polish society from quite early on. Confessional religious diversity eventually made its appearance in Poland on account of several factors. Among them was the economic one. The ruling class attempted to modernize the state by inviting skilled immigrants. Mostly coming from overpopulated Germany, these immigrants brought with them a variety of skills from crafts to agriculture. Thus initially this phase introduced ethnic rather than religious diversity. Among these early immigrants, however, were also Jews looking for a securer abode in Europe. The pogroms to the west of the Polish state during the fervor of the Crusades contributed members to this community that settled in Poland, and they would be joined in later centuries by similarly persecuted brethren, creating in the host country what was known as the Paradise Judeorum. To some extent economic necessity fostered a measure of religious tolerance, but this was not the whole story. And if the tolerance the Jews met with in Poland was relative—that is, positive in relation to that of Europe at the time, but hardly able to meet today's standards—it nonetheless was sufficient for the community to flourish as in few of their European Diasporas.

Substantial religious diversity resulted from the politics at the twilight of the Piast dynasty, as the founding dynasty of the kingdom of Poland was called, which, having more or less secured the western boundary of the state, decided to expand into the remnants of Kievan Rus after the Mongols had taken over its core. Thus a large Orthodox Christian population was incorporated. An immeasurable impact on the Polish state in its various later incarnations and boundaries followed from this, since several neighboring states—Ukraine, Belarus, and modern Russia—would eventually emerge from the Kievan progenitor, and the blend of religion and politics at the ethnic cross sections would be toxic at a number of junctures.

This phase culminated in the Middle Ages when the dynasty died out at the end of the fourteenth century and the gentry convinced the ruler of Lithuania, Ladislaus Jagiello (originally Iogaila), to become their king, creating a personal union with the latter's kingdom. Lithuania at that time was a dynamic pagan state that had likewise taken advantage of the power vacuum in the remains of Kievian Rus overrun by the Mongols, divvying out such large portions that the conquerors became a minority in their own realm. The prerequisite for the Polish crown was Jagiello's acceptance of Christianity and the subsequent conversion of his realm. With this event, the last major pagan realm in Europe formally accepted Christianity. It might be added that besides the Kievan Orthodox Christians the Grand Duchy of Lithuania also included, among others, a diaspora escaping persecution from the Islamic Caliphate, the Armenians, a Christian group, but one with their own rite and doctrine. The state military effort was likewise augmented by Tatar immigrants, who maintained their Islamic faith, along with a number of much smaller religious communities, for example, the Karaites.

Under the leadership of King Jagiello the two states, united in a personal union reminiscent of, but more binding than, that of the Stuarts in England and Scotland a few centuries later, became engaged in a military campaign that would provide the reason for the earliest articulation of the spirit of tolerance John Paul II so highly praised. The story harkens back to the period of feudal fragmentation of the Polish state, not uncommon for medieval times, when in the thirteenth century one of the border princes, harried by Baltic pagans to the north, invited one of the military orders that had been formed during the Crusades to convert them and thus strengthen the security of his realm. Typical of such an arrangement where unwary local politicians employed shrewd international players, the Teutonic Knights were extremely good at looking after their own interests and ended up becoming a threat to their hosts. Moreover, since the Poles had no dependence, not even at the symbolic level, on the Holy Roman Empire, the Teutonic Knights, as one historian puts it, "saw the Poles as dubious Christians and unworthy members of the European family of nations."[10]

At a critical moment of the conflict in the ensuing military engagements, which included one of the largest battles of the medieval period in Europe at Tannenberg, or Grunwald, in 1410, victory on the battlefield was not enough. At the Council of Constance several years later, which was the equivalent of a court of international law, the Teutonic Knights accused the Polish Lithuanian alliance of unfairly using non–Christian forces—pagan Lithuanians and Muslim Tatars—to attain the victory over the order at Grunwald. While the issue was unresolved—given the wide diplomatic support the Teutonic Knights enjoyed, this in itself was a major accomplishment—Paweł Włodkowic (Paulus Vladimiri), the head of the Polish legal delegation, was given a forum to present forceful arguments concerning the rights of non–Christians. Włodkowic claimed that the natural right to political independence held equally for pagans and Christians. As one scholar puts it, "Neither before or after Vladimiri was there anyone so eloquent, so sincere and complete a champion of the principle of friendship between Christians and non–Christians, based on the mutual recognition of equal rights."[11] Needless to say, Włodkowic was vehemently against "conversion by the sword," asserting that "faith should not be accepted under duress."[12] One should recall this was uttered a century before Las Casas! Moreover, his work had an impact on the seventeenth-century Dutch jurist Hugo Grotius, who also pondered on natural law and international relations.

The council was also the site of the execution of Jan Hus for heresy. Hus had followers in Silesia, and the Polish delegation, including Włodkowic himself, gallantly intervened on his behalf. This incident might be looked upon as a prelude to the storms of diversity that would engulf the Polish-Lithuanian Commonwealth approximately a century and a half later with the onset of the Reformation.

*   *   *

One of the more absurd incidents after the Christian Democrats won the largest bloc of members of the European Parliament in the elections of 2009 occurred when the Poles and the Italians, the two largest national groups in the victorious bloc, put forward their respective candidates for the president of the European Parliament. In the heat of lobbying for his country's candidate, the Italian prime minister Silvio Berlusconi accused the Poles—what could be more terrible!—of forwarding a non–Catholic. Indeed, the Polish Christian Democrats, Catholic almost to a man—and woman—had chosen as their candidate Jerzy Buzek, a very popular politician in Poland, who subsequently did win the presidency, but a Lutheran.

Buzek is an exemplary representative of a Polish community with roots extending almost as far back as the beginning of the Protestant Reformation in Europe. The Reformation in Poland had a powerful effect on society, both culturally and numerically. By the 1550s the majority of the deputies to the Sejm, the Commonwealth's parliament, were Protestant. Since the Sejm was a relatively independent political body in the sixteenth century, a Polish national church was even considered at one point; more surprisingly, one of the primates of the Catholic Church was favorably inclined toward the idea. The more interesting question in light of the early strength of the movement is the reasons for its ultimate decline.

Part of the answer is relatively banal. At the time of the Partitions of the eighteenth century there were still a substantial number of Protestants in the Commonwealth, but they were by and large absorbed by the partitioning powers (among them was Protestant Prussia, formerly a vassal of Poland) since they were concentrated in territories that were ultimately lost to Poland when the country regained its independence in the twentieth century. This process was concluded during the final partition of Poland in the course of and after the Second World War and its aftermath. Similarly, a circumstance that mitigated against a greater impact of the Reformation in Poland was its diffusion: both the Lutheran Church and Calvinism had a grip on the gentry and townsmen, which meant their efforts were not very coordinated. In a related manner neither group made significant inroads in the largest portion of the population, the peasants. In his discussion of the question, historian Adam Zamoyski suggests another aspect of the Polish religious experience that served as something of an inoculation against overreacting to Protestant demands, namely the presence of Orthodox Christians in the Polish realm: "The Christians of the Orthodox rite had always enjoyed three of the demands of the Protestant movement: the marriage of priests, the use of the vernacular in the liturgy, and communion in both kinds. The Protestant demands were therefore less shocking and novel in Poland than in other Catholic countries."[13]

A common claim is that Poles were simply less interested in religion than a number of European countries. While it is difficult to measure genuine religious feeling, it may be true that in the course of the union with Lithuania and the Ruthenian lands, the gentry were involved in an exciting experiment of building a polity based on republican and libertarian values of which they were particularly proud, and which they realized was quite appealing. As an influential sixteenth-century writer put it, "Could Poland have conquered the ancient and more numerous people, such as the [Kievan] Rus', otherwise than by these liberties?"[14] This project might have tempered their religious zealousness, which if too excessive could easily have sabotaged it.

The "proactive"—from the perspective of Catholicism—part of the story is more complex. Among the factors that worked in favor of the long-term relative ineffectiveness of the Reformation in maintaining its gains in Polish society is the fact that it arrived several decades later than in its countries of origin, as close as those happened to be. Although this time span is not great, it was enough to nearly coincide with the development of the Counterreformation.

In fact, Poland had one of the leading representatives of that movement in the figure of Cardinal Stanislaus Hosius, perhaps the last figure in the Polish Catholic Church to have a substantial impact on the Church in Europe until Karol Wojtyła became pope in the twentieth century. A prominent contributor to the later stages of the Council of Trent, he was also the author of *Confessio fidei catholicae Christiana* of 1553, an influential exposition of Catholic principles that ran to thirty editions within his own lifetime in a number of European languages. Highly engaged in the Counterreformation, his attitude toward this enterprise was of seminal importance. Among others, Hosius was horrified by the bloody turn of events in England once Mary Tudor was on the throne, warning, "Let Poland never become like England."[15] Lamenting the fact that Poland had become a land of heretics, he nevertheless preferred the route of persuasion to force. Hosius was instrumental in introducing the Jesuit order to Poland. The Jesuits lost no time in establishing their schools throughout the Commonwealth. Highly reputable throughout Europe, they were practically without competition in Poland, and their high standards convinced numerous Protestant gentry to place their children under their care. Needless to say this was an important step in the return of the gentry to the Catholic fold.

However, the person who most evidently fits the need of a Polish usable past with its emphasis on the "state without stakes" is Sigismund II Augustus, the last monarch of the Jagiellonian dynasty. In religious matters he took after his tolerant father, who had been scolded by Henry VIII (during the latter's *fidei defensor* stage) for his lax attitude toward schismatics.[16] Since he thought a monarch had no claim to his subjects' conscience, Sigismund was famously against the principle *cuius region, eius religio* ("the ruler dictates the religion of the land"), which the rulers of the German-speaking states and Charles V, Holy Roman Emperor, agreed to in principle at the Peace of Augsburg (1555), ending internecine religious conflict. The irenic attitude of the last of the Jagiellonians helped cool the temperature of the debates and ensured that they remained only that, debates.[17] Rather exceptionally in the European context, as one historian puts it, "the growth of Lutheranism and several kinds of nonconformity did not plunge the nation into war."[18]

The fact that the monarchs at this crucial juncture were fairly enlightened and, perhaps more importantly, unwilling to bend under external pressure, be it the Vatican or other Catholic bishops, while the leading churchmen were also willing to be patient, undoubtedly had its effect on the Catholic Counterreformation in Poland. As Piotr Skarga, a leading figure in the new Jesuit order put it, the gentry would return to the Catholic fold, "not by force or with steel, but by virtuous example, teaching, discussion, gentle intercourse and persuasion."[19]

This is indeed what to a large extent happened, but not before the Protestant input helped author one of the remarkable documents of the period that influenced the course of that process.[20] If there was a pivotal moment for the success of "religious and national diversity" that John Paul II claimed pervaded Polish Catholicism, it is the working out of the Confederation of Warsaw in 1573.

Shortly after the Union of Lublin in 1569, which created the Polish-Lithuanian Commonwealth and a constitutional monarchy, the last of the Jagiellonians passed away. The gentry were understandably nervous, especially after events like the St. Bartholomew's Day Massacre in France, that a king from another dynasty might not be so tolerant of Protestants. Together with their Catholic peers they helped enshrine freedom of religion. Its memorable clause includes the invocation,

> [W]e swear to each other, in our name and in that of our descendants for ever [W]e, on our honor, our faith, our love and our consciences, that albeit we are *dissidentes in religione*, we will keep the peace between ourselves, and that we will not, for the sake of our various faith and difference of church, either shed blood or confiscate property, deny favor, imprison or banish, and that furthermore we will not abet any power or office which strives to do this in any way whatsoever.

As Norman Davies puts it, "Certainly, the wording and substance of the declaration of the Confederation of Warsaw of January 28, 1573, were extraordinary with regards to prevailing conditions elsewhere in Europe; and they governed the principles of religious life in the Republic for over two hundred years."[21] However, one can also look at the declaration as a form of covenant, which, as Jonathan Sacks argues, is a form of agreement fundamental to civil society.[22] Covenants were more typical of Protestant societies of the next couple of centuries, but this is a rare instance of one between Catholics and Protestants.

The confederation became part of a pact that each elected monarch—

the polity was now a constitutional elective monarchy—would have to accept before he could reign over the commonwealth. And although there were pressures to which some monarchs succumbed from the Catholic Church to overturn them once the tide turned in its favor, this effectively rarely happened, even though by the end of the Commonwealth, in its period of decline, the toleration was becoming frayed.

One more point is worth noting with regard to the diversity of the Jagiellonian period and subsequently of the Polish-Lithuanian Commonwealth. A number of commentators have observed that this flourishing was achieved in no small measure through the Catholic laity going against the wishes of the Catholic Church. Kłoczowski notes that even in the seventeenth century when Catholics once again dominated the institution, "the Sejm was far from giving way to the Church's demands concerning many significant issues: for example, it was out of the question for the state to confirm the sentences of the Church courts or to suspend the resolutions of the Warsaw Confederation."[23]

By the eighteenth century when Catholicism had become predominant among the nobility, there were a number of setbacks for Protestant nobility, and they were slowly excluded from political power. Nevertheless, this rising Catholic intolerance was accompanied by paradoxical tolerance by the ruling class of Protestant and Jewish faith among their subordinates, even in responsible positions, much to the chagrin of the Church authorities.[24]

If the above seems somewhat rosy, there were setbacks, depending to some extent on the personality of a given monarch and other factors. For instance, the traumatic Swedish occupation of the mid–seventeenth century was the occasion of the only collective expulsion of a Protestant group: "The weakest of Poland's Protestant groups, Socinians became the scapegoats for the Deluge."[25] Moreover, there is a major development of the Commonwealth's religious history that balances the picture and had a far more ambivalent effect. It should be remembered that whatever their differences, the Protestant and Catholic churches were essentially thriving in the sixteenth century. Both sides built upon the European Renaissance, and the term "reformation" could apply to either of them, if more dramatically to the Protestant side. This was hardly the case for the third major Christian party in the Commonwealth. Besides being generally in a less favorable position in the polity, the Orthodox Church as a whole suffered from stagnation after the collapse of Byzantium, which had resulted in the subordination of the patriarch of Constantinople to the Muslim Ottoman Empire since the end of the fifteenth century.

In the last quarter of the sixteenth century the Jesuits started proposing a union with the Church of Rome by the Orthodox Church in Poland. The hierarchy of the Orthodox Church was interested since the idea was that they would retain their eastern rite and simultaneously gain a portion of the prestige of the Catholic Church in the Commonwealth, whose bishops, among others, sat in the upper house of the Sejm. Except for a couple of abstainers, the Orthodox bishops decided to accept the union, which was announced at the synod at Brest in 1596.

However, instead of leading to the desired reform of the Eastern Church, the union created a schism within it. Alongside the abstaining bishops lined up against the union were a number of lay fraternities, which played a crucial role in the Orthodox Church. These had substantial patrons, such as Prince Konstanty Vasil Ostrogski, the most powerful Ruthenian magnate of the period. A period of conflict ensued, and for some time the "disuniates," as the members of the original church were called, were not recognized by the state. There were riots and martyrs on both sides, not to mention that during their ruinous insurrections half a century later the Cossacks saw themselves as defenders of Orthodoxy.

Nonetheless the Union of Brest, as it came to be known, did act as a wake-up call for the remaining Orthodox hierarchs, who realized that their church needed thoroughgoing reform. The metropolitan of Kiev, Piotr Mohyla, was instrumental in this. Educated in Paris, he stressed the need for an educated clergy and founded a college, called the Mohyla Academy, instituting a program of studies that included Latin and Polish culture. Already in Mohyla's lifetime this had a profound effect. As a Ukrainian historian puts it, "It consisted in the general raising of the level of Kiev's intellectual life, in imbuing Ruthenian youth with Western cultural notions, and thus providing the elite with cultural self-confidence with respect to the Poles."[26] By the second half of the seventeenth century Kiev was already a part of Russia, yet the academy continued to exert its influence: "When Tsar Peter I started his 'Europeanisation' of the Russian Church, the bishops who realized this project were from the academy."[27] To this day there are millions of faithful who belong to the Uniate Church, primarily in Ukraine. Still, the Uniates remain a bone of contention between the Church of Rome and the Orthodox Church.

If the Commonwealth did not experience internal wars of religion, this does not mean wars of religion did not come to it: the seventeenth century witnessed an invasion from Protestant Sweden and wars with Orthodox Russia and the Muslim Ottoman Empire. This resulted in a growing sense of the Commonwealth's role as the "Bulwark of Christianity" (*antemurale christianitatis*). In turn, this was part and parcel of Sarmatian ideology that developed the idea of the uniqueness of the Commonwealth and its liberties. Western ideologies were seen as corrupting, and, ironically, "they were much more tolerant of the oriental influences that reached them through the Turks and Tatars, against whom the Sarmatian Commonwealth waged constant wars under the banner of Christianity."[28]

One particularly meaningful event was the halt of the Swedish "deluge" at the siege of Jasna Góra monastery, the home of the Black Madonna icon. King John II Casimir caught the symbolic meaning of the event by declaring the Blessed Virgin Mary the Queen of Poland. Unfortunately, the siege mentality remained and, together with the Commonwealth's general decline, negatively affected the attitude toward religious minorities in the country for the last years of its existence.

*　*　*

Anyone who watched the televised transmission of John Paul II's funeral toward the end of April 2005 would have noted the contrasting liturgical robes of a number of the Eastern Rite Catholics, who were given the opportunity to perform some of their rites after the Roman rites were concluded. Half a decade later in Warsaw the funeral for the deceased president Lech Kaczynski and his fellow passengers after the catastrophic airplane crash of April 10, 2010, also bore witness to religious diversity. The three major Polish Christian groupings, the Catholics, the Protestants and the Orthodox, all took part in the funeral service, while the chief rabbi of Poland and representatives of the community were in attendance: a symbolic memento of the religious heritage of the Polish-Lithuanian Commonwealth.[29]

In the second half of the eighteenth century the Polish-Lithuanian Commonwealth came to a rather abrupt end after three successive partitions. Although it would take more than a century, Poland and Lithuania would reemerge as separate states after World War I. Finally, following the collapse of the Soviet Empire, several other nations would also emerge from what were once the lands of the Commonwealth, most notably Ukraine and Belarus. Obviously this process and the shattering events along the way have had an enormous impact on religion in Poland. However, before we continue with this complex history, let us look at the actual religious communities before the watershed event of the disappearance of the Polish state. Since the non–Christian religions were presented most briefly up to this juncture, we will begin with them.

The largest of these groups, also with the deepest historical roots in Polish territory, was the Jewish community.[30] The first significant numbers of Jews go back to the end of the eleventh century. In fact, the early settlement recedes so far back in time that it even became shrouded in legend. Among other things, the name for Poland in Hebrew was considered a good omen, since *Polin* meant "here you should dwell." As in other parts of Europe, the Jews settled in the towns since the law forbid aliens to buy farmland. This obviously influenced the professions and trades that were available to the community. As a religious caste with their own customs and lifestyle, they were tolerated in the Commonwealth but hardly liked. And even at the best of times they were not completely safe from persecution. Nevertheless, in contrast to many parts of Europe, "in Warsaw, Krakow and other towns, synagogues and churches stood side by side, Jewish and Christian streets interlinked."[31] Moreover, within their communal autonomy they could select their own rabbis and authorities and were even permitted to collect their own taxes for the state. And as long as they maintained their sequestered existence—which was to some extent a mutually beneficial arrangement[32]—there was no pressure from the dominant Christians to change their religion. As one scholar summarized their position in the Commonwealth, "[t]he mid–sixteenth to mid–seventeenth centuries could rightfully be called the Golden Age of Polish Jewry, a time of unprecedented corporate autonomy, economic privilege and religious creativity."[33]

If the Jews seemed fairly homogenous to the gentile population, a number of internal divisions were present or developed over the course of centuries. The oldest group apart from the mainstream was the Karaites, brought to Lithuania from the Crimea by Grand Duke Witold. A fundamentalist group within Judaism, they followed a literalist interpretation of the Hebrew Scriptures that rejected the Talmudic tradition.

The Jewish community suffered profoundly during the Chmielnicki Rebellion of the Cossacks in the middle of the seventeenth century, while the Commonwealth had been severely weakened by wars with Moscow and Sweden, which led to a substantial decline of tolerance for the Jews, not to mention other religious groups. Accusations and charges of ritual murders and desecrations of the Communion host became more common.

In the eighteenth century during its period of decline the Polish-Lithuanian Commonwealth was home to approximately four-fifths of the world's Jewish population. The decline affected the fortunes of the Jews, and many of them experienced great poverty. In light of the above it is hardly surprising that a number of messianic sects arose within the community. Among the earliest sects were the Sabbateists, followers of the "false Messiah," Sabbataj Zevi, who died in 1676. Next were the Frankists, the followers of Jankiel Lejbowicz (1727–91), later known as Jakub Frank, one of the greatest religious charlatans of the Commonwealth.

More or less parallel to the Frankists was the rise of Hasidism, the most substantial of the movements. The Podolia region where it arose was especially depressed economically. Israel Ben Eliezer, known as Baal Shem Tov, was born around the turn of the eighteenth century in Okopy in Podolia, now in Ukraine. He began his career in a nearby town as a *baal shem*—a miracle worker who could bring about healing and cures—and in 1740 moved to Międzybóż, the site of the largest Jewish community in Podolia, where he spent the last twenty years of his life.

In the eighteenth century there were a number of similar groups to the one gathered around Baal Shem Tov, often led by kabbalists. However, thanks to the founder's particular genius and charismatic nature, along with the organizational abilities of his followers, his was the group that generated a movement which in a short period of time was to spread from the southeast corner of the Commonwealth throughout most of it, and subsequently through the Jewish communities in Hungary and beyond. Its rapid spread and spiritual creativity, touching numerous aspects of Jewish life, meant that above and beyond its religious dimension Hasidism became the most important cultural development in modern East European Jewry before the development of Jewish political movements such as Zionism.

Some saw Hasidism as a threat to Orthodoxy, but its innovations never challenged the Torah or the Commandments. Eventually the movement took the side of tradition in the face of the challenge from the Haskalah—or Jewish enlightenment—in the nineteenth century, in the process becoming one of the rare splinter movements of Judaism that became accepted by Orthodoxy. Nevertheless tensions persisted. Within Orthodoxy, for instance, were the Misnagidim, as the Hasidim called them, who remained fervently against their more emotional fellow Jews well into the twentieth century, as is captured in the delightful Isaac Bashevis Singer story, "A Piece of Advice."[34]

Baal Shem's insistence that it was important to "serve God in joy" was quite remarkable at the time. From this postulate an ecstatic prayer-centered regime that critiqued the strenuous asceticism of earlier Jewish mystics evolved within Hasidism. The emphasis placed on joy as essential to the good Jewish life and crucial in the worship of God resulted in the importance of Hasidic song and dance as expressions of piety among the followers and aided in building community cohesion. These practices found their place among the external elements that identified the movement.

A major reason Hasidism worried Orthodox leaders was on account of its apparent similarity with earlier messianic movements that had stemmed from the Sabbatean movement, which taught that under the right eschatological conditions *halakhic* rules no longer bound the Jews. Sabbateans also felt that sin might be a source of redemption by provoking the Messiah to come. Indeed, some scholars have discerned what they call a neutralized messianism in the movement. However, Norman Lamm, among others, has argued that the radical elements in Hasidism were less prominent than they were made out to be in the heat of polemics.[35]

Initially Hasidism had virtually no organization. Baal Shem Tov can more accurately be called the first among equals in a circle of mystics and kabbalists that was formed in the middle of the eighteenth century in Międzybóż. He gained his reputation as a *baal shem*, and it is in this role that the local Jewish community supported him. It is also in this role that non–Jewish sources register him.[36] He was also known as a mystic who had experiences of the "ascent of the soul." These heavenly journeys were undertaken to plead for his fellow Jews, which was a noteworthy departure from the tradition that a soul ascent would be used by a *baal shem* primarily to gain divine knowledge. The Besht was initially not known to a wider public, nor does it seem he strived for one. Rather he was an inspirational figure, certainly quite an original one, who played a central role in the foundation myth of Hasidism established by his enterprising colleague-disciples. As a scholar of the period puts it, one of the keys to Baal Shem Tov's stature was the fact that "he took on himself, and he did this without holding office and without communal sanction, the task of defending the whole people of Israel."[37] This role was partly taken over by the *tzaddiks* and was one of the keys to the movement's widespread influence.

The oldest Muslim community, as mentioned earlier, was an inheritance of the Polish-Lithuanian Union. The Tatars were part of the Golden Horde that overran Kievian Rus. During the course of internal power struggles a group of approximately four thousand decided to take refuge by migrating to the grand duchy of Lithuania in the late fourteenth century, offering their military services. At the beginning of the fifteenth century, Witold, the grand duke of Lithuania, guaranteed the community the freedom to practice its faith, with the right to build mosques and cemeteries. At various times the community was further augmented; for instance during the course of the Commonwealth's wars with the Tatars of Crimea, prisoners were settled in the polity. Their numbers have been estimated at as much as one hundred thousand before the partitions, although for some scholars that number seems exaggerated. Nevertheless, as one historian puts it, "this population had no counterpart in central or western Europe, where in the early modern period there were only two types of Muslim community: slaves and, until their expulsion [from Spain], Moriscos."[38]

In different military campaigns the "Polish" Tatars of necessity fought alongside Commonwealth forces against their own Muslim ethnic attackers and raiders. Their response to entreaties in the sixteenth century to turn against their hosts by joining their aggressor coreligionists has an almost apocryphal air: "Neither God, nor the Prophet commands you to rob, and for us to be ungrateful. We consider you robbers, and our sword that defeats you, kills rogues, not our brothers."[39] Whether some such response was actually given or not, instances of unfaithfulness to the Commonwealth, although they did occur, were rare.

At one point in the seventeenth century when the community had approximately one hundred mosques in the Commonwealth, the notion of baptizing the children of mixed marriages arose, but generally the community was left alone.[40] After the Tatars valiantly aided King Sobieski during a major battle with the Ottoman Empire in the second half of the seventeenth century, the monarch granted them additional land in the Polish part of the Commonwealth, and it is primarily the descendants of these settlers that still reside in contemporary Poland,[41] with historical wooden mosques in the Bialystok region like the one visited by Prince Charles during his visit to Poland in 2009.

Although the Tatars maintained a separate identity on account of their religion, in many other ways they became assimilated to the society at large. The first stage was giving up their nomadic lifestyle together with gaining land. By the time of the Partitions of the Commonwealth, the Tatars no longer spoke their original languages, having absorbed the dialect of the surrounding populace in their places of settlement. Cultural assimilation was accompanied by elements of religious syncretism on account of the community's centuries-long separation from mainstream Sunni Islam.[42]

Another religious group that entered Poland both by way of the Grand Duchy of Lithuania and the Piast conquest of the outskirts of Kievan Rus were the Christian Armenians. Numerous invasions of their kingdom, especially by Seljuq Turks who annihilated their capital in the eleventh century, led to the mass emigration of Armenians. Involved in trading, some of them eventually made their way to Kievan Rus, from where they finally made it into the orbit of the Poles and Lithuanians and later the Commonwealth. They specialized in trading with the East and also mediated in matters of ransomed Christians in Tatar and Turkish bondage.

In 1635 the Armenian Church entered the Union with Rome which had earlier been established with the Orthodox Church in the Commonwealth. Although it was an Apostolic Church with an ancient tradition, as a Monophysite church it meant that accepting the Catholic teaching of the nature of Christ required a greater doctrinal change than for their Orthodox predecessors. They likewise kept their own rite, while their diocese in Lviv attained the rank of an archdiocese.

A result of the Union was a more rapid assimilation of the denomination and its subsequent Polonization, which was accompanied by greater participation in the Commonwealth's culture. Armenian's likewise started to identify with the Commonwealth. The Church also changed; unlike the Ruthenian Uniate Church, the Armenian Church now required celibacy from its clergy. The separate rite was the only thing that kept the community from complete Polonization. Consequently, "while in a given locale the Armenian Church existed, the Armenians kept up their separate identity; when a parish disappeared, they dissipated into a sea of other nationalities."[43]

One major context that differentiated the situation of the Christian Orthodox Church in the Commonwealth from other Christian churches was its Slavic nature. The eleventh century saw the break between Rome and Constantinople with the schism of 1054. Even before the Piasts conquered outlying Kievan principalities there had been intermarriages between bordering aristocrats, not to mention a short period in the eleventh century when some of these principalities were under Polish rule.

At any rate, Orthodoxy did not come to Poland; the Kingdom of Poland and its successors came to possess Orthodox territories, with which it had contact for centuries. When it did arrive, Orthodoxy came with a church structure that had been intact for centuries, and only minor changes were incurred. The social structure of the Orthodox Church was quite different from the Catholicism of that period. The Catholic priest was originally from an upper-class background, while the Orthodox priest was married and from the peasant class. Consequently, as has been noted, "the Orthodox priest was usually someone connected with the local community in numerous ways: marital-familial, with quotidian farm duties, living at the same financial level as his faithful and without any of the special privileges that eased the life and raised the prestige of the Catholic priests."[44]

The rise of Muscovy, with the subsequent establishment of the patriarch of Moscow in 1589 by Ivan the Terrible, had ramifications for the Orthodox Church in Poland. Russia could hardly be neutral with regard to the Union of Brest. It was the pro–Orthodox stance of Bohdan Chmielnicki that finally led him to subordinate his Cossacks to Moscow, which resulted in the loss of Kiev by the Commonwealth. Later, during the decline of the Commonwealth in the eighteenth century, the Russian Empire had an enormous influence on the Orthodox Church in the polity. There was an attempt at the end of the eighteenth century during a flurry of reform to bring the Orthodox Church in Poland directly under the auspices of the state and for it to become doctrinally dependent on the patriarch in Constantinople, but this was largely wishful thinking just before the final Partitions took place, that placed the majority of the Eastern church, Uniate and Disuniate, directly under the care of Moscow.

Since Luther was a German monk, with the proximity of the country to the Commonwealth it is hardly surprising his was the first Protestant church in Poland. Although the major impact on Polish gentry was in the middle of the sixteenth century, the German states subordinate to the state were affected almost immediately. The Teutonic Order was secularized, becoming Ducal Prussia, and accepted Luther's teachings. It soon established a university in Konigsberg of a clearly Lutheran character. The university attracted many Polish students. Much the same was the case in other territories adjacent to Germany or with significant German populations, like Wrocław. The latter Silesian city became an important Lutheran publishing center. In commercial centers like Gdansk, Elbląg and Toruń the guilds and the middle class were receptive to Lutheranism.

It was under the tolerant Jagiellonians that the Reformation started having a stronger impact on ethnic Poles, although primarily the nobility. While the substantial German population remained the most affected by Lutheranism, a number of Polish Lutheran communities also arose, especially in Pomerania and Wielkopolska, or Greater Poland. During the period of greatest toleration a number of persecuted groups from other parts of Europe came to Poland. For instance, Mennonites, persecuted in the Netherlands, settled in the Vistula Delta. More radical Protestant groups also sought refuge in the Commonwealth. Among them were the non–Trinitarian Arians, also known as the Polish Brethren, who broke away from the Polish Calvinists. An interesting cocktail of beliefs from a variety of religious groups, including an obscure Orthodox sect, they practiced an Evangelical egalitarianism with an extraordinary freedom of discussion that held no dogmas sacred. This was often too much even for Polish Protestants: "In their attempts to communicate, the Polish Protestants were always leaving the Polish Brethren aside."[45] Their works, however, were studied by intellectual leaders in Europe and were a precursor to Enlightenment thought. A number of dislocated German Protestants also came to Poland after the Thirty Years' War, strengthening their number, although not enough to make up to the losses of the Polish Protestants that frequently converted to Catholicism in those years of the Counterreformation.

One can contrast the treatment of Protestants in the Polish-Lithuanian Commonwealth with that of the Polish Protestants who were outside its bounds, primarily in Silesia. While it was under the control of the Jagiellonians the situation was much the same; when the dynasty died out and Silesia passed into the hands of the Habsburgs in the early seventeenth century, however, the Protestants were no longer allowed to say mass or hold services, and at one point even their churches were confiscated. An unexpected breakthrough for the Lutherans of Silesia was after the Commonwealth lost the "Northern War" in 1707 with Charles XII of Sweden, who interceded with the Habsburgs, which resulted in the permission of single churches in six towns of the region.

As mentioned above, a weakness of the Protestant movement in Poland was its lack of unity. There were attempts to coordinate the efforts of different denominations, such as the Sandomierz Agreement of 1570, which bound the Lutherans, Calvinists and Bohemian Brethren to common enterprises: "Declaring that the dogmas of the three expressed the same faith, it promised that the confessions would aid and support one another in the fight against papists and anti–Trinitarians."[46] But these had no lasting effect. Moreover, during the height of the Reformation there was no cooperation between the

Protestant and Orthodox churches in the Commonwealth. The latter neither felt threatened by nor particularly interested in the former.

Since much of the history above concerns the Catholic Church as such, we will conclude this part with a look at the final years of that church in the Commonwealth. Among other matters, the Church in eighteenth-century Europe had to deal with the impact of the Enlightenment. Catholic rulers, especially absolutist monarchs, subordinated the Church to their own purposes, placing a great deal of emphasis on the utilitarian aspect of religion. In the Commonwealth, instead of absolutism there existed an elective monarchy with a highly decentralized state. There was a strong sense among elites that the Commonwealth was in jeopardy and needed reform, and education was one of the key tools of working for the common good. On the one hand, at a time when the Catholic Church had gained greater preeminence in the Commonwealth, secular ideas along with anticlericalism affected prominent members of the intelligentsia and even clergy.[47] On the other hand, religious thinkers participated in the drive for reform within the polity. A number of teaching orders, especially the Piarists under the leadership of Stanisław Konarski, were willing to introduce this more practical, and patriotic, education. Among other things, this spirit translated into a greater concern among enlightened priests for the human aspects of Christianity that no longer accepted the contrasts of the earlier period, "where the glamour and splendor of the great [baroque] Churches increasingly contrasted with the poverty of the people."[48]

An example of this new attitude is found in *The Proposal to the Church of Krzyzanowice*, by Hugo Kołłątaj, a Polish Enlightenment luminary who was himself a vicar: "A vicar should be all things to all men following the example of St. Paul, the teacher of the nations. Therefore in his parish he should be a teacher for the blind, a benefactor to people in need, a doctor for the ill, an arbiter between the quarrelsome, an example of a good ruler, especially in the virtues, on which a good life depends."[49] Kłoczowski argues that this emphasis on education would become of paramount importance for the challenges the Church faced in a stateless nation, where it was one of the few institutions left to fill such a role.

From the Partitions Through Independent Poland

Anyone currently visiting the city of Lublin in the southeast of Poland can admire an ornate gate topped with an onion dome at the entrance to the Christian Orthodox section of the municipal cemetery at the periphery of the city's center. If the visitor came to the city by bus he or she would have possibly noticed a substantially different Orthodox Church situated on the outskirts of the main bus station. This church is likewise crowned by a dome, but it is a far simpler one and is more characteristic of the Eastern Church architecture of the Commonwealth. The architectural style of the cemetery gate is clearly Russian Orthodox and is a witness of the time of the Partitions in the nineteenth century when it was erected. What is noteworthy is that the somewhat older Catholic entrance just a few meters on is far more modest, clearly demonstrating the power structure of the Partitions where Orthodoxy was the religion of the ruling class, and Catholicism that of the subjugated—at times oppressed—majority. In fact, rightly or wrongly, the large Orthodox Church that was erected during the period in a central square in the city was demolished as a symbol of repression shortly after Poland regained its independence after the First World War.

In terms of European history, the partitioning of the Polish-Lithuanian Commonwealth was an event without precedent: over the period of 1772, 1793, and 1795, respectively, a fairly advanced historical state was "deliberately annihilated" by Prussia, Russia and Austria, each taking a share. "The only excuse given," as historian Norman Davies notes, "was that the patient had not been feeling well."[50] While it is true that the Commonwealth had been practically unreformable after the failure of the so-called Silent Sejm of 1717, the last decades of its existence had been witness to serious attempts at reform in a number of key fields, suppressed at each phase by the Russian Empire. In fact, the last Sejm of the independent Commonwealth planned fairly far-reaching reforms concerning the status of the churches.[51]

As a result of the partitions the Polish and Lithuanian paths diverged—especially after the failure of the major uprisings in the Russian Partition—while the Ruthenians were slowly transformed into Ukrainians or Byelorussians, at various rates depending on the partitions, or even the part of the partition. Like the Poles, the Jews were in all three partitions, but there were fewer of them in the Prussian Partition, and they were more mobile there; for one thing the similarities between Yiddish and German made it easier for them to succeed; thus many of them eventually migrated to Berlin. As members of a former non–Absolutist multiethnic state, even the Poles, or rather their elites, did not initially have a "national" consciousness, at least not in the sense of one based on ethnic identity. They had essentially been a political nation. Now, as political historian Andrzej Walicki defines their paradoxical situation, they were a "stateless political nation," which in practice meant that a critical percentage of the former Commonwealth's conscious population "felt themselves to be citizens of an invisible *res publica*, ruled by an informal 'moral government,' composed of the most authoritative representatives of the national elite in the three parts of the partitioned country."[52]

While memory of the Commonwealth was strong, such a stance more or less held, although with variations. One tradition with some support was the multicultural conception, which idealized the multiethnic and multireligious tradition of the Commonwealth. The historian Joachim Lelewel dreamed of a Poland where "no differences would exist among the people that composed it." This Romantic tradition is also present in Adam Mickiewicz's great opus, *Master Thaddeus*, which begins with the invocation (in Polish!), "O Lithuania, my fatherland."

The Romantic tradition tried to universalize the task of Poland's historical mission, which explains the slogan of the first major insurrection, the November Uprising of 1831: "For your freedom and ours." But it was an untenable position in the long run, especially since without statehood Poles were forced to depend more heavily on nonpolitical factors to maintain a sense of common mission, among them the surprisingly potent literary tradition. Albeit inadvertently, this was not without narrowing consequences, since the growing importance of literary language "prepared the ground for defining the nation linguistically rather than politically."[53] However, on account of the uprising, much of the Polish intelligentsia that had instigated it ended up in exile, and the heart of Polish culture was in Paris. The one substantial essentially Polish institution that remained in place and spanned the three partitions was the Catholic Church, which continued to include the vast majority of ethnic Poles, from all stations of life. To some extent unintentionally, if not necessarily unwillingly, on account of its virtually organic relation to Polish culture it became dragged into the process of nation building: "The connection of traditional Polish culture and all its customs with religious practices was so complete that in the people's eyes they could easily be identified with each other; and this was promoted by contacts with Protestant Prussia and Orthodox Russia after the partitions."[54]

No Christian Church was persecuted like the Uniate Church in the Russian Partition where parishes were taken away at once, and from 1838 to 1839 (in 1875 in the "Polish" part of the empire) it was liquidated where it remained, while the faithful suffered persecution, with a number of priests becoming martyrs. One of the immediate effects in all partitions was the loss of substantial autonomy on the part of the Catholic Church. All the partitioning powers—whether Protestant Prussia, Orthodox Russia, or Catholic Austria—were absolutist monarchies that subordinated the churches to their policies. Even at the best of times church lands were confiscated and religious orders were hampered, if not closed. The fact that priests were given salaries was not without significance: they were thus effectively relegated to the role of public servants. This imposed order was claimed to be divinely ordained: "The argument that the rulers were appointed by God was repeated by all three partitioning states. Appointments to the senior posts in the Church had to be acceptable to secular powers and consequently the bishops tended to be elderly and incapable."[55] Moreover, in a revolutionary era in Europe, the popes were not too sympathetic toward an independence movement, especially after the Napoleonic Wars. This state of affairs disturbed Polish patriots and their attitude toward the Vatican.

To some extent this created a two-tier church. The upper echelons were more dependent on the partitioning powers and generally more submissive, while the lower-order priests were increasingly closer to the patriotic mood where it existed. The January Uprising of 1863 in the Russian Partition witnessed the greatest participation of priests in a patriotic insurrection, many of them paying for it with their lives. Even the bishop of Warsaw at the time, although a personal nominee of Tsar Alexander II, ended up exiled for many years after writing a patriotic letter to the tsar. This type of response strengthened the moral authority of the Church.

Initially the relationship of the elite to the Church was ambivalent. Although they were somewhat less anticlerical in the Commonwealth than in other parts of Europe, the Enlightenment nonetheless had had its effect; among others, the gentry did not see anything the matter with the state subordinating the Church. This slowly changed after the collapse of the November Uprising. The Romantic generation of the insurgents had a greater appreciation of religion and combined it with their patriotism. Within this vein there was also a dream of a Polish-Jewish brotherhood, which to a limited extent even met with a positive response among the Jews of Warsaw up until the January Uprising. Related to this sentiment was a tendency to imbue Polish patriotism with an Old Testament stylization. As one historian puts it, "Polish messianic poets were compared to Biblical prophets, freedom fighters were identified with the Maccabees, Poland was referred to as Zion, and Warsaw as Jerusalem."[56] There were idealized stories of the brotherhood, like "the Jew with the cross," based on an event during a demonstration in Warsaw in 1861, where a Jew took a cross from a dying clergyman and was himself killed by a Russian soldier, which received a number of literary treatments.[57]

The most persuasive synthesis of this messianism appears in Adam Mickiewicz's *Księgi narodu i pielgrzymstwa polskiego* (*Books of the Polish Nation and the Polish Pilgrimages*) of 1832, which symbolically had a biblical form. In this work he intimated that Poland and its sacrifice could work as a collective messiah, which he later modified. As historian Brian Porter-Szücs put it, "whether Poland was to be the agent of apocalyptic transformation or the vehicle for a for a personal messiah, the link between the nation and a dynamic vision of historical time, culminating in a utopia of peace and brotherhood, was spread throughout Mickiewicz's work."[58] The role played by Mickiewicz and others in augmenting the role of religion in Polish nation building can hardly be over-estimated. Kłoczowski summarizes their contribution: "Without this peculiar mixture of religion and patriotism of the romantic-insurgent generations, without its overcoming the dangerous loyalty of the clergy, the process of realization as well as preservation of traditional religious practices and customs would have taken a completely different form."[59]

However, the Church had other serious problems to confront than nation building. A number of weighty social problems existed, some inherited from the Commonwealth and beyond its powers, such as the necessity of the emancipation of the serfs. In Galicia, the Polish part of the Austrian partition, the peasants revolted, killing numerous gentry. Although churches were not destroyed along with manor houses, the attempts of priests to quell the violence were brushed aside. Each of the partitioning powers dealt with the problem of emancipation at their own pace. The last power to release the peasants from villeinage was Russia, in 1865 after the defeat of the January Uprising. Although intended to punish the gentry for their rebellion, the move actually exposed the Polish peasants to the arbitrariness of the Russian administrative bureaucracy, which inadvertently taught them the meaning of their Polishness.

In Galicia, where emancipation had occurred earlier, as one of the more educated members of the community, the village priest initially served as its spokesman and helped to organize agricultural circles, village stores, credit cooperatives and local schools. However, as the peasants started becoming politically active, conflicts of interest arose. The situation has been summarized thus: "Once peasants began to establish political organizations to promote their own needs clerical leadership was compromised. Ecclesiastical authorities believed that the peasantry could not both govern itself and also accept the traditional social hierarchy."[60] Paradoxically, when a radical priest, the Rev. Stanisław Stojałowski, who published popular newspapers promoting peasant needs, was imprisoned by the authorities and condemned by the Church, it provoked the initial anticlericalism that was to mark peasant political parties right up to the Second World War.

More within the range of the Church's capacities was the problem of alcoholism. Initiated in Upper Silesia in 1844 after a pan–European movement started by the Catholic Church, sodalities of sobriety were established, reaching hundreds of thousands of Poles in various regions of the partitions. Authorities, however, suppressed the movement, afraid of the influence of the Church it demonstrated.[61]

Social transformations were important in destroying the Romantic vision of Poland, or at least it could not be maintained without serious revision. The defeat of the January Uprising of 1863 together with its repercussions—for example, the loss of the last remnants of Polish autonomy in part of the Russian Partition and even the cessation of basic Polish language instruction—gave rise to various positivist programs. Some of these programs incorporated the importance of the Church for defending traditional "Polish-Catholic" values, while another strain concentrated on economic progress and modernization within it. A narrower, ethnolinguistic conception of the nation became common to both strains. However, interethnic conflicts during the industrialization of the Russian Partition, where, for instance, "the Polish workers in the thriving textile industry in Lodz had to face the fact that their factories were owned by Jews or Germans and managed by German foremen,"[62] fostered the emergence of narrower forms of nationalism and its frequent handmaid, anti–Semitism. Religion played a role in the latter, along with imported ideas. As has been noted, "Although Catholicism certainly played a far more important role in the ideology of Polish anti–Semitism than in Germany, Austria, or France, the image of the Jewish capitalist, journalist, and 'freethinker' began to appear in Poland, too."[63]

As the nineteenth century drew to a close the National Democratic Party was formed by Roman Dmowski. Inspired by social Darwinism, the founder of the party believed the "Polish nation ... is a living, organic whole to which the individual belongs, or should belong, entirely and to which he owes an unlimited, undivided loyalty."[64] The Endecja, as it was known for short, tolerated Catholicism at the time, but considered its universalism ultimately a hindrance to national unity. The idea of the Commonwealth had not died, but it had serious contenders.

Although the fit was hardly exact, nationalism often coincided with religion. But even when the religion was the same, nationalism could trump this similarity. Albeit of different rites, the Poles and the Ukrainians were both predominantly Catholic, but this did not ease tensions between their respective Roman and Uniate rites. What perhaps eased the religious situation in Galicia was the end of Josephinism in the middle of the nineteenth century. Consequently the churches were able to refer directly to the Vatican to solve their internal problems. For instance, the Roman and Greek Catholic churches, as the Uniate Church was renamed in Austria, met with Pius IX in 1863 to deal with a number of outstanding issues, like the problem of mixed marriages.

This situation was in marked contrast to the Prussian Partition, which was transformed during the unification of Germany. Chancellor Bismarck's policy of *Kulturkampf*, aimed at suppressing the Catholic Church throughout the empire, was particularly harsh against the Poles. The suppression of the Church in the Russian Partition hardly needs mentioning. After the major uprisings it was particularly brutal.

Social transformations created their own problems that the Church barely had the resources to deal with. The poverty in Galicia was particularly striking and engendered one of the largest emigrations from Central Europe. The emigration is estimated to have included approximately four and half million inhabitants, including Poles, Ukrainians and Jews, a significant portion of which passed through Ellis Island on their way to the United States. Meanwhile the population growth in cities like Warsaw and Lodz wreaked havoc on existing parish structures, which were completely inadequate to deal with the huge parishes. Yet a rich popular religion thrived in the countryside and was to be the source of much strength for Poles in the future.

*   *   *

On August 17, 1989, Tadeusz Mazowiecki met Lech Wałęsa, who offered him the position of prime minister in the new government that was to be formed after the elections of June 4, in a contractual Sejm negotiated at the Round Table Talks between the Communists and the democratic opposition. Several weeks later Mazowiecki formed the first non–Communist government in postwar Poland, ushering in the end of Communism in the country and setting off a domino effect throughout the socialist bloc. However, before he accepted, Mazowiecki asked for a few days to consider the decision. A deeply religious man, he spent those days in Laski, at a center for the blind run by a suborder of Franciscan nuns, established by its first abbess Sister Róża Czacka in 1921. While diligently carrying out its mission with the blind, the center became a popular retreat for the Catholic intelligentsia. Mazowiecki had earlier written of Laski that it was "a particle of Christianity and a particle of Poland, forged through suffering and through openness toward people; it is one of those places in the world that were and are given to be a sign on the road for others."[65] Fittingly, in this center Mazowiecki sought the peace of mind he needed for his milestone decision. Laski was also a place of calm in the interwar period, a rare haven in one of the most hectic peacetime periods in Polish history, both in the political and social sphere.

Poland regained its independence in 1918 after the conclusion of the First World War. Due to the alliances of the partitioning powers, the Poles had tragically fought on both belligerent sides, and the front had crossed the republic-to-be a number of times, leaving many of its potential resources in ruins. To top off this misfortune, practically all of the borders of the "independent" nation were contested, and plebiscites, uprisings, military operations and wars were the order of the day for several years before borders that pleased no one— one of which sparked the Second World War—were established.

Within those borders approximately one-third of the population was composed of non–Polish minorities, but even the Poles themselves were initially quite foreign to each other. For well over a century they had been separated in three partitions, each of which had required different strategies of cultural and economic resistance, and each of which had experienced different growth. Nonetheless, they had the right to feel at home since approximately two-thirds of the population consisted of ethnic Poles. As one political historian sums up the situation, in a metaphorical sense, "the Polish cultural and political authorities, as well as the military authorities said: 'Listen, reborn Poland must be a Polish state in the same way that France is a French state. And that means that we are not a multiethnic empire.'"[66] The problem was that Poland possessed a smattering of the multiethnic empire pulling it one way and the ethnic nation-state another. Although a major political group, led by Marshal Józef Piłsudski, had aspired to recreating a federation inspired by the Jagiellonian tradition, and although after a military coup in 1926 the group held sway, political reality during its period of rule gravitated it toward a more nationalistic practice. Among other things, toward the end of its existence the state would become tolerant of anti–Semitic excesses within sectors of Polish society; moreover, of its own accord it would be responsible for the brutal suppression of Ukrainian nationalists. While it is true in the latter case that the state was provoked by terrorist acts, its indiscriminate dealing with the issue aggravated Ukrainians, paving the way to retaliatory acts during the Second World War. In sum, according to one historian, toward the end of its existence, "the relationship of the government to a substantial proportion of its citizens had so deteriorated that, on the eve of World War II, a virtual condition of 'undeclared war' existed between the state and the leading minorities."[67] This to no small degree reflected the relationship between the dominant religion and the smaller communities, since ethnoreligious identities often coincided.[68]

Although finding itself in a fledgling twentieth-century secular democracy without a state religion, Catholicism was definitely the first among equal religions, as was awkwardly but clearly stated in the country's constitutions of 1921 and 1935. The Church had inherited a good deal of prestige during the partitions. The nation's military struggle with the atheistic Bolsheviks in 1920 also had an effect, cementing a process in which "Catholicism became more national and nationalism became more Catholic,"[69] by creating a common front against an enemy that seemed deadly then, but later turned out far more powerful than could be imagined. Thus although it was more patriotic than nationalistic, the Church nonetheless allowed itself to be courted, and in no small measure seduced, by nationalistic currents in Polish society, for whom— acknowledging the now proverbial link of "Pole-Catholic"—a state with a confessional character was appealing. Initially the nationalistic National Democratic Party did not make strong inroads into the Church. One obstacle was the party's social Darwinism–derived rhetoric of the need to foster the nation's ego mentioned earlier, which went against Christian teaching. The party eventually tempered that rhetoric while emphasizing the historic role of the Catholic Church in the development of the nation, which strengthened its overall influence within the Church. "Nonetheless," notes a Polish author, "in the end the Church did not officially support any political party, and the clergy divided its support among the National Democrats, the Christian Democrats, and the [ruling] Sanation movement."[70]

In 1925 the Polish state signed a concordat with the Vatican that gave the Church a free hand in many issues. One of the few concessions to the state was that the Vatican would consult it before appointing any foreigner head of a religious order. Despite its privileged position, after years of suppression the Church faced many challenges. A major project at the time for the Church was the financing of the University of Lublin, later to be known as the Catholic University of Lublin, which had the task of educating Catholic elite in the country. From a handful during the partitions, hundreds of Catholic periodicals and even a daily newspaper were published in independent Poland. Some periodicals were quite popular, while others, like *Verbum*, which was published by Catholics associated with Łaski, were directed toward the elite and spread the ideas of innovative Catholic thinkers like Jacques Maritain. Efforts at bringing Polish Catholic thought up to date were also attempted by the Rev. Antoni Szymański, who as the editor in chief of the theological periodical *Ateneum Kapłańskie* appealed to clergy to participate more in dealing with the social problems of the faithful, which was also crucial in a period of the expansion of socialist thought.[71]

The Church also wished to activate lay Catholics and this was achieved by the creation of Catholic Action, an umbrella group for lay initiatives inspired by the Italian Azione Cattolica and promoted by Pius XI. As a hierarchical organization it lacked flexibility, although some of its initiatives were successful in the Polish context. An important outreach group that gathered Catholic university students was Odrodzenia (Rebirth), which focused on social and cultural problems. Among people associated with it were the Rev. Stefan Wyszyński, the future primate of Poland, and Jerzy Turowicz, the future editor in chief of *Tygodnik Powszechny*, the only independent Catholic weekly in the Communist bloc.[72] There was also the Marian Sodality, which helped spiritually form a number of the leaders of the so-called "open Church" during the period of the totalitarian regime, like Stefan Świeżawski, a philosopher who was close to Karol Wojtyła, subsequently John Paul II.

The relatively privileged position of the Church in the state was sharply criticized by different secular political groups like the socialists and the anticlerical peasant party. As historian Neal Pease puts it, "Apart from an avowedly Catholic minority, Polish intellectuals, like their counterparts elsewhere in

Europe, were far more inclined to irreligion, anticlericalism, and radical sympathies than the Polish nation as a whole."[73] There was a culture war between the secular intelligentsia and Church journalists. On one side of the barricades religion was generally considered anachronistic, while Church supporters responded by treating the intelligentsia as a threat not only to religion, but also to the nation.[74] After the more levelheaded August Hlond became primate of the Church, the situation settled somewhat, and despite the nationalist leanings of much of the clergy, the Church as a whole avoided extremes, which was crucial in the face of the rising threat of Fascist and Communist totalitarian systems in Europe.

One of the vital internal issues was the relationship with the sister church, or the Greek Catholic Church, whose clergy and head were supporters of Ukrainian national aspirations. The priests also helped Ukrainian society organize many cooperative and self-help societies in Poland. Archbishop Andrey Sheptytsky had even lobbied for an independent Ukrainian state during the first years of independence. Polish Ukrainian tensions from the period of the partitions had been aggravated by a tragic war of 1918–19. For this reason Ukrainian Greek Catholics, as they came to be known, were not trusted by either the Polish government, the Polish Catholics or the Vatican to conduct missions among the Ukrainian and Belorussian Orthodox "because of its strong propensity to promote Ukrainian nationalism and separatism, as well as the 'latinisation' it had undergone since 1596."[75] Eager to take advantage of the collapse of the Russian Orthodox Church to which the Church in Poland had been subordinate, the Vatican thought up a Byzantine Slavonic Rite, in other words a neounion, that would be more effective at convincing Orthodox faithful to return to Rome, as they saw it. However, whatever hope for success such a plan had was strongly hampered by the lack of cooperation from both the Polish government and Polish Catholic priests, neither of which felt that maintaining the Orthodox Rite would change the national consciousness of the Ukrainians or Byelorussians, which was a major concern from their perspective.[76]

A further problem likewise resulted from relations with another religious minority. If the National Democratic Party changed some of its rhetoric about the nature of the nation in independent Poland, it did not change its stance toward the Jews, which it grouped together with freemasons and Communists as involved in "conspiracies with foreign powers." Unfortunately, this rhetoric had its supporters in the Church as well. For instance, an influential Catholic journalist, the Rev. Stanisław Trzeciak, favored and disseminated conspiracy theories. In more general terms, there was a wide consensus within the Church of the wealth of Jewish petty retailers and tradesmen, which hampered the success of Poles in these areas. A significant portion of Church circles supported an "economic anti–Semitism," which aimed at strengthening Polish enterprise at the cost of its Jewish counterpart. This latter included any form of legal deterrents to Jewish economic activity.

At times the Church sent mixed messages, like in the Lublin diocesan publication that in March 1919 advised "in the matter of the Jewish question, [priests] should not incite hatred. They should speak prudently and in the spirit of Christian love, but also warn people of the bad influence of the Jews."[77] Somewhat later, in 1936, the primate of Poland, Cardinal August Hlond, wrote a pastoral letter in which he admonished Poles not to hate people from "a different camp," but he went on to accuse Jews of "fighting the Catholic Church, being freemasons," along with the usual calumny, only to revert to a different tenor, stating "there are many Jews who are honest, just, kind. In numerous Jewish families the sense of a family is very constructive. We know Jews who are ethically outstanding, noble and venerable people. I am warning you against the imported ethical approach which is basically and arbitrarily anti–Semitic. It is against the Catholic ethic."[78] Although bearing some noble sentiments, the mixed message at a time when a radical splinter group from the National Democrats was escalating violence against the Jews could hardly turn the tide against such reactions, if anything could.

To summarize the position of the Church before the outbreak of the Second World War, considering all the problems it had to surmount and some of its nationalistic prejudices, there were nevertheless some modest accomplishments. With some qualifications, Katarzyna Jarkiewicz's assessment can be accepted: she notes that the period witnessed the gradual transformation of the Church toward a less defensive stance regarding traditional religiosity, while encouraging in the younger generation "an ideal of Catholicism by choice, accepting religious values not because they are given but because of the task they invoke, [all of which] clearly liberated the Church from a 'fortress of faith' complex. With all its flaws, especially the urgent problem of Christian anti–Semitism, all this had enormous significance for enduring the dramatic war and occupation."[79]

*   *   *

Although religious life in independent Poland obviously differed from that under the Partitions, there was at least some continuity. For instance, the religions that had been identified with particular geographic regions essentially flourished in the same territories, or rather what remained of them: the Orthodox Christians predominantly in the east, the Catholics in the center and in various urban centers throughout the country, and the Jews in different small towns and urban centers they had inhabited toward the end of the Partitions. In other words, some semblance of the Commonwealth remained within rather truncated borders. This was to change radically during the maelstrom of the Second World War and its aftermath. Of necessity we have focused on the Catholic Church, since it was so closely connected to Polish national aspirations. Before proceeding we will now take a somewhat closer look at the other religious groups.

Of all the religious groups in the new republic, the position of the Orthodox Christians changed most radically. With good reason historian Edward Wynot calls the Eastern Orthodox Church in Poland a "prisoner of history."[80] Through no fault of their own, at the end of the eighteenth century its faithful became associated with the dominant partitioning power, which was to ruthlessly crush the Uniate Church and use the Orthodox Church in an attempt to eliminate any vestiges of Ukrainian national consciousness. Under the rule of the Russians, the Church was successively placed under stricter control of the patriarch of Moscow.

The liquidation of the Union of Brest in 1839–75 caused more than just untold suffering and the martyrdom of clergy and lay Uniates. The parish structure and even family structure of the communities were hit hard. As a historian on the topic observes, "This resulted in the spread of Protestant groups, often sects, as well as the popularity of anti–Church revolutionary movements."[81] At this point the Orthodox faithful remained predominantly native born, including the descendants of former Uniates who either willingly or unwillingly accepted the faith, but they were joined by various officials—bureaucrats, policemen, teachers, and their families—that either were sent or decided to make their careers in the western marches of the empire. Some of them stayed on after Poland regained independence, especially those unhappy with the Russian Revolution. Moreover, in 1905 when the tsar liberalized the law that forbade conversion from Orthodoxy, a significant portion of former Uniates, although unable to return to their previous denomination, decided to become Roman Catholics.

In the Republic of Poland, the Orthodox Christian population reached over three and a half million, which constituted over 11 percent of the entire population. This was composed of three main ethnic groups: Ukrainians, Belorussians and a small group of Poles, not to mention a smattering of Russians. These were concentrated in the three eastern voivodeships, or provinces, bordering the Soviet Union, where the Orthodox constituted the majority of the population. Much as had been the case in the Partitions for the Poles and their relationship to the Catholic Church, many Ukrainians and Byelorussians saw the Orthodox Church as a means of protecting themselves from the formal and informal repression of the Poles.

Repression as such was either spontaneous, as in the instance of the Orthodox Church that was destroyed in Lublin and several other similar instances, or sporadic. However, in the Lublin voivodeship a more ominous instance occurred in the district of Chełm, where a substantial number of Orthodox churches were deemed superfluous by the authorities on account of their allegedly small membership and destroyed in 1938. An earlier contentious issue had been reclaiming Uniate churches taken over by tsarist authorities.

Another problem was the governance of the Orthodox Church. Formally, it was still governed by the patriarch of Moscow, who was under the control of the Soviet authorities. The Polish authorities could not countenance such a state of affairs, and efforts were made for a Polish Autocephalous Church, that is, an independent national Orthodox Church. This was not easy, since the hierarchy of the Church remained Russian, and eventually it formally would require acceptance by Moscow. Finally, the state acted of its own accord, formally decreeing an autonomous Orthodox Church, independent of secular and external authorities. Wynot notes that, "strictly speaking, it was not a canonical body under Orthodox law, since it had bypassed its Russian Mother Church in the process of gaining autocephaly. Nonetheless, for the first time in its history, a Polish state had defined the legal framework within which this faith would function within its borders, a fact of considerable future significance."[82]

If we continue in this part of the overview geographically in the *Kresy*—the eastern voivodeships, or provinces—south of the Orthodox Christians were the Uniates, or Greek Catholics as they had been renamed by Maria Theresa in the Austrian Partition in 1774. Unlike in the case of their unfortunate brethren in the Russian Partition, the Habsburgs were rather positively inclined toward the Greek Catholics. And so, among other things their status improved somewhat while their priests received a similar salary to their Latin Rite colleagues. Although in many cases they had to support their families on this sum, it was still an improvement. Toward the end of the nineteenth century more Greek Catholic dioceses were added to the existing ones, and educational opportunities opened up, including a seminary associated with the University of Vienna. Among the agreements between the Roman and Greek Catholics in the "concordia" meeting in Rome in 1863, the faithful were no longer able to change rites without permission from the Vatican. This was quite significant, since some wealthy Polish landlords had been guilty of forcing Ukrainian peasants to change their rite to the Latin one.

On account of the predominantly peasant culture of the Ukrainians in Galicia, to a much larger extent than with the Poles the Greek Catholic priests played a dominant role in nurturing the growing national consciousness of their faithful. An outstanding figure in this regard was Andrey Sheptytsky, the metropolitan archbishop of the Greek Catholic Church from 1901 until his death in 1944. Born into a Polish Ruthenian aristocratic family, he became a Basilian monk after the order had been reformed in order to serve the poor Ukrainian peasants. He became so taken with the Ukrainians that he became a champion of their cause, for which he had problems with Polish authorities once Poland regained independence.

In the interwar period the metropolis of Halicz and Lwów had about three and a half million faithful and was divided among three dioceses. The Uniate, Greek Catholic Church officially enjoyed the same rights as its Roman sister church; however, authorities were distrustful of its separatist Ukrainian leanings. Nonetheless, at the level of pastoral work much progress was made during the period of Polish independence. The Church also had a lively press with a variety of publications, both high-end and aimed at the popular readership of faithful. In 1928 Sheptytsky founded the Greco-Catholic Theological Academy in Lwów, which served as a proxy university for the Ukrainian community. He also introduced mandatory celibacy for new candidates to the priesthood. Unfortunately, much like the Catholic Church, the Greek Catholic Church could hardly deal with the rising nationalistic radicalism and terrorism spawned within its community, and calls for moderation were generally ineffective. Naturally, the archbishop also condemned the "pacification" of his fellow Ukrainians by the Polish government in 1930. Jerzy Kłoczowski asks the pertinent question: "Today we are led to ask: what did those two powerful Churches of Lwów—the Greek and Latin provinces—do, and what were they able to do, to stop the growing hatred?... It seems unquestionable that in Ukrainian society the clergy's influence started to decrease in favor of the extreme nationalist secular intelligentsia."[83]

It is of interest that among Catholic bishops of the interwar period the only voice to criticize nationalist anti–Semitism was Hryhory Khomyshyn, the Greek Catholic bishop from Stanisławów (currently Iwano-Frankowsk). In an interview for a newspaper in Lviv he emphasized, "No one is of less value as a human being because of religion, nationality or class." One historian observes, "His own minority status obviously made him more sensitive to the plight of others in the same situation."[84] As true as that may be, unfortunately being treated as a member of a "second-rate nation" did not always produce such an effect of commiseration.

A less controversial Christian group based in Lviv was the Armenian Catholics. Like their Uniate brethren, they lost their parishes in the Russian Partition and only survived in the Austrian Partition, although here they also declined. There number was marginally augmented by the new diaspora that managed to escape genocide at the hands of the Turks. Of the eighteen parishes they had at the beginning of the partitions only eight remained up to the advent of the Republic of Poland. The process of assimilation continued, and it was rare for any of the faithful to speak Armenian, which was retained primarily as a liturgical language.[85] Indeed, the Armenian Catholic archbishop of Lwów during most of the interwar period was a member of the nationalistic National Democratic Party; that is, he was fully accepted as a "Pole."

As a small diaspora spread over a sizeable territory it was difficult for the Armenians to remain in touch with each other. In his memoir, a Polish Armenian recalls the parish fairs that were held in Kuty, one of the larger regional concentrations of Armenians in Eastern Galicia: "Here, on June 13, were held the ceremonial parish fairs, on St. Anthony's Day, which was the occasion for crowded gatherings of Armenians. It was noisy then in Kuty, with dances and festivals, most everyone taking advantage of meeting family members scattered throughout the region."[86] Worth noting is that the feast day he mentions is actually Roman Catholic: the Armenians were celebrating St. Anthony of Padua.

Another group, non–Christian in this case, which lived mainly in the *Kresy* borderlands were the Tatars. They were concentrated in a few of the eastern voivodeships, only one of which remains within the present borders of Poland. The Tatars had fought in the Polish Legions during World War I, and their patriotism was highly regarded. In some places where they had resided for centuries the Polish Tatars retained an almost idyllic way of life and the period is regarded with nostalgia, as evidenced in this description by the former Imam of Gdańsk of the place where his grandfather lived: "The priests from both churches [Orthodox and Catholic], the rabbi and the mullah knew each other well in everyday life, they often helped one another out in various neighborly matters, and sometimes they gathered together and played cards ... and drank beverages that the mullah most certainly should not have drunk."[87] The total population reached approximately eight thousand at its height in that period, and they even published a couple of periodicals on Tatar life. In 1936 the Muslim Religious Association was formed, with nineteen Muslim parishes, each one with an imam at its head and its own mosque and a religious cemetery.

Although assimilation did take place in the Polish Jewish community, it was hardly visible among the more traditional Hasidic and Orthodox Jews, the most numerous non–Christian religious group of the small towns and cities of the central and eastern parts of the Republic of Poland in the interwar period. By the early twentieth century the traditional Jews of Eastern Europe even had a specific dress code, which was actually the fashion from an earlier period, frozen in time, as it were, but now serving as "a highly visible marker of identity"[88] for the community. The entire Jewish population in interwar Poland reached over three million, which was in the vicinity of 10 percent of the overall population of the country. By some estimates, about a third of it was quite traditional; a small percentage of the population was thoroughly assimilated, while the remainder ranged in between.

The intense religiosity of the Hasidim made quite an impression on some Poles. The Polish landowner and writer Stanisław Vincenz describes his impression from a visit to a Hassidic prayer house in Kołomyja during the Feast of Yom Kippur, the Day of Atonement: "I experienced there a form of prayer so fervent, that all traces of 'modern' convictions, that prayer in itself is a type of self-persuasion, a delusion or illusion, fell away from me.... What spiritual power hid beneath the unassuming gabardines! On one small street, close to the Great Library, the march of the newest thoughts is followed, on the other—the fire hasn't gone out even for a moment, it burns as hotly as in ages past."[89]

Although coexistence was troubled in many parts of the country, there were communities where Jews, Poles, Ukrainians and others got along relatively well. For instance, the Jews often were innkeepers, so weddings frequently enough were held at their inns in rural areas, while Jewish musicians would play at Christian weddings. In his tetralogy *On the High Uplands*, Vincenz writes about encountering an old Hasidic Jew who recounts the beliefs about a local cave where according to legend Baal Shem Tov had resided during one of his journeys "and walked an underground path all the way to Palestine and returned in the morning."[90] The area he writes about is not too far from where Hasidism had been founded. By the interwar period, in the independent Republic of Poland, the movement had already been international for some time, having crossed over to the United States, among other places, with many of the Jews that emigrated from the impoverished Galicia. One reason Hasidism spread so quickly among poorer Jews was that its teachings were partly conveyed through appealing stories. These narratives eventually gained special appeal to later Jewish thinkers such as Martin Buber or Elie Wiesel who transmitted them to a wider audience and gave the impression that Hasidism was primarily a folk religion. What attracted these twentieth-century thinkers repelled earlier members of the Haskalah, or Jewish enlightenment, which emerged in the nineteenth century during the period of the Partitions. They considered its folksy nature and ecstatic practices as signs of ignorance, which were obstacles to Jews in their assimilation with the host society. However, the attraction of Hasidism was such that at its height its communities were able to penetrate Haskalah strongholds such as Vilnius. In order to do so it had to attract many well-off patrons, which runs counter to the typical assumption that the better-off Jews were solely inclined toward the Haskalah.[91] Moreover, the impression of folksiness is only partly correct; in his examination of Hassidic thought the scholar Norman Lamm in his monumental study *The Religious Thought of Hasidism* has discerned a surprisingly high degree of sophistication present within it from the very onset of the movement.[92]

As mentioned earlier, Hasidism formed an alliance with Orthodox Judaism in the face of Haskalah innovations. The demarcation line between these most religious Jewish communities became rather fluid. In general terms, it might be possible to repeat after sociologist of religion Rodney Stark that "Jews persisted in [Eastern Europe] because Jewish encapsulation persisted, even increased. And eastern Jews chose to remain a distinctive, socially isolated community because God ordained it."[93] However, this does not mean that the community did not recognize the challenges of the present. One of the great experiments of that group in independent Poland was the establishment of the Yeshivat Chachmei Lublin. Lublin had been an important cultural and political center for the Jews at the time of the Commonwealth, and Rabbi Meir Shapiro capitalized on this past glory to mobilize the Jewish community to fund this impressive modern institution of higher Talmudic learning: "Its goal was to modernize higher learning and offer renewed recognition to the activity of learning itself."[94] However, since it inaugurated its activities in 1931, the bold Orthodox experiment did not have time to fully develop before the outbreak of the war.

If Yeshivat Chachmei Lublin was a response to the times on the part of Orthodoxy, cautiously appropriating some of the ideas of Haskalah by including a partly secular program, already during the period of the Partitions modernity was making secular inroads in the Jewish community in many of the urban centers: most notably through the Zionist movement and the socialist bund. These differed in that one saw the hope of Jews in creating their own country, while the other option focused its efforts closer to home. The division was expressed linguistically in the Zionists' effort to revive Hebrew as a modern language, while the Bund socialists supported Yiddish, which was used on a day-to-day basis by Ashkenazi Jews. Some larger cities like Warsaw, Łódź and Lviv had quite sizable Jewish populations. As mentioned, toward the end of the period the community experienced various forms of persecution, economic boycotts, and even violence at the hands of nationalistic elements in Polish society. Historian Istvan Deak summarizes the situation as follows: "Although there was a tremendous rise of political anti–Semitism in independent Poland during the interwar years, Jewish political and cultural activity flourished there."[95]

As we can see, the richest variety of religious life in the partitioned lands and in the independent Republic of Poland was in the eastern regions. Nonetheless, some western voivodeships had their share of diversity. In the Prussian Partition, and to some extent in the Austrian Partition, a number of German Lutherans augmented their Polish coreligionists. Naturally, in the two German partitions, German Lutherans had increasingly identified with their new states.[96] Nevertheless, much like their Catholic counterparts, the

Polish Lutherans of Greater Poland and Silesia had kept up a Polish identity. During the course of the Partitions, Germans also moved to Warsaw on account of investment opportunities. They ended up largely Polonized but maintained their Lutheran faith. And so Warsaw eventually became the Protestant capital of the lands of partitioned Poland. Some of its leaders, like Juliusz Bursche, consciously harkened back to the liberal sixteenth-century Jagiellonian traditions and favored the joining of part of Protestant Silesia to the new Republic of Poland, which partially occurred. The Polish Evangelical Church was the largest Lutheran body in Poland, growing from 53 parishes in 1918 to 194 in 1939. It was largely governed by trustworthy Poles (from the perspective of the government), but the faithful were about half German.

The first census in independent Poland determined that there were a million Lutherans in the country. In 1926 at a congress in Vilnius an ecumenical Council of Evangelical Churches in Poland was established, uniting the majority of different Lutheran churches in the country. Once the Department of Evangelical Theology was established at the University of Warsaw in 1921, for the first time ever it was possible for Lutherans to study their own theology in Poland at the university level, which also influenced the qualifications of pastors.

The Lutherans were the largest Protestant group in the country, but there were a dozen other communities. Although fairly small, the Polish Reformed Church had historical roots almost as deep, but it had been influenced by Calvinism. Among the larger communities were the Baptists, numbering over twelve thousand, even though they were only established in Poland well into the Partition period. Groups that broke away from the Catholic majority also arose during the time of the Partitions. In the early twentieth century the Mariavite movement was the most important among these. As their name suggests, they developed a strong cult of the Blessed Virgin Mary and introduced Polish into the liturgy. They were also quite receptive to the needs of Polish workers, and so they flourished in the new working-class districts within Warsaw and Łódź. In several years they managed to expand to a dozen or more parishes, serving approximately a hundred thousand people. In independent Poland their vitality ebbed, but they maintain a presence in Poland to this day.

While this canvas hardly paints the entire religious scene before the Second World War broke out, there are a number of smaller groups that have not been discussed and within larger ones there was even more diversity. However, even with the little that has been presented, some impression of the "religious and national diversity" that marked the internal life of religion in Poland is obvious. What is also evident, however, is how at the time this wealth was not always valued.

Charles Taylor summarizes the characteristics of religion in Europe of the period: "Powerful forms of faith wove four strands together in this age: spirituality, discipline, political identity, and an image of the civilizational order. These four strands had been present in elite religion in the two preceding centuries, but now this had become a mass phenomenon."[97] On account of their different resources and circumstances, this description fits some of the groups in Poland better than others, but to the extent that it does fit, the various religious communities were taking similar steps and undergoing similar processes which reflected the times, but they were largely marching in their own directions.

2

Inferno, Purgatory and Beyond

*Religion from World War II
to the European Union*

Inferno: Religion in the Wake of World War II

Early in Andrzej Wajda's film *Katyń* of 2007, a scene occurs that documents an occurrence shortly after the Soviets invaded the country on September 17, 1939, on the heels of the Nazi invasion initiating World War II two weeks earlier. The inhabitants of the Nazi and Soviet occupations of Poland meet on a bridge at a river dividing the two zones. They are trying to escape to the other occupied territory and warning their countrymen who, in turn, are attempting to escape the other way. Many Poles and other citizens of the country lost their lives trying to outguess the occupiers. The occupiers, on the other hand—initially allies, later at each others' throats—seemed to be engaged in a macabre game of one-upmanship in terror. Historian Timothy Snyder calls the lands in between where Hitler and Stalin carried out their policies taking millions upon millions of lives "bloodlands" and argues, "Often the Germans and the Soviets goaded each other into escalations that cost more lives than the policies of either state by itself would have."[1]

Wajda's film depicts one of the crimes against humanity perpetrated by the Soviets with the summary execution of roughly twenty thousand Polish army officers at a particular juncture of the war. Indeed, in the first two years of war, the Soviet occupation zone was far crueler than that of the Nazi zone for the ethnic Polish population, with mass executions, arrests and deportations.[2] Of course, one of the prime candidates for *the* crime against humanity was, among other locations, methodically conducted on Polish territories from 1942 until the end of the war. It is well known that in the Holocaust the entire European Jewish population was marked for methodical extermination by the Nazis. Much of that population was found on Polish soil—over three million members—which is one of the prime reasons the largest Nazi concentration and death camps were constructed there, not to mention that it was far from the witnesses that counted in the allegedly civilized West. At that bridge depicted in Wajda's film, there is no question of which direction offered more hope for the Jews' survival, but at the outset of the war, not all of this was clear yet, and some Jews from the Soviet occupation attempted to return to the General Government on the German side.[3]

But there is one more horrible aspect of the maelstrom of this war that requires mentioning. In order to make it easier for their relatively small numbers to control the large populations they overran, virtually each of the ethnic groups and nationalities of Poland were played off against each other by the occupying powers. This did not always work,[4] but hardly any group did not allow itself to be provoked into exposing its darker side in some form or another. Incidents of neighbor turning against former neighbor—one perhaps a Pole, the other a Ukrainian, or vice versa—seem to gruesomely verify Rene Girard's counterintuitive thought: "Order, peace, and fecundity depend on cultural distinctions; it is not these distinctions but the loss of them that gives birth to fierce rivalries and sets members of the same family or social group at one another's throats."[5] Girard's intuition introduces a corrective to the common formula that the stigma of being the "other" leads to atrocities in such circumstances, but that stigma nevertheless still inspired aggression, such as the Jews experienced at the hands of their "neighbors." Although the atrocities in these cases pale in comparison to those of the occupying powers, these crimes are in some ways the most difficult to come to terms with, especially for the separate perpetrating groups, now often largely behind different borders, because it has meant giving up at least part of the victim status that most groups nonetheless still deserve. Fortunately, that is not the whole story, but the story of religion in the region is related to both the heroism and depravity that each of the ethnic groups and nationalities demonstrated in varying degrees.

However, there is a more interesting question from the perspective of this study. The very last image on the screen in Wajda's *Katyn* is a rosary in the hands of an executed officer about to be covered with earth, moved by a bulldozer, over the mass grave. Images of the overt powerlessness of religion in the face of a ruthless atheistic aggressor are strategically placed throughout the film. The officers themselves had been detained in a former Orthodox church before being shipped out to the forest where their fate was sealed. However, the viewer who knows his or her history will also be cognizant of the fact that in the long run it was actually religion that was at the heart of Polish resistance to the regime and played a major role in bringing it down. No one is more aware of this than Wajda, and implicit in his excruciating depiction of the powerlessness of religion at that historical juncture seems to be a sense of amazement at the astonishing role it would eventually play in his country's fate. Understanding this journey from powerlessness to empowerment is perhaps the most fascinating recent historical question concerning religion in Poland and will be the focus of much of this chapter.

This is naturally not a new question. Most people who deal with religion in Poland during the Nazi occupation and Communist regime confront it to some extent. What gives a slightly different dimension to the discussion at this juncture are the recent negative disclosures concerning the covert cooperation of priests and bishops with the totalitarian state apparatus. Beyond doubt this shows that the priests and people who faced the state apparatus were very human and given to failings. Paradoxically, this makes the overall accomplishment of the Church in the period all the more astounding, since it was not the feat of some otherworldly beings but of flesh-and-blood Poles, prone to fear like anyone else—a fear that some did indeed succumb to.

Overall the dramatic nature of this struggle provided moral capital for the Church, but this is nonetheless no guarantee for its success in the face of new challenges, which is the other side of the story that is currently unfolding. But that is after much water had flowed under our now metaphorical bridge at the onset of the war and will primarily be examined in later chapters.

The situation of the Catholic Church at the onset of World War II differed quite radically depending on which part of a given occupation it happened to be situated in and—after the new partitioning powers stopped being allies—where the front ran. The worst situation was where the Nazis incorporated parts of Poland directly under German rule. There the Church was divided into Polish and German, with the former virtually eliminated and many priests and nuns taken to concentration camps. Mainly on account of priests from this region, as George Weigel puts it in black humor, "the Dachau concentration camp outside of Munich became the world's largest presbytery, housing at one time or another 1,474 Polish priests and hundreds from other occupied countries."[6]

In the General Government, that is, the Polish territory that was incorporated into the Greater German Reich but not directly into Germany—later to be joined by the Eastern voivodeships taken over after Operation Barbarossa and the attack on the Soviet Union in the summer of 1941—the situation was less dramatic. Despite the occupation with its repressions, the churches were not closed, and generally religious life at a basic level was allowed to continue. However, any more dynamic forms of religious activity were severely restricted, like that of Catholic youth groups, many of whose members were nonetheless involved in clandestine activities.

The situation of the sister churches, especially the Greek Catholic Church in Galicia was different again. After the Germans expelled the Soviets from

Lwów, Metropolitan Sheptytzky openly cooperated with the Nazis, although he privately rescued two rabbis. Thus while Polish schools were closed in Galicia, the Greek Catholic ones remained open; similarly, the Polish seminaries were closed, while the Greco-Catholic Theological Academy was allowed to operate. Ukrainian society at that time had no leadership. The Nazis trained about 11,600 Ukrainians in a Galician SS division. Sheptytzky had even supported volunteers, reasoning that it was "desirable as the nucleus of a future Ukrainian army."[7] But there were a number of radical groups, such as the Organization of Ukrainian Nationalists, known as OUN. In Volhynia one of the OUN groups engaged in the ethnic cleansing of Poles, killing tens of thousands of them. Kłoczowski accurately indicates the partial culpability of Poles for this state of affairs: "The fact that the Poles failed to comprehend Ukrainian aspirations, and that they undertook a campaign of military retaliation, led to tragic bloodshed and conflicts which have had serious consequences ever since for both nations."[8] But at this juncture among the Ukrainians internecine brutality was also rampant. Snyder suggests that "although no one has taken up the subject, it is likely that the UPA [an OUN splinter group] killed as many Ukrainians as Poles in 1943."[9] While the matter does indeed require research,[10] it demonstrates how volatile the situation was. It is hardly surprising that Sheptytzky, despite all his authority, had virtually no influence over such fanaticism.

A less ambiguously outstanding church figure during the war was the aristocratic Adam Sapieha, archbishop of Kraków. Among other things, he cooperated with the Polish government in exile. He helped create the Central Welfare Council, one of the few Polish social organizations allowed to operate legally in occupied Poland. Operating primarily on volunteer efforts of thousands, approximately eight hundred thousand Poles received aid from it yearly. Sapieha is currently best known now for his clandestine seminary where the young Karol Wojtyła studied to become a priest. The seminary was very risky, but it corresponded with Sapieha's conviction that "the revitalization of Polish Catholicism after the war required a well-educated and dynamic corps of priests."[11] It was Sapieha who promoted Jerzy Turowicz as the head of a possible Catholic weekly once the war seemed to be coming to an end—a superlative choice, as it turned out.

Both occupiers wanted to annihilate Poland's intelligentsia to leave the country without potential leadership. Having incorporated parts of prewar Poland into the Byelorussian or Ukrainian soviets, the Soviets deported any Pole with professional or social standing, together with a number of Jews— by some records approximately a million civilians—deep into Siberian work camps, where a considerable number died.[12] Wajda's *Katyń* shows the professors of the Jagiellonian University rounded up in Kraków and taken to Sachsenhausen concentration camp, at which a good number of them died. A significant number of professors of the Catholic University of Lublin were also arrested, with some of them summarily executed. On account of the closing of all schools above the elementary level—Poles and Slavs were considered unfit for any occupation above labor, so higher education was considered redundant—a network of underground schools were created, which was a dangerous enterprise. Approximately two hundred priests lost their lives teaching at these institutions. Nuns were particularly active in running orphanages and smuggling food to prisoners in concentration camps, as well as many other risky activities connected with aiding the neediest.

A high price was paid for all these activities. Thousands of priests and members of male and female religious orders suffered repression during the war. Poland was also the only German-occupied country where bishops were arrested and taken to concentration camps, while 1,932 parish priests, 580 religious and 289 sisters ended up paying the highest price, not to mention the repressions numerous lay Catholics suffered. However, the gains were also considerable. Kłoczowski's assessment can hardly be denied: "The Catholic Church suffered terrible losses, but by means of its total identification with the vicissitudes of the Polish community it strengthened its prestige and significance for society as a whole."[13] This moral capital was to be of immense significance when the next trial befell the Polish nation. However, the story is not complete without examining a more ambivalent chapter both for the Polish society and the Church.

Maximilian Kolbe was a Franciscan friar who founded and supervised the huge monastery of Niepokalanów near Warsaw. During the war he gave refuge to countless refugees at the center, including approximately two thousand Jews. For this he was arrested by the German gestapo and eventually wound up in Auschwitz, where he became renowned for having offered to exchange his life for a fellow prisoner who was chosen to be killed by starvation. This action was deemed sufficient for him to attain the status of a martyr in the Catholic Church, and he was canonized by John Paul II in 1982. Kolbe was not alone in such activities. A number of monasteries also gave shelter to Jews; for instance the congregation of the Franciscan Sisters of the Virgin Mary's Family, with its superior, Matylda Getter, were particularly courageous in their efforts. It should be recalled that Poland was one of the rare countries under Nazi occupation where the penalty for assisting Jews in any way was death.

What makes Fr. Kolbe's case ambivalent is the fact that the publications of his monastery in the interwar period were quite anti–Semitic.[14] Overall the attitude of the Catholic Church was ambivalent toward the plight of the Jews during the war. To no small degree this can be attributed to the silence of the

Vatican on the Holocaust. Both accusations and defenses have been aimed at or proffered for Pope Pius XII, who was interned at the Vatican by Italian Fascists and officially remained silent on the plight of the Jews. However the pope is judged, the result of the silence itself is that national churches were rudderless in the matter. In her examination of Christians who rescued Jews in Poland, Nechama Tec, while acknowledging that Pius XII himself rescued Jews, argues persuasively that,

> in the absence of clear directives from the Vatican, Polish clergy had no unified policy toward the Nazi extermination of Jews. The result was a multitude of personalized expressions. At the two extremes, the clergy and lay Catholics could lean on religious anti–Semitism or on Christian teachings of charity and universal love.[15]

Evidence bears out this variety of responses. Positive responses from priests and religious are given above. Tec gives the example of a pious peasant who saved a group of Jews despite reporting to them that his priest encouraged them to deliver Jews to the Nazis. To the alarmed group who heard his report and knew of his deep faith, he sagaciously responded, "The devil finds his way even into the church."[16] The devil did indeed seem to get the upper hand on religion in many parts of former Polish lands.

As hardly needs repeating, for the Jewish population of Poland, the German occupation was a death sentence. The death knot closed in on the community inexorably with practically no escape. First there were the ghettoes, and then deportations to the concentration or death camps. Returning to Wajda's bridge, escape to Soviet occupied Poland was a temporary reprieve, not to mention the good fortune of the considerable number of Jews who initially resided there. However, after the Nazis invaded that part of the country, even there havens were few and far apart, although the Jews living there were slightly better prepared for the onslaught, as evidenced by the story of the Bielski brothers—appropriated by Hollywood in the movie *Defiance* (2009). Moreover, the Nazis came later and were expelled earlier from this part of the former Polish territories, which had some bearing on the chances for survival there. As was partly described above, at great risk to themselves some Poles rescued Jews, whether through organizations such as Żegota, the Council of Help for Jews, created in 1942, or individually, while not a few others turned them over to the Nazis. Most of the population, on the other hand, remained passive; the terrors of the occupation did not necessarily foster empathy. And a much larger proportion than previously suspected of the Polish population collaborated with the Nazis, turning Jews over to the occupiers or, more gruesomely, carrying out pogroms themselves. Paradoxically, apart from the rare cases of escape from Europe as such, those Jews in the Soviet occupation who were deported to Siberia and other areas of the Soviet Union to work camps had the best chance of survival, despite the fact that on account of the inhuman conditions the death rate was appallingly high, but nothing like what awaited them with the Nazis.

Although the sordid story of the Holocaust is quite well known, one of the lesser-noted aspects is that despite drastically changed circumstances, religion continued to be an essential issue for many Polish Jews. For instance, despite the challenges to practicing religion in the ghettos—before the deportations to the concentration and death camps—one scholar notes that for many Jews, religious beliefs and practices were a major source of inspiration and support: "Community observance of banned rituals can also be seen as a form of spiritual resistance, which maintained Jewish beliefs and identity in the very face of death."[17]

An anonymous account of a survivor from the Radom memorial book bears this out.[18] Despite the fact that the synagogue was closed, Jews would meet at the different ghetto residences of rabbis and pray. Even the yeshiva operated clandestinely where the Torah was studied.[19] An account from the Łódź Ghetto, on the other hand, suggests that while after a period of time communal prayers were lessened, a different matter was saying Kaddish, the prayer for the dead. With the constant deaths, this was a major practice, involving much of the community: "Many children, lined up in rows, come from their schools, to say Kaddish."[20] Amazingly, despite the inhuman conditions of the ghettos and the presence of death at every corner, there was a relative infrequency of suicides. A chronicler of the Warsaw Ghetto is astonished by "this will to live," claiming, "It is a wondrous, superlative power with which only the most established communities among our people have been blessed."[21] It seemed to the chronicler that the Hasidim stood out in this respect with their will to live.

Some religious groups, on the other hand, did not experience particularly drastic problems from the occupying powers, even in comparison to the Poles, let alone the Jews. Most of the Polish Orthodox Christians initially ended up under the control of the Soviets. However, the Germans had prepared for dealing with the Orthodox under their occupation by building up a cadre of Orthodox priests, including a bishop, for key posts. This turned out to have been almost unnecessary, since the Polish Metropolitan Dionizy, although he initially abdicated his position, finally convinced the Nazi leadership of his loyalty and, after pledging obedience, received his jurisdiction back.[22]

The Polish Lutheran community was in quite a difficult situation. The stereotype of Poles as Catholics and Lutherans as Germans worked to the community's detriment in that some Nazis expected their support, with charges of betrayal when it was not forthcoming. Within the General Government, Polish Lutheran parishes were separated from the German ones, while masses in Polish were banned. Many church buildings were destroyed and aid groups closed down. Quite a few of the ministers who claimed to be Polish were arrested, of which the majority ended up in concentration camps. Bishop Juliusz Bursche, who had done so much for the Church in interwar Poland, lost his life there. The huge Warsaw parish, of approximately twelve thousand, bravely resisted such a division. On account of its patriotic stance, the smaller Polish Reformed Church of Poland likewise suffered similar repressions, both under the Nazis and the Soviets.

Despite the critical situation, both churches were forward looking and together with a number of other smaller Protestant Churches established a national Temporary Ecumenical Council. In itself this was an act of defiance that had to be carried out clandestinely, since the Nazis considered any ecumenical activity on the part of the Evangelical Churches a betrayal of their "German soul."[23]

Purgatory: Religion Under the Communists

The so-called castle in Lublin presently houses a fine museum; an adjacent chapel from the Middle Ages is magnificently adorned with world-class Byzantine frescoes. During the war, however, on their way to concentration camps, for shorter or longer stays, over forty thousand prisoners, mostly people resisting the occupation, passed through the jail that the Nazis maintained there. And while vacating it just hours before the Red Army entered the city, the Germans brutally massacred over three hundred ethnic Polish and Jewish Polish prisoners held there at the time. Hardly had the blood been washed out of the prison, though, and Poles were once again placed there, this time by the Ministry of Public Security for resisting the Communist regime, with thousands imprisoned temporarily and several hundred executions taking place there over the span of a decade.

As this one minuscule sample demonstrates, initially the lower rungs of purgatory were just barely more livable than the inferno the nation and its communities had survived. Behind the Red Army that successively expelled the Nazis from mid–July 1944 on through its slow march to Berlin the new regime was installed, initially against ever-weakening armed resistance of the former Home Army that had actually helped the Red Army drive out the Nazis. After that the terror was directed at large swathes of Polish society.[24] All the while on account of international agreements ending World War II, borders were changed and populations transferred, moving groups from where they had lived for centuries to new homelands in which their ethnic brethren resided in larger numbers. As one historian summarizes the situation, "Anyone believing that massive wartime and postwar migration produced a systematic 'un-mixing' of peoples, the placement of like with like, would surely be flummoxed by descriptions of everyday life in much of Poland in the late 1940s, descriptions redolent with tales of intercommunal strife and clashes of civilizations."[25] As if those forces were not sufficiently insurmountable for the battered nation, the new injuries the national and ethnic communities had recently received from each other during the Second World War weakened their resistance to the new totalitarian state, and were burning issues in their own right.

The most widely discussed issue concerns relations between the Poles and the Jews of the destroyed republic. Tales of bravery and assistance offered by Poles at incredible risk to save tens of thousands of Jews were easily forgotten in light of other events. As mentioned, some Poles collaborated directly with Nazis, turning over their fellow countrymen to a certain fate. Elsewhere, it is hardly surprising that Jews in the eastern borderlands welcomed the Soviet occupants as an alternative to the Nazis, and, especially where the Polish nationalist extremists had been most abusive, as a possible improvement to earlier mistreatment. This, also unsurprisingly, was considered by Poles as a betrayal of Poland, and when the Nazis temporarily drove out the Soviets, there were cases of collective revenge. At the end of the war, on the one hand, some Poles were loath to give up the Jewish houses they had occupied when the latter had been removed to the ghettos by the Nazis, going as far as killing a substantial number of returning survivors; on the other hand, a number of Jews were prominent members of the new government, not to mention a disproportionate number of officers in the security forces. Stanisław Krajewski describes the conundrum Jews found themselves in:

> Communists could be seen as the only force that could effectively defend Jews against anti–Semitism. This resulted in a vicious circle: the more Jews were afraid, the more they relied on communist authorities—and at the beginning of the period on the Red Army itself—the more they were threatened, and the more afraid they became.[26]

The vicious circle of resentment and fear all round is easy to imagine. Most horribly, in these killings and several pogroms, possibly as many as a thousand Jews or more died after the Holocaust. The majority of the upwards of 400,000 survivors, ended up leaving Poland for Palestine or somewhere else. Thus, ironically among the two peoples that suffered the most from the Second World War, although in hardly a comparable manner—as it has been aptly put—"an unbridgeable chasm opened between the two groups, with each barricading itself behind a set of concepts, images, and memories that left its mark."[27]

Relations between Poles and Ukrainians were just as complicated, and the border shift along with population transfers rendered them even more so. Of course these facts along with similar ones are the end results of extremely complicated situations and will likely be discussed for some time. Not to mention that years of Communist censorship hampered earlier discussion, so in some cases the wounds currently seem as fresh in Poland as if they had just been inflicted.

These are just some factors to bear in mind while looking at the story of religion in Poland, now overwhelmingly Catholic, after the rest of Europe on the other side of the Iron Curtain, was in the process of healing its wounds and largely forgetting the war. While officially atheist, until the falsified elections of January 1947 consolidated their political power, the Communist regime had been relatively soft on the Catholic Church, recognizing within it the strongest social force within the country. It had allowed many of the nonpolitical functions that the Church had carried on before the war to be resumed. The Church reopened hospitals, its charity organization Caritas was reestablished, and religious instruction was even allowed in schools.

In recognizing the status of the Church within society, the regime was unmistaken. As mentioned previously, having suffered alongside the Polish population, the Church had amassed enormous moral capital. And it had charismatic leaders, with Archbishop Adam Sapieha at the fore. And unlike the Polish primate, Cardinal Hlond, he had spent the entire occupation in Poland. Upon his returned from the ceremony in Rome that had made him a cardinal early in 1946, he was given a hero's welcome by the people of Kraków.

Among others, in March 1945 he established the Catholic weekly *Tygodnik Powszechny* [*Universal Weekly*], edited almost from the beginning until his death in an independent Poland by Jerzy Turowicz, which demonstrated Sapieha's concern for the formation of a Catholic elite. A pastoral letter in the summer of the same year showed he was just as sensitive to what ailed the demoralized Polish society at the time. Among others he writes, "If discord was the sin that led our country to its downfall, then an even heavier sin, even a crime, is the widespread injustice, spitefulness, seeking revenge and gaining profits from one's own brothers. With a heavy heart we must admit these incidents are quite frequent here."[28]

No matter how high the prestige of the Church at the time, ultimately it was no match for a regime that had brutally muscled its way into the country. Here one can compare Andrzej Wajda's *Katyn* of 2007 with his *Ashes and Diamonds* of 1958 to see different versions of the imposition of Communism— one uncensored version and the other made under the regime—to have some idea of the censorship Poles endured, even though by 1956 much more truth was allowed than under the Stalinist regime. That the Church was aware from the onset of its limitations under the totalitarian regime explains the fact that it did not officially condemn the clearly manipulated elections of 1947 legitimizing the Communists. As a Church historian argues, it is this deed that shows how early the Church initiated "its strategy of delay tactics and optimalizing concessions."[29]

Once its hold on power was complete for a time, the Communists played with attempting to appropriate Church support for the regime,[30] but soon they no longer bothered to hide their intents with regard to religion, and many of the earlier concessions were quickly withdrawn[31]: hospitals and much Church land was confiscated, religion was no longer taught in school, many clergy and even a bishop were arrested for criticizing the regime, and active lay Catholics were intimidated. Subterfuge was likewise undertaken, with the Ministry of Public Security attempting to lure priests into cooperating with the regime, and a group of "patriot priests" were enlisted, who took the part of the regime against the bishops. As Weigel observes, the strategy to control and eventually destroy the Church was threefold: "confrontation and direct attack when tactically feasible; cooptation when possible; and, withal, a slow strangulation of the Church's evangelical mission through relentless pressure on both Church leaders and the Catholic populace."[32] It was a devastating strategy that worked effectively in neighboring countries, and even in retrospect it seems almost providential that it failed in Poland.

It was the new primate, then Archbishop Stefan Wyszyński, who was eventually to perfect the strategy of the Church against the seemingly invulnerable regime and exploit its weaknesses once they did arise. He was an extraordinarily pious and humane man whose spirituality discerned between the sin and the sinner. A few years later when he was incarcerated by the regime and he learned that the first secretary of the Communist Party, the man who was responsible for his imprisonment, had died in Moscow, he magnanimously wrote in his diary, "I wish to pray for God's mercy for the man who harmed me so much. Tomorrow I will offer Mass for him; already now I forgive him who trespassed against me, confident that the just God will find better deeds in his life that will secure for him God's mercy."[33]

In part, the strength of his position was due to Pius XII, who recognized that extraordinary measures were called for with the impending Communist take-over and granted the primate of the Polish Church wide-ranging plenipotentiary powers so that it would not be handicapped by Church formalities. After he became primate in 1948, Wyszyński was able to make full use of this relative independence. In the atmosphere of mounting reprisals in 1950 Wyszynski signed an agreement with the Communist authorities at their behest, although not before rejecting an earlier version. Among others, the bishops were to accept the collectivization of agriculture, to condemn subversive activities against the state, and even to oppose the Vatican's policy of

Church administration in the "regained territories," that is, the ones incorporated from Germany.[34] In exchange Wyszyński was promised that the persecution would be lessened and religious education would be maintained in schools. Furthermore, the Church would be able to maintain the Catholic University of Lublin, and several other concessions were made.

The agreement was criticized by the Vatican, which felt the Polish Church had conceded too much to the regime. Moreover, the regime itself wasted no time in reneging on the agreement as soon as the document was valid. Repressions increased instead of declined. The rector of the Catholic University was arrested, as was the abbot of Jasna Góra monastery. Soon a bishop was arrested, Czesław Kaczmarek of the diocese of Kielce, and underwent torture on trumped-up charges of spying on behalf of the Americans.

After three years Wyszynski finally put his foot down. In a memorial to the regime he catalogued all the abuses and vehemently opposed the last measure, the intent on the part of the authorities to interfere in appointments to Church posts. This was his famous *non possumus*, and he did not have to wait long for the government's response. Four months later on September 25, 1953, he was arrested. His detention lasted for three years and was to have a devastating effect on the bishops, who were left rudderless and were thus more amenable to the regime's pressures and enticements. Wyszyński himself expressed profound disappointment with the bishops' weakness in his prison journal.[35]

Nevertheless, as is well known in Poland, Wyszynski was eventually vindicated in his policy. Once the political climate changed on account of workers' unrest in Poznan in 1956 and the initially genuinely popular Władysław Gomułka was made first secretary of the Communist Party, it was clear that Stalinism had come to an end. Although Wyszynski was cut off from all news of what was happening, he shrewdly played his cards when the new authorities negotiated with him, realizing they would not bother doing so unless they genuinely needed his help, which was indeed the case. The situation corresponded to the general truth of church–state relations expressed in one assessment: "[The] high position in the church in the eyes of the Roman Catholics, especially in the eyes of the working class—the 'ruling class,' 'the owners of the state,' according to communist ideology—made it difficult for the Communist-dominated government to destroy the Church structures, or even weaken them in any significant way."[36]

This pressure from below largely protected the primate, but it is only part of the story. Once the authorities "had" him, in a sense he eventually started dictating terms to them. When he sensed their weakness, for instance when they inexplicably moved him to a place of lighter incarceration or eventually promised him freedom, Wyszynski effectively negotiated for the authorities to guarantee the independent institutional activities of the Church.[37] The unbending primate returned as a hero. As should be apparent by now, Wyszynski's courage was backed by a strategy, possibly the best one imaginable under the circumstances. As Weigel puts it, "[if] Wyszynski was moderate in his demands, [he was] extremely immoderate in defending them. His demands were consistent with the Church's integrity and the dignity of conscientious people: he asked that the Church be allowed to contribute to building Polish society without compromising its principles."[38]

The comparison has been made by a number of scholars between the responses of Wyszynski and Mindszenty in Hungary: the latter very quickly stood up firmly against the Communists, allowing no room for dialogue. Unsurprisingly, Mindszenty spent most of the time in Communist prisons, where he was in no position to guide his Church. Upon his release he was forced to leave the country. The situation was substantially different in Hungary where Catholicism did not play the same role in society—when imprisoned Wyszynski had the Polish society behind him, and even during the worst period of his detention he was not mistreated the way the Hungarian primate was—but leadership was nonetheless crucial. Wyszyński was as staunchly anti–Communist as Mindeszenty, but he knew when to bend and when to stand firm, and so the Polish Church was in the hands of a strong leader at a crucial moment in its history.[39]

Naturally the political situation at a given juncture played a role: the open persecution during the Stalinist period was replaced by more subtle forms of repression, for instance, during the period of détente in the 1970s. But overt repression was always an option. After the occasional tactical thaws, repression would inevitably return; a few years after Wyszyński's release from custody, for instance, the authorities started treating the Church in a heavy-handed manner that hardly differed from the Stalinist period. Grassroots resistance was crucial. Often enough the faithful would defend buildings about to be confiscated and generally stand up to the regime, like the famous case of the workers of Nowa Huta who in 1960 defended the cross erected by the young Bishop Wojtyła on the site of their future church. Further to the west in the same year in the town of Zielona Góra the largest such confrontation occurred when the authorities sent special forces to confiscate a Catholic cultural center where catechism lessons were taught. A crowd of five thousand parishioners barred their way. Reinforcements came from as far away as Poznań while skirmishes lasted into the night, but the repression several hundred participants endured lasted much longer.[40] The need to use such force in such instances was an indication of the failure of Communist policies.

After each thaw, however, the backlash that followed was never as deep as the period preceding the thaw. The imposition of martial law in December

1981 was aimed primarily at Polish society, but the Church also had its martyrs, of which the Rev. Jerzy Popieluszko (who actually was killed after martial law had been lifted) is only the most well known. Jerzy Kłoczowski assesses the overall situation: "In each individual case the confrontation between tradition, religion and the party line found its own solution. These solutions varied, and in practice they were often not very integrated."[41] The regime may have had to make concessions to the times in its own manner, but its goal remained constant.

The observation has been made, however, that while the Church grew stronger, so did Communist propaganda. The regime had at its disposal all the instruments of mass communication, such as the press, television and radio, not to mention the entire educational system. All the while, it must be noted, Polish society was being modernized, albeit at a much slower rate than Western Europe, which at the outset had the benefit of the Marshall Plan underpinning its efforts. The Church had a small press, but its primary instrument remained the Sunday sermon and personal contacts with the faithful.

Under the circumstances, in light of the fact that the Soviet Union had intervened on different occasions in both Hungary and Czechoslovakia, the Church generally followed a course of political neutrality. Underlying the Church's efforts at mediating between the regime and society was a sense of its prophetic voice that, although it refrained from direct involvement in politics, could be highly critical if, as it was expressed in the mid–1980s in *Tygodnik Powszechny*, government actions impinged on "the dignity and rights of man, in particular on his right to be a subject, to form his own destiny."[42] In this way the Church acted as an informal opposition party right up to Solidarity, and when the latter was banned, the Church "persisted in its endeavors to be a link between the rulers and the ruled."[43]

Moreover, in part thanks to these circumstances, unlike in other socialist bloc countries, eventually an underground political opposition did develop that linked various strands, including disillusioned former Communists. As Brian Porter-Szücs puts it, "With people like Michnik picking up the concept of *dignity* and people like Wojtyła propagating the idea of *rights*, the vocabularies of the secular opposition and the Church were converging."[44]

*   *   *

Alongside a country road outside of Lublin heading toward the village of Wojciechów there is a small roadside shrine with an image of the Black Madonna of Częstochowa that one sees all over the Polish countryside and often enough in the cities as well. Underneath the main part of the chapel—not much larger than a birdhouse and similarly perched on a pole—is fastened a small plaque with the words, "In this place on 7 June 1966 an act of desecration of the picture of Our Lady of Czestochowa took place." The plaque is dated 1981: in other words it was written in during the period of Solidarity when Poles could express their concerns more openly.

What the chapel silently commemorates is an event that happened during one of the crucial symbolic struggles between the Church and the regime after Wyszynski's release. Right after his release in 1956, the primate came up with the idea to celebrate the millennium of Poland's acceptance of Christianity in 1966. This turned into the Great Millenary Novena, starting with a tremendous meeting on Jasna Gora in 1957, continuing with many carefully planned events, and culminating in a gigantic meeting in Czestochowa. The state authorities would not interfere directly, but they did attempt to compete with the program by staging competing events, which invariably lost out to the Church events.

The whole program was carefully planned as a manner of an extended nine-year-long national catechism. Conceptually, however, Wyszynski was particularly concerned with the regime's manipulation of the nation's past, which was a key to Polish identity. The state would no doubt attempt to reduce the acceptance of Christianity in 966 into a mere beginning of statehood. As Weigel puts it, "The Great Novena, would ... challenge the communist attempt to separate the Polish people from their past in order to subjugate them in the present."[45]

Among the initiatives undertaken by the Polish bishops was an invitation in 1965 to the German bishops to take part in the main celebrations, which included a call for mutual forgiveness that was roundly criticized by the regime, ending with oft-quoted words: "We extend our hands to you, pledge forgiveness and ask for it." Inspired to some extent by the spirit of the recently ended Second Vatican Council where the bishops of the two nations had had the opportunity to meet, the letter worked at more than one level. As it has been observed, "The courageous message of forgiveness formed the first attempt to bridge the chasm between the two neighboring nations and quell the historical antagonism fed by official propaganda."[46]

A key to the program consisted of a copy of the Black Madonna taken to various dioceses. The faithful would often line the streets at the approach of the icon, which would be carried in a solemn procession as it neared its destination. For devout Poles, it represented "a journey of the Blessed Mother in and through Poland."[47] The scheme was so successful that in frustration the authorities decided to intervene. After a meeting at the Catholic University in Lublin, the icon was being transported to Warsaw by a side road during which time it was "arrested" and taken back to Warsaw. This is the event that is mutely commemorated in the roadside chapel. However, Wyszynski brilliantly capitalized on the deed by continuing the program with the empty frame of the icon, and the faithful continued to flock to the arrival of the absent icon. The regime was shamed into returning the icon. If the chapel on a rarely traveled road gives the impression of the event having been forgotten, interviews with people who were even a few years old demonstrate that the memory of the "imprisonment" or "arrest" of Mary is still alive.[48]

The Great Millenary Novena deserves particular attention beyond the duel between the Church and the illegitimate regime which despite its state apparatus proved powerless against a master strategist supported by the Polish people. The Novena had a powerful pastoral effect by bringing Poles out into the open so they could see themselves in a way suppressed by the atheist regime. It needs little insight to see that Karol Wojtyła learned a great deal from the event and appropriated its lessons for his future papacy. For instance, there is not such a great step from the Great Novena to John Paul II's World Youth Days. Charles Taylor explains that in our consumer society, "people still seek those moments of fusion, which wrench us out of the everyday, and put us into contact with something beyond ourselves."[49] In the midst of the mind-numbing grayness of the Communist era, this need was all the greater, and the Great Novena provided this for Poles.

Before we examine the period of religion in Poland that bears John Paul II's personal stamp, we will look at the other religions in Poland under Communism right up to the period before the Solidarity movement, after which they will be treated in a separate chapter.

* * *

In May of 1991 the First International Gathering of Children Hidden during World War II was held in Manhattan at the Marriot Hotel. A small delegation of survivors arrived from Poland; among them was Hanna Krall, a well-known writer in Poland. In her fictionalized account of the event she describes the hospitality of the American Jews, who were inadvertently a living testimony to what, if not for the Holocaust, Jewish life in Poland could have been like but too obviously was not. The fact that the American hosts had full families, they knew how to keep a kosher household, and many other factors effectively separated them from the Polish survivors: "The women from Poland didn't know how to bless the Sabbath candles," writes Krall. "They didn't know how to pray in a synagogue."

Despite being steeped in the tradition of their ancestors, these American Jews were nonetheless quite modern in their attitudes molded by their pace of life: they wanted their coreligionists from Poland to be able to recount their experiences in quick, digestible capsules, which made it impossible to transmit the horror of the wartime experiences in a manner that would do them justice, especially with regard to the memory of those who did not survive.

Toward the end of the actual event when visitors from the public asked questions, a common belief harbored toward the small delegation came to the fore:

> "And you're going back to Poland?!" they asked in horror. "To what? To graves?" They had Jewish graves in mind for they did not understand that the ladies were returning to their Polish graves. To mothers who were not their mothers and to the Jewish void of their real mothers.[50]

Krall's brief story itself encapsulates the situation of a good number of Polish Jews after the Second World War, who, if they had been children, often enough had been raised by the Christian families who had saved them. Although all Jews had been targeted by the Nazis, religious Jews were particularly hard hit by the war, since practicing Jews, with their highly distinct dress, not to mention standing out from the Polish or Ukrainian and Belorussian masses in various other ways, "had negligible chances of surviving the Holocaust, and very few of them survived."[51] Out of the two and a half thousand rabbis in Poland before the war, approximately one hundred survived.[52] Those Jews that survived had invariably lost families and their traditions, which in a religion that places such a high value on *halakhic* practices is a particularly discouraging circumstance.

At the time of the event in New York at the beginning of the 1990s there was thought to be from eight to sixteen thousand Jews living in Poland, which in dispersed communities meant that it was often difficult for a *minyan* to be formed, that is, the requisite ten men needed to say prayers in a synagogue. Right after the war, however, albeit decimated, there was still enough of a Jewish community to warrant hope for at least a modest revival of Jewish life in Poland.

About fifty to seventy thousand Jews survived the war in Poland under the occupation, while Jews from among the Polish citizens repatriated from the Soviet Union over the next couple of years added a further quarter of a million to the number. In other words, only about 10 percent of the prewar Jewish population survived the Holocaust. As mentioned above, they were not exactly made welcome by the Polish population, who were in the midst of a losing struggle with a new occupational force, along with some of the other factors discussed. Under these circumstances, not to mention obvious psychological factors, such as the difficulty of living in a country where the vast majority of one's family and relatives had been violently killed, with entire communities decimated, many Jews started emigrating. Many religious Jews also knew quite well that under an atheistic regime there would be problems and left the country. After the Kielce pogrom of July 1946, this overall trend increased.

Initially the new regime was somewhat accommodating, since it was ideologically opposed to anti–Semitism. But anti–Semitism soon returned in the guise of anti–Zionism. The regime permitted a number of Jewish secular organizations and a limited number of religious organizations to be established. These were primarily self-help organizations that received assistance from the American-Jewish Joint Distribution Committee.

As can be imagined, among religious Jews that survived the war, returning to all the earlier traditions was virtually impossible. For instance, the distinctive attire characteristic of the Orthodox community was no longer worn. In part this was from fear of standing out among the Poles, which posed a danger, but additionally "there was a widespread feeling that the great trauma of the Holocaust ruled out the restoration of the old traditional life."[53] Not to mention that its devastating effect disheartened many Jews from religious practice even when circumstances permitted it. In light of the above, it is hardly surprising that in a survey conducted in 1948, 56 percent of Jews declared themselves nonbelievers.[54]

Just as in the case of the Catholic Church, the falsified referendum and consolidation of power by the regime likewise brought about a drastic cutback in the toleration of the pluralistic groups within the Jewish community. One small Jewish organization was founded in the Stalinist period to monopolize all Jewish cultural activity, and the religious organization responsible for the congregations was severely restricted. For a longer period there was not even a rabbi to serve the congregations, while those communities that could not form a *minyan* for communal prayer were reduced to branches of larger congregations. All the while Jews were allowed to emigrate, and the community continued to contract. For a while after the political thaw of 1956, Jewish cultural life at least was allowed to develop at a healthier level, but this turned out to be a passing stage.

In 1968 due to an internal struggle within the Communist Party in which the proportionately large number of Jewish members of one of the factions was used against it, anti–Semitism again reared its ugly head in Polish society, and a majority of the Jewish community were either pressured or felt pressured to leave in the following years, most of them having been well assimilated to Polish society. However, if there is a light at the end of this sordid tale it is that this government campaign finally snapped something in the minds of at least a part of the countercultural elite. In the 1970s, for instance, the Catholic Intelligentsia Clubs organized a number of "Weeks of Jewish Culture" that raised the issue of Polish Jews and their culture and Polish–Jewish relations. Helena Datner claims, "The moral significance of such initiatives was highly significant for the smashed—literally and metaphorically—community, that is for those Jews who remained in Poland."[55]

The postwar Polish Orthodox Church, at approximately 450,000 members, was also reduced to a tenth of its prewar size, but this was largely due to the border changes and to some extent to population transfers.[56] In addition, on account of military operations against the Ukrainian Insurgent Army, nearly 140,000 Ukrainians were resettled by the communists from their indigenous territories to western and northern Poland in order to remove their guerrilla base, although some of these were Uniates.[57] Since the Orthodox Church leadership had essentially collaborated with both of the occupational powers, the current situation with only one of those powers remaining did not alter matters substantially. Formally the autocephalous status from prewar Poland was repudiated, only to be granted from the Moscow patriarch to a hierarchy acceptable to the new regime. Even the bishop who had collaborated with the Nazis was released from prison and temporarily reinstated to his position as the head of the Church before he was retired from his duties.

The formal structure of the Church was incrementally adapted to the new borders: a convent and monastery were founded close to the eastern borders of Poland in the late 1940s, more or less at which time an additional diocese was formed. An Orthodox Theological Seminary was opened to train future priests in Warsaw. When the Moscow Synod finally granted a metropolitan of Warsaw and Poland in 1951, the new hierarch set to work at Polonizing the Church by reducing the influence of its Ukrainian and Belorussian aspects. He also took advantage of the favor of the regime to assume control of a number of Uniate churches that had in turn been confiscated by the prewar Polish authorities. Partly due to his own organizational abilities but obviously through the favor of the regime, Archbishop Macarius was able to develop the Orthodox Church in Poland into a "respectable ecclesiastical body which enjoyed comparatively more privileges than the Roman Catholic Church."[58]

The succeeding decades under Communist rule saw an increasing grassroots demand for Ukrainization of the Orthodox Church in Poland as many of the faithful and clergy were Ukrainians, to which the hierarchy made only minor concessions. Some suggest that behind the regime's reluctance to make any concessions toward a Ukrainian Orthodoxy lurked "fears that a more far reaching Ukrainization of the church might well produce similar demands for a religious revival among its own [i.e., the Soviet Union's] Ukrainian population."[59]

If Ukrainians made up a substantial portion of the Orthodox Church in Communist Poland, they overwhelmingly formed the population of the Uniate or Greek Catholic Church, with a far more complex state of affairs after World War II ended. For one thing, a territorial Church that in prewar Poland existed in one state, the Church was now split with the major portion of believers and its dioceses in the Ukrainian SSR. Apart from the border change breaking up the structure of the Church, putting such a large number of Uniates under the control of the Soviet regime meant that their fate on the other side of the border affected their treatment in Poland to a larger degree than other religions. Their connection with the Vatican was a strong point against them, as was the political nature of the Greek Catholic Church with its close association with Ukrainian national identity: "The Greek Catholic Church was seen as a bastion of Ukrainian national and cultural identity, for which in the uniform, internationalist Soviet society there was no place."[60]

In the Soviet Union the Church was liquidated and the hierarchy imprisoned, and soon the remaining bishop in Poland and his assistant were also imprisoned because they did not "volunteer" to emigrate to the Ukrainian SSR. The bishop was tortured and died a couple of years later. The seminary was also closed down, and the mass was prohibited. Censorship also prohibited the use of the terms "Greek Catholic" or "Uniate" in any sense other than historical, which is a reason why it is now difficult to accurately chronicle the fate of the Church in the Stalinist era.

The deportation and dispersal of the Ukrainians mentioned above was to no small measure also aimed at destroying the Church as a prerequisite stage toward assimilating the Ukrainian population in Polish society. The population was spread out in the so-called recovered territories which were taken from Germany at Potsdam. In no place was there to be a concentration of Ukrainians greater than 10 percent of the population.

Thus the Church was effectively restructured from a territorial one to an underground Church serving the faithful throughout Poland. The masses were clandestine until the political thaw following the end of the Stalinist period in 1956. Even then no Greek Catholic parish was reestablished or permitted; rather masses were allowed at Latin Rite churches. Only the religious Order of St. Basil the Great was reinstated in Warsaw. From 1964 Greek Catholic priests were trained at the Catholic seminary in Lublin. By the time of Solidarity in 1981 the first priests were also being ordained in Przemysl, a city in the southeast corner of Poland, where a couple of small parishes outside the city had existed throughout the entire period, and whose small population had avoided deportation.

Unfortunately Roman Catholic priests, and even some bishops, were not always hospitable to the needs of the Greek Catholics. A journalist from *Tygodnik Powszechny* reports that in parts of Poland, Roman Catholic priests had no idea such a rite existed and were quite suspicious, but knowledge was not the only barrier:

> In southern and southeastern Poland where the rite was known, good will toward it was sometimes lacking. Occasionally a Greek Catholic priest came to a bishop, but he would not be seen, since the bishop did not want to talk to him. So he

would go to a village and present his documents to the parish priest. That priest would laugh at his papers: "What are you showing me, I've got my Primate in Tarnów." And at times for years a mass, baptism, or even funeral would not be said in the rite of the believer.[61]

The faithful of the remaining Catholic Rite, the Armenians, on account of their high assimilation to Polish society, suffered at the hands of Ukrainian nationalists in the former eastern Poland during the German occupation. A large number of them were killed in Kuty where they had a relatively large community. However, the above was also a factor in many Armenians being "repatriated" to Poland after the border shifts from the eastern border-lands that were now in the nearest Soviet republics, that is, the Ukrainian and Belorussian ones. The few Armenians who remained in those republics lost their church, since the rite was treated the same as the other Eastern Catholic rites: it was banned. In the new Poland their minuscule population was dispersed. Although their numbers now did not merit their own churches—nor, it must be stated, did the host Latin Rite churches show great sensitivity to this minority—they brought with them icons from three of their former churches, and these were located in three Polish Roman Catholic churches in Gdansk, Gliwice and Kraków, where their masses were said.

The last of the religious groups from the former borderlands was also largely dislocated by the border changes. The Tatars had already suffered tremendously for their strong resistance during the September campaign against the Nazis at the onset of the war. The latter retaliated by decimating the Tatar intelligentsia. After the war only two of the community's centers remained within the boundaries of the new Poland. Despite pressure against their decision, a couple of thousand Tatars from beyond its new borders decided to resettle in the country—mainly intelligentsia from the towns and cities, who had greater political awareness. But in the reconstituted Poland they were scattered across the country and did not have access to mosques or religious cemeteries. Moreover, the Poles they now lived among had little knowledge of their culture and attachment to Poland. These factors naturally had an impact on the Polonization of the group's members.

An increasing number of Tatars moved to the Bialystok region, close to the only remaining historical centers of their community, including two tiny mosques, where it was possible to maintain their religion and traditions. As a historian notes, "It was only here they were not aliens, here a handful of their coreligionists had lived for centuries, like in the parts where they had originated, peacefully and in a neighborly manner with their Catholic and Orthodox neighbors. Here no one was surprised by a Tatar, and a Muslim was not associated with the Arab world."[62] However, the process was not without some tensions within the group, since the local Tatars led a rural lifestyle, whereas the newcomers were more urban and better educated.

Slowly organizational structures of the community were enhanced. In 1969 the government allowed a congress of Polish Muslims, which resulted in the creation of a Muslim Religious Union of Poland. In the above context, the existence of the community must be acknowledged as quite a phenomenon. "Its survival," it has been noted, "in a predominantly Roman Catholic country ruled for forty years by a polity whose ideology was avowedly atheistic, is remarkable."[63]

Of the remaining historical Christian religious minorities the proportion of Protestants also changed drastically after the war. The number of Lutherans decreased on account of the transfer of the German population accompanying the border changes. Since many of their churches were then taken over by Polish Catholics "repatriated" from the eastern *kresy*, there was much rancor toward the dominant faith for decades. A number of the Czech Brethren left for Czechoslovakia, weakening the Polish Reformed Church of which they were a part, while a number of other Protestant groups that had lived in the eastern borderlands were not repatriated. The general weakness of the remaining Lutherans made it difficult for them to confront the totalitarian regime. In addition, a number of the Polonized Lutherans of German descent, especially in the Mazurian region, left Poland in the decades following the war right up to the 1980s, which further reduced their number to about sixty thousand at that time. The remnant of the rather small Polish Reformed Church managed to rebuild itself to the extent that in 1957 they resumed publication of their prewar periodical *Jednota*, which they continue to publish to this day.

One must not forget the internal diversity within Poles that is often overlooked, and which is to some extent still present in the country. This was particularly evident in the "recovered territories" granted to Poland after World War II in compensation for those taken away, where autochthon Catholics mixed with "repatriated" Polish Catholics. Bishop Kominek presided over the diocese of Opole during the postwar period, where this painful transition took place. Among others, he wrote about the healing role of pilgrimage sites such the one at Annaberg (Góra św. Anny), where "purely Silesian" Catholics would meet the newcomers, and how over the course of time "previously mutual injustices and score-settling slowly recede into oblivion."[64] A number of the "Silesians" were actually Germans, the descendants of whom currently constitute the largest ethnic minority in Poland. Significantly, bishop Kominek was the author of the famous letter of the Polish bishops to the German bishops mentioned above.

Although the list of minorities remaining in Poland after the Second World War is not complete in the above discussion, even with their addition they would hardly total beyond a small percentage of the population, which remains the current proportion. Thus it takes a discerning eye to spot the "religious and national diversity" that John Paul II claims is a part of every Pole. Nonetheless, as we will see more and more, Poles see it that way. But that is a somewhat later story. At the time Poles were concentrated on simply surviving the totalitarian system with a minimum of dignity, and maintaining this was religion's primary role in the totalitarian state.

Heaven? Religion from John Paul II to the European Union

Few Poles who watched the funeral of John Paul II on television in April 2005 will forget the scene of the wind blowing the pages of the open Gospel that had been laid on his coffin. For them, the image symbolized the end of a chapter in Polish history, indeed of world history. Rarely have similar events ever drawn so many heads of state and ordinary people to witness it, not to mention approximately a billion viewers worldwide watching the funeral on television. From the time of his election to the throne of Peter at the head of the Catholic Church on October 16, 1978, to his passing away, Poland had gone from a country subjected to a totalitarian state—somewhat "softer" than during its worst periods, but still capable of criminal actions against its society—to a member of the European Union. The Cold War had ended and, despite an ongoing war on terrorism, many more countries had democratically elected governments than during the closing years of the 1970s. Although no one person can be credited with these changes, the marked impact that John Paul II had on events is undeniable. By the time of his death many of these changes were already taken for granted, and it required considerable effort to remember the point of departure.

Right up until his election as pope on October 16, 1978, Karol Wojtyła had largely remained in the shadow of his mentor Cardinal Wyszyński. This was an essential strategy in that the regime would have given much to drive a wedge between the key players in the Church and thus be capable of manipulating it. Moreover, for all his stature and deft leadership of the Polish Church, Wyszyński was a known entity and was becoming predictable. Karol Wojtyła was different. Initially it seemed the quiet professorial bishop would not cause substantial problems. It soon turned out he possessed unbounded stores of charisma and could command a public. He was also astute. Among other things, as has been noted, "his defense of religious freedom was increasingly sharp-edged and struck the regime at its most vulnerable point, its claim to be a true representative of the Polish people."[65] One of the Communist rulers' great concerns was that Wojtyła would become the next primate. As Weigel dryly notes, "That turned out to be the least of their worries."[66]

The election of Wojtyła as pope stunned his countrymen, Catholic and non–Catholic alike. The authorities were shocked—both in Warsaw and in Moscow—but could only try to put up a good face despite the fact that they had at least some notion of what to expect. Party leader Edward Gierek rationalized the situation for himself and his Soviet overlords: "Every Pope has to take into account the reality he operates in, and the Church's overriding interest."[67] The most astute—even prophetic—observer outside the country, Alexander Solzhenitsyn, from his exile in Vermont exclaimed to his family: "It's a miracle! It's the first positive event since World War I, and it's going to change the face of the world!"[68]

Initially John Paul II used the conventional means at the disposal of his office to make his position clear. His first encyclical makes the point: "Even the phenomenon of unbelief, a-religiousness and atheism, as a human phenomenon, is understood only in the relation to the phenomenon of religion and faith. It is therefore difficult, even from a 'purely human' point of view, to accept a position that gives only atheism the right of citizenship."[69] It was clear from this that the pope was making an ideological point. This was evident for the Catholic leadership in Poland and was not lost on the non–Church opposition to the Communists. In a letter to the pope the members of the KOR (an acronym for Workers' Defense Committee) opposition group wrote, "We see in Your Holiness a spokesman for the best values of Polish culture, a culture free of narrow nationalism, based on tolerance and pluralism, linked to the Christian world of values."[70]

It is in this context that John Paul II's historic pilgrimage of 1979 must be placed. Ostensibly the visit was intended to be part of a celebration of the nine hundredth anniversary of the death of St. Stanisław, a bishop martyr from the Middle Ages who had opposed a powerful Polish prince. The Polish regime obviously knew they could not keep the Polish pope away from his homeland indefinitely, but they were hesitant about the date. "In the communists' minds," Weigel concludes, "Stanisław's resistance to the civil authority of his day had uncomfortable parallels to the current Polish situation."[71] The likelihood of this appraisal shows the weakness of the regime and its general paranoia at the time.

At the very outset of the visit the contrast between the homecoming pope and the resident head of the occupational regime could hardly be greater. The head of the Communist Party, Edward Gierek, stressed the importance for Poland of its alliance to the Soviet Union. John Paul reminded him that lasting peace could only be built upon the respect for basic human rights, including the right of a nation to freedom and its own culture. The importance of culture in relation to national identity would be a key theme in the pilgrim-age. To a group of young people in Gniezno the pope said, "Culture is, above all, a common good of the nation. It was decisive for us throughout history, more decisive than material power, more decisive than boundaries.... In the works of Polish culture, the soul of the nation is reflected."[72] At one juncture he gave a pointed Christian critique of Marxist-Leninism: "Remember this: Christ will never agree to a man being viewed only as a means of production, or agree to man viewing himself as such. He will not agree that man should be valued, measured, or evaluated only on this basis. He will not agree to that!"[73] It is evident what impact such words later had on Solidarity.

Thirteen million Poles saw John Paul II in his homeland in those few days. The ex–Marxist dissident Adam Michnik called the pope's pilgrimage a "lesson in dignity," "Poland's second baptism." He enthused that John Paul simultaneously "spoke to all of us" and "each of us individually."[74] Fr. Maciej Zięba, who was twenty-five at the time, remarks on the moment that so many felt was pivotal—when John Paul prayed at the meeting in Victory Square, "Come Holy Spirit, renew the face of the earth ... of this land!"—that people knew that "*something* had to change." His personal feeling then was that "we might have to live and die under communism. But what I wanted was to live without being a liar. The 1979 visit gave us the hope that this was possible."[75]

A remarkable matter was that such a revolutionary event took place in a peaceful atmosphere. The Poles had passed a test in human dignity. As Weigel summarizes this aspect of the pope's visit, "In other circumstances, under other leadership, and inspired by other themes, the mass demonstrations of disaf-fection that took place in June 1979 could have led in short order to cataclysmic rioting and bloodshed. Instead, they led to the solidarity from which came Solidarity."[76]

Few statements summarize the seminal event that led to the creation of Solidarity from the perspective of the impact of John Paul's visit better than Lech Wałęsa's later account. The leader of the historic strike at the Lenin Ship-yards in Gdańsk refers to it as "a kind of revolution on the knees in which prayer protected us against a totalitarianism limited by the existence of the Church, private individual farms, the historical consciousness of the popula-tion, and the presence in the Vatican of a Polish Pope with an explicit reminder that Poland was a part of Europe and its Christian heritage."[77] The irony of the movement was not lost on Leszek Kołakowski when he remarked that Sol-idarity was the first genuine workers' revolution in history: "It follows that the first workers' revolution in history was directed against a socialist state, and has proceeded under the sign of the Cross and with the blessing of the Pope. So much for the irresistible laws of history discovered scientifically by Marxists."[78]

Nevertheless, it should be noted that albeit the rise of Solidarity may have had a strong religious inspiration, it took the Church somewhat by surprise. Porter-Szücs goes as far as to claim, "The [obvious] religious overtones of the worker's revolt were ... an example of popular appropriation of religious imagery in defiance of the wishes of the Church leadership."[79] However, once the cat was out of the bag, so to speak, the Church's role during the August strike was supportive of the workers in a number of ways. It was the bishop of Gdańsk who proposed that allowing a priest to give pastoral services to barricaded workers would help keep things calm. At another juncture when one of Cardinal Wyszyński's sermons calling for "calm, balance, prudence, wisdom and responsibility for the whole Polish nation" was distorted by the state media and had dispirited the workers, the bishops responded immediately; as Weigel reports, "That same night they issued an emergency communiqué stressing that civic peace was impossible without freedom, including the freedom to form independent trade unions—the point on which the Gdańsk strikers had decided to make their stand."[80]

While the eyes of the world were rightfully turned on the mushrooming trade union, something else extraordinary was taking place below the level of the media radar: a civil society was born almost overnight. Developing civil society had been one of the ideas that dissident groups like KOR were forwarding, especially since any other forms of resistance to the regime were futile. Once Solidarity was established, little time was wasted in implementing it. As David Ost observed, "In the first months of existence [Solidarity formed] discussion clubs, political forums, independent social organizations, diverse newspapers, numerous ad hoc organizations." Befitting civil society, these were "ends in themselves."[81] He also observed that during Solidarity's height, a new morality took control in cities like Gdańsk and Szczecin: "No one drank, no one caused trouble, no one woke up crushed by a stupefying hangover. Crime fell to zero, aggression disappeared. Total strangers felt they needed each other."[82]

Certainly the above was not always the case and varied in different parts of the country, and the leadership bickered and the movement could not fully be controlled, which the regime scrupulously utilized to its own ends; nevertheless, Timothy Garton Ash's insights still quite appropriately summarize the accomplishment of the movement: "It is hard to think of any previous revolution in which moral goals played such a large part; not only in the theory but also in the practice of the revolutionaries; not only at the outset but throughout the revolution."[83]

History was now on the side of Solidarity, but the regime still had a few blows left to deal. Although the assassination attempt on John Paul II on May 13, 1981, could not be and still cannot be definitively attributed to Soviet instigation, the suspicion of Poles that this was the case cannot be considered irrational. The pope had been the object of extreme criticism in the Soviet Union and its satellites for several months before the event. As Weigel summarizes the various loose ends surrounding the mystery, "The simplest, most compelling answer to the question, Who benefitted? will keep alive the intuition that the Soviet Union was not innocent in this business."[84] The imposition of martial law now seems like the desperate act of a flailing regime, not to mention the killing of several priests, most notably Fr. Jerzy Popieluszko, over the next several years. Nine priests died in unexplained circumstances in the last couple of years of the regime alone, well after Popieluszko's murder.

This last event resulted in a sign of the regime's decline. The operation was botched and a witness turned up. Since martial law had temporarily crushed the opposition but had stripped away any legitimacy the Communists still maintained, the Polish authorities had little choice but to put their own agents on trial, where they eventually ended up serving long-term sentences. Davies aptly assesses the significance of the trial of Popieluszko's murderers: "In a society where the communist dictators had never been held to account, this event was a milestone."[85] The affair coincided with the emergence of Gorbachev as the first secretary of the Communist Party in Moscow. It took some time for him to realize that a new line would be necessary to possibly salvage the Communist system, and from this latter perspective his efforts were a failure. But the route he took meant that a return to past practices of censoring discussion wholesale were no longer possible.

In comparison to its hero-priests, the Church as an institution was somewhat timid. Cardinal Glemp did not possess the charisma of his predecessor as primate, who had died of cancer before the imposition of martial law. But it is difficult to say whether Cardinal Wyszyński would have taken a different line even if his style might have differed. Davies gives a fair assessment of the line taken by the Church in those trying years: "As an institution the Church remained rock solid in its determination to propagate an alternative vision of the nation's future. And the Primate's Council of mixed clerical and lay composition consistently acted as the most powerful medium of mediation."[86] One can also say that the Church partially took over Solidarity's role in promoting civil society through its continued support of independent culture, albeit in much more inauspicious circumstances. To some extent the regime attempted to curry favor with the Church in its difficult situation by granting an unprecedented number of permits to build churches. Since the proportion of parishes quite heavily favored the countryside while over the decades from the war the population had become highly urban, this was indeed a pressing ecclesial need.[87] Among the reasons for lower church attendance in cities was simply that the churches were not there for the faithful when they arrived from the country. Needless to say the edifices were built with the funds raised by the Church itself from an impoverished society.

John Paul II also continued to strengthen his fellow Poles' spirits, visiting the country shortly after martial law was lifted in 1983 and then again in 1987. In fact, it has been noted that "there were moments during his third Polish visit when the Pope spoke as if communism were already over."[88] The last visit was quite clearly meant to buttress the slowly recovering underground trade union by delivering a series of sermons on the theme of Christian solidarity. When the regime was finally exhausted and after a series of strikes in April and May of 1988 along with a series of pro–Solidarity demonstrations across the country, it tried to play the "Catholic card" by suggesting that Church leadership represent "society" in negotiations over any changes. The Church refused and the regime had to begin a dialogue with Solidarity after a seven-year hiatus. The famous Round Table Talks resulted in the first quasi-free elections on June 4, 1989, with Solidarity-backed candidates winning all the openly contested seats in the Polish parliament, and ninety-nine out of one hundred seats in the senate.

* * *

In a powerful poem written a couple of years after Poland regained its independence in 1989, Czesław Miłosz laments that there was no apt expression of gratitude marking the event. Entitled "Why?," Miłosz expresses wonder at the lack of any appropriate symbolic response on the part the Poles, whose "prayers" within the depths of their humiliation had "been heard."[89] Commenting on the poem in a homily soon after its publication, a priest in Lublin further contrasted the event and the subsequent meager response of Poles to that of the Israelites, who having crossed the Red Sea made a thanksgiving offering, while for the Poles a momentous passage had gone practically uncelebrated.[90] The historical magnitude of the downfall of Communism could appropriately conjure up biblical metaphors. However, granting the metaphorical interpretation of the transition and that no symbolic offering was made, nonetheless like in the biblical parallel, Poland had several years of crossing the wilderness in front of her.

For instance, Tadeusz Mazowiecki, the first prime minister of independent Poland, famously compared the terrible state of the economy when he formed his government to that of a skidding car that the Communists had abandoned and said: "Here, take over the steering wheel." The country was facing runaway inflation and had to make the transition to a market economy while the economy of its largest trading partner, the Soviet Union, soon to break up, also collapsed, leaving Poland scrambling to fill in the gap crucial for exports. Structural problems were likewise enormous in the government and its administration. Cataloguing the problems facing the new government would require a great deal of space. Social problems were another issue. Just to take one glaring issue, while the Polish economy has grown substantially, and its middle-class along with it, twenty years after the fall of communism 90 percent of families with four or more children lived in poverty, up from the 37 percent at the onset of independence.[91] Similarly to the Israelites during their exodus, for a time some Poles complained that it had been better under slavery, during Communist times.

While many problems were dealt with, some better, some worse, a particularly intractable legacy of totalitarianism influencing Poles' responses to numerous issues—from politics to daily life—has been the dearth of social trust affecting Polish society. It is this lack of social trust, among others, that has limited the potential for structural changes that can possibly affect the stability of economic growth in the long run, however impressive the current accomplishments appear. For instance, regional policy is a crucial area to address economic differences that have their roots all the way back to the Partitions. Economist Piotr Zientara assesses the problem from this perspective: "If social capital, by enhancing cooperation, plays a critical part in region-level learning and, by extension, regional development, then in Poland the prospects for the implementation of such strategies are not bright. How can a learning region be built if local inhabitants are distrustful, unwilling to compromise and disinclined to cooperate?"[92] Needless to say, the parting of ways of many of the members of Solidarity, with the trade union becoming a shadow of its former self, likewise reflects a crisis of trust.[93] This problem will be dealt with in greater detail in the next chapter. Suffice it to say that since religion to no small extent reflects society, this general problem of social trust affects it as well and doubtlessly plays a role in aggravating the crises that intermittently seem to overwhelm the Catholic Church in Poland, along with the divisions within it. Certainly the wilderness has not been crossed yet, and though it may not be the whole story of religion in Poland, its effect creates a significant undertone to a number of its developments.

Among the first concerns of the Catholic Church after the triumphant elections of 1989 was the return of religious education to the public schools. In short order the bishops issued a communiqué calling for its restoration; in August of the following year a subcommittee of the government and the Conference of Bishops announced it. The constitutionality of the move was challenged by the ombudsman, but the Constitutional Court of Poland upheld the decree. Fears that this was unfair to minorities led to the eventual opening up of the possibility for their organizing religion classes where the latter had the organizational wherewithal to do so. In practice this primarily meant some Protestant groups in Lower Silesia and Orthodox Christian communities in eastern Poland. Although the fact that religious instruction was introduced by a decree met with public criticism, the classes themselves soon became popular, as one scholar notes, "with Catholics and non–Catholics alike valuing them as a unique occasion on which to discuss metaphysical questions in an open way."[94]

Another issue important for the Church was that of concluding a concordat with the Vatican to replace the one broken by the Communist regime during the Stalinist period, which would allow such absurdities as the state not recognizing Church marriages to come to an end. This turned out to be surprisingly controversial, although the basic aim of the agreement was simply to protect the Church in carrying out its mission of evangelization from the vagaries of political change. Indeed, one of the reasons that the agreement— which had already been prepared in 1993—took until 1998 to come into effect was the interlude of a post–Communist government that would not confirm the negotiated agreement on account of its anticlerical electorate. Some critics, among others, contended that the recognition of Church marriages by the state would violate the division between the state and the Church, despite the fact that a number of democratic states—Austria, Denmark, Canada, and Finland—accepted such marriages.[95] Similarly, critics felt the concordat would move the country toward a Catholic state religion. The constitution, however, when it was passed, clearly spoke of the "independence and autonomy" of the state and Church. "Autonomy" was an important term, since it was more positive than separation: "In the situation, where the majority of the population belongs to both, the necessity of cooperation between State and Church should be stressed for each person's well-being," a statement by the Conference of Bishops explained.[96] Again, as in the case of religious education, all legal benefits that the Catholic Church accrued from the concordat were then gained— on an individual basis—by the major remaining religious communities.[97]

Certainly a "naked public square"—to use Richard John Neuhaus's memorable expression—does not exist in Poland. While some of the critics that claim the existence of an excessive civil religion in the country might have grounds for their complaints, there is no threat of a state religion, even if sometimes a lesser or even larger number of priests—occasionally bishops—overstep the boundaries of noninvolvement in political campaigns of various sorts. One of the more evident lessons in this regard from the pre-EU period has been that the less the Church has seemed to involve itself in politics, the greater confidence has been bestowed upon it by the public. For instance, after a decline in public approval, a politically restrained Church regained its esteem in 2003[98]—during the rule of a post–Communist government no less!

The various issues that arose between the Church and the state along with other social issues, as the Catholic public intellectual Jaroslaw Gowin puts it, were part and parcel of the fact that "the fall of communism signified the return of Poland to the mainstream of western civilization, with all the positive and negative effects of this fact." Ironically, one might add, despite its avant-garde rhetoric, the "scientific socialism" of Communism had kept Poland behind the European mainstream. Gowin continues, "From the perspective of the Church, perhaps the most important aspect of this return was a confrontation with the phenomenon and processes signified by social thinkers under the term 'modernity.'"[99] Although after Gowin, we could say much of the remainder of this book will look at different aspects of this confrontation, at this point we will present some of the more notable early reactions to this tremendous transformation.

The difficulties the hierarchical Church faced in adapting to the new circumstances were shared by the entire country and met with different responses. Some parts of the Church and faithful had greater problems in dealing with them. One nominally Church organization that thrived upon these troubles, attracting worldwide attention in the process, was and remains Radio Maryja. In 1991, Fr. Tadeusz Rydzyk of the Redemptorist Order established the station in Toruń. Initially the station kept a proper religious profile, broadcasting religious programs, prayers, news, and calm religious music. It soon started promoting a nationalistic Catholicism, which, as Weigel succinctly describes it, was overly clerical and "longs for a national political party tied to the hierarchy, and a large, paternalistic state."[100] Significantly John Paul II ignored the radio station during his visit in 1997 that included Toruń; while his spokesman went as far as to officially state that in his comments on the pope's visit, Fr. Rydzyk spoke only for himself. Eventually, even the cautious primate, Cardinal Glemp, issued a statement in 2002 openly critical of the station's activities. Compared to a televangelist with his own agenda,[101] the director of the station is a superb organizer, and although he has garnered much criticism, even within the episcopate, and some halfhearted attempts at controlling him, he seems untouchable. He is at once an entity unto himself and an embodiment of a significant split within the Church in Poland. The split also has a dynamic that creates a self-perpetuating cycle.

Moreover, the more the country's liberal media paint the radio almost exclusively in negative terms, the stronger the backlash effect, claims Ireneusz Krzemiński, a prominent sociologist: "The black image of Radio Maryja and the campaign against the station inclines some to stand in its defense."[102] He has further suggested that conflict strengthens the supporters of Radio Maryja, which was demonstrably true in a confrontation that arose concerning the television station sponsored by Fr. Rydzyk. For several months in 2012 a conflict of varying intensity ensued—including a major demonstration supported by one of the political parties—in which the denial of access for Telewizja Tram to a modern package of air-wave concessions was viewed by supporters as suppression. At one point even the Polish branch of Helsinki Watch agreed it was an attack on the station's freedom of expression. As a result of the conflict, a significantly larger number of listeners tuned in to the radio station and watched the existing television program. The Polish episcopate has officially supported this demand.[103]

If the existence of Radio Maryja generally acted—and acts—as a foil for the split in Polish Catholicism, the latter became quite visible in an early post–1989 crisis. A controversy broke out over Christian crosses planted near the entrance of the former Auschwitz concentration camp in 1988–89. This was the culmination of a crisis with roots back in Communist Poland, when Carmelite nuns established a convent near the former camp in 1984 to pray for all the victims, regardless of their religion and nationality. However, this went against Jewish sensibilities, who felt it was an appropriation of the camp where so many Jews had died, and a number of Jewish organizations expressed their outrage. Eventually the convent was moved in 1993 after negotiations; however, a cross that had been part of a ceremony conducted by John Paul II at Auschwitz in 1979 had been erected in 1988 close to the location "to commemorate the spot where 152 Polish prisoners had been shot by the Nazis in 1941."[104] Since Jews insisted they cannot pray in the presence of a cross, Jewish opposition mounted and an agreement was finally reached to move the cross in 1998. This evoked a grassroots response by a Catholic group calling itself the Cross Defense Committee, which—egged on by Radio Maryja—started planting numerous crosses next to the papal cross. The leader of the group used the media attention to denounce Jews as freemasons and "enemies of Poland."

In response, the chief rabbi of Poland at the time, Pinchas Menachem Joskowicz, together with the Israeli government and the Yad Vashem Holocaust Martyrs' and Heroes' Remembrance Authority protested the presence of the crosses. Cardinal Glemp countered that the Israeli protest was an attempt to "impose foreign will" on Poles. Eventually, with subtle prompts from the pope that dialogue was necessary, Glemp came to change this opinion, and it was decided that a nondenominational center for dialogue would be established near the camp. What the crisis demonstrated is aptly summarized by sociologist Genevieve Zubrzycka in her study of the crisis: "The 'War of the Crosses' highlights the divisions within Polish society and the different ways in which social groups actually articulate, 'on the ground' and in the public sphere, the relationship between national identity and religion." Although it started as a Polish Jewish issue, she further claims, "the controversy came to be interpreted as a largely internal affair: as a debate among Poles about Poland, and a discussion among Roman Catholics about Catholicism in post–

Communist Poland."[105] This conclusion is borne out by the War of the Crosses that took place the summer of 2010 after the presidential elections following the airline catastrophe of the flight to Smoleńsk, where the entire conflict was a "Polish"–"Polish" affair, largely among Catholics with a different vision of their Church—and country! The affair will be discussed later in some detail.

Other problems have included those specific to post–Communist countries as well as those that recently are affecting the Church in developed countries as a whole. Emerging evidence of Church collaboration with the secret services of the Communist regime has been a sensitive issue, and a number of priests waited until the evidence was unassailable before admitting to having done so, while others have used the opportunity to carry out witch hunts.[106] Altogether it has been estimated that approximately 15 percent of the Catholic clergy collaborated as informants in Poland, which is nevertheless considerably less than in other Communist countries, not to mention other professions within the country. As one historian puts it, "Recent revelations of extensive collaboration by priests ... provide a valuable correction to the historical record but do not greatly detract from the image of the Church overall as having resisted communism."[107] What surprisingly seems to have raised little attention is the problem of the priests and laypeople who openly collaborated with the regime in organizations of patriotic priests and the like—roughly 10 percent of the clergy. There was a period in the mid–1990s when the main organization of this type, PAX, published a daily newspaper, and since it seemed like the only successful Catholic daily, it had the blessing of the bishops, even though the organization made no genuine atonement for its former activities.

Sexual abuse scandals have not particularly rocked the Polish Church, perhaps in part because the Church was not involved in educating youth in institutions on a larger scale. Moreover, when a small number of incidents were initially uncovered, their impact was diffused on account of media exposing sexual scandals in a number of different fields: for example, almost simultaneous to the Polish public learning in 2002 of a case of an archbishop homosexually molesting seminarians in Poznań, the case of a renowned child psychologist abusing children came to light—what had been separated in time as media events in a number of Western countries occurred simultaneously in Poland. Moreover, the fact that cases come up intermittently rather than a collective report being issued as in some other affected countries likewise seems to have lessened the impact among the faithful. Although the problem certainly exists, and there is speculation that it may be larger than is apparent, the available evidence indicates the problem is smaller than in any other country in Europe.[108] Regardless of the size of the problem, there have been instances of quite insensitive handling of the situation by members of the hierarchy.[109]

One of the undoubted successes of the Church, on the other hand, has been in reinstating its charitable activities. First and foremost among them is reactivating Caritas, which is the largest charity active in Poland. The Polish branch of the Catholic Youth Organization boasts approximately twenty thousand active members and organizes charity drives, while numerous other Church organizations run hospices, orphanages, homes for single mothers, and soup kitchens for the poor. These are a drop in the bucket of Poland's social needs, and the question is what more the Church can do in this regard. One Church historian makes the point that the problem of poverty "can scarcely be solved by the passage of a few laws in Warsaw."[110] However, according to the religion journalist Jonathan Luxmoore, the Church could weigh in on stronger action from the powers that be. Luxmoore claims that the Church has been "remarkably reluctant to take on a prophetic public role as defender of the poor and marginalized. Although it has sometimes talked about the current injustices, it has yet to address their underlying causes."[111] Considering, among others, that poverty among children in Polish society is among the highest in the EU, this is indeed a pressing issue.

The charge is to some extent confirmed by Bishop Andrzej Czaja of the diocese of Opole, who in an interview for the Catholic Information Agency claims the Church is too absorbed with itself and admitted that Poles in backward areas like the former state farms, among the most depressed parts of Poland, have a right to feel abandoned by the Church. (*Gazeta Wyborcza*, October 6, 2010). Nevertheless, the above should not detract from those who have devoted themselves to alleviating poverty in a more direct manner, for instance Sr. Małgorzata Chmielewska, the charismatic nun who heads the Bread of Life Community, which runs seven homes for the homeless and raises funds to subsidize educational needs for children from poor homes.[112] Known for her tough-love approach, she has perhaps the best claim to be called the Polish Jean Vanier.

In other fields there has been a degree of adaptation to the new circumstances. A noteworthy development in 1993 has been the establishment of the Catholic Information Agency referred to above. It has grown to be the largest religious news agency in East Central Europe and the second-largest in Europe as a whole. Indeed, it is the second-largest news agency in Poland, which is a measure of its success, but also of the interest the Polish media generally have in religion.[113] Naturally religion is also a sensitive issue, but on the whole for the first two decades after the fall of Communism, more clearheaded commentators from both the liberal and conservative wings of the Church agree that Polish media—although they certainly have not covered them up—have been rather restrained in reporting Church scandals, like the ones mentioned above.[114] Although, after the presidential elections of 2010, the trend has been toward removal of the kid gloves. Conversely, a number of religious media, especially Radio Maryja and its affiliates, are hardly unbiased in presenting secular news. These matters will be dealt with in more detail in the final chapter.

A number of erstwhile supporters of the Catholic Church in Poland are currently unhappy with the direction it has allegedly taken. Adam Michnik complains that the Polish bishops have difficulty coping with pluralism; as a result, "The intolerant conformism of Radio Maryja is gaining the upper hand over the positive legacy of John Paul II."[115] Even among people in the Church camp, there are those who share the impression that the Church is largely drifting. From among the members of the episcopate, Bishop Czaja says very much the same, claiming, "During the last few years, especially after the death of John Paul II, we primarily respond to what the external world throws at us and to its accusations. This is an apologetic and polemical vision, but not very proactive."[116]

Symbolically the end of an era came in 2005 when the primate and president of the Polish Conference of Bishops stopped being the same person. These functions had become separate in the Catholic Church after the Second Vatican Council with the purpose of increasing the collegiality of the Church, but remained connected in Poland on account of the existence of the totalitarian regime in order to avoid the possibility of a divided Church through providing the Communists with an avenue for manipulation. In Poland the functions had become separate in 1994 in independent Poland, but the Polish bishops voted Cardinal Glemp as their president in order to honor his position as primate. When Cardinal Glemp declined to run for the presidency in 2005, they were finally split in fact and not simply in principle.

The last substantial issue in which John Paul II left his direct imprint was the question of the entry of Poland into the European Union, which culminated in 2004, a year before his death. The Polish episcopate was understandably wary of the EU. They had little need to be informed by the opinion expressed on various occasions by sociologist Peter Berger, a social scientist who does not accept the inevitability of secularization in America but concerning the European context claims that,

> quite apart from the *acquis* to the EU, there is an *acquis* to what I call the "European package"—an aggregate of attitudes, beliefs and lifestyles, which has a cultural fusion effect within the borders of the EU, but which spills across these borders with varying force. *Secularity is an important element of the "European package."* Whether they are initially aware of this or not, countries that come under the influence of this new European culture *ipso facto* open themselves up to secularization— a decline of traditional religion in the public sphere and in the lives of individuals.[117]

However, at an early stage EU officials included the Church in the process of unification. A delegation of Polish bishops was invited to Brussels in November of 1997 on a fact-finding mission, where they were satisfied that no threat was posed by EU institutions. In a survey conducted on Catholic priests a year later, 84 percent declared themselves in favor of European accession, and two-thirds felt the membership would not affect the Church's position. Although there was a concern that integration would expose Poles to materialistic values, more than half felt that this would be the case whether Poland entered the EU or not.[118]

Of course John Paul II had never withheld his criticisms of European materialism, together with its "culture of death," but he nevertheless insisted from quite early on that Poland's place was within the EU. During his visit to Poland in 1991 he quite emphatically stated, "We do not have to become part of Europe, since we ourselves created Europe. We created it, enduring greater hardship than those now credited, or crediting themselves, with being the keepers of Europeanness."[119] And there was his slogan mentioned during the meeting with Polish pilgrims on the eve of their country's referendum on access to the European Union in 2004: "From the Union of Lublin to the European Union." This effective summary of Poland's position was quite influential in the outcome of the referendum.

Where does this leave Catholicism in Poland at present? Although that question will be an ongoing concern throughout the remainder of the book, one point deserves preliminary attention. Pointing out that the "European 'norm' of secularization warrants some more critical scrutiny," sociologist Jose Casanova goes on to give one of the best summaries of the opportunities and challenges currently facing the Catholic Church in the country:

> Let *Polonia semper fidelis* keep faith with its Catholic identity and tradition while succeeding in its integration into Europe, thus becoming a 'normal' European country. Such an outcome, if feasible, could suggest that the decline of religion in Europe might not be a teleological process necessarily linked with modernization but a historical choice Europeans have made. A modern religious Poland could perhaps force secular Europeans to rethink their secular assumptions and realize that it is not so much Poland which is out of sync with modern trends, but rather secular Europe that is out of sync with the rest of the world.[120]

Casanova suggested a number of conditions that were a prerequisite for such an optimistic scenario. Obviously from the perspective of the Church, this would also be the optimal result of the entry into the European Union, and the chances of its success or failure will be examined particularly in the last chapter.

An example of the challenges facing the Church is featured in an event that occurred in late summer 2010. During the crisis concerning the "defenders of the cross" after the Smoleńsk tragedy referred to above, with the help of Facebook a group protesting the "defenders" organized a spontaneous anti-

Catholic happening, heaping ridicule on the mottled group. Berger, rightly pointing out that such an event would have been largely unthinkable just a few years earlier, commented on the event: "I would say that we are witnessing here a process of 'Europeanization.' This is a *cultural* process, reinforced by incorporation into the European Union but independent of this political development, and preceding it in time."[121] No doubt there is more than a grain of truth to such an assessment. However, in an interview in the September 6, 2010, edition of *Gazeta Wyborcza*, Krzysztof Michalski, who had been closely associated with John Paul II and Solidarity priest Jozef Tischner, indicates another, less obvious but traditional aspect to the gathering, despite its modern form. Much like a number of Catholic countries, Polish Catholicism has a deep tradition of anticlericalism harkening back to the Partitions that was put on hold during the Nazi and Communist occupations, and that extended to the end of John Paul's reign. This anticlericalism is not necessarily against religion and can have a purgative effect on some of the Church's excesses. One can add from this historical survey of religion in Poland that at times the phenomenon of Poles going counter to the Church, such as with the Confederation of Warsaw of 1573, in the long run has had a salutary effect on Catholicism.

As the above demonstrates, the Church is not simply the hierarchy, which has largely been the focus within these historical chapters. Rather, the relationship between the hierarchical Church and the faithful is dynamic, and a closer look at this relationship, together with the lived religious experience of the various religious groups of contemporary Poland, both Catholic and non–Catholic, will also be a primary subject of the remainder of the book.

PART II

The Varieties of Polish Religious Experience

3

From Popular Religion to Religion's Role in Civil Society

Popular Religion Past and Present

Shortly after the airline catastrophe on April 10, 2010, when the president of Poland and ninety-five passengers and crew members perished and a tremendous surge of national grief ensued, the author Jerzy Pilch commented during a TVN24 broadcast on the form that the major spontaneous sites of commemoration had taken: "Poles have gained mastery, certainly remarkable virtuosity, in two fields: in lighting candles, illuminating cemeteries, or creating sites that are quasi-cemeteries, and in setting up crosses out of flowers."

Naturally Pilch was being ironic, but he nonetheless hit upon something characteristic for the Polish popular religious sensibility, especially in its dominant Catholic version. At this juncture a bit of what might be called theological sociology is in order. According to the theologian David Tracy, the theistic religious imagination is on the one hand dialectical, picturing God as distant from creation, on the other hand it is analogical, wherein God is also felt to be close to the world and to people.[1] Although the relationship of these two tendencies is dynamic and rarely found in pure form, the Catholic imagination inclines toward accepting the close proximity of God to creation. Sociologist Andrew Greeley summarizes the different sensibilities in more traditional terms: "Catholics tend to accentuate the immanence of God, Protestants the transcendence of God."[2] This, among others, is evidenced by the importance for the former of the sacraments, which suggest the availability of grace to God's creatures. The religious sensibility that evolves from this perspective has a proclivity for multiplying metaphors demonstrating the proximity of God to humanity, and, among other things, values human community. In contrast, the dialectical imagination, more likely for the Protestant sensibility, tends to view community as an obstacle to a more direct relationship with

88

God. Tracy stresses the complementarity of the two religious sensibilities—
at times one acting as a corrective to the other's extremes—and that neither
is superior to the other, while Greeley has studied how they become embodied
in the art, literature and attitudes of society, particularly in the United States;
he concludes there is a connection between the religious imagination and how
people live and the themes that permeate their creativity. Due to the tendency
of the analogical imagination to see grace virtually everywhere Greeley often
refers to it as the "enchanted" imagination, obviously in contradistinction to
Weber's "disenchanted" modernity.

The division suggested by Tracy and augmented by Greeley is perhaps a
little pat, but it does offer a pertinent point of departure for a discussion of
religion in Poland—all the more so since, as it was pointed out, even in its
variety religion is and was dominated by theism in the country, and thus the
diverse forms of the theistic imagination. One can see, for instance, in the
example proffered by Pilch that the religious sensibility which the Poles exhibited at that tragic juncture is sacramental despite its spontaneous, grassroots
expression. The same can be said for the even greater outpouring of grief at
the death of John Paul II several years earlier.[3] It proves what Greeley argues
that the sensibility is also a part of lived religion, and not just of the high religion of the Church hierarchy and religious elite. And it might help to note in
reference to the suggested complementarity of the two poles of religious sensibility that although he was not alone in his critique of this particular facet
of Polish religiosity at the time, Pilch happens to be a Lutheran, with his opinion typical for the dialectical imagination—elsewhere he emphatically explains
that the ritual of lighting candles at graves is not Lutheran[4]—and such commentary as his is certainly helpful at times in piercing excesses in the specific
expressions of the Catholic religious imagination. There was a tremendous
amount of genuine grief that Poles felt at that historic moment of the catastrophe, and the form was largely appropriate for its expression, but there was
also an element of pomp and spectacle that was hardly negligible.[5]

A problem in applying this bipolar concept of the religious imagination
more extensively to Poland lies in the fact that both Tracy and Greeley are primarily interested in the theological and sociological problems of their native
United States where the Protestant and Catholic denominations are dominant,
and so they have not, nor has anyone else to date, attempted to apply it to
Orthodox Christianity, nor to Judaism or Islam. However, if we agree that it
is a dynamic concept that pertains to the theistic imagination,[6] I would speculate that in Judaism, for one, where the written "Word" dominates, it is likely
that the dialectical imagination is primarily at work, but not entirely. For
instance, the Sabbath practices in Judaism can be counted as sacramental.
Moreover, we can take the Polish case of classical eighteenth- and nineteenth-

century Hasidic thought, which its Haskalah critics accused of pantheism but is more accurately termed panentheism,[7] in which everything is in God. Although the distinction may be a fine theological one, the conception evidences the analogical imagination, which at times brings theism to the brink of pantheism. This largely accounts, as shall be seen later by the Polish example, for the phenomenon that "Catholicism (in its better moments) has not hesitated to make its own the practices, customs, and devotions of the nature religions wherever it has encountered them."[8]

For the Hasidim, everything, including the entire cosmos, was a garment of the divine. And so "it follows implicitly by extension," argues Aryeh Wineman, "that all the cosmos be considered a kind of parable."[9] Indeed, the parable was a formidable teaching tool of the Hasidim. Hasidism also taught that people must worship and cling to God, that is, attain *devukut*, not only during the practice of religious observances, but in all aspects of life—business, social contacts, and daily affairs. Moreover, the founder of Hasidism Baal Shem Tov's insistence that it was important to "serve God in joy" was quite remarkable at the time. From this postulate an ecstatic prayer-centered regime that questioned the strenuous asceticism of earlier Jewish mystics evolved within the movement. The emphasis placed on joy as essential to the good Jewish life and crucial in the worship of God resulted in the importance of Hasidic song and dance as expressions of piety among the followers and aided in building community cohesion. All this implies a high degree of the analogical imagination operating both at the conceptual—"theological"—level and in lived religion.

At any rate, it is beyond the scope of this book to prove the above concepts, and it is not my intent to apply them to all religious traditions in Poland. I will primarily utilize them as a relevant point of departure in the further discussion of popular religion, which is perhaps among the most distinctive forms of lived Catholicism in Poland and will be the subject of the first part of this chapter. To put it another way, in the concept of the analogical imagination Greeley finds a theological affirmation of lived religion in its variety. In this survey I share Greeley's enthusiasm for the popular tradition in Catholicism, arguably the most richly developed aspect of Polish Catholicism, as the few salient examples below might demonstrate. The greater part of this section of the chapter will look at historical aspects of the phenomenon, and here the analogical imagination will be more implicit. Among other things, in keeping with the conceptual model of the analogical imagination, I will examine what might be called "enchanted time and space," referring to phenomena like the wayside shrines, but also the evolution of sanctuaries and paraliturgical practices. A particular aspect of popular religion that accompanies the above phenomena is the dynamic relationship between the high tradition in Catholicism—largely borne by the institutional Church—and the popular tradition, or "poetic Catholicism," as Greeley calls it. Having established a number of its salient historical features, I will end with a discussion of the current state of popular religion, which will especially concentrate on some of the areas of its transformation. The remainder of the chapter will then focus briefly on lived religion in the face of catastrophe, which ethnic Poles and most of the minorities, needless to say especially the Jews, experienced during World War II and to a somewhat lesser degree under Communism, and then to a larger extent I will concentrate on the problem of religion in the face of modernity, particularly—at least in this chapter—its role in building civil society after the collapse of Communism.

*   *   *

If we accept the existence of the analogical imagination we gain a partial explanation for observations anthropologists offer such as, "Catholicism has long encouraged a considerable amount of internal diversity."[10] Greeley boasts, perhaps unfairly, that from among the primary theistic religions—Judaism, Protestantism, Catholicism, and Islam—"Catholicism has the most richly developed popular tradition because it is least afraid of the imaginative dimension of religion."[11] The popular tradition of Catholicism in Poland is most commonly associated with folk religion or religiosity. One of the seminal features of this type of religiosity is the importance of tradition, or the "faith of our fathers." Put simply, "the dominant conviction [in folk religion] is that patterns of conduct transmitted by past generations are important and worth perpetuating. This type of culture, and its inherent religious elements, are treated as something essential and constitute—in the conviction of the faithful—an integrated whole with the divine plan."[12] Considering that to this day approximately half of Poles attribute their faith to tradition, the impact of folk religion remains quite significant.[13]

According to Church historian Jerzy Kłoczowski, the nineteenth century is in many ways a key to the contemporary phenomenon. Life in the largely agrarian society of the period was steeped in religion: "Names that were used, the attitude toward animals and God's gifts such as bread, the formulas used to greet people, the feeling that everything depended on God's decision, the habit of crossing oneself on many occasions, all manifested deep religious sensitivity."[14] It was then that popular religion likely reached its peak—at a time, in other words, when some parts of Europe were experiencing de–Christianization: it is estimated between 90 to 95 percent of Poles were regularly engaged in religious practices then.[15] It was a period when the Church carried out a widespread catechism of the faithful along with more regular internal missions.[16]

Naturally, lived religion has changed considerably over time, even in tradition-bound environments such as the agrarian areas where folk religion continues to dominate.[17] Still, up until the period Kłoczowski describes and beyond, it was possible to discern what has been claimed to be characteristic for religion in premodern Europe; in rural areas, "the entire local setting had something of a 'sacred overlay.' All the people in the community knew numerous spaces where they could readily contact the divine—a votive shrine at a crossroads, a holy well, a home altar, a standing stone or cairn."[18] Perhaps the main difference would be that by the nineteenth century the "standing stones" and "cairns," examples of the more pantheistic bent of agrarian residents— with which the analogical imagination likewise has an affinity—would also be replaced by crosses and shrines to patron saints or the Virgin Mary. It should be added that to this day there is an impressive number of these roadside shrines and crosses in Poland. By some accounts, the number of religious shrines is more reminiscent of Nepal than Europe.

The crosses are an effect of the institutional Church. Although according to sources freestanding crosses appeared in villages by the sixteenth century,[19] in the seventeenth century parish priests were instructed to erect holy crosses wherever possible to deepen the religiosity of the faithful during the Counterreformation. This campaign became a sign of patriotism during the Partitions and so started to resemble a grassroots movement. Crosses were erected for a number of reasons: among them to protect travelers against evil forces; imposing penance to forgive sins; to receive requests for good harvests, successful journeys, and the like; and as memorials to commemorate places, persons, or events.[20]

If the institutional Church instigated the cult of crosses, to a great extent wayside shrines seem to have multiplied on the initiative of the faithful from the sixteenth to seventeenth centuries[21] and on to the present, although they likewise possibly indicate the effect of the long-term presence of the churches.[22] Indeed, some of the more elaborate shrines are like miniature churches. However, this did not stop the believers who erected them from occasionally incorporating older beliefs, like the importance of holy places and trees: to this day one finds small shrines placed up on trunks of trees, sometimes at the edge of a field or by a forest road. Moreover, various patron saints were popular depending on the needs of a community or settlement: "Thus the figure of Saint Roche was displayed in pastures to protect cattle and Saint Nicholas against wolves. Saint Ambrose protected an apiary and Saint Jan Nepomucen ... stood beside the water and bridges on a graceful counter column."[23] Some of the saints had a high tradition and a low tradition—for instance, in wayside shrines—like Saint Adalbert of Prague, whose martyrdom was instrumental in establishing the Polish Church, and whose cult is maintained in parts of the country to this very day.[24]

Early in Andrzej Wajda's film *Man of Marble* of 1976, the viewer witnesses a fictional Stalinist documentary in which the bricklayer hero leaves his village and passes a wayside shrine, ostensibly leaving folk religion behind to build the industrial future in Nowa Huta. What is not well known is that in some cases such shrines were brand new, especially during the Stalinist era, when building a church bordered on the miraculous. Alongside the date they bear cryptic but appropriate religious inscriptions. For instance, on the side of a shrine outside of Wilków on the Vistula erected in 1951, the faithful inscribed the invocation, "*Od powietrza, głodu, ognia i wojny zachowaj nas Jezu*" (Protect us Jesus from airborne plagues, hunger, fire and war), a variation on a traditional invocation, but obviously appropriate for those troubled times.

Religion scholar David Morgan makes the salient point that "[d]evotional images ... participate in a visual piety that encompasses a range of interacting, interdependent forms of meaning-making."[25] Frequently these wayside shrines were the site of special practices or even social events; among others things, priests in the countryside would bless the fields annually, and these ceremonies would take advantage of the proximity of a wayside cross or shrine. Some practices would evolve in connection with a particular site. In a wooded area on the outskirts of the town of Urzędów a chapel dedicated to St. Odile of Alsace is located. A bishop who for a time in the 1960s was the parish priest of the town describes one of the traditions connected with the shrine: "There is a beautiful custom of going for water to the spring by St. Odile's chapel on Good Thursday. Folk belief says the water is helpful for eye diseases, headaches and sore throats."[26] The intercession of the patron saint—concerning the listed ailments—is thus connected with the regenerative powers of water, as in a "holy well." Unsurprisingly, shrines and chapels are not infrequently situated close to springs.

On a more social level, an elaborate but otherwise typical historical example of various practices connected with shrines are the customs surrounding an elegant St. Jan Nepomucen shrine on a column at the edge of the town of Bilgoraj in the current voivodeship of Lublin that was erected in the first quarter of the nineteenth century. Soon it became popular with sieve makers, an important group to the economy of the vicinity. An ethnographer recorded how after they made their wares, the sieve makers would take journeys into the depths of the Russian empire to peddle them. Since these journeys were full of hardships and even hazards, before setting out on them their wives and friends would join the sieve makers at the shrine of St. Nepomucen, the patron saint of long journeys, and drink a number of toasts to the success of the journey, only to meet again at its completion to celebrate the safe return.[27] It is obvious in such customs that the boundary between sacred and profane could be fairly fluid, which is typical for folk religion. This is not to say that a distinction between sacred and profane did not exist and was not essential for the agrarian sense of the good life. As a popular saying goes—now a part of the Polish vernacular—an ideal partner was supposed to be fit, both for "dancing" and "praying": "*do tańca i różańca.*"

In many cases—or longer than communal memory could say—it is apparent such local practices "confirmed community social bonds and ties with the land."[28] Such localism, it must be mentioned, had its downside, including a suspicion of outsiders. Jews and Roma were often outcasts, and alongside a number of demeaning customs that utilized them they were often incorporated into warnings disciplining children to get them to behave.[29] But the "other" did not have to be a member of a different ethnic group. In some circumstances it be could one village against another, and the same religion was no shield. Before the First World War in Eastern Galicia, the Hutsul villagers of Bystrec in the Carpathian Mountains—a place too small to merit its own parish— had to attend a parish church at a more distant village, rather than in the nearby town of Żabie, where feelings of animosity were mutual. Author Stanisław Vincenz describes the run-ins that took place: "While riding to church more than once it happened that they would be assaulted passing through Żabie, which sometimes resulted in injury or they would be tossed into the river."[30]

However, if the emphasis was on communal practices, folk religion was flexible enough to meet particular needs. During the interwar period agrarian political leader Wincenty Witos describes how the prayers said at home could be quite varied, "depending on what patrons the household had and what concerns worried the family."[31] Yet if some of the practices at the shrines were idiosyncratic and specific to the locality, the middle of the nineteenth century brought an impetus to the traditional folk culture of Polish religious life that would proffer a common denominator to many regions. This was the time of the spread of May Devotions to Our Lady, the Live Rosary, and later in the century came October Rosary Devotions. These practices took place at the village churches, but the latter could be fairly distant for the faithful, while the shrines and crosses were much closer to home. In the late nineteenth century such private group devotions in the country were encouraged.[32] To this day in a good many regions of the Polish countryside one sees these crosses and shrines decorated around Easter time, which, in turn, prepares them for the May Devotions. These are organized spontaneously by the faithful, although occasionally a priest might participate when invited. The care taken in maintaining these shrines throughout the country is a phenomenon worthy of closer study and testifies to their continuing significance for the local communities.[33]

Wayside shrines have not escaped the attention of artists, and they are finally capturing the imagination of urban religious authors, like Piotr Wojciechowski, who praises their qualities: "A wayside shrine is the point where the landscape meets God. It is a human presence in the landscape that doesn't disturb it, but humanizes it. The ecology of Polish shrines is an unwritten book."[34] In the latter point he is certainly correct; wayside shrines and the practices surrounding them are a fascinating aspect of Polish religiosity, and though they may be attracting the interest of ethnographers and anthropologists, they have yet to receive a treatment that does the phenomenon justice.

The crosses and wayside shrines were intended to augment the parish churches and sanctuaries, the representatives of high tradition in smaller centers. But even within these, especially the sanctuaries, the boundary between high and popular religion could be fluid. This can be illustrated by the story of a church belonging to the Order of Bernardines in Rzeszów. Within the order's cloister there is an impressive basilica. To some extent the entire cloister with the basilica can be considered an adjunct to a late Gothic Madonna found in one of the transepts. An account of the origins of the cult surrounding the Madonna was published by the order in 1765, demonstrating the dynamic relationship between the high and popular tradition. Early in the sixteenth century a poor farmer on land that was then the outskirts of Rzeszów is said to have first heard the voice of the Blessed Virgin invoking praise for her son and promising succor for those in need.[35] The voice came from a pear tree, which in folk tradition was associated with the tree of life, as was Mary on account of her bearing "fruit." This perhaps explains why a similar vision is recounted pertaining to a sanctuary not so distant in the region, at the town of Jarosław, which also includes a pear tree. According to the related tradition the farmer built a chapel on the spot of the revelation. In 1531 a church was built replacing the chapel, and it became one of the earliest churches in the Małopolskie region dedicated to the cult of Mary, which at that juncture was not so common.

That part of Poland was subject to attacks by Tatars. In the same year that the church was erected the latter tried to burn it down during one of their raids, but, as the account relates, "in a miraculous manner neither the church nor the statue were burnt and as if it were Moses' burning bush they remained whole within the flames."[36] The motif of holy images remaining unscathed by flames was not uncommon in accounts from that period. Generally, according to a local historian,

> Within the descriptions of the aid which the faithful attained through miraculous intercession after praying before the statue the dramatic events that the entire community experienced are chronicled: wars, epidemics, plagues on cattle. Aside from these were the individual ailments—diseases, accidents or Polish plait. They reflected the conditions of the age in which people lived.[37]

People from many stations of life were affected and came to the figure to pray for intercession in their needs.

The current church and cloister were erected in the first quarter of the seventeenth century, and in 1629 it was offered by the benefactors to the regional chapter of the Bernardine Order who were renowned for their devotion to the Blessed Virgin Mary. The cult of the miraculous figure continued to grow, as the votive offerings attested; consequently, in the middle of the eighteenth century the prior started the prerequisite process for the statue to be crowned. This involved an application to the Vatican in which the duration and miraculous nature of the cult were to be confirmed.[38] Out of hundreds of Marian shrines in the Commonwealth, only twenty-nine received this status.[39] The account of 1765 was obviously intended to commemorate the figure's coronation of two years earlier. At the time of the coronation, two tableaux were offered to decorate the transept, on which roughly a hundred different miracles attributed to praying intercession gained through by the figure are illustrated, providing contemporary visitors with a vivid visual document of the time.

The presence of the religious order naturally gave the local cult greater credibility, allowing it to flourish, but it must be stressed that the cult came first. The high and popular tradition formed a symbiosis. The legends and tales at the base of the impressive baroque church in what were then the outskirts of Rzeszów are not uncommon for most historic religious edifices in Poland. The seventeenth and eighteenth centuries were periods from which many of the country's Marian shrines and sanctuaries date, a good number of them, like the sanctuary in Rzeszów, known for their efficaciousness.[40] At that time the coronation of Marian images was part of a larger campaign on the part of the Vatican in confirming the value of religious images that had been questioned by the reformers. The custom was appropriated in folk religion through images of Mary with wreaths of flowers which also became popular in Poland.[41]

As the above example demonstrates, if in the nineteenth century agrarian Poland was a bastion of Polish Catholicism, in the earlier Commonwealth period religion radiated from the towns and through the gentry.[42] Even the wayside shrines in the countryside of the seventeenth and eighteenth century were still largely funded by the gentry landowners.[43] The peasants were as of yet not very religious, or were so in a manner that was considered crude on the part of their social betters. Currently it is difficult to say, for instance, whether peasants, who as late as in the eighteenth century were sometimes accused of poor church attendance, were simply not very religious or rather were exhausted from their trying lifestyle.[44] It must be recalled that in contrast to much of Western Europe in the seventeenth and eighteenth centuries the situation of the Polish peasants degenerated rather than improved, because of the response of the gentry to the economic decline that both accompanied and fostered the political decline of the Commonwealth,[45] not to mention that the peasants' religious practices were viewed from the outside by a different social class.

However, even the high tradition in its Sarmation version tended toward the sensuous expression, which is witnessed in the presence of certain folk practices and the lack of more demanding ones. For instance, during the period of the Commonwealth the town of Urzędów had a hospital that served the region. On account of the importance of the latter the town chose St. Odile as its patron. This resembled folk religion, where, understandably, saints who were patrons for diseases, epidemics, and natural disasters were quite popular.[46] Although according to the official liturgical calendar the feast day for the patron was December 13, the inhabitants of the town customarily celebrated it the day following the Feast of the Pentecost, which in Poland is known as *Zielone Świątki*, a folk name connecting the Christian tradition with the vegetative cycle.[47] The visiting bishops in the late eighteenth century did not see anything wrong with this custom, but coaxed the parish priests to apply to the Vatican for the appropriate permission to formalize it. Apparently the latter followed these recommendations, since the local tradition was approved by the Vatican in 1836.[48]

One manner in which the Polish Catholicism of the period differed in comparison to Catholicism further west in Europe was that Poles were apparently largely unamenable to a deeper spiritual discipline. A foreign observer in the first half of the seventeenth century, for instance, noted that there were no Carthusians in the country. He interpreted this as evidence of a "restless Polish spirit which could not submit to the quiet solitude" of that strict order.[49] Although the claim was not strictly true,[50] it had some substance, and one might note that the observation still has a degree of validity. More or less at the time that Philip Gröning's documentary *Into Great Silence* (2005) was popular in much of Europe, with its profound depiction of Carthusians, a Polish filmmaker, Jan Jakub Kolski, produced a fiction film, *Jasminum* (2005), about monastic life from the perspective of popular tradition showing a derision of contemplative orders, albeit lighthearted, while praising an earthy Franciscan spirituality.[51]

The above does not mean that certain depths were not expressed in the religiosity of the Commonwealth period. At the literary level there was the religious poetry of Mikołaj Sęp Szarzyński, a pioneer of baroque in Poland and the greatest representative of the metaphysical movement of the era in Poland. However, a work from 1707 that touched every level of the period's religious sensibilities is a Lenten song cycle entitled *Snopek miry z Ogroda Getsemańskiego, albo żalosne gorzkiej męki Syna Bożego*, commonly known as *Gorzkie żale*, or *Lenten (or Bitter) Lamentations*. Currently considered by some critics to be a "pastoral and literary" masterpiece,[52] the cycle developed from what was then a relatively recent Lenten devotion. The *Lamentations* incorporated major elements of the Spiritual Exercises of St. Ignatius Loyola, among which reflections on the Passion of Christ hold a prominent place. The original version, published by the Congregation of the Mission Order in Poland, quite popular in itself, subsequently underwent various modifications. As one scholar notes, "Over the years communities developed their own melodic versions, their own ceremonies—as well as particular and indigenous forms of experiencing" the service.[53] This was especially true in rural Poland in the nineteenth century, and so it came to be known as a folk service.

Another—more evident—instance of high tradition filtering down to popular tradition is the founding of a number of Calvary sites, most spectacularly Kalwaria Zebrzydowska, founded by Michał Zebrzydowski, the governor of Kraków, in 1602. The name *Calvary* often refers to sculptures or pictures representing the scene of the *crucifixion* of Jesus, or a small *wayside shrine* incorporating such a picture. But the tradition in Poland was initiated by larger, more monument-like constructions, with Kalwaria Zebrzydowska setting the pattern—although the unique blend of landscape and sequestered scenes created an inimitable contemplative atmosphere there.[54] Zebrzydowski invited the Bernardine Order to maintain his site.

Initially Polish high culture participated in the Passion plays that became associated with these sites. As they became more popular, however, the elite lost interest in the pageants, "even exhibiting enmity and disdain toward them."[55] This process reached its apogee during the Polish Enlightenment in the eighteenth century. However, the elite did not turn their backs on the Passion plays for all that long, and a renewed interest at the turn of the twentieth century occurred, focusing initially at Kalwaria Zebrzydowska. There were subsequent waves of interest, obviously influenced by historical circumstances, not the least being John Paul II's visit to the sanctuary in 1979. This set off a renaissance of Passion plays that approached a comparable intensity to that of the seventeenth century.

The Bitter Lamentations were part of the rich paraliturgical developments in Polish Catholicism that supplemented the post–Tridentine mass, which—as has been noted—"did not satisfy the needs of most of the faithful."[56] The lamentations and the Calvary pageants presented the Gospel events in an accessible manner for the uneducated, but without significant distortions. The reasons for this are rather obvious. As theater scholar Dariusz Kosiński notes, "[e]ven such 'folk' dramatizations as the mystery plays of Kalwaria Zebrzydowska took place and continue take place with the support of the Bernardine Order and can hardly be imagined without them."[57] The lamentations were also experienced in a church setting from the nineteenth century and thus were partially controlled.[58]

Perhaps because of the spectacle involved, the Passion plays are among the popular religious traditions that not only maintain a tentative link with Polish high culture, but have also crossed the boundary between a largely agrarian to an urban practice. For instance, the Salesian Society of Poznań, one of the country's metropolises, now stages the largest Passion play in Poland in the city's spacious Cytadela Park. Approximately a hundred thousand spectators attend, with special buses arriving from Warsaw several hours away. Despite an audience that in size is more reminiscent of a rock concert at a stadium, the religious atmosphere is largely maintained. An actor who has played Jesus for over a decade observes, "Crowds come, but there is silence and a prayerful atmosphere. The mystery play strikes a chord in our spiritual needs."[59]

In its "enchanted" phase, folk religion answered the question of the believer's place in the cosmos. The traditional worldview of agrarian society tended toward a pantheistic opposition of forces in which Christianity plays a mediating role. Significantly, a popular image of Jesus on the cross placed him between the two thieves—the good thief on one side and the bad one on the other. Mary is also a mediator who brings mercy to the strict justice imputed to her son.[60] The focus on mediation is one of the explanations, according to a Polish anthropologist, for why in some ways the preparations for holidays seemingly take precedence over the holiday itself, as in the case of the unusual regard Poles place on Christmas Eve over Christmas Day.

A number of elements of the traditional folk Christmas Eve indicate pre–Christian origins. For instance, the tradition of placing an extra plate on the table for the main meal dates back to the several feasts for the dead that were so important in Slavic culture, one of which was appropriated by the Christmas Eve traditions and in turn left its impact on a number of the traditions connected with its celebration. Some of the latter have disappeared, like the tradition of eating the meal in silence in a number of locations; some have been reinterpreted—the empty plate has come to symbolize a place left for the stranger who might knock on the door. This interpretation fits in with the troubled history of Poland, where during the Partitions and world wars many, through no fault of their own, were far from home during the holiday, and on that holy day no one should be without a place at a table. It might be claimed that this tradition has opened up toward more contemporary needs, such as organizing special Christmas Eve celebrations for the homeless in public places.

Traditional Catholicism tolerated social division, but these were symbolically annulled during communal holidays like Christmas. Nevertheless Christmas Eve was primarily a time to be with one's family, and a number of ceremonies and rituals strengthened its ties. Among them was carol singing.

Christmas stimulated the poetic imagination, and many of the carols sung during the evening were of folk origin—*pastorałki*—and a number of these have now entered the canon of Polish carols, some of them sung in Church. A special place was and is given to sharing the *opłatek*, or Christmas wafer, which is reminiscent of the Communion wafer at mass. The custom started in the homes of the gentry in the eighteenth century and slowly spread throughout the country during the time of the Partitions, to reach Silesia in the interwar period of the twentieth century. In the eastern parts of Poland, Orthodox Christians have a similar tradition; instead of a wafer they use a roll blessed by a priest.[61] The custom takes on an additional cosmic meaning when in the countryside peasants would take the wafer, or perhaps part of the evening's meal, out to the livestock. In Władysław Reymont's classic novel *Peasants* of 1924, before the master of the household goes to the stable for this purpose, he proclaims to his family attending the meal, "Christ ... was born at this hour; therefore let every creature feed upon this holy bread."[62]

The cosmic unity of man and beast, household and nature, symbolically enacted during the evening, was then crowned by the tradition of attending Midnight Mass, which introduced Christmas Day. The enchanted theology that integrated all the aspects of the traditional agrarian religious worldview has been persuasively summarized: "All the mediatory figures form a hierarchical, symbolic structure, through which the different levels lead to the Savior, in many ways identified with God the Father as Re-Creator, *Weltordner*, a second Creator."[63]

*   *   *

One of the factors that had a broader impact on Polish Catholic religiosity was its proximity to Orthodox Christianity. Since in the Middle Ages relics of saints were not available to the extent they were in Western Europe, icons stimulated the religious imagination of Poles to a much larger extent. Much of the Marian tradition, according to an authority, centers on the importance that Poles attached to images, and "designating such a high position to the face of Mary in Polish religiosity should be attributed to the—derived from Eastern Christianity—exceptional cultural function of images as an instantiation of divine power and a palladium in the struggle against external (enemies of the faith) and internal enemies (Satan)."[64] Significantly, the best-known image of Mary connected with Polish religion is the Black Madonna of Częstochowa, quite possibly originally an Orthodox icon.

And certainly the most characteristic expression of popular Catholicism in Poland is its deep veneration of Mary. John Paul II revived the practice of coronating Marian images in Poland, while his profound devotion to Our Lady of Częstochowa is common knowledge. The badge adorned with the face of that icon constantly accompanied Solidarity leader Lech Wałęsa on his lapel, creating an iconic image in itself.[65] For anyone traveling through Poland the image of the Black Madonna seems ubiquitous; on those wayside shrines mentioned above the image has come to dominate over the earlier variety of saints, or even Christ figures. Although not the only venerated image of Mary, Our Lady of Częstochowa certainly prevails. And she has received special veneration after the fall of Communism. The monastery of Jasna Góra where the icon is housed now receives approximately four and a half million visitors a year. The support for the Catholic Church might vacillate in accordance with how it responds to various situations that arise, but the cult of Our Lady seems largely unaffected.

Yet if the cult of Mary is at the heart of popular religion in Poland, it is another aspect of the folk tradition that has filtered down—or even been appropriated—from high tradition. When Poland accepted Christianity, the cult was developed in both eastern Orthodoxy and Roman Catholicism. In the latter, during the High Middle Ages, the cult of Mary as Mater Dolorossa developed—not without influence from Byzantium—as witnessed by the poem *Stabat Mater* that has versions in many different countries.[66] The *Snopek miry* version of the Bitter Lamentations discussed earlier has a verse likely inspired by the tradition.[67] An even earlier Polish text inspired by *Stabat Mater* is "Lament świętokrzyski" (Holy Cross lament) from the fifteenth century, with the moving line, "Oh my son, beloved and chosen, Share your wounds with your mother," which was incorporated by Henryk Górecki into his *Symphony of Sorrowful Songs* in 1976.[68] Indeed, the work, Górecki's "most powerful essay combining the themes of motherhood and death, images of human and heavenly suffering,"[69] demonstrates the inspirational force this presentation of Mary carries in the high art of Poland to this day.

An illustration of this religious cross-fertilization can be given on the example of the possible travels of that most famous icon that eventually settled in Częstochowa. The original icon—attributed by tradition to St. Luke—was painted on linden wood somewhere in the Byzantine cultural sphere. Its exact origin is unknown, with the exclusion of Ruthenia, likely in the twelfth or thirteenth centuries. Somewhere in the fourteenth century the icon came into the hands of a painter familiar with the Sienese tradition, who renovated the painting.[70] Only after these two traditions had their input did the icon make its way to Poland, where Prince Ladislaus Opolczyk brought it to Częstochowa in 1382, symbolically in a country where both primary pre–Reformation Christian traditions meet. Our Lady of Częstochowa is also one of the rare major Marian shrines not connected with a miracle at its origin, but the presence of an image. But in Polish religiosity, miracles and images are closely interconnected; at any rate, the miracles came later.

During the Commonwealth it has been estimated that there were approximately a thousand shrines venerating Mary. Their number decreased somewhat during the Partitions, and after the postwar border changes is currently roughly seven hundred.[71] Each of the regions of Poland had their special sanctuaries. Among the best known aside from Częstochowa is the Blessed Virgin Mary Mother of Mercy at the Chapel in the Gate of Dawn in Vilnius (Matka Boska Ostrobramska). These various centers attracted a thriving movement of pilgrims, to say the least.

The Polish inclination for going on pilgrimages is outstanding on a European scale. Toward the end of the twentieth century an estimated five to seven million Poles took part in religious pilgrimages annually, constituting 15 percent of the Polish population and approximately 20 percent of the Christians engaged in this activity in Europe.[72] Of course not all pilgrimages are to Marian shrines: currently the center in Niepokalanów attracts many visitors, as does the grave of the martyr priest the Blessed Jerzy Popieluszko in Warsaw. The Łagiewniki Center for Divine Mercy, now more closely associated with the Blessed John Paul II, attracts its share of pilgrims. But these are only a fraction of those that visit Marian shrines and sanctuaries.

The tradition of pilgrimages to Marian sanctuaries started in the Middle Ages but developed most rapidly from the sixteenth century on, reaching its height in the seventeenth century. One might say the Calvaries, in a sense competitors for pilgrims, were so far behind in the pilgrims they attracted that a number of them, including Kalwaria Zebrzydowska, acquired miraculous images of Mary in order to attract more visitors. As mentioned, the sanctuary at Częstochowa stood out from other sanctuaries quite early, even before the "miraculous" victory there against the besieging Swedes in the middle of the seventeenth century gave it an added impetus. Moreover, over 95 percent of its pilgrims came from over forty miles away, testifying to its national character. At that juncture it is difficult to talk of a folk religion, since peasants, in servitude, could not participate in such peregrinations. Only in the eighteenth century was the importance of the religious practice recognized to the extent that peasants were exempt from their servitudes for the duration of such a pilgrimage.[73] To some degree Our Lady of Częstochowa also came to them, as copies of the icon were made and in this manner found their way in other churches. The late Commonwealth period also witnessed the beginning of the now renowned pilgrimages on foot to Jasna Góra from Warsaw.

The time of the Partitions initially diminished the movement of pilgrims as the partitioning powers were generally against them. Eventually, when Galicia became autonomous after 1865, pilgrimages became relatively unhampered within its bounds, but the Russian authorities realized the unifying symbolism of the shrine in Częstochowa and made it difficult for Polish pilgrims from the other partitions to visit. Despite the obstacles, Jasna Góra was the primary sanctuary that united all Poles. Moreover, the turn of the century witnessed specialized pilgrimages, often by different trade and professional groups. During that period Our Lady of Częstochowa figured in songs and hymns, not to mention her special position in Henryk Sienkiewicz's popular *Deluge*. It is hardly a wonder she emerged in independent Poland as "one of the most familiar images of national symbolism,"[74] although, it must be added, this dominance was rather ambivalent for many in the new multinational state. This "nationalization" of the Marian cult coincided with the same process occurring with folk religion, where folk religiosity generally went hand in hand with a strong patriotic bent.

Catholic and Orthodox Christians were not the only ones who practiced pilgrimages in Poland during this period. Jewish pilgrimages predate Christianity and were practiced by Polish Jews in the Commonwealth, but what gave the practice a genuine impetus was the rise of Hasidism at the end of the eighteenth century. Although according to the teachings of Hasidism all faithful were open to direct contact with God, in practice the *tzaddikim* were felt to be privileged. To this day "[a] blessing by the rebbe is held by the believer to have almost talismanic power and to facilitate positive benefits."[75] And pilgrimages evolved from this conviction, whether to famous living *tzaddikim*, or to their graves. It is this latter practice that after the fall of Communism brings many contemporary Hasidim to Poland, not to mention the Ukraine.[76] In independent Poland of the interwar period, some sites were the centers for pilgrims from different faiths. For instance Góra Kalwaria, as the name suggests, was the site of a renowned Calvary, but also the location of a famous dynasty of Hassidic rebbes. Some holy men were even revered by all faiths. Near Nowogródek close to Lithuania, the grave of a Tatar Muslim holy man attracted Catholic, Orthodox and Jewish women who wished to have children.[77]

During World War II, pilgrimages were obviously quite difficult, although individuals and small groups continued to make their way to Jasna Góra monastery. Initially Communist authorities did not impede pilgrimages. In 1946, for instance, approximately two million pilgrims visited Częstochowa. After the clampdown in religious practices in the Stalinist period, the number of pilgrims dwindled sharply. Despite the spectacular success of Cardinal Wyszyński's Millennium Novena, which attracted huge crowds to the Black Madonna for specific events, the number of pilgrims did not increase significantly until the end of the 1970s when Cardinal Karol Wojtyła became pope, and again after the imposition of martial law when an additional protest motivation was added. This national element, it must be noted, went hand in hand with a deepening of the religious motivations of the pilgrims.

To a degree pilgrimages, especially those on foot, help strengthen social bonds across the country. Hiking for a number of days across the country, pilgrims would meet with residents of various regions of Poland, who often prepare meals and help them in numerous impromptu stations along the way. These people come from various occupations and are residents of cities and villages. As geographer Antoni Jackowski puts it, "An invisible thread of reconciliation is sewn and a particular sense of community is developed that is simultaneously religious, social and national."[78] In the late twentieth century there were approximately 150 group pilgrimages on foot to Częstochowa, varying in size from 175 people to over several thousand. Currently the pilgrimages from Warsaw—still the largest—average eight to nine thousand pilgrims.

The unique quality of these pilgrimages has attracted an increasing number of foreigners. In the late twentieth century, anywhere from ten to fifteen thousand foreigners from twenty-five countries—mainly European—participated in these pilgrimages. Nonetheless, the shrine predominately attracts Poles. At four to five million visitors a year, Jasna Góra is the third-largest Marian shrine in the world, but only 4 percent of the visitors come from outside Poland, quite a small number for a major shrine. Nevertheless this "sanctuary of Polishness" attracts a particular kind of Pole—at least in the statistical sense. During the time of their revival under John Paul II, the social makeup of the pilgrims changed considerably. Whereas earlier the pilgrims were older, after that period a younger pilgrim appeared. Just over 45 percent of the pilgrims were now between eighteen and twenty-nine years of age, while the pilgrimages on foot stopped being the domain of the agrarian population and poorer city folk.[79]

Moreover, bearing in mind the basic split we mentioned in the Church, the Catholics visiting Jasna Gora—in contrast to those visiting its main current competitor at Licheń[80]—tend to be a more open, less nationalistic group. One study pertaining to pilgrims at Częstochowa has determined that "whereas, for instance, three-quarters of the Polish population consider it very important for a Pole to be a Catholic, this figure is considerably lower among Polish visitors of Jasna Góra (60 percent). Polish visitors to Jasna Góra are more oriented toward Europe and tend to have a relatively more open attitude toward other cultures and religions than their fellow countrymen."[81] As Cathelijne de Busser and Anna Niedźwiedź put it, "Marian veneration will certainly continue in future times to be a master symbol of Polish culture, both for the Polish nation and for individual believers, since Mary sustains 'the hope of the nation in the victory of good, freedom and truth. So it was for centuries of Polish history, so it is today.'"[82]

* * *

As can be seen in the examples above, at times it is hard to draw a fixed line between the Catholic high tradition and the popular tradition: what is high tradition at one point can be transformed into popular tradition, and the latter can sometimes influence the former, as when a popular cult was accepted by the institutional Church. Moreover, it is not without meaning that a large percentage of the rural population was illiterate when popular practices reached their peak in the nineteenth century. As was mentioned in Chapter 1, the spread of literacy in agrarian Galicia was accompanied by a rise in anticlericalism. Popular religion has never been immune to external pressures and has been to some degree a distorted mirror of the religiosity of other classes. But the reverse also has a grain of truth.

I started the chapter with a spectacular example of spontaneous sites of commemoration. However, the tradition of visiting "conventional" cemeteries is still very much alive. During most major holidays such as Christmas and Easter, the departed are not forgotten. Be that as it may, it is at the feast days of All Saints and All Souls on the first days of November—whether in the cities, towns or villages—that the cemeteries are especially full. People, young and old, sometimes traverse the country to commemorate their nearest and dearest departed, as they have been doing for generations. This extends to historical memory, where candles at major cemeteries are lit at shrines commemorating historical events and national tragedies, such as the Katyń massacre. Historical memory can be magnanimous at this time; for instance candles are often placed on graves of Red Army soldiers, bearing in mind that so many of its members lost their lives on Polish soil and were not personally responsible for the totalitarian state that was their legacy.

Indeed, the holiday is another example of the analogical imagination at work, since the custom predates the Christian period in Poland. But biblical culture is also implicit in the tradition: according to Harvard pastor Peter Gomes, the Bible is permeated with the sense that an "awareness of death is the first key to the discipline that contributes to the good life."[83] By this he means that an awareness of death helps to properly order one's life. In this sense popular religion continues to order the life of Poles in correspondence with its deepest transcendent roots.

From the earlier discussion it is obvious that some popular practices, however transformed, have survived. With some practices it is difficult to say what the future holds. Catholic journalist Szymon Hołownia praises the Live Rosary and seems to understand what the elderly ladies who say the rosary daily gain from the practice. Yet, he declares, "each time I see [them] by the entry to a church attempting to convince boys in dreadlocks or girls in skimpy dresses that they should say the rosary daily I'm deeply moved."[84] Youth usually regard their seniors with pity, oblivious of the strength that the practice has given so many for centuries, at times under the starkest of circumstances. But nothing is certain even in such cases; as witnessed above, a number of traditional practices like pilgrimages attract a different group of practitioners than not too long ago.

Regarding pilgrimages, one of the few religious groups in Poland beyond the Catholics that can claim a popular tradition at this point are the Orthodox Christians. Considering the fact that approximately one hundred thousand faithful participate in pilgrimages a year, which constitute 20 percent of their number, the tradition is exceptionally strong in the community.[85] Due to the border changes after World War II along with the imposition of Communism, some of the earlier sanctuaries were no longer open to the faithful from Poland, and national ones took their place. In fact, on account of the relative religious freedom in the country during that period, the sanctuary at Grabarka came to have a significance beyond its borders, and faithful from as far away as Finland would come to celebrate major feast days there. Festivals of Orthodox choirs, like the one at Hajnówka near Białystok, attract an interdenominational audience.

Unsurprisingly, the expanding consumer society has made an impact on numerous religious practices and traditions. There is the concern common to many countries that consumerism has tainted the traditional Christmas. However, superficially Christian elements have always been present in its celebration, such as various ludic customs connected with caroling, which traditionally lasted several days.[86] Not to mention that contradictions existed within some crucial traditions, such as the fact that the Christmas Eve meal is supposed to be an Advent fast meal, but is only so by being meatless; otherwise, for those who can afford it, in many parts of Poland it has been more feast than fast, as the family meal is quite sumptuous.

Bearing in mind the atmosphere of friendliness that accompanies the commercialized Christmas in the United States, sociologist Peter Berger claims that "*[t]he secular celebration of Christmas is a celebration of civil society at its best. Put differently: The generalized good will of the secular Christmas is a heightened expression of civility.*"[87] The spread of the retail business in Poland has undoubtedly likewise resulted in an increase of civility, and after its degeneration during Communism, civility is sorely needed in the country, whatever its source. Moreover, despite all its secular trappings, Christmas in Poland still fairly clearly echoes its transcendent source, if predominantly in a more enchanted analogical mode rather than a contemplative one.

Worth noting in this context is the custom of setting up Christmas trees in homes, which initially arrived in Poland from Germany in the late eighteenth century and slowly spread eastward, largely replacing parallel customs native to the country.[88] The cosmological significance of the "evergreen" was easily assimilated in Christian religious practice, and Christmas trees are present in most churches in Poland during the holiday season. However, currently there is an additional significance to the practice, reflecting what a cultural historian has noted concerning Christmas trees in American homes: "Today's Christmas tree is one of the few purely aesthetic objects created by families and individuals."[89] The care with which most families dress the trees, even though the decorations are bought rather than personally made, and quite often the trees themselves are artificial, satisfies a deep need for creating beauty that remains at a time when other practices such as singing carols at home are in decline (replaced, as elsewhere, by listening to commercial recordings).[90] Here we might note an intuition at work evoked by the analogical imagination that at Christmas is entertained by many non–Catholics as well: beauty—even if it is of the kind that primarily exists in the eye of its beholder—is a medium for grace.

A more serious incursion of consumerism to the holiday spirit is the phenomenon of not a few Poles now simply using the period to take a small vacation.[91] A thorough study of the phenomenon has yet to be carried out; however, more might be involved than simply consumerism. The fact that the celebration of Christmas places such a strong emphasis on family helps strengthen that battered institution; conversely, some people do feel excluded from the holiday on account of that very emphasis. In the late 1980s Krzysztof Kieślowski gave a powerful expression of the excluded in *Decalogue Three*, the third episode of his made-for-television *Decalogue* series, which features a Christmas Eve drama. At present some of the better-off excluded might simply take a holiday trip to get away from an atmosphere that reminds them of their situation.

One might further argue that even in the midst of major religious rites, consumerism, the most insipient and ubiquitous form of secularization, has virtually undone over a century of discipline during which the Church attempted to gain control of the "old festive Christianity"[92] that was a mark of Polish—and not only Polish—folk religion. Now, for instance, religious rites of passage such as First Communion, while heartfelt and spiritual for many Poles, for a significant number seem to largely constitute an excuse for expensive gift giving and the family banquet that follows, not infrequently at restaurants. Yet even here a vestige of sacramental value can be detected in the integrative function of the event, bringing the extended family together. The First Communion creates "a pretext to meet in a wider familial group and discuss important matters and family problems, or perhaps it provides a distinctive 'family theater' with a religious background, in which the main role falls to the young child, not fully conscious of its essence and meaning."[93] *Communitas* remains a key to lived religion, as it was in the past.

In the examples mentioned earlier it was demonstrated that a number of popular traditions such as Passion plays have continued to thrive and have even gained participants from new sectors of Polish society. What seems to link these traditions is the element of theatricality involved: the Poles love different forms of spectacle, whether in religious holidays and practices or otherwise.[94] Of course John Paul was not thinking in these terms when he came up with the idea to celebrate World Youth Day in 1986,[95] but his sensitive interest in dramaturgy certainly contributed to their success.

A co-organizer of the successful World Youth Day that took place in Częstochowa in 1991 was Fr. Jan Góra, a Dominican. He soon came up with the idea of celebrating a Polish version of the event known as the Poland-wide Youth Meeting Lednica 2000. The first such gathering took place on the eve of the Pentecost in 1997 near Lednica Lake—where it is believed Mieszko accepted Christianity—and continues to do so annually. The meetings attract thousands of youth. Set in an attractive landscape with symbolic significance for Poles, Kosiński observes that the event also gains its particular emphasis on account of "taking advantage of 'archetypical' symbolism of the elements, and above all collective actions dramatically sequenced in order to evoke a deep spiritual experience, all this contributes to the fact that Lednica has become a contemporary mass religious paratheater of a quasi-countercultural character."[96]

This "quasi-countercultural character" stems from elements of pop youth culture that have been incorporated in the event. Some scholars note that popular culture has entered Polish religiosity in a similar manner to the ludic element in traditional folk religion. The question remains, what of folk religion as such, particularly in its agrarian setting? Certainly, a number of traditional elements remain. As mentioned, the cult of Mary remains strong, especially among women, who see her as a more accessible intercessor than her son, but also—it would seem—through her they see something of the feminine in the divine.[97] However, many of the forces affecting lived religion in Polish agrarian society are similar to those that affect the country as a whole. A rural sociologist points out that "[c]ontemporary studies indicate a deepening religious pluralism of Polish society, both in the village and in the city."[98] This includes greater selectivity of what is accepted from the Church's teachings. At another level, continuity includes change. Maja Narbutt, a reporter for a national paper, covered a religious retreat at Licheń for victims of substance abuse addiction. When she brought up the case of a woman with an alcoholic husband to the priest running the retreat, the latter offered an analysis and advice that were pretty much from contemporary therapy. When she asked what about religion and grace, the priest retorted ironically: "What did you want me to tell her? My daughter, suffer, because He also suffered. Carry your cross, it's a part of life" (*Rzeczpospolita*, August 6–7, 2011).

As in the past, the role of the Church includes channeling the spontaneous side of popular religion and its practices. For instance, much as in a fair portion of Europe and beyond,[99] memorial crosses are currently being erected on the site of fatal road accidents. Reporter Paweł Smoleński relates how at the outskirts of a medium-sized town in northeastern Poland a civic engineer approached a parish priest when he wanted to straighten a road with a number of dangerous curves. A number of deaths had occurred at different spots on the road, and naturally crosses had been placed at the site of the fatal accidents. It was the priest's task to negotiate the removal of these crosses in order to enable work to begin on the road. Among others, he had to conduct ceremonies at the sites where a grieving family relocated the crosses (*Gazeta Wyborcza*, October 23–24, 2010).

Roughly a third of Poles live in the countryside, which remains deeply religious, even if this religiosity is comparatively less "enchanted" than it was in what might be called its classical phase discussed earlier in the chapter. This figure, however, does not reflect the importance of the agrarian inheritance that according to some scholars forms a collective unconscious or reservoir of Polish values.[100] Such a claim may be overstated, but it bears substantial validity in a country that experienced delayed urbanization before World War II, and where subsequently large numbers have migrated from the country to towns and cities; in a place like Warsaw the same phenomenon occurred together with the city having been heavily depopulated during the war.[101] Consequently on account of this great influx of people from the countryside, for a time after the war in the capital city of Poland, "the dominant model of lived religion was folk religion."[102] Elements of traditional folk religion are visible in towns and cities up to the present, such as flowers placed at the base of religious shrines or crosses within the municipal bounds, not to mention popular practices such as Corpus Christie processions streaming out into the neighborhoods surrounding numerous churches. However, this urban-agrarian religious fusion evokes complex emotions, in part due to prejudices on one side and complexes on the other quite possibly originating from the fact that the gentry was the nation building class in Poland, and it held the peasants in disdain. Poles generally seem to be simultaneously fascinated with and averse to the agrarian part of their cultural roots.[103]

After long-standing incomprehension, even scorn, with roots stemming from the Enlightenment when a popular tradition was distinguished from higher religion—accused, although not without reason, among others, of shallowness and empty ritualism—folk religion is gaining some contemporary defenders. For her part, sociologist Izabella Bukraba-Rylska complains that critical views are often one-sided or selective and that on account of its communal character, folk religion is not treated seriously by scholars, who cite many familiar urban stereotypes concerning their subjects. "By what rationale can we assume that an intellectual and personal experience of *sacrum*, characteristic of members of Protestant Churches," she asks, "is preferable to a faith

that is communal, steeped with emotionalism?"[104] In essence she defends the
Catholic imagination. Bukraba-Rylska refers to studies indicating that where
this communal lifestyle has survived, vigorous social capital is considerably
stronger than in Polish urban centers.[105] Anthropologist Anna Niedźwiedź
defends folk religion in a similar manner:

> Some researchers speak of the mass nature of folk religiosity claiming it does not
> allow any deeper spiritual experience. I vehemently disagree. My experience as an
> ethnographer, as someone who talks to people and listens to what they have to say,
> confirms that representatives of this type of religiosity have a very deep spiritual
> life. This type of religiosity is very direct, which results in an especially intense
> experience—a spiritual experience.[106]

While recognizing the existence of certain excesses, the Church itself at
the level of hierarchy is fairly positive toward folk religion. Addressing the faithful in Zakopane, John Paul II claimed that this religiosity "is often a genuine
expression of a soul filled with grace and developed in the fortunate meeting
of the work of evangelization with a local culture."[107] Another prominent
Church intellectual appreciative of folk religion was the Rev. Józef Tischner,
who himself had roots in such a community in the Tatra Mountains region. In
her evaluation of folk religion, Bukraba-Rylska also points out that historically
a number of its seeming weaknesses proved useful in some crucial circumstances:
for instance the simple religiosity and stubbornness of agrarian society inoculated
it to a much greater extent than the rationalism of the elite against the attraction
of Communism. This fact was acknowledged by the prewar intellectual Aleksander Wat, among others, and was one of the foundations of Cardinal
Wyszyński's resistance to the totalitarian regime. Bukraba-Rylska challenges that
portion of the Polish elite critical of this agrarian religious inheritance:

> If trust—that possibly most important component of social capital that guarantees
> progress—is transmitted through custom and moral norms, and is manifested in
> the form of a number of "irrational" phenomena like religion or traditional ethics,
> then—if one believes sociologists, who have provided much evidence of their exis-
> tence—we can look to the future [of Poland] with optimism.[108]

To some extent we can accept the arguments of the defenders, but the
dark side of popular religion cannot be ignored—as witnessed through its partial appropriation by Radio Maryja with its more nationalistic vein of Catholicism. Folk religion can also coincide with intolerance, as in the instance of
members in smaller towns who have been rejected by the community for
informing the civic authorities of priestly abuses toward themselves. There is
the well-known case of a woman in Tylawa who felt forced to leave her community even though the priest in question was proved guilty of sexually abusing
her as a child.[109]

On a more benign level, too much can be expected of folk religion or it can be manipulated, as in the case of the parish priest of Ślebodzin, who mobilized his parishioners in a rather vainglorious campaign to build a 108-foot Christ—larger than the renowned one of Rio de Janeiro—and completed the project in 2010. The Rev. Sylwester Zawadzki was reported as stating: "I hope this statue will become a remedy for this secularization."[110] Moreover, the current situation of an increasing number of Catholics with a post-secondary education for whom religion will to a greater extent be a matter of choice and not primarily received tradition is bound to have an impact on popular religion in the country. However, the somewhat analogous coexistence of popular culture and higher education demonstrates that what that effect might be is not altogether predictable, as the presence of numerous educated youth in the pilgrimages on foot attests.

Like most aspects of Polish religion, folk religion is not as simple as it appears on the surface, and any deeper evaluation must take into account its many facets. As a living tradition, folk religion is bound to change despite continuities. What Archbishop Józef Kowalczyk, the current primate of the Polish church, said of the tradition of pilgrimages largely goes for folk and popular religion as such:

> If, on account of different factors, interest in pilgrimages wanes, this should not be considered a tragedy; if people will not walk from Warsaw to Częstochowa in the same numbers as before, this does not mean that the Church has weakened, but only that the means of experiencing faith are changing [*Gazeta Wyborcza*, December 20, 2010].

In the second movement of his *Symphony of Sorrowful Songs*, Górecki uses the words of the eighteen-year-old highland woman Helena Wanda Błażukowniak, who came from a little town in the Tatra Mountains close to Zakopane. During World War II she had been tortured by the Gestapo and placed in a cell to await execution. Whatever her fate, which remains unknown, she scrawled on her cell wall the words "*O Mamo nie płacz—Niebios Przeczysta Królowo Ty zawsze wspieraj mnie*" (Oh mama do not cry—Immaculate Queen of Heaven support me always).[111] It is difficult to find a more eloquent testimony to the depths folk religion can reach than in that brief supplication.

Confronting Catastrophe: Lived Religion in War and Under Communism

In December of 2003 the Catholic periodical *Znak* published a Polish translation of Charles Taylor's essay "A Catholic Modernity?" and asked

Czesław Miłosz to comment upon it. Known to a broader thinking public for his breakthrough opus *Sources of the Self* of 1989 in which he demonstrated his mastery of Western thought, in this essay the Canadian philosopher turned his reflections toward the religion he himself practices. Miłosz, approaching ninety but mentally quite astute, summarized the thinker's analysis: "Taylor's well-ordered thought can be accused of being rather tame, in other words it lacks a sense of the tragic, and obviously looking at humanity today, we must acknowledge that thought lacking a sense of the tragic is incomplete at best."[112] The difference between Taylor and Miłosz on the topic of Catholicism is telling. The Canadian is someone who has wrestled to the best of his considerable intellectual abilities with the thoughts that have created our contemporary ethical and intellectual baggage, or "social imaginary," to use his own term, whereas Miłosz has experienced some of those seminal ideas put brutally into practice by two totalitarian systems in the twentieth century. Although we will look at it rather briefly, the response to catastrophe cannot be overlooked in any discussion of religion in Poland.

The experience of World War II and Communism is like nothing else Poles, and much of humanity, have previously experienced. Poles may have had their state and identity grievously assaulted by the Partitions, and brutal repression did take place at various times, all of which has left an indelible mark on them—to this day the resultant messianic vision erupts on occasion, now often as a caricature of its former self—but the Nazis and Communists imposed either a living hell, on the one hand, with the "bloodlands" in diabolical, seemingly common effort, or, on the other hand, a perverse utopia largely based on terror. And this is before we consider the Holocaust, which afflicted such a large part of the Polish prewar population—the Jews constituted one out of ten citizens—and thus left its indelible mark on the entire society.

Regarding the Holocaust we encounter an aspect of twentieth-century experience in which even Miłosz's sense of the tragic is inadequate. It can likely only be treated with any semblance of adequacy under the metaphysical term of "evil." Hannah Arendt has claimed that on account of the Holocaust, evil became the greatest problem for contemporary thinkers to deal with.[113] This has hardly been the case; evil for some has been largely "disenchanted"—to use Max Weber's term—and thus reduced, but this leaves us with more problems than it solves. During an interview with Polish journalists, Hungarian historian Istvan Deak claimed that the horrors perpetrated during World War II cannot be explained away by any of the social sciences. Almost in exasperation he added that no better explanation can be given than that humans have an inclination to sin (*Rzeczpospolita*, June 2, 2002). Evil, it seems, is one problem that ultimately cannot be disenchanted.

If the ethnically Polish population confronted catastrophe primarily from the onslaught of the Nazis and under the occupation of the Communists, Polish Jews experienced it much earlier. The Cossack revolt from 1648 to 1649 under Bogdan Chmielnicki essentially brought the golden age of Polish Jewry to an end. Nevertheless, since the massacres of the Jews by the Cossacks corresponded to a communal memory that extended well beyond the Polish experience, the response to the catastrophe essentially fitted Jewish tradition. As David Roskies puts it, the catastrophe "simply added new impetus to the earlier response: to the writing of historical chronicles and dirges and to the further standardization of *Kiddush Hashem* [among others, it refers to a Jew being prepared to sacrifice his or her life rather than transgress any of God's cardinal sins] as the Jewish way of death."[114]

The Holocaust radically changed this. To start with, the rabbis were faced with the extremely difficult task of offering consolation to the faithful in near impossible circumstances. All the while, when they were in the position to do so, they were engaged in the tradition of *responsa*, where they would answer questions of *halakha*, or practices concerning the faith which arose in the camps, or wherever circumstances found them: unthinkable questions such as how to atone for having suffocated a crying baby that would otherwise have given away a group of Jews when Nazis were in the vicinity of their hideout.[115] One of the astonishing records of an attempt to go beyond individual cases are the sermons of the Hassidic rabbi Kalonymus Kalmus Shapiro, the rebbe of Piaseczno, who turned his home in the Warsaw Ghetto into a combination of soup kitchen and synagogue. He regularly gave sermons from there until July 18, 1942, just before the Great Deportation. He wrote these sermons down in Hebrew. Fortunately they were discovered by a Polish worker after the war and were published in Israel in 1960 under the title *Esh Kodesh* (Fire of Holiness).

The sermons demonstrate an evolution and profound religious response to the catastrophe engulfing the faithful. As Roskies puts it,

> the destruction of the European Jewry ... was perceived by Shapiro to be a war against God, and in this war, Jews were his soldiers. This meant that Jewish suffering, no matter how great, was ancillary to His. It also meant the catastrophe was occurring not for any sin, large or small, committed by Israel, but simply by virtue of Israel's identification with God.[116]

At times the burning faith of simple Hasidim was virtually all they had to face an impossible adversity. This saved few but allowed some to keep their dignity—as mentioned earlier, the Hasidim very rarely committed suicide—and in some instances it even led to survival. There is an account in Yaffa Eliach's *Hasidic Tales from the Holocaust* of a rabbi from a town near Gdańsk who before the war had the habit of greeting everyone he came across, Jew or non–Jew, with a warm "Good morning!" using the interlocutor's proper name and title if he knew it. He ended up in Auschwitz, and during a selection where his life was on the line, he recognized in the officiating SS officer a former German neighbor and greeted him, "Good morning, Herr Müller!" The rabbi was then transferred to a safer camp. Many years later he would summarize his experience: "That is the power of a good-morning greeting. A man must always greet his fellow man."[117] It could happen that the Hasid's belief in his own rabbi would save him. One dramatic account relates how at a camp in Austria a fourteen-year-old child from Bobov near Lviv was slowly freezing to death during a midwinter roll call that lasted extra long, when he recalled a Zohar melody that his rabbi used to chant, and he began to dance to its rhythms. While many of his fellow inmates died during the incident, he survived.[118]

These experiences and many like them were later spun into tales, which form a powerful element of Hasidic tradition. Eliach who collected many of these "tales" acknowledges that they do not answer the question of the "tales" of those who did not survive. It is true that even for numerous Jews who did survive the experience of the Holocaust shook the foundations of their faith. As was mentioned earlier, many Jews in Poland after the war questioned their faith. While the dispersal of the community was a factor, wartime memories of the Holocaust played a role. In a survey conducted in 1948 one of the respondents confessed, "Before the war I was a believer, experiencing the wartime tragedy unfortunately deprived me of my faith."[119] One can add that survivors often struggled with the sense of evil in the world for their entire lives. This is visible, for instance, in the work of Roman Polanski: perhaps only in *The Pianist* of 2002, the film in which he finally confronted the ghosts of the Holocaust head on, did he allow glimmers of light to enter through the depiction of Christians who helped the protagonist survive, one of them even a Nazi officer.

The Christian response of Poles to wartime catastrophe was to no small extent conditioned by the occupier and varied tremendously. In addition to what was discussed in the historical outline, the Church attempted to support the faithful wherever it could deploy clergy. Catholic chaplains, for instance, accompanied Polish soldiers during the September campaign at the onset of the war and later supported the Home Army underground resistance, including the Warsaw Uprising, where they died alongside the insurgents. Poignant surviving documentary footage of that episode captures a young couple that decided they would get married within the inferno: a sign that the struggle itself was for human dignity.

But even under less extreme circumstances religion was important simply to make sense of the whole wartime environment. "The religious life, deeply hidden but inspiring, helped people keep their belief not only in God but also in man," claims Jerzy Kłoczowski, a historian who actually experienced the Warsaw Uprising.[120] For instance, there is the phenomenon of the shrines built in the courtyards of Warsaw buildings during the war, especially from 1943 up until the Warsaw Uprising of the following year. The sense of terror in the city had been escalating for the remaining citizens since the Warsaw Ghetto Uprising of 1943 that witnessed the tragic end of the city's Jewish community. Curfews were imposed; Polish citizens also were frequently arrested. Religious life was restricted to Sundays, while processions and public gatherings were banned. In this case the tradition of erecting shrines in the countryside was adopted in the enclosed courtyards, "any place where after the gates were closed in the evenings and it was thought to be safe to gather in common prayer."[121] Although most were destroyed during the uprising in 1944, some of the surviving shrines are looked after to this day. A longtime resident at one such site even reports the rather unusual event of how at the Marian shrine in her courtyard the customary gathering from the period of occupation has endured to the present.[122]

For the hundreds of thousands of Catholic or other Christian Poles in various concentration camps, a clandestine religious life took place under the most adverse circumstances. This was also the case among the hundreds of thousands of Poles and Jews and some other minorities from the eastern borderlands who were deported into the Soviet labor camps by the invaders from the east, the infamous gulags. Above and beyond the often life-threatening regime of the camps, an ideological component was present that attacked religious belief head on. Prisoners were often deprived of any religious objects they possessed upon arrival at the camps and could be assigned heavier chores or have their already limited rations cut simply for admitting to belief. The camp routine was a sore trial for the ordinary believer, especially during religious holidays. A camp survivor wrote in his diary, "Christmas Day has passed unnoticed. Perhaps it's just as well, since holidays and memories soften us up, making us weak. Why do these thoughts come to me? Why do I bother to write them down? God has forgot about us, why should I remember about God?"[123] Indeed, a loss of faith was not uncommon. The atheistic propaganda itself was especially effective among children, while in adults, a loss of faith in God was often accompanied by a loss of faith in humanity. A loss of humanity was not infrequently accompanied by the dehumanizing of the "other," as we have seen in the historical outline.

Nonetheless, if religion was driven underground, for a few, faith became all the more fervent. Prayer could not be taken away, although not many had strength left to utter it. Some went to great lengths to revive the vestiges of religion. As in Nazi camps, rosaries were fashioned by Catholics from bits of bread and string. One camp denizen recalls the near mystical experience that supported him: "I sat on a boulder under the high wall of the barrack and said the rosary.... I remember an uplifting, blissful peace which spread over me and a feeling of certainty, that no harm will come to me."[124] Prayers were even turned toward forgiveness of the oppressors, as in this poetic meditation on what under the circumstances must have been the most difficult petition in the Lord's Prayer to utter in all sincerity:

> Forgive the murderers / of our husbands and brothers, the perpetrators of their demise! / Let it be according to your words, Christ... / And lead us not into temptation... / Lord, when the hour of our liberation strikes, / keep us, keep us from the temptation to seek revenge, which lurks within us.[125]

The Soviet gulags also subjected believers from different faiths to the same level of persecution, and instances of cooperation in the face of it occurred. The camp memoirs note such cases as, "In the room Catholics are celebrating mass, the Jews are standing guard outside." "The Muslims were celebrating their holiday. According to the agreement the Catholics and Orthodox Christians would take their place at work."[126] At times a spontaneous ecumenism emerged; for instance, when lacking priests or pastors of their own denomination, the faithful would look for spiritual guidance, or even sacraments, from those of another.

If catastrophe could strain faith to the limit and beyond, for some from nonreligious backgrounds religious experience entered through the back door, so to speak, through the experience of evil. For instance, from his earlier Communist leanings, Leszek Kołakowski eventually moved to the conclusion that "sense can only come through the sacred; ... the sacred reveals itself through sin, imperfection, and evil; and evil, in turn, can be identified only through the sacred."[127] More dramatically, during his stay in Soviet prisons the writer and former Communist sympathizer Aleksander Wat felt the presence of evil so strongly he later wrote that currently only someone blind "doesn't believe in the existence of the devil."[128] Indeed, through the experience of evil, whether in the extreme form of the camps or witnessing the effects of Stalinism on others, a number of previously secular Polish intellectuals and writers—such as, besides the above mentioned, Czesław Miłosz and Gustaw Herling-Grudziński, and others—came to respect Christianity, some to the point of conversion.[129] It is interesting to note that Peter Hitchens, a former leftist agnostic British journalist, experienced something similar after his professional stay in the declining Soviet Union, observing that he has "seldom seen a more powerful argument for the fallen nature of man, and his inability to achieve perfection, than those countries in which man set himself up to replace God with the state."[130]

As is well known, in the course of the decades of Communist dictatorship, the grip of the totalitarian regime eventually lessened. As Wat might put it, over the course of time the "devil" became less overt and more absorbed in the details. The majority of Poles simply tried to make the best of life as they could under the circumstances. Nevertheless, even during the relatively lax 1970s, people felt the oppressive atmosphere. In this atmosphere people started returning to the Church. People were converting to Catholicism or recovering their lapsed faith. As one sociologist put it, "One can metaphorically say that social life was sick in the 1970s and the Church had the only available cure at the time: faith."[131] By all accounts the phenomenon markedly increased in the 1980s, playing a seminal role at key junctures. Writer Janusz Głowacki was at the strike at the Gdańsk shipyard in August 1980 that gave birth to Solidarity: "At the shipyard I spoke with people who were terribly confused. Some believed that they would succeed, others didn't; some were afraid and wanted to return home as quickly as possible. What helped quite a bit—and this was Wałęsa's idea—were the masses, they strengthened [the strikers] and gave hope."[132]

The decades-long experience of almost palpable evil set the Polish religious experience apart from much of Europe. The Rev. Józef Tischner who spent a great deal of time in Vienna observed, "It is interesting that when the evil of communism is discussed one is not understood in the West. When the word 'evil' comes up, the thread of understanding breaks."[133] Misunderstanding is one matter: one of the darkest cards in Western European intellectual history is the support that part of its elite proffered Communism, especially during the Stalinist period while so many suffered east of the Iron Curtain.[134]

Among the quotidian totalitarian evils—present from the severe Stalinist repressions to the various "thaws"—was the numbing sense of unreality that was compounded by the lack of freedom inherent in the system. Regarding this experience, Tischner observed, "When in the middle of the totalitarian world a free man was born the occurrence had the semblance of a miracle."[135] Due in no small part to the faith of much of the nation that played an astonishing role in breaking down the Iron Curtain, this "miracle" virtually encompassed the entire society in a much shorter period of time than anyone could have foreseen and is one of the matters we will look at more closely now from the religious perspective.

The Long and Winding Road: From an Ethics of Solidarity to Building Social Trust

During a visit to Warsaw after Poland had enjoyed European Union membership for a few years, journalist Kay Hymowitz witnessed the following scene:

After my Lot Airlines flight from New York touched down at Warsaw's Frédéric Chopin Airport a few months back, I watched a middle-aged passenger rush to embrace a waiting younger woman—clearly her daughter. Like many people on the plane, the older woman wore drab clothing and had the short, square physique of someone familiar with too many potatoes and too much manual labor. Her Poland-based daughter, by contrast, was tall and smartly outfitted in pointy-toed pumps, slim-cut jeans, a cropped jacket revealing a toned midriff … and a large, brass-studded leather bag, into which she dropped a silver cell phone.[136]

The *City Journal* author used the incident as evidence of globalization. Those who currently visit Poland, especially its larger cities—if they don't happen upon some extraordinary period, such as the time of national mourning that introduced this chapter—will likely see more that is typical of contemporary European countries than evidence of the past. And, yes, the appearance is more than skin deep. As Hymowitz notes, many of the elements of that European— global, if you will—lifestyle are embraced by the younger generation, and by their elders as well, if to a lesser degree. Documentaries portraying the worst aspects of Polish society before the country hosted the Euro 2012 soccer championships frightened some European fans away from the country, but those tens of thousands that came praised the hosts. At the end of the first decade in the new millennium, Poland ranked a quite respectable thirty-ninth on the UN's Human Development Index—with, among other things, the numerous opportunities for women in the job market contributing to that rank.

Nevertheless, after having survived five decades of war and two devastating totalitarian regimes it is hardly surprising that all is not as it seems—even more than two decades after the collapse of Communism. The undoubtedly higher standard of living for much of the population goes hand in hand with an entrenched poverty. Surprisingly, the latter is accompanied by a shocking indifference to its existence, especially, declares theologian Gerald Beyer, "in the country of the great Solidarity revolution."[137] On account of the low level of social trust that quite likely is the most toxic inheritance of Communism,[138] civil society in Poland has a fairly wobbly foundation. This might be surprising for some, since building civil society was among the primary foci of the movement that was seminal to the emergence of the freedom that Poland, not to mention the countries of the former Soviet bloc, currently enjoys. However, for a number of observers of Poland after the evident collapse of the ethic of Solidarity—symbolized by the often divisive politics of the eponymous trade union—this initial focus is all but forgotten, and an often fractious pluralism seems to prevail.

Returning to the vignette above, if the middle-aged woman in it was quite possibly an adherent of folk religion or popular religion in general, what about her hip daughter? This question is related to the conditions under which religion must flourish—or fail to do so—in a society that has regained its liberty after decades under a totalitarian regime. Before we ponder these and other questions, particularly those related to religion and social trust, we will turn in somewhat greater detail to the birth of the "miracle" of independence—to use the Reverend Tischner's term—and the seminal role religion played in the liberation from Communism.

Many have noted a strong link between John Paul II's pilgrimage to Poland in June 1979 and Lech Wałęsa's signing of the Gdańsk Agreement with the Communist authorities on August 30, 1980, creating the Solidarity Free Trade Union at the Gdańsk Shipyard. From that juncture the subsequent full-blown Solidarity movement—the apex of opposition to the totalitarian state—emerged almost overnight but had been long in the making, with roots much earlier than the Polish pontiff's visit.

The Church, and with it religion, was influential at a number of different levels in these changes, some of which were touched upon or implicit in the brief historical outline given earlier. Sociologist David Herbert delineates four levels in which religion contributed to the democratic transition in Central and Eastern Europe,[139] all of them valid in Poland, and most to a greater degree than elsewhere, one can add. First, religion created the prerequisite institutional space within the totalitarian regime, enabling various forms of opposition to Communism to germinate and, on occasion, flourish. Second, "religion provided a symbolic resource, or fund of collective memories, which were mobilized to oppose or subvert state imposed communist ideologies." One need merely think of the absurdly oversized pen, which blatantly bore an image of John Paul II, that Wałęsa used to sign the agreement of 1980. Third, largely on an institutional level, religion proved to be an ideological link with the outside world. The role of the Polish pontiff is obvious, but in East Germany, for instance, the Lutheran Church had connections with its western counterpart. Fourth, religion possessed a bank of intellectual resources on which the opposition could draw. The existence of the Catholic University of Lublin, or periodicals like *Więź* and *Znak*, were intellectual havens that to some extent eventually forced the regime to create similar outlets.[140]

If the Church in Poland played a key role in the democratic transition, it was to some degree a side effect of its primary mission. Although Cardinal Wyszyński had consciously created a "religious nationalism," as it has been called, which played a key role in laying the foundations for the transition, he did not lose sight of that seminal mission. "The Church, while conceding 'politics' to the Communists," observes Maryjane Osa, "wanted to maintain authority over private life: the family, especially, individual morality, child-rearing, and religious education."[141] The Church's public role was partially subservient to this priority, which I believe was crucial to the growth of precious human capital in the country. This mission is an area of the Church's activity under Communism that has been undervalued and not well documented. However, the high rate of intact families in Poland in comparison to most of the Soviet bloc is indirect but suggestive proof of the success of this policy—at the historic juncture when Poland gained independence, fewer than one in five marriages ended in divorce.[142] This despite the fact that the Communists denigrated the traditional family almost to the same extent as religion, since individuals segregated from its influence could more easily be manipulated.[143] Among the factors that likely played a role were the fact that family farms—uniquely in the entire Communist bloc—were largely saved in rural Poland, while in towns and cites the labor market was less mobile than in the more economically developed Western Europe. Nonetheless, the latter factor did not save the family elsewhere in the Socialist bloc. A witness to "family" life in the Soviet Union during the twilight of its existence in the early 1990s was the British correspondent Peter Hitchens, who observed that "in mile after mile of mass-produced housing you would be hard put to find a single family untouched by divorce."[144] While only a journalistic impression, it nonetheless gives some notion of the demoralizing reality connected to the family that to a greater or lesser degree affected much of the Soviet bloc.[145]

A number of commentators have argued that for much of the period under Communism, Poles concerned themselves primarily with their families and virtually ignored the common good.[146] This may be largely true, but with the caveat that the regime effectively controlled the means for creating the common good. If the prerequisite for contributing to the common good is a civil society created on the basis of voluntary association, then this was virtually impossible under Communism, which held that the separation of civil society and the state was ideologically unacceptable.[147] True civil society was stymied, and there was practically no common good to which the family could contribute. But the point is that Poles had their families to fall back on, while the families, in turn, leaned on the Church for support. For instance, in a study of the letters of supplication that the sanctuary Kalwaria Zebrzydowska received from 1965 to 1979, prayers for the family were among the most frequent requests.[148] It might be argued that the wealth of intact families created a reservoir of human capital waiting for an outlet.

For a time the Church created a symbolic space for common good that was unavailable elsewhere in totalitarian society. It is true a number of Church associations were eventually permitted shortly after the Stalinist era concluded, like the Light and Life movement by Fr. Franciszek Blachnicki, who organized "Oasis" summer camps for youth and families since 1954 (the movement further expanded after the Second Vatican Council). Barring such limited exceptions, the Church was largely hampered by the regime from creating lasting social structures beyond the parish itself. As an alternative strategy, primarily under the inspired guidance of Cardinal Wyszyński, the Church formulated a "pastoral mobilization" program, as it has been called by Osa. Initiated during the Great Novena celebrating the millennium of Polish Christianity described earlier, the structural key to this mobilization was its temporal and spatial strategy; for instance, "the different anniversaries and feast days of the Blessed Virgin temporally marked occasions for collective celebrations."[149] Spatially, the faithful would converge on significant central points, like the monastery at Jasna Góra, or participate in aligned celebrations at the parish level, as with the peregrinations of the copy of the icon of the Black Madonna. Eventually, John Paul II's visits to Poland, with their symbolism and patriotic rhetoric, likewise fit into this sense of pastoral mobilization.[150] However, their scale and the pope's authority gave them an impact that simultaneously augmented and transcended Wyszyński's program

While Osa stresses the collective nature of these celebrations, it is not as if the Church waved a magic wand and the masses appeared. Especially in the program's early phase, each participant had to make a serious—sometimes risky—decision to participate. Nevertheless, the lack of a structural permanence to the program meant that the human capital tapped by these decisions to participate in the events was not transformed into social capital on a larger scale. Be that as it may, an example was set that had momentous consequence. On a smaller scale, notes Osa, "Religious activists developed (cooptable) social networks, provided organizational resources ... and created an action repertoire for strategic resources for strategic opposition."[151]

It was more or less at this juncture that the democratic opposition, inspired to a large extent by a Christian ethos and initially spearheaded by KOR (Worker's Defense Committee) activists, found common ground with the worker opposition to create a new form of civil society under the aegis of the Solidarity Free Trade Union. Besides its political import, what is striking about the movement, argues one political scientist, is that the "unified commitment to a Christian ethos ... helped moderate the centrifugal forces that are innate to civil society but [under the circumstances of Communist rule] would have meant death to the Solidarity movement."[152]

Among the achievements of the movement from this moral perspective was the fact that it managed to indeed promote a palpable sense of solidarity in a fractured society suffering from a dearth of social trust. As a number of people reported at the time, "the most important thing was an unusually intense experience of community. The most essential meaning of the initial solidarity was the widespread awareness of the deep bond with others."[153] Befitting a worker's movement, the dignity of work was stressed. In one of his homilies during the Solidarity Congress in Gdańsk, the Reverend Tischner points out the sacramental nature of work. Referring to the offertory of the mass during which bread and wine become the Holy Eucharist, he points out that bread and wine are the fruits of the earth but also the work of human hands and infers, "Work that created bread and wine paves the way toward God."[154]

The duration of the initial Solidarity movement witnessed many conversions, some religious, some ethical, or both. Political philosopher Zbigniew Stawrowski points out that "even God-fearing Catholics converted, including priests, who thanks to the community of *Solidarity* noticed that their hearts had been narrow and sensitive only to the matters of the sacristy."[155] Moreover, in the context of the ongoing experience of catastrophe, as Beyer puts it, "despite their cognizance of the depths of human evil, most horribly exemplified at Auschwitz and Kolyma, during the height of the Solidarity era Poles believed in the human ability to do good."[156] And this conviction was at the base of the movement's crucial commitment to social change without resorting to violence, which set it apart from so many of Poland's bloody, but ultimately unsuccessful, historical insurrections.

One could go on discussing this extraordinary experiment in civil society, but what is undeniable is that despite the intensity of the Solidarity movement and its political success, after 1989 a dramatic failure to transfer the ethic of the movement to post–Communist Poland ensued which has baffled some observers, both in Poland and abroad. This has even led some to discount different elements of the movement. One scholar comments on the low level of its union membership in independent Poland: "This suggests that Solidarity functioned more in the manner of a social movement rather than a trade union of the type typical of Western and Northern Europe."[157] On account of the disappearance of social cohesion once the Poles gained independence, Osa questions whether Solidarity can be said to have created a genuine civil society. "Since 'civil society' is a social structural variable, it cannot disappear overnight," she observes.[158]

The latter is a valid point and is a matter for political scientists to debate. However, for the sake of argument if we grant that Solidarity as a "social movement" indeed contributed to the emergence of an "ethical civil society,"[159] then the fact that it evidently had fragile roots should not be surprising. Considering civil societies typically take generations to develop,[160] the sixteen months that the movement lasted before it was brutally suppressed by the regime was hardly enough for a lasting transformation, even if the transformation—and some evidence suggests this[161]—was genuine. After that point, Solidarity pertained primarily to an elite underground movement and not to a social movement. In other words, the social cohesion likely disappeared—except, significantly, for its brief reemergence during the campaign culminating in the seminal election of June 4, 1989—well before Poles regained their independence. Indeed, some of the descriptions of post–martial law Poland suggest as much: for instance the Reverend Tischner's description of the country prior to John Paul's visit in 1987, which is as much a description of the sense of hopelessness as it is of the actual state of affairs:

> This is Polish society! The number of people who have left the country has risen drastically. Alcoholism has not decreased, but gone up; the black market measures the value of Polish currency against the value of vodka! The number of abortions is rising, caused by the dramatic lack of living space.... The ecological situation of the country is also catastrophic. The Church continues to preach an ideal moral ethic from its pulpits and cathedrals that cannot be realized on account of the lack of apartments, the lack of medicines, the lack of food, the lack of books, and the dearth of strength.[162]

At any rate the state of Polish society after 1989 might be compared to a patient who has just undergone a lengthy and heavy operation; while the patient struggled heroically to survive the operation, after the anesthetic wears off along with the initial elation at surviving, he or she is weak and wobbly for a good period of time. Like a necessary surgical operation, Solidarity helped the patient when his life was threatened, but now upon "regaining consciousness"—that is, independence—his problems have radically changed. For one thing, although the cancer of totalitarianism had been removed, the patient, initially extremely weak, is still convalescing in many ways, and there is no known therapy for what ails him. Poles commonly say that a new generation must come that has not experienced communism before the Polish mentality changes, but looking at postcolonial countries—and the experience has reasonably been compared to colonialism—even one generation may be too little. Moreover, considering that to this day the Partitions have left their mark on the country,[163] it can be expected that some effects of communism will likely also linger for generations. Even a view that people are agents and history is not fate must take into account that it nonetheless leaves its undeniable stamp.

The author of a study on post-communist societies points out, among other things, that they suffer from "the legacy of mistrust of all formal organizations caused by forced participation in communist organizations"[164]; conversely, members of such societies have not yet learned to trust the new capitalist and democratic systems. The factors a Polish sociologist enumerates as contributing to a "syndrome of mistrust"—high unemployment, political instability—in the first five years were aggravated, he suggests, by the unrealistic expectations that had been aroused by independence, one might say "a product of the 'glorious year of 1989.'"[165] Over the next decade and a half there has been marginal improvement, but the current European recession at the time of writing, accompanied by a return of high unemployment, especially among the young, might hamper the positive process.

Of the problems connected with mistrust, an old one remains—corruption; virulent in Communist societies, it has at length somewhat decreased may but nevertheless persists. During one of the public debates that took place at the Catholic University of Lublin before the referendum concerning accession to the European Union, one of the participants said, "How can we boast about the Christian values that we will contribute to the EU when we are such a corrupt society?" A newer problem is a flourishing culture of litigation. For instance, many public contracts face seeming eons of paralysis when disgruntled bidders use every legal loophole available to challenge unfavorable results. A phenomenon indirectly pointing to mistrust is the mushrooming of gated communities in Warsaw, which reportedly surpasses most EU metropolises in this respect. On another front, even though the number of NGOs and foundations is growing—currently there are approximately seventy-five thousand associations and nine thousand foundations—Poles generally do not trust them: in a survey from 2010 it was found that 48 percent feel these organizations are corrupt and have their own interests at heart.[166]

Thus, despite high church attendance on a European scale, in light of the above it is less surprising that in a study of civil society in post–Communist societies Poles came out quite low even in membership of religious organizations.[167] Placed at about 7 to 10 percent, membership in various Church organizations is fairly low when compared to other European countries. Of course the Communist regime curtailed all such organizations for much of its duration. The pastoral mobilization during communism that Osa describes did not contribute to restoring lay participation in organizations probably on account of its being largely conducted by the clergy. What might be described as the partially guerrilla nature of Church mobilization perhaps worked against a deeper or steady involvement by lay Catholics. Moreover, because of the possibility of their infiltration by Communist agents, parish councils were not formed by the Polish Church after the Second Vatican Council. The Church was a giant in moral capital but seems to have stimulated very little lasting social trust through organizational initiatives.

Another possible explanation for low participation is that a great deal of Church involvement was—and some of it remains—unofficial and partially hidden. For instance, during Communism parishioners were often voluntarily involved in building new churches, but this left no organizational trace as such. This is borne out in statistics such as the low membership in Church organizations mentioned above that contrasts to the 40 percent who declare that they occasionally help out around their church.[168] Additionally, the amateurism of the past is no longer sufficient in some cases; as Kazimierz Nycz, the archbishop of the diocese of Warsaw, points out in relation to the above example, "Today it is difficult to build a church in such an amateur manner because the bylaws connected with the construction of a public building are just too demanding."[169] Nonetheless, compared to a number of European countries, to this day churches or other religious institutions receive limited state subsidies—at least not for their cult and the edifices they erect on its behalf—and 80 percent of their expenses are financed by the donations of their members. We will return to this problem later; for now we will simply observe that to some degree this means the churches must compete for attendance, not just in terms of the quality of their religious services and homilies but also in matters related to the consumer society, with demands such as comfortable, well-heated churches in the winter increasing their operational costs.[170] One also notices that wherever they have the space to do so, contemporary parishes are building parking lots to make it easier for their parishioners to come and go.

A third factor to be considered is the relative inertia of a mass church. It may be true that the members of the Catholic Church are more active in France, for instance, but over time they have been pared down from a mass church to an elite one: like the biblical Gideon's three hundred, so to speak. The 5 percent of the population that attends church in that country is quite conscious of why they do so in a way that the approximately 40 percent of the Polish population that does so is not. It is hardly surprising that most of the Catholic renewal movements in Europe come from Western Europe.[171]

Before discussing the relationship between social trust and religion in Poland in greater detail, some idea of the general state of religion in the country upon regaining its liberty is necessary. Among the challenges that emerged and which most western societies take for granted are cultural pluralism, a reorientation of values, and secularization. One might say the social mistrust inherited from the former system is further exacerbated by what Francis Fukuyama has termed the "Great Disruption" of information age societies[172]: the largely positive growth of individualism that is nonetheless accompanied by divorce, consumerism, and so forth, which cuts into the human capital of the family that was arguably the strong point of Polish society. In the Polish version of the phenomenon, in order to make up the difference in prosperity between themselves and their better-off European neighbors, Poles are concentrating on work and careers. Now that the labor flow is relatively free, many are working in EU countries, with children often staying in Poland deprived of one or both parents for a time. In sum, they are spending less time with their families, let alone devoting it to society in any meaningful way through volunteer work. The young are also putting off marriage in part because many wish to become established in their careers and be relatively free of material concerns before setting up a family. Additionally, alternatives like cohabitation are making inroads, quite often intended as a trial marriage, but with a life of their own once practiced. All the latter pressures negatively affect the growth of social capital in developed countries, let alone in one with such a low point of departure.

It is hardly a wonder then, that—at least in hindsight—after the moral clarity of the pre–1989 world, some Catholics have seen liberty itself as the problem because it offers many alternatives to religious values; conversely, others accept its Western expression uncritically. Still others see it as a challenge that requires a dynamic approach according to which "[t]he priority is to educate people, especially the young, to live under freedom so that they wish and know how to choose wisely and well. People must be taught to think according to values."[173]

Naturally enough, a free society tends to leave no authority unquestioned. The Church has also been open to criticism, some warranted, some derived from groups similar to those in a number of European countries and in North America that believe in a naked public square: that is, groups—some blatantly anticlerical—that feel religion should not express any opinion about public matters. Conversely, other groups in Poland feel quite the reverse. The Rev. Janusz Mariański summarizes this aspect of the current situation: "On the one hand there are fears about the dominating presence and meaning of the Church in society, on the other hand there are fears of its marginalization in public life and of its diminished presence in social life. The criticism or even partial crisis of the institutional Church is part and parcel of the crisis of all institutions in the world currently."[174] This crucial topic will be discussed in greater detail in the final chapter. One might add that Catholic teachings are adhered to selectively, even by people who practice fairly regularly. Poles are rather lax in following or accepting the sexual ethics of the Church; on the other hand, 80 percent consider marital betrayal unacceptable, and approximately two-thirds are against abortion on demand.[175]

Moreover, under democratic conditions the Church no longer has a monopoly on the role of a guarantor of patriotic values nor is it the only place where civic aspirations can be expressed. Nonetheless, patriotism, religiosity and civic virtue are still highly valued in Polish society. According to sociologist Tomasz Żukowski, "Polishness is constituted by a conglomeration of values that are individualistic and communitarian."[176] This makes Poland more akin to Britain and the United States than to its continental neighbors. Żukowski argues that the triad of values offers an explanation for why Poland has been able to undergo modernization without the frequently accompanying secularization.[177] These values are present to various degrees in different segments of Polish society or individual Poles, leading to the odd but understandable statistic that several percent more declare themselves Catholics than declare belief in God: rather evidently following from the patriotic need to identify with the Church even at the expense of one's deeper beliefs—or lack of them.[178]

Another paradox is the survey finding that while three-quarters of Poles feel that Polish Catholicism is and will remain exceptional in Europe, at the same time a similar percentage (70 percent) feel that contemporary people are less religious.[179]

On the basis of a major study from October 2007 probing its hierarchy of values, Polish society places family life on top, together with its constituent elements: marriage, children, and love. Regular employment came next, with religion following behind these concerns. Different values connected with self-realization came lower still.[180] Regarded by many as quite a traditional society, in fact currently the model family in Poland is predominantly a partnership rather than a patriarchal model, with both parents working and sharing domestic tasks, if not always equally (as in most societies, even working women tend to do more at home). While the divorce rate has indeed risen, it still affects less than a third of marriages. Despite its somewhat lower position in the overall hierarchy, 41 percent of respondents considered religion very important in their lives, and only 17 percent considered it unimportant. On the basis of this survey it has been suggested that, "since the religiosity of the Poles seems to be a lasting phenomenon and seems to be rooted, more strongly than we used to believe, in a mystical and a communal (as opposed to institutional) vision of the Church, one can hardly assume that it is the traditional authorities, rather than spiritual needs, that are the source and main cause of the religiosity of the Polish people."[181] If this is correct, and an even more recent survey seems to corroborate the earlier one,[182] then this goes some way toward explaining why despite the variations in approval of the institution, the religiosity of Poles remains fairly high.

There is naturally more variance in this global picture when specific sectors of the Polish population are examined. It is worth looking more closely at the young in Poland, upon whom in one way or another the future of the Church rests. To the extent that she represents her generation, the young woman mentioned at the beginning of this section is better educated than her mother, probably has worried about employment at one time or another, although with far more opportunities once she gets that job than a woman of any previous generation, and—as Hymowitz makes quite evident—she is immersed in a consumer culture. What is her—as well as her peers,' not to say "cohort's"—attitude toward religion? Further, what are her generation's values?

Regarding their value system, studies indicate Polish youth are largely caught up in the contemporary ethos of authenticity,[183] although it must be added that this ethos has many sources for them, running the gamut from tradition to consumer society. As one authority puts it, "More frequently than the rest of society the young are likely to claim that their conscience is the ultimate authority, without worrying too much how that conscience has been formed."[184] This "conscience" does not differ too much from that of their European peers as far as sexual mores are concerned, considering that even there the sexual revolution has partially run out of steam—casual sex with numerous partners tends to be frowned upon—but if the mutual feelings are deemed to be genuine then there are few qualms to sexual activity.[185] On the other hand, the family is virtually as important for the young as for their elders, with 91 percent of those who responded to a World Values Survey in 2005 holding the family as important or even very important. This placed Polish youth as the most family oriented in Europe, although not by much. Where they differ is in their attitude to the right to life. Polish youth are not only the most pro-life Europeans of their generation, with 71 percent against abortion on demand, but as the authors of a Polish report put it, "in Poland the youngest [the eighteen- to twenty-nine-year-old cohort] are the greatest opponents of the right to abortion."[186] This might not be all that surprising considering that their parents are a generation that was raised in Communist Poland where abortion on demand was the norm.

As for religious practices, like their parents approximately 95 percent of Polish youth declare belief in God, but they attend Church services somewhat less: 45 percent report they attend mass weekly against 50 percent reported by their elders. Again this puts them near the top of attending European youth. It should be remembered, however, that the overall Church statistics for attendance is lower than the self-declared ones generally given, but it is not broken down by categories of age, so the actual attendance of the young can only be speculated. Moreover, there have been no longitudinal studies to determine whether those who stop attending Church—often after the sacrament of confirmation which is a precondition for Church marriages—return to it once they establish families, a common pattern in the United States, but there is indirect evidence to suggest that this might be the case.[187] To a greater extent than church attendance, what differentiates Polish youth from their parents is that in contrast to the latter their sense of belonging to any particular parish is weakening. This may be part of the consumer culture attitude of looking for a parish that suits their spiritual needs better than their local parish; however, it also might reflect their greater mobility, both on account of higher education institutions away from home and the necessity to move to where there is employment.[188]

The Church possesses a modest arsenal at its disposal to reach the young. There are—frequently criticized as ineffective—religion classes in public schools, mentioned in Chapter 2, and pastoral programs at institutions of higher learning. Internet pages devoted to religion are quite popular, with over two million users annually, and the number is growing; while these are not exclusively aimed at the young, 29 percent of internauts in the fifteen- to twenty-four-year-old age range visit such websites annually.[189] Special events are geared toward the young, as Lednica 2000 discussed above. Many special retreats with a festive air take place in the summer and are rising in popularity.[190] Moreover, pastoral outreach programs have been attempted at some of the more prominent secular youth events. A good example is Przystanek Jezus which has been established at Przystanek Woodstock, a youth festival featuring rock music organized by the Great Orchestra of Christmas Charity Foundation, ostensibly to reward its volunteers for participation in the NGO's annual charity campaign. Przystanek Jezus was initially unwelcome at the festival, which attracts the better part of half a million young people for several days in the summer, and now that it is accepted the outreach program must compete with other groups. The Rev. Andrzej Draguła, a spokesman for Przystanek Jezus, points out that it is not rare for Polish youth to go to Woodstock to have a good time and then participate in a pilgrimage. He claims they are "primarily looking for a space where they can be together. They experience such a community of getting together with peers at Lednica, and on pilgrimages, and at Przystanek Woodstock, as well as at Przystanek Jezus."[191]

Dubbed by some—for a brief period after the pontiff's death—the "JPII generation," a possible impact of the pontiff on young Polish Catholics is bringing the wider Church into their purview. Maria Rogaczewska attended the World Youth Day 2000 in Rome where the pope met with two and a half million participants. She claims,

> John Paul II, addressing us in a dozen languages, seemed someone very close, yet a "citizen of the world": a personal model of a Catholic of the twenty-first century, in other words someone who understands that the old divisions and conflicts— between nations, religions, people of different races and sexes—are no longer valid in a world in which small groups can have a destructive or blessed impact on the lives of larger groups.[192]

From this perspective young Polish Catholics appear to be simultaneously the most selective and most "Catholic" generation in the history of Polish Catholicism. At a qualitative level young Catholics have applied themselves to a number of the cutting-edge initiatives intended to keep the Church in step with the challenges that currently face it. They are crucial to new Catholic institutions and think tanks that have been formed, like Instytut Tertio Millennio, Dzieło Nowego Tysiąclecia or Centrum Myśli Jana Pawła II.[193] Some of these groups, like the one centered round the periodical *Fronda*, are best described as Evangelical Catholic (see Chapter 5), accusing some of the more established Catholic elite periodicals of promoting a Polish version of Christianity lite. More generally, young Catholics are involved in numerous volunteer efforts.

The situation of the aged in Poland is at the other end of the religious spectrum. Although their religiosity is considerably higher than that of the young, and they are far more closely connected to their parishes, their needs are not always met by them.[194] Many are confused by the radically different situation of the country, to which they do not always have the resources to adapt. The most controversial and yet possibly effective religious outreach program geared toward aged Poles is Radio Maryja. The station—along with its affiliated media—offers them a sounding board from which their voice is heard in the public sphere. Similarly the Friends of Radio Maryja Circles total approximately twenty thousand members and are found in a large number of parishes throughout the country, creating social capital for those involved,[195] although it can be termed as a "bonding" rather than a "bridging" social capital. One sociologist recognizes how Radio Maryja activates the elderly like no other organization, but this comes at a cost: "It creates a circle that is closed, convinced of its infallibility and uniqueness, and which questions the order that—paradoxically—allows it to develop."[196]

Studies carried out through Europe unsurprisingly demonstrate that countries that have experienced Communism have a low level of social capital—its members do not cooperate well with each other. Countries like Poland that had a democratic opposition fare somewhat better in this respect than those like Bulgaria or Romania where none existed. Still, almost two decades after the collapse of the totalitarian regime only a little over 10 percent of Polish citizens declared that they had participated in some type of social organization.[197] Moreover, although the number of volunteers is steadily rising, Poles nevertheless tend to participate in temporary campaigns rather than contribute their time systematically.[198] The Great Orchestra of Christmas Charity campaign mentioned above is a good example. The massive goodwill generated by the event is nothing short of phenomenal on a national level, yet it only lasts a few days during the year.[199]

Herbert maintains that religion remains one of the prime stimulators of social trust in contemporary societies, albeit "no longer through the vertical legitimizing relationship through which faith traditionally produced social cohesion."[200] Although after the transformation nothing like the civil society experienced during Solidarity emerged, religion remains the primary engine for building social capital in Poland. In the commentary accompanying a survey conducted in 2008 on the topic by the Center for Public Opinion (CBOS), it was found that in determining whether a respondent would be engaged in dealing with local problems the most important factor was the frequency of religious practice, followed by his or her level of education.[201] Summing the relationship of religion to volunteering in Poland, one Catholic journalist puts it thus: "Although in Poland only a quarter of the people are involved in volunteering in comparison to the United States, in [deriving its inspiration from religion] our country is more reminiscent of the USA than like the states of Western Europe."[202]

The authors of the *Better Together* report of the Saguaro Seminar led by Robert Putnam insist that "religious faith provides a moral foundation for civic regeneration."[203] One can say that moral capital is connected to social capital. The authors of *Better Together* also optimistically acknowledge, "Because faith has such power to transform lives, faith-based programs can enjoy success where secular programs fail."[204] Thus it is worth looking a little closer at the nature of the social capital developed directly by religion in Poland. Social mobilization taking place within the Church usually focuses on charitable campaigns of a nonsystematic nature, for instance preparing Christmas packages for the parish needy, or fund-raising drives after natural catastrophes, like the floods that intermittently ravage the country.[205] Catholic thinkers in Poland feel the Church could do more to develop social ties among the faithful. Zbigniew Nosowski suggests, among other things, that "[i]n dioceses and larger centers there should be a pastoral program supporting volunteers that could facilitate the meeting and interpenetration of various groups. Many people involved in social organizations report the problem of potential burnout and need a spiritual foundation for their work."[206]

The message from such concerned Catholics is that much remains to be done within their Church for it to fulfill its potential role in enriching the social life of their society. It is partly in this sense that Rogaczewska's following observation must be understood: "The institutional Church in post-communist countries, in a fashion similar to the modernizing societies, is 'backward.' It is only after a long delay that it is returning to the mainstream of the changes occurring in the universal Church."[207] Certainly in terms of its contribution to activating its members this accusation has substantial clout. Rogaczewska feels that the blame for this falls on the vertical legitimizing relationships—that is, their hierarchical nature—between the priest and the faithful that are still the predominant pattern in the country. This is illustrated by a comment a young Pole wrote on the Catholic website Opoka.org: "In my parish it is better to be just a listener. I am waiting, maybe our parish priest will break down and recognize that we might be of some use to him."[208] Rogaczewska mentions the need to activate the parish councils that often have a largely symbolic role in many dioceses and exist in only one out of ten parishes. However, the problem is not just one of the hierarchical nature of relationships in the Polish Church, but also the passivity of the Polish faithful. This passivity is related to many matters, such as schools, where Poles complain about problems but look for solutions to come from above. In line with such an attitude, it has been observed, "People complain about priests and the

Church, but place the responsibility for the state of affairs in the hierarchy and not in themselves."[209]

Largely in light of the above context some of the social initiatives currently taking place within the Polish Church shall be examined, beginning at the parish level. At the onset of the millennium, following a reorganization of the parishes in Poland that was completed during John Paul II's pontificate, there were just over ten thousand parishes in forty-one dioceses. Although the identification with the parish is weakening, it nonetheless constitutes the strongest religious identification of Poles, valued more than membership in the Catholic Church itself.[210] A parish is primarily concerned with the pastoral care of the faithful, which includes administering the sacraments. There are complaints that this function is carried out in a fairly perfunctory manner. Nonetheless, outstanding pastoral programs do exist that are largely taken for granted, such as the "*kolęda*," in which once a year, shortly after Christmas, each and every parishioner is visited at home by a priest—a process lasting a couple of weeks and occupying several priests in a large city parish. Not everyone accepts the priest into their homes—in Gdańsk, for instance, the percentage is approximately 70 percent, while in Warsaw it probably does not reach 50 percent—but a far larger percentage of the faithful accept a visit than attend church each week. Although many parishioners are on their best behavior then, the priests nonetheless get a better idea of what is going on in their parishes at that point than any sociological study can tell them. And—in some cases—"miracles" occur, such as when the priest is able to help someone with a serious problem.

A parish's contribution to civil society stems by nature from its constituting a certain network of relations and social ties—relations which, typically, but not in every instance, are localized in a given territory.[211] The fact that the better part of half of Polish society attends mass with a good deal of regularity, along with the inclusive nature of the Church, has a large significance from this perspective. "In contrast to numerous clubs and associations," it has been pointed out, "a religious community remains a place in which the poorer members can feel themselves full members, while through the dedication of a little time and effort—they can fulfill an essential function, respected by the community. It is difficult to find a better example of what sociologists describe as 'bridging' capital."[212] Paradoxically, this role is perhaps diminished in large urban centers, where practicing Catholics are generally better educated and thus more selective. Hence they tend to select a parish that suits them for whatever reason, and the diversity of parishioners might be lessened.[213] However, if—as mentioned—charitable campaigns are the primary form of a more significant involvement of parishioners, it needs pointing out that the parishes throughout the country are not equal in this respect. Generally, where religious participation is higher, the social activity of parishioners corresponds. And so in a study it was observed that parishioners of the largely agrarian diocese of Tarnów are engaged in charitable activities far more frequently than those of highly urban dioceses like Gdańsk or Warsaw, which according to Church statistics have a lower percentage of attendance at mass as well.[214]

According to a major study published in 2010 it is estimated that throughout the country perhaps up to two and a half million parishioners are engaged in different parish groups or faith-based organizations.[215] On average five groups are active in each parish, but this varies substantially from those parishes where as many as thirty groups are active to those where there is not even one group. Most of the activities are religious—anything from prayer circles to organizing pilgrimages—or connected to helping run the parish. Others are related to charitable or cultural and recreational activities. Although professional and nonprofit organizations are involved in more specialized help, such as psychological assistance or dealing with substance abuse, parishes still deal in these activities at the periphery of their other involvements.[216] Among the newer activities are the steadily improving parish gazettes and websites, some of which engage a whole team of specialized volunteers who also provide a genuine service to the local community.[217]

Unsurprisingly, the personality of the parish priest plays a significant role in whether a parish has a number of active organizations or not. For instance, in the history of his parish in Krasiczyn, the Rev. Stanisław Bartmiński—who became a consultant for a popular television series about life in a country parish—richly documents the life of his flourishing parish in a small town in the southeast of Poland. The parish has boasted an active parish council reaching back for decades, and numerous organizations that run the spectrum of religious groups; parish charities; cultural groups—among others, Cardinal Adam Sapieha grew up in this parish, and his memory is cultivated there—and educational groups, not to mention its care of imprisoned Solidarity activists during martial law in the early 1980s. In his account we find how activities become transformed over time, as in the case of how the energy devoted to a traditional harvest festival—*dożynki*—that had its own committee in the parish was largely redirected to a fund-raising fair after parishioners lost interest in the traditional event.[218] His person may be almost absent in the account, but he was a key to the wealth of activities that take place there.[219]

Although a few of the religious groups in parishes have deeper historical roots, others were initiated after the Second Vatican Council. These became particularly active in Poland in the 1980s shortly after John Paul II was elected to the Holy See. Some, like the Catholic Charismatic Renewal or Fokolari, came from outside of Poland; the Light and Life movement is the best-known renewal movement that was initiated in Poland, and it now even has branches outside of the country. Among the problems these groups face remains the great dependence of the Polish faithful on clergy; a group tends to vegetate or decline if for any reason a member of the clergy is no longer present for a longer period.[220] To some extent tension exists between these movements— which are nationwide or even international—and the traditional parish, which is firmly rooted in a given locality, but some research available on this account suggests that this fear on the part of parish priests is largely unfounded.[221] Nevertheless, on account of the comparatively greater mobility of Polish society, particularly the elite, the local parish cannot fully satisfy the spiritual needs of all Poles. There was mention above of the young requiring a special type of pastoral care, especially when they move from home, for instance, to an institution of higher learning. At the various colleges and universities, young Poles have a chance to attend the academic pastoral programs active there.

These academic pastoral programs are in many regards at the cutting edge of the changes in the religious landscape of Poland. They have a tradition that goes back to Communist times when during Solidarity they had a prestigious role in opposing the regime, a role that makes their current one seem more prosaic to the uninformed. At that time their role was more intellectual, and they typically arranged meetings that discussed censored topics. Now Poles have access to information from a great variety of sources, and the academic pastoral programs have had to adapt to a vastly changed post-secondary educational scene in the country: an array of private and state universities and colleges as well as a number of institutions that never existed before. Most importantly, they have had to adapt to the different spiritual needs of today's youth. Their programs are voluntary and participation fluctuates, so it is difficult to say how many young Poles take advantage of them. As in the parishes, the role of the coordinating priest can be a crucial factor, and a charismatic and creative priest can inspire participation. At a private university in Pułtusk, for instance, at one point one the priests even arranged a motorcycle cavalcade in the town square to raise funds for a hospice in Vilnius, Lithuania. However, the most positive aspect of the current academic pastoral programs is how they inspire the young to come up with programs that meet their own needs.

At one of these programs run by Jesuits in Toruń, students could choose from different groups interested in gender and spirituality, a theater group, and choir, as well as a discussion group of difficult topics, to name a few. A coordinator at the program reports, "New groups emerge all the time. What's most important though, is that students form them by themselves; they come to us with various ideas, organize everything and it works."[222] A Warsaw priest enthusiastically claims,

It is in the Academic Pastoral programs, and not in the parishes, which are often dominated by the clergy and the role of the lay Catholics can be quite minimal, that I learned that the laity are prepared to discern their mission in the Church, to play a role in which the priest cannot replace them. The Pastoral program was a time for them to prepare them for future responsibilities, to undertake projects in the Church, educate them to be active in their parishes. It is in them that the new elites are created.[223]

Beyond the parish there exist Church organizations or faith-based initiatives that contribute to Polish civil society, often assisting its neediest members. When Nosowski wrote of the need for larger centers to organize support groups to stimulate and uplift social initiatives, he quite possibly had Centrum Duszpasterstwa Młodzieży (Pastoral Center for Youth) of Lublin in mind, which was initiated by the archbishop of the diocese and run by the Rev. Mieczysław Puzewicz. The center coordinates youth volunteer efforts in the diocese, along with some regular programs. The latter include first-aid help that is offered to the homeless, volunteer work at Lublin's children's hospital, and an outreach program to small communities where volunteers run extramural activities at schools. Among others, volunteers also look after small children at the regional refugee center's daycare. The Reverend Puzewicz claims the center attempts to build John Paul II's "civilization of love" in a practical form.[224]

The largest nationwide charitable organization connected with the Church in Poland is—as mentioned in the previous chapter—Caritas, revived shortly after the collapse of Communism. However, charity is only one of its fields of operation. Its main fields of activity include aid to the sick as well as to single mothers. Caritas is also involved in assisting the unemployed in returning to the workforce; some of its programs in this regard make use of European Union funds. It also coordinates volunteer work throughout the country, which includes conducting leadership training camps where volunteers from Ukraine and Belarus participate. Beyer summarizes the organization's efforts: "Caritas is already doing the work of solidarity in many ways."[225]

Encouraging participation happens among the better-known faith-based initiatives not directly connected with the Church, such as Sister Małgorzata Chmielewska's Bread of Life Community centered in Warsaw, mentioned in the previous chapter. Another group that has garnered much deserved attention is Stowarzyszenie "U Siemiachy" ("At Siemiach's" Society). Initiated by the Rev. Andrzej Augustyński in 1993 in Krakow, the concept for the society actually is based on the efforts of the Rev. Kazimierz Siemieszko ("Siemiach" is the nickname from that name) at the turn of the twentieth century, who believed that in order to raise the moral level of impoverished parishioners one needed first to raise their standard of living and he subsequently initiated a broad scheme of social programs. The aim of the contemporary association is to gather people inspired by Christian values to assist needy children and youth: "The organization's mission is to help youth and support their full and conscious development."[226] The community formed at the different homes run by the association rubs off on the charges, with not a few of them becoming community workers themselves after they have left.[227] "U Siemiachy" has now expanded to a number of Polish cities. The Reverend Augustyński has been adept at fundraising for a new ambitious program that fits the changing times. Since so many young people now spend time at malls, he has further organized community centers at or nearby a number of malls, like the mall located in the Bonarka district of Kraków, where the center is found in a spacious area at the mall's top level.[228]

Characteristic of Bread of Life Community and "At Siemiach's" Society and the variety of programs they have developed is the fact that despite being initiated by a nun and a priest, it is the lay Catholics who develop and maintain the different programs; they have gone much further in transcending the "vertical legitimizing relationships" so typical of much of the earlier efforts. Whether or not they are harbingers of things to come for the Polish Church remains to be seen.

Although these Church and faith-based organizations play a substantial role in developing social capital in Polish society, there are still numerous NGOs that are neither connected to the Church nor faith based. With so many genuine problems to deal with under the new circumstances there is obviously room for all initiatives. However, regarding the more serious problems, solutions are more effective when there is cooperation. A good example is the care of AIDs victims. The problem originated during the time of Communism, but the regime preferred not to inform Polish society about serious social problems, nor did it feel obliged to consult with any social group about the solutions it implemented. One of the early NGOs in independent Poland that attempted to establish group homes for victims was MONAR, an organization that helped drug-abuse victims, founded by the charismatic Marek Kotański. Initially the organization was rather hostile to the Church, especially toward its policy on the use of condoms. On the other hand, on its own it had great difficulty in dealing with the public opposition to the group homes. Eventually Kotański changed his attitude toward the Church and the work of both parties in tandem—much good work was done by Fr. Arkadiusz Nowak, who established a number of group homes for victims[229]—to markedly change the public attitude toward the problem. One of the outstanding NGOs in Poland is Polish Humanitarian Action, founded by Janina Ohojska. In 1992 she organized an aid convoy to Sarajevo, just as she had seen French donors do to help her own country. Over the next decade, Ochojska organized a number of convoys to troubled areas of the region—Chechnya, and Kosovo—

from which efforts she eventually forged her organization, now "the country's largest independent aid agency, with projects in dozens of countries."[230] Although the organization is secular, Ohojska has roots in the academic pastoral programs before 1989, and she is supported by different Catholic lay groups.

The above examples are doubtlessly positive; nevertheless, the overall picture is less optimistic. Sociologist Jan Herbst bemoans the fact that currently the Church volunteer sector and the nongovernmental sector are not particularly well integrated. Not only is this to the detriment of those that would better receive aid from such a coordinated effort, but, Herbst insists, "for church circles such an institutional opening up would mean joining in on the modernization processes [in Poland] and influencing them as well."[231] Two factors significantly influencing the ability of a society to produce social capital are religion and education, but they can also produce different priorities. Tensions exist at some junctures, and they are unlikely to disappear.

If religious faith, as the *Better Together* report puts it, "provides a moral foundation for civic regeneration," it can further be argued that faith likewise helps in economic development, which also requires a moral foundation. A Polish economist argues for the connection between moral capital and economic development: "trustworthiness, industriousness, promise-keeping and honesty are all qualities that underpin the functioning of the markets and condition long-term value creation."[232] Naturally, it is not as easy as that; most Poles, for instance, tend to place religion—more specifically Church teaching—and work in different spheres.[233] However, this is the attitude the Instytut Tertio Millennio attempts to instill through a program intended to inspire Christian leadership in all walks of life. The institute developed from a series of summer school seminars held in Kraków co-organized by the Polish Dominican Fr. Maciej Zięba and *First Things* editor the Rev. Richard John Neuhaus.[234] The summer schools have focused on everything from aspects of Catholic social teaching to the *Federalist Papers* and have been attended both by Polish students and students from the United States, as well as from East Central Europe. The seminars have continued, now with the participation of the Washington-based Ethics and Public Policy Center, but the institute has considerably enriched its program. Furthermore, for businessmen and entrepreneurs themselves, there is the Pastoral Program for Entrepreneurs and Employers "Talent," with which approximately seven hundred people are involved. Established in 1999, the members understand the relationship between Christian values and business quite differently, but the basic values mentioned above are fundamental to them all.[235]

Among the more prominent active political leaders hailing from the Solidarity generation in Polish society that admits to being indebted to Catholic social teaching is Rafał Dutkiewicz, the popular mayor of Wrocław, under his stewardship one of the more flourishing metropolises in the country. A friend of Fr. Zięba's, Dutkiewicz is familiar with the works of liberal Catholic thinkers—in the economic sense—like Michael Novak, and tries to combine the modernization of Wrocław with a regard for fundamental values. In his creedal book *Nowe horyzonty* (New Horizons) he focuses extensively on economic matters and their impact upon the future of his city, but insists "I attempt to write about economics without losing sight of other spheres of social life."[236] From this perspective he turns to John Paul II's social teaching that underpins the deepest understanding of his responsibilities as mayor: "An economy worthy of the person. That goal must be my task. I must do everything so that ... the person would never be seen simply in categories of his productive worth."[237] He emphasizes that work and leisure are necessary for the dignity and flourishing of the human being and are the basis for civil society. Dutkiewicz's creed might seem overly optimistic if it were not for the fact that few people in Poland have done more to make its ideas a reality. If such a stance is unusual at the national level of politics where politicians either dutifully participate in the heavily Catholic civil religion or treat religion instrumentally, at the level of municipal politics Dutkiewicz might be the near epitome of a particular stance, but by no means is he the exception. Naturally there are other philosophies of municipal government that are practiced, to say the least.

Although none of the other religious denominations has the potential of the Catholic Church for creating social programs, the comparatively larger ones also have organizations that conduct charitable work or tend to the social needs of their faithful. The Orthodox Church in Poland has a number of organizations that mirror aspects of its Catholic counterparts described above. As small as it is, the Polish Reformed Church likewise runs a number of homes for the elderly or disabled. One of their more dynamic initiatives is Ośrodek Profilaktyki i Rozwoju Osobowości (the Center for Prevention and Personal Development) in Bełchatów. Their mission statement includes the goal of "creating opportunities for education and trying out positive models of behavior as an alternative to pathological ones."[238] Despite its small size the Jewish community likewise has a number of organizations serving the needs of its members.

The bright spots enumerated above are significant, but the fact remains that civil society in Poland at present remains poorly developed and faces numerous obstacles, many of them internal. No doubt if economic stability increases and, what tends to go hand in hand with this, Polish society becomes better educated, social capital will increase. For its part the Polish Church, as Nosowski and Rogaczewska argue, may not be living up to its potential for contributing to civil society—as an institution it is also learning how to cope in the new situation—but it is nonetheless currently a major if not the major force that contributes to the development of social capital in the country, and will likely continue to be so for the foreseeable future. As the Church modernizes, no matter how slowly, its impact on the richness of social ties in the country might increase, although likely not without occasional setbacks. How effectively the Church will contribute in this sphere depends on a number of factors, not all of them within its domain. For instance, how cooperative secular NGOs will be in the years to come with faith-based initiatives, and in what spheres, remains an open question. However, since social trust also concerns the problem of pluralism in society, we will now turn to the situation of the other religious groups in the Poland and their relations with the dominant Catholicism.

4

Diversity and Dialogue

Minority Christian Denominations and Non-Christian Religions in Poland at Present

More than once in the historical overview, reference has been made to John Paul II's insistence of the importance of the Jagiellonian era for Poland's religious identity, citing in this context his optimistic claim of the "religious and national diversity" which form a crucial element of Polish identity. Quite significant are the words that Poles "bear *within* themselves" concerning this identity. At one level it can be extrapolated from this thought that essentially diversity is in fact currently absent. Although traces of the historic diversity remain, Poland in the Jagiellonian sense is indeed gone and was largely gone after World War II. If anything, diversity has decreased since then on account of the dispersal and frequent intermarriage of members of the rather minuscule minorities with Polish Catholics. John Paul admitted as much in the same interview when he added, "It seems ... that the 'Jagiellonian' dimension of the Polish spirit, mentioned above, has sadly ceased to be an evident feature of our time."[1]

Witnesses to life in prewar Poland played an important role in encouraging an awareness of the tradition for several more decades after the Second World War, but slowly they too have mostly passed away. If one were to choose a symbolic moment of its passing in this sense, then aside from the death of John Paul himself, one such moment could be the funeral of poet laureate Czesław Miłosz in 2004. Born in what is now Lithuania in 1911, with his last years—after many earlier ones in exile—spent in Kraków, in his life Miłosz embodied and defended the Jagiellonian ethos the Polish pontiff praised. A troubled Catholic, but later in his life not a lapsed one—since his mid-forties he attended mass fairly regularly—Miłosz was open to the various traditions of Poland's past and lamented lost opportunities for mutual enrichment, for instance, among Jews and Poles. He also wrote the powerful poems "A Poor Christian Looks at the Ghetto" and "Campo de Fiori" in 1943 in response to the Warsaw Ghetto Uprising, among the first Polish literary responses to the Holocaust.

After a mass at St. Mary's Basilica in Kraków where a letter from John Paul II was read, and following a ceremonial procession during which the cardinal of the city followed his coffin on foot, Miłosz was interred at the crypt for outstanding Poles at St. Stanislaus Church at Skałka. Significantly, a symbolic remnant of Jagiellonian Poland was mutely present at the service preceding the internment. While outstanding living Poles, among them Nobel poet laureate Wisława Szymborska, delivered eulogies, a curious priest stood silently in the background among a row of other priests, drawing attention to himself during the televised ceremony primarily on account of his unusually colorful priestly robes. This was the Rev. Tadeusz Isakowicz-Zaleski, pastor of the Armenian community in southern Poland, and his robes represented the Armenian Catholic rite. Several years later he was elected as the representative of the Armenian community at the National and Ethnic Minorities Unit of the Ministry of Interior and Administration.

At present only three priests serve the Armenian Catholics in Poland, and only two of them are actually versed in the rite of the faithful. The number of members of the Armenian Catholic Church is approximately eight thousand. After the collapse of the Soviet Union a number of Armenians have immigrated to Poland. Needless to say, upon arrival these immigrants have little in common with the now comparatively minuscule minority that has lived in the country or has been connected with its history for centuries—Armenian Catholics who, when they still identify themselves as such, are fully assimilated, and whose religion is their main distinction from other Poles. Moreover, as the Soviet Union was much more thoroughly secularized than Poland, the members of the new wave of immigrants usually have less to do with religion, and in the instances that they do it is rather with the tradition of the ancient Armenian Apostolic Church. Nevertheless, since that Church has no representatives in Poland, writes the Rev. Isakowicz-Zaleski, "the faithful often resort to the services of Armenian Catholic priests."[2] The new Armenians relate to their historic brethren on account of their significant presence in Poland, among others through the cultural institutions they have organized, while the newcomers have imprinted on their largely Polonized counterparts a greater awareness of the concerns of the Armenians abroad. A symbolic instance of this: in 2004 a *khachkar*—a cross-bearing carved memorial stele—was erected outside a church in Kraków to commemorate the Armenian victims of massacres in Ukraine and the genocide at the hands of the Turks shortly after World War I.[3]

Another religious group with deep historic roots, likewise going back to Jagiellonian times, but currently affected by an influx of coreligionist immigrants, is the historic Muslim community of Poland. Here the difference is not only cultural but also ethnic. The Polish Muslims are predominantly descended from the Tatars. Other Muslims did come over time from the nineteenth century to the interwar period, but their numbers were insignificant, and they generally assimilated with the existing group. Presently Muslims from countries with Arab and other populations have arrived, and although not in as great numbers as in other European countries, they are still large enough to be the dominant practitioners of Islam in the country. At most, five thousand of the estimated twenty to thirty thousand Muslims in Poland are Polish Tatars.

As an ethnic group, not a great deal has changed for the Tatars after the downfall of Communism. At the organizational level the Organization of Tatars of the Polish Republic was founded in 1992 and started publishing *Rocznik Tatarów Polskich* (The Polish Tatar Yearbook). Presently, despite the estimated four to five thousand Tatars in Poland, only 447 declared themselves as such in the 2002 census. Gathered within six communities, mostly in the eastern part of the country where they have the deepest historic roots, each community has an imam. One of the more active Tatar communities in Poland is located in Gdańsk. Among the changes that occurred after the rise of Solidarity, but not directly related to the event, was the permission granted by the city in 1983 for the community to build a mosque. This project helped energize the community, strengthening its identity.[4] When the mosque was ready for use, among other guests the archbishop of Gdańsk attended the opening ceremony on June 1, 1990. The Tatar community is accepted by Polish society and participates with other ethnic groups in festivals and various cultural events.

For the majority of Polish Tatars their religion and ethnicity are virtually the same. An anthropologist who has studied the group points out the importance of communal religious practices for the community: "Praying and spending holidays together not only integrates the group, but also provides its members with a sense of mutual participation, identification with the same world of beliefs, values and attitudes, which impart a feeling of security, self-fulfillment and self-definition."[5]Although there is an increasing awareness that their brand of Islam has accrued many changes on account of the centuries of isolation from the mainstream, which has led to the emergence of "reformers" who wish to introduce a purer practice of Islam, most Tatars are happy with their religious practices as they are.

Already at this juncture the group of more recent Muslim newcomers is several times larger than the historic group.[6] Some settled in Poland during

Communist times, when, among others, Arabs from the then socialist regimes studied in universities in Eastern Europe and ended up staying in Poland. Others have arrived after the change of the system when Poland became a more attractive country for immigrants. Still more are in the country as refugees, for example, on account of the ongoing civil war between the Russians and Chechens. This, one might say, while formally belonging to the responsibilities of a modern nation, is also a nod toward the Jagiellonian tradition, where various refugees came to the commonwealth. One more group of Muslims that is relatively sizeable is that of Polish converts to Islam; sometimes Poles take on the religion of their Muslim spouses. Whatever the reason, members of this group do not always find understanding among their relatives and friends.

The Polish Tatars founded the Muslim Religious Association in 1925. It was shut down during World War II and was reactivated in 1947. Although non–Tatar Muslims have joined the association, a number of other associations have been founded as well, the most important being the Muslim League in Poland, which was registered in 2004. This organization primarily serves non–Tatars. Some Muslim groups, like the Turks who now live in Poland, although they are quite religious do not belong to any religious associations and only a relatively small percentage of the estimated Muslims in the country are registered in either association.[7]

The plight of the Polish Tatars and Armenians was severely affected by World War II and its aftermath, through violence at the hands of Nazis and Ukrainian nationalists, respectively, and through dislocation after the subsequent border changes. Although nothing can compensate for these blows, on account of the opening up of Poland after 1989 both groups have nonetheless been bolstered in recent years, either through an influx of co-nationalists on the part of the Armenians, or coreligionists on the part of the Tatars. The situation of the Polish Jews, far more dramatic in the first place, has little hope for growth from immigrants. Nonetheless, on account of assistance from outside Poland that has strengthened Jewish cultural and religious institutions, a number of the assimilated Jews who remained in the country have recovered their roots. This is one of the reasons why, quite surprisingly all things considered, the end of the Jewish presence in Poland no longer seems eminent. As small as the group became after the last major exodus stemming from the Communist regime's anti–Semitic campaign of 1968, there have actually been a couple of revivals, for lack of a better word, taking into account the small number of people involved.

The onset of the first revival slightly predates Solidarity but was augmented by that great awakening of Polish society. In the second chapter, we concluded the pre–Solidarity history of the Jewish community with the moral support it received from the Catholic elite, among other things by promoting the discussion of largely taboo Jewish matters. Some of the younger assimilated Jews of Warsaw who attended such events were encouraged by this to further self-exploration, establishing the Jewish Flying University. Despite debating the essence of Jewish identity, the efforts of the clandestine organization hardly produced dramatic changes. There were practically no role models for the young Jews—indeed, the future of the Jewish community seemed in doubt—and the debated solutions varied radically, while much of the knowledge participants gained about Jewishness was secondhand from books, usually in English. As one of the founders of the Flying University put it, despite finding various pertinent outlets for Jewish identity, "[we] remained 'Poles of Jewish origin,' albeit with much more knowledge of the Jewish component of [our] identity and a strikingly more positive attitude toward it."[8]

These young Jews were hardly encouraged by their elders from among the remaining elite. In part this stemmed from the former's enthusiastic involvement with Solidarity. For their highly secularized elders Solidarity's overt Catholicism made them wary; this caution was somewhat warranted since even at that idealistic juncture the movement had an anti–Semitic fringe. But likewise for older Jews who were not put off by Solidarity there seemed something artificial about the initiative. "You are not for real," claimed Marek Edelman, the last surviving leader of the Warsaw Ghetto Uprising of 1943.[9] It was largely incomprehensible to the "old" Jews that the younger assimilated generation would seek a Jewish identity which seemed an unnecessary burden. It took some time for the older group to accept the younger one.

During Solidarity the Jewish Flying University expanded its activities to other cities and for a time the activities were overt, which made the institution vulnerable when martial law was declared in December 1981. But the base had been established. Still, no matter how one looks at it, the numbers involved in this "revival" were not large, while the responses to Jewish identity were quite individualistic. Significantly, some of the group did become interested in the religious aspect of their identity, and this core was crucial for the next phase of the growth of the community. For instance, among them was Konstanty Gebert, the future founding editor of *Midrasz*, a journal examining cultural and religious matters from a Jewish perspective.

Nevertheless, although the movement vitally affected involved individuals from the Jewish community, the overall post–1968 trend of the shrinking religious community was not reversed. In 1988 the official organization for religious Jews in Poland had a meager 1,560 members, about a quarter of the Jews registered in any Polish organizations. And since they had no rabbi of their own, a rabbi had to be invited from Hungary to celebrate major holidays in Warsaw.[10]

However, if the Communist regime curtailed the activities of the Jewish

Flying University, by the mid–1980s, eager to gain some international validity, the state authorities were finally more supportive of the official religious organization, among other things restoring and in 1983 returning the Nożyk Synagogue to the community in Warsaw, the only surviving prewar house of prayer in Poland's capital. Slowly regular Jewish religious life returned to Warsaw, with the first Bar Mitzvah in twenty years taking place in 1985, and a rabbi was finally arranged for the Polish Jewish community in 1989.

A few years after the downfall of Communism, the Ronald S. Lauder Foundation started supporting Jewish education in Poland, financing an educational complex in Warsaw starting in 1994 that encompassed preschool to junior high school. Among other things, students could gain knowledge of Jewish traditions, learn some Hebrew, and celebrate holidays. Later a similar school was established in Wrocław by the foundation, and together over three hundred students attend the schools, some of them from outside the Jewish community.

In the early 1990s the religious community became the center of the entire Jewish community under the new name of the Union of Jewish Religious Communities [Związek Gmin Wyznaniowych Żydowskich], partially restoring the institutional *kehillah* from before World War II. The move raised some criticism from the cultural organization that had dominated the community under Communism. Formally it was also a key toward the restitution by the state of the property confiscated by the Nazis from the religious community and not returned by the Communists.[11]

In accordance with the *kehillah* tradition, an important feature of the organization is its form of self-governance which allows for going beyond strictly religious matters, for instance, in dealing with crucial matters such as social assistance to needier members. In 1997 a ruling was passed that had seminal significance for adjusting the rules for membership in the Jewish religious community under postwar circumstances: from that time on, non-*halakhic* Jews were permitted to join the community. This was essential in that there were conversions to Judaism by Poles of mixed backgrounds, that is, with a partially Jewish background, but without a Jewish mother. Under a strict adherence to Orthodoxy these converts could not be considered Jews. But since most "Jews" in Poland were now from mixed families, they were a key to the flourishing of the community. Effectively, the rules for admission to the community were patterned after the right of return to Israel.

Despite the controversial rules, orthopraxy remained the rule for religious life in the new circumstances. The somewhat paradoxical life of the community has been described by its researchers in the following terms: "On the one hand, the Jewish religious community performs all religious practices in the form prescribed by Orthodox Judaism; on the other hand, only a minority of its members is followers of this version of Judaism."[12] This flexibility has permitted a modest growth of the religious community, which, having fallen to approximately 1,200 at its nadir, now numbers in the vicinity of 1,600 members. Nevertheless, only a small minority of the members follow the practices of their religion outside the major holidays. The largest congregations are in Warsaw, with almost a third of the Polish total, followed by Wrocław and Kraków.

Together with several other cultural and combatant organizations, the number of Jews in various organizations totals up to approximately four and a half thousand members. The Jewish population in Poland is estimated at some at eight thousand,[13] although only a little over a thousand admitted to being Jewish in the 2002 census. Polish scholars conclude a study on the religious life of Jews in Poland with the claim, "The identity of most Polish Jews today is based solely on the memory of the Shoah and their ancestors, opposition to anti–Semitism, and solidarity with Israel, but it lacks a solid cultural foundation."[14] In part this explains why the religious organization is the single largest organization of Jews in Poland. This shift can also be considered a logical extension of the fact of the disappearance of the rich secular culture of the prewar Polish Jews, of a trilingual character with a Hebrew and Polish, and especially of a vital Yiddish culture.[15]

In 2008 the Rabbinate Council of Poland—numbering seven rabbis— was formed, in some ways a culmination of the above organizational process. At its founding it was headed by Michael Schudrich, the chief rabbi of Poland. Taking into account the fact that there had been a period in the not too distant past of over two decades when the Jewish community had no rabbi, this was a memorable moment. Most of the rabbis were from abroad, but one member, Maciej Pawlak, was a native of the country. Like not a few Jews in the country, Pawlak had only learned he was Jewish after some time, when he was sixteen.

The extraordinary contrast between the past when Poland was a major center of the Jewish world and the present creates its own problems. And so, despite the destruction by the Nazis and additional damage from the passage of time and neglect, the rich material heritage creates an enormous strain on the resources of the remaining community, even with the assistance of foundations from abroad. Rabbi Schudrich realizes that his first priority is to support the living community, but the above problem is always close at hand. As he puts it,

> This heritage raises many complex questions that call for resolution. For example, how many synagogues and *cheders* can we possibly hope to restore? Which ones will we rescue, and why those over others? When teaching young and old, the question remains: how much does one focus on what will be and how much on what was? There has to be a balance; neglecting the future for the past is not reasonable.[16]

The list of pressing questions for the community goes on.

Considering the rich variety of Judaism practiced in places like the United

States, although there are currently a couple of Reformed rabbis as well as an ultra–Orthodox Chabad center, another striking feature of the Polish Jewish community is its overall uniformity, at least in its orthopraxy. Polish Jews are aware of the possibilities offered by their faith as it is lived in the world, but there is a sense that circumstances in the country do not allow for many options. Where does that place the experience of the Polish Jewish community in today's Judaism?

According to Rabbi Jonathan Sacks of Britain, "the seminal Jewish experience for the past two centuries has been what I call the 'flight from particularism.'"[17] Quite obviously the destruction of the Orthodox community from before the war during the Holocaust and the strong forces of secularization within the remnant community accelerated this dynamic process for Polish Jews. Nevertheless, in reconstructing their identity, some form of search for the essence of their religion has returned. In this context, Stanisław Krajewski, one of the lay leaders that emerged from the first revival, has expressed his deep concern about the current situation and the direction which he sees forward:

> We are too few and the existing divisions are already painful. Even more important, I have come to realize that proper reform, be it slight or deep, can only mean a reform *of* a tradition. You cannot start with a reform of an empty space devoid of religious traditions. We need a traditional Orthodox background.[18]

As the above faith communities demonstrate, although the two are by no means identical, there is nonetheless a strong correlation between religion and ethnicity in Poland. This is also partly the case in the Orthodox Christian community in the country, currently at over five thousand members constituting the largest single religious group outside of Catholicism. However, ethnicity is complicated in the case of the Orthodox, since it involves two larger ethnic groups, or rather nationalities—the Byelorussians and Ukrainians—that are rather different from each other, and a number of smaller ones, especially the Russians. Even a number of Romani are Orthodox Christian. A host of other complex issues are likewise involved with this religious group.

During the Solidarity years and their aftermath, the Orthodox hierarchy maintained an ambivalent relationship with the state authorities that benefitted the Church structurally, and which also had a beneficial impact on its religious life by creating new parishes. Together with other non–Catholic Christian churches that belonged to the Polish Ecumenical Council, the hierarchy pressed the regime for the same access to the radio broadcast of its masses and services that had been accorded to the Catholic Church in the Gdańsk Accords of 1980. However, together with those same members it subsequently supported the military regime during martial law, gaining praise from the minister of religious affairs for "praying vigorously for the authorities in power."[19] For instance, the hierarchy even remained silent after the murder in 1982 of the Rev. Piotr Popławski, an Orthodox priest who had been known to be a supporter of Solidarity, even though independent sources in Poland and abroad protested the official claim of "suicide." Among the benefits accrued from such a policy was the approval of an Orthodox diocese of Przemyśl-Nowy Sącz in southeastern Poland, a region where there had been an Orthodox presence but that had been dominated by Ukrainian Greek Catholics before the Second World War. Moreover, the Church not only received permission to build a cathedral in Białystok, where there was a sizeable Orthodox community, but— which was indeed rare under the Communist regime—also received some state funding for the enterprise. As historian Edward Wynot, Jr. puts it, "Clearly the Polish Orthodox Church had profited from its accommodation with the prevailing political forces."[20]

However, the above is far from the whole story of Orthodoxy in Poland at the time. For instance, in the late 1970s and early 1980s a group of Orthodox youth studying at the Orthodox section of the Christian Theological Academy started reviving the tradition of pilgrimages to the Holy Mountain of Grabarka. They also wished to register a Fellowship of Orthodox Youth, but the idea was too much for the Communist regime to swallow. Nonetheless an Orthodox student organization at the Christian Theological Academy was permitted and this was enough of a foothold for a semiofficial national youth group to form. The group even managed to form contacts with Finnish Orthodox youth, the first such external contact from among the entire socialist bloc. By the early 1980s, the Easter pilgrimages to Grabarka were attracting thousands of Orthodox youth, and the group was publishing a bulletin that reached a larger number within the faith community. The Fellowship, as it was unofficially called, was the first Orthodox Christian youth group within the Communist bloc, as well as the first Orthodox mass movement within the bloc initiated by lay members.[21] Not without meaning were the changes toward the end of the period connected with perestroika in the Soviet Union across the eastern border of Poland, which permitted closer contacts with Orthodox communities with which the Polish community had deep historical roots, such as the Byelorussian, Ukrainian and Russian Orthodox churches.

Following the lead of the Catholic Church, which was undoubtedly initially in a privileged position after 1989, the Orthodox Church gained much more freedom of self-organization—especially after the legislation in 1997 that spread many of the rights gained by the Catholic Church on to the other major faith communities, including—most importantly—full internal autonomy. For the Orthodox, the new legal situation also included the restitution of church property confiscated by the Communists and, in some cases, by the authorities from interwar Poland. The case of property confiscated in the Chełm region in the late 1930s was particularly important in this respect.

A number of new parishes were founded, and churches constructed in the 1990s. By the end of the decade the Church had 219 parishes and over thirty branches in Poland. However, effects of assimilation were also felt, and places where the Orthodox population had been particularly dispersed experienced a reduction in members. Moreover, Orthodox parishioners now often enough expected sermons in their own languages, such as Ukrainian, which had been denied under the Communists. This demand was matched by a change in the education of the seminarians, who were now taught in these languages, while the Orthodox section of the Christian Theological Academy initiated a course on minorities in Poland that had a sizeable Orthodox population. Training of seminarians was generally upgraded, and their program was eventually acknowledged by state authorities as the equivalent of a bachelor's degree. The Orthodox Theological Seminary finally attained the status of a university college in 1998. At a more basic level, Orthodox religious education was permitted in schools where the communities were large enough to warrant this. In practice this pertained to parts of the Białystok Voivodeship.

The indigenous historic Orthodox communities are in the eastern part of Poland, the poorest part of the country. The diminishing number of faithful in some places meant that historical churches were difficult to maintain and restoration was very expensive. Once Poland entered the European Union, funds became available for the restoration of some of the more significant historical churches, for instance in Szczebrzeszyn in eastern Poland, where the oldest historic Orthodox church in the country is found.

Significantly, the Polish language became more and more frequent in sermons and the liturgy, which testified to the assimilation of a larger body of the believers, especially among the younger generation. The Orthodox young were particularly active at this time. A couple of years after the end of Communism in 1989, the Fellowship of Orthodox Youth was legalized and expanded its earlier activities. The pilgrimage to Grabarka each spring remained a key event. The Fellowship also started publishing newsletters and maintaining an Internet site. Cooperation with the World Fellowship of Orthodox Youth Syndesmos was established. As mentioned earlier, the Orthodox Church also became involved in charitable work. Centers were established to assist needy members of the faith community in a number of the dioceses, which after a while were coordinated in Warsaw.[22]

Besides the sanctuary in Grabarka, Orthodox pilgrims also visited a number of other sanctuaries, such as the monastery in Jabłeczna or the sanctuary in Supraśl, which also drew pilgrims from abroad. The freedom to travel after the fall of Communism also meant that the Polish Orthodox faithful could visit sanctuaries outside Poland with ease, especially those in the former Socialist bloc, such as in Belarus, Ukraine or Russia. On the other hand, the cult of local saints was not forgotten: their number was also increased, since the Orthodox Church of Poland started canonizing new saints, something it had historically never done. Especially meaningful was the canonizing of the martyrs of Chełm and from Polesie, who died in the Second World War.

The latter was a sign of the democratic processes in Poland allowing difficult issues to be raised. Historical memory of the faithful is a particularly important issue, which was impossible to foster on a larger scale under the Communists, when it was not suppressed outright. As one historian observes, "A result of the diversity of the Orthodox faith community in Poland is that historical memory of the Orthodox Church in various regions is quite differentiated."[23] For instance, knowledge of their history is generally weak among the Orthodox; nevertheless it is growing. One might add that Orthodoxy plays a different role in parts of Poland depending on the national or ethnic group involved and plays a different role in their identity. For instance, in the case of the Byelorussians their attachment to Orthodoxy comes before their ethnic identity, while for the Ukrainians the reverse is true.[24] In the latter case, as we have seen, the issue is further complicated by the Ukrainians being attached to two separate denominations: along with Orthodoxy an even larger percentage of the group are attached to the Ukrainian Greek Catholic Church.

It was mentioned in Chapter 2 that the Orthodox Church has the most vibrant popular religion in Poland after the Catholics. Besides the pilgrimages, there remain parts of Poland, particularly close to the Ukrainian border, where much of the enchanted worldview that has virtually disappeared elsewhere continues to nourish religious traditions, which anthropologists scrupulously report.[25] In due course after 1989 the higher religious cultural life of the community also began flourishing. To some extent this is a necessary process connected with the growing urbanization of the Orthodox: there are now an estimated twenty thousand members in Warsaw alone. The founding of the Orthodox Cultural Center in Białystok in 1999 was a milestone in this major diocese, imitated in a number of other ones. Some festivals, like the annual International Festival of Orthodox Church Music in Hajnówka attract visitors from abroad, and resonate outside the Orthodox community in the country. The Internet has offered further resources for a number of its communities, such as Internet radio stations, which two Orthodox dioceses run, as well as a host of websites.

Despite the rich culture of the Polish Orthodox Church, it still struggles with questions of identity. One of its more provocative thinkers of recent years was the theologian and painter Jerzy Nowosielski. He maintains that the Church has been influenced by the Russian Orthodox Church to too great an extent from the Partitions on and it should relate more to the older traditions of Orthodoxy from the Polish-Lithuanian Commonwealth.[26] Whatever manner the discussion may develop, or fail to develop—Nowosielski, who died in 2010, seemed pessimistic as to the intellectual potential of the Church—at least the Orthodox in Poland are in a position now to conduct it for themselves.

Undoubtedly the continued Polonization of the Orthodox community will be a growing concern. It may be slower in the case of the Orthodox on account of the size of the particular ethnic groups to which it pertains, but it proceeds inexorably. Moreover, either on account of the earlier dispersal or because of people looking for employment or higher education, in some parts of the country where the faithful found themselves, Polish was the language that connected the believers from different national or ethnic groups. Still, it is not likely the factor that will play the greatest threat to Orthodoxy as such, since, in all likelihood, the outreach of the Church will be more effective in this circumstance than in other threats to its integrity, which will be discussed in the next section. Here Sacks's law, as we might call it, after a statement by the chief rabbi of Britain, will likely maintain: "ethnicity per se does not last. It fades over time.... What lasts is religion."[27]

The case of the Ukrainian Greek Catholic Church has some similarities to the Orthodox Church in being historically and strongly connected with an ethnic minority: as mentioned, the Ukrainian nationality, together with a number of Lemkos, an ethnic group that is split between those who identify more with Ukrainians and those who feel themselves to be Carpatho-Ruthenians. By the 1980s the situation of the Church had improved slightly, with two auxiliary bishops of the primate of Poland caring for the faithful. The regime relaxed its suppression of the denomination further but tried to pass the responsibility for it on to the Roman Catholic hierarchy, no doubt expecting the major Christian denomination to be fully aware of the political circumstances and their inherent limitations. Indeed, after martial law, not wishing to provoke the Soviets, the Catholic hierarchy was quite cautious in extending any further aid to their coreligionist brethren. Much like in the preceding period, the Ukrainian Greek Catholic Church was dependent on the goodwill of Roman Catholic parishes for liturgical access, which was not always forthcoming despite greater support from the hierarchy. However, John Paul II was definitely on their side, and by the end of the decade perestroika had liberalized Soviet attitudes and provided more latitude in the treatment of Greek Catholics. Nevertheless, to this day in parts of the country where their numbers are not large enough to sustain their own parish, Ukrainian Catholics remain dependent on Roman Catholic parishes.[28]

The structure of the Church was strengthened in 1989 when it gained its own bishop. This was followed by the reactivation of the Ukrainian Catholic diocese of Przemyśl two years later. In 1996 the Vatican opened a special province of the Ukrainian Greek Catholic Church made up of the Ukrainian Catholic archeparchy of Przemyśl-Warsaw and the Ukrainian Catholic eparchy of Wrocław-Gdańsk, which is suffragan to the former. This period also witnessed the restitution of a number of the churches that had been taken from the denomination in 1947. Relations with the Ukrainian Greek Catholic Church in the Ukraine are consciously fostered, with the Church in Poland actually taking on the same name, and despite the fact that their bishops are a part of the Polish Conference of Bishops, they regard the major archbishop of L'viv as their spiritual superior.[29] Nevertheless, decades of being dependent on Roman Catholics for religious services as well as centuries of earlier Polish–Ukrainian coexistence, have led to a degree of "Latinization" of many Ukrainian Greek Catholic practices. "At the same time," observes Juray Buzalka, "Greek Catholics—both older devout women and young intellectuals—claim they look to the true tradition as their source of inspiration."[30] These traditions, such as specific icons, are sometimes sought in Ukraine.

Toward the end of the first decade of the twenty-first century, the Church had approximately 120 parishes in Poland, with an estimated 110,000 to 160,000 faithful. The latter figure is significant, since in the census of 2002 only about 27,000 Polish citizens admitted to belonging to the Ukrainian national group.[31] It might be true in part what an Orthodox historian has suggested to the author in regard to these statistics that to some extent Ukrainian respondents did not trust the surveyors and were afraid to come out with their identity. Nevertheless, despite the fact that the Ukrainians have a more developed sense of national identity than the Byelorussians, their dispersion after 1947 has affected their sense of identity quite strongly. As in the case of the Orthodox, however, religion remains stronger than ethnicity.

One of the Christian denominations mistakenly associated with ethnicity is that of the Polish Lutherans. A significant portion of Lutherans are indeed of German descent, but the German minority that lives in Poland is predominantly Catholic. Albeit historically this nationality did play a larger role among the Lutheran minority, after World War II, with numerous Polish Germans leaving for Germany for various reasons, the ethnically Polish Lutherans came to heavily dominate the denomination. These statistics have less significance for the religious life of the faith community than for the fact that they go against the Polish stereotype concerning the Lutherans, who with somewhat over 80,000 members constitute the largest mainstream Protestant group in Poland.

Much like other religious groups, the Lutherans slowly gained increasingly greater legal space for their activities in the 1980s.[32] The Polish Protestant

Association of which they were a founding member was reactivated in 1983 and allowed to function nationwide; several other associations were also permitted. After the fall of Communism the Lutheran Church successively gained more rights and expanded its activities, contributing to Poland's slowly developing civil society. Among these activities religious education of the faith community's young is very important. As mentioned, the Lutherans are well enough organized and large enough that in some regions this education takes place in public schools. Where there is a sizeable presence in a town or city, but not large enough for full classes in particular schools, religious education takes place in Church facilities, with the children receiving credit from the local school boards. Although religion teachers can be prepared for their work in the Protestant section of the Christian Theological Academy in Warsaw, the University of Silesia provides such preparation for Lutherans at their branch in Cieszyn, which is the center with one of the largest Lutheran communities in Poland.

In 1994 the Lutheran Church gained internal autonomy within the Polish polity and was able to take steps for the restitution of confiscated property. In 1995 the Lutherans were able to provide pastoral care for members of their faith community serving in the armed forces. Moreover the Church's contacts with other Lutheran communities abroad were no longer subject to any impediments.

At an estimated 5,000 members, much smaller than the Lutheran Church but possessing equally deep historical roots in Poland, is the Polish Reformed Church, the Polish church that holds to the Calvinist tradition. As such it is fully congregational. The Polish Reformed Church is likely the most liberal of the Christian churches in the country. For instance, since 1991 the Church has ordained women as pastors. The Church also publishes *Jednota* (Unity), one of the best-known Protestant periodicals in the country, which, in keeping with the traditional stress on tolerance of the faith community, has championed causes such as establishing legal equality for minorities in Poland's legal system.

For a number of years the periodical's editor in chief was Krzysztof Dorosz, one of the country's most critically acknowledged authors on religious thought. If we wished to indicate an example of the dialectical imagination—the religious imagination that runs counter to the analogical imagination prevalent in Catholics—then a good place to start would be in the reflections contained in Dorosz's book published in 2010, *Bóg i terror historii* (God and the Terror of History). Among other things, the author reflects on the expansion of the ego in the twentieth century, which moves people away from God. Where the dialectical imagination emerges in this analysis of the religious tenor of the age, however, is in the solutions the author sees, or rather where he fails to see them. For Dorosz, symbolic mediators are not efficacious, be it the church or any other religious institution, and thus he states, "In order recover to the relationship between contemporary people and God, it is not enough to refer to the Christian roots of Europe, nor to insist on the presence of Christianity in the preamble to the [EU] constitution or of the cross in the public sphere.[33] The road to faith is difficult and must be conducted individually.

This steep path for the faithful is more than just a theological stance; in many ways it reflects a survival strategy for a denomination as small as the Polish Reformed Church. Bishop Lech Tranda relates how he perceives his mission on account of the situation of his flock: "One of my tasks, which I see as a priority, is leading people to Christ, and not to church. I feel this is my main task, because the members of my church in Warsaw live in Diaspora, at some distance from the church and from each other as well, in constant haste in the big city.[34]

Alongside these historical mainstream denominations, there are a plethora of Protestant denominations active in Poland, ranging from those that nevertheless have comparatively lengthy historical pedigrees on the one hand as well as some that are recent arrivals on the other hand. Seniority among them belongs to groups like the Baptists, which arrived in Polish lands in the mid–nineteenth century, during the Partitions when there was no Polish state. Presently the Baptists are approximately four thousand strong and growing.[35] At just over twenty thousand members the Polish Pentecostal Church is the second-largest Protestant church in the country. With a total population in the vicinity of 160,000, Protestants in Poland run the gamut from mainstream denominations, through various Pentecostal and even non–Trinitarian ones. They are primarily found in urban centers. Some parts of the country have longer Protestant traditions, and there seem to be a greater concentration of diverse denominations found there. For instance, the Cieszyn area near the border of the Czech Republic, a Lutheran stronghold, boasts approximately twenty-six different denominations.[36] Another feature common for many of these denominations is their close connection to their respective international religious communities. This, among other things, helps to provide all the necessary literature for a contemporary church—most of the Polish religious literature for smaller denominations comes from translations—which would be difficult for such small communities to produce on their own.[37]

If, as mentioned above, among the Protestants the Lutherans are often associated with the German minority although most of their church's members are ethnically Poles, there is the reverse myth of the equation of the ethnic Pole with Catholicism. Although largely true, at present there is a small but growing number of Poles with no religious belief. Even historically, however, there was at least a limited national and ethnic diversity among Roman Catholics in Poland. In the Middle Ages, for instance, there was a sizeable

German minority in a number of cities and towns. This group assimilated into the Polish population over time, but not before leaving its cultural signature. Tourists in Kraków gaze in admiration at the fifteenth-century altarpiece in St. Mary's Church. The magnificent altarpiece carved by Veit Stoss (in Polish, Wit Stwosz) was commissioned by the German community of the city in 1477 at great cost through the donations of its members.[38] Germans have arrived in Poland in many different waves, and at approximately 150,000, currently Germans constitute the largest national minority in Poland. Besides the small group in southwestern Poland that are largely Protestant, Germans are the largest non-ethnically Polish group of Catholics. Many of these Germans live in Silesia and have distinct religious customs. This "local piety" has survived because in the years following the war the local bishops used these autochthons as a model for the influx of Poles from the eastern *kresy*. As one historian puts it, it was understood that "[f]or those driven out of their homes and struggling to establish regular devotional habits, who could provide a better example than those who had managed to stay put?"[39]

The early German Catholic community may have largely assimilated into the Polish populace, but the same is not the case with the historic Lithuanian Catholics, most of whom live in the Lithuanian state, but some of which remain within Polish borders to this day. One matter that unites the Lithuanian Catholics in Poland is their struggle to be able to attend mass in their own language, which requires a priest capable of conducting the liturgy, along with providing pastoral care, in Lithuanian, as well as a church where the mass can be conducted. During the Communist years Polish Lithuanians struggled with the bishop of Łomża for decades to get a Lithuanian mass in Sejny, where they had a large community. Only in the early 1980s did a new bishop finally resolve the matter. However, the struggle in other places, quite intense at times, continued until the early 1990s.[40]

Another historical ethnic group that is largely Roman Catholic is the Romani, traditionally called Gypsies. Here one must add a caveat: the Romas were traditionally nomadic, so while their presence in Poland goes back a number of centuries, a stable population only dates back to post–World War II, when the Communists forced them to give up their traditional lifestyle. Initially their Catholicism was largely symbolic, in part a defense mechanism of a nomadic people wishing to gain at least partial acceptance within a sedentary European context. Once the Romani who happened to be there were largely settled in Poland—a painful process—in the late 1970s and early 1980s, some Catholic priests undertook pastoral missions among them. The Rev. Edward Wesołek, for instance, was among the first Polish priests who learned the Romany language and conducted masses along with delivering homilies in it. He also translated a number of prayers and hymns into Romany. A Roma parish was also established at that time close to Limanowa, the site of a Marian sanctuary not all that far from Kraków, but in a different diocese. The latter sanctuary also became the locus of the largest annual Romani pilgrimage in that part of country and it continues to this day. In part it is an occasion for the Roma to gather.

The Romani largely accept Catholicism under conditions that suit them.[41] Their children are baptized at the age of four to six years, and most Roma receive a Catholic funeral. Other sacraments are treated less strictly. For instance, marriages are rarely taken in church, but this is not so much due to a lax interpretation of Catholicism as the fact that the church ceremony is simultaneously a civil ceremony, and the Roma are wary of public institutions. Priests and various Catholic volunteers that work with the Roma are generally accepted by the community—a community that has many needs!—in part acting as mediators for it to the society at large, but there are few religious callings from within it. Partly this harkens back to their nomadic tradition which never sustained any priestly cast. The Roma Catholicism also coexists with a number of beliefs and practices that stem from their traditional world-view.

As unconventional as their Catholicism may be deemed, and though some belong to other Christian denominations, considering they are among the more numerous ethnic minorities in Poland, aside from the Germans, the Roma community likely holds the largest number of Roman Catholics who are not ethnic Poles (which does not prevent them from being the group that draws the greatest amount of negative feelings). Whether this will remain the case depends on what immigrants settle in Poland in the future—their number may be relatively small now, but as the country is a member of the European Union, the situation may slowly change—along with the religious mix they bring with them. Currently the immigrants come from mixed religious backgrounds and are largely presented in the media by country of origin, with rarely a mention of their religious background. For instance, there is little information whether Nigerians settling in Poland are Muslim or Christian, and Poles are not particularly interested. Unfortunately, for the general public race plays a larger role for the reception of African immigrants, and racism is a problem. One might add that the most high-profile Nigerian immigrant in Poland at present is John Godson, a Protestant minister who is a member of the Polish parliament, and who, among other things, has been active in a committee on the persecution of Christians in the contemporary world: something which Polish Christians already have behind them for some time, but is quite topical for an African Christian.

It should be remembered immigrants are often enough not entirely representative of their home populations with regard to the religions they hold.[42]

This question has not been thoroughly researched in Poland, and it is hard to say, for instance, to what extent the sizeable Vietnamese population in Poland has a greater proportion of Buddhists than Christians. As of yet, the Buddhist group is not very organized, although it has invited Vietnamese monks from France to assist the community.[43] Often enough Buddhist parents send their children to Catholic religious education in the public schools in order for their children not to stand out from the majority. As concerns the smaller group of Christian Vietnamese, suppressed in their own country by its Communist regime, the community found a receptive space in its host country. The Society of the Divine Word, a missionary order, runs a center for immigrants in Warsaw where many of the Vietnamese come and attend masses. Currently a Vietnamese priest also has organized a center close to Warsaw where he provides the community with religious instruction. Naturally not all the Vietnamese Christians participate in such missions; some are more isolated in smaller centers, while others drift into religious indifference amid the struggle to get along in the new country.[44]

The different faith community groups mentioned above does not end the list of religious diversity in Poland. There are smaller religious groups with an older or more recent presence in the country, among the largest being the Jehovah's Witnesses. There are also new religious movements, commonly known as sects, which attract less-committed or otherwise frustrated Catholics or other Poles into their fold. New Age or Neo-Pagan groups along with various related groups of spiritual renewal are likewise part of the religious scene. The latter also occur with a modicum of syncretism; a number of Catholic Poles experiment with different movements while remaining somewhat attached to their traditional faith community. In other words, Poland is currently a relatively normal developed country: in fact, the presence of a dominant religious group is probably more unusual than the above phenomenon.

All in all, while the religious variety is scant, it remains a fact. Among the questions it evokes are, firstly, what has been the effect on the minorities of having such a monumental partner; secondly, and closely related, what is the relationship of the dominant group, that is, Catholic Poles, with the minorities; and, thirdly—returning in part to John Paul II's assertion—to what extent does the existence of diversity affect the attitude of the Roman Catholics to their own religion?

From Coexistence to Dialogue

On September 16, 2000, a symbolic event took place during the first Congress of Christian Culture in Lublin organized by the new archbishop of the diocese. A theatrical group and educational center named Teatr NN organized a happening in which the soil from two destroyed "temples"—a Catholic church in the historic center of the city, which had collapsed from neglect during the time of the Partitions of Poland in the nineteenth century, and the main synagogue of the prewar Jewish community, that like many Jewish places of worship was destroyed by the Nazis during World War II—was mixed in a pot and a grape vine was planted in it at a site symbolically halfway between the two ruins.

The soil from the synagogue was carried by Michael Schudrich, the chief rabbi of Poland from Warsaw. In itself this was symbolic of the fate of Judaism in Lublin and further in the country. Once the thriving heart of the rich Jewish life in Poland, with centuries-deep roots, now not only did the remnants of Lublin's community not have its own rabbi, but it did not even have a *minyan*, the minimum number of Jewish men needed to hold a prayer meeting, while the chief rabbi of the country with the formerly largest Jewish population in Europe had to be recruited from abroad.

Józef Życiński, the archbishop of Lublin at the time, greeted the Jewish delegation at the appointed spot. Broadly smiling he intoned in English, "I am Joseph, I am your brother. Welcome!" In his allusion to the biblical bearer of the coat of many colors, the archbishop can serve as a metaphor for the wealth inherent in Poland's religious past and—as we have seen, to a much lesser extent—also the present. The archbishop was quite close to John Paul II and also valued the Jagiellonian tradition.[45] His warm greeting to the rabbi in Lublin gives some indication of the distance both groups have traveled toward each other.

However, the Congress and its relation to the above event implicitly expresses that today to no small extent the memory of what these groups once represented relies on the goodwill and initiative of Catholic Poles. In independent Poland an increasing number of Catholics have begun to take this heritage seriously, helped among other things by the ecumenical and interfaith dialogue taking place within the country—largely initiated after the Solidarity movement, spurred on by John Paul II's meeting with representatives from various groups in Poland, and flourishing without any external restraints after the fall of Communism—acknowledging its importance for their own religious and national identity. Members of minorities also refer to this tradition. For instance, the former imam of Gdańsk, Selim Chazbijewicz, summarizes the position of his people: "The very fact that the Polish Tatars use such a multi-layered identification makes them a living relic of the former Sarmatian nation of the First Commonwealth of Poland.[46]

For ideological reasons, among other things, validating the postwar border changes, the Communist regime fostered the vision of a uniform Poland—

and, what follows, censored topics countering this vision. Thus before regaining independence, awareness of this multicultural and varied religious past was primarily maintained in elite, usually secular circles, like Jerzy Giedroyć's émigré group that published the *Kultura* monthly in Paris. Somewhat later, a small group of Catholic intellectuals in Poland centered at the Catholic University in Lublin took up the call, from 1976 on publishing the samizdat journal *Spotkania* where this tradition was discussed. Both periodicals were read clandestinely, so they could not have a broader impact. The weeks of Christian culture mentioned earlier were also elitist. However, it was the rise of Solidarity that allowed the issue to return to a broader public awareness. For instance, during the First National Congress of Solidarity in October of 1981, a resolution was passed stating,

> With concern for the development of a Polish culture open to the accomplishments of other nationalities, we express our willingness to show the greatest care so that Polish citizens belonging to other nationalities and ethnic groups—Byelorussians, Gypsies, Greeks, Lithuanians, Lemkos, Germans, Ukrainians, Tatars, Jews and other nationalities—should find in the fatherland they share with Poles adequate conditions for the free development of their cultures and the transmission of them on to their subsequent generations. In this way we wish to be faithful to the tradition of the [Polish-Lithuanian] Commonwealth of many nationalities.[47]

Nevertheless, despite matters of censorship having been removed, partly in the wake of the transitional problems mentioned earlier, after regaining independence one might say that to a greater extent Poles have been inclined to self-absorption, which in part explains the reemergence of a significant nationalist streak also discussed earlier. While religious minorities have many of the legal benefits of a country that meets the standard requirements for the freedom of conscience and worship in the EU, and there are no particularly significant conflicts between the Catholic majority and religious minorities, what the future holds is not so certain. To give one example, "It seems to me," states an expert on minorities, "the problem of the protection of national and ethnic minorities will systematically grow in Poland, because the number of immigrants from different countries that gain Polish citizenship is systematically growing.[48] Moreover, even in the case of historical minorities, there is the general problem of ignorance toward non-ethnic Poles or non–Catholics in the country. The picture varies somewhat with each religious and national or ethnic minority.

* * *

Jerzy Pilch is catching a taxi for the Rev. Adam Pilch's funeral. As the highest-ranking Lutheran involved in the pastoral care of his faithful in the Polish army, the Reverend Pilch had the honor of being invited by the president of Poland to participate in the delegation to Smoleńsk on that fateful flight on April 10, 2010, where the Polish officers executed by Soviets at Katyń were to be commemorated, but which ended so tragically for all aboard. Now, through death, for a brief period he became a part of a national pantheon.

An award-winning Polish author and a Lutheran, Jerzy Pilch is irritated. Part of him is thinking about the near invisibility of his coreligionists in Polish society, despite the unexpected renown of his personal friend so recently deceased. He decides to test the taxi driver, someone who knows the city like the back of his hand. "Take me to the Lutheran church on Puławska [Street]," he says, without further explanation. The cabbie, as Pilch relates, is momentarily dumbfounded:

> [O]n the face of the driver I detected classic impotence and Catholic cognitive panic. I remained silent. He remained all the more silent. In the deathly silence I rehearsed the slights my brethren and I experience. Well, now! No one knows where our churches are! We hide in the catacombs! I whispered in my soul.[49]

The test may seem unfair, especially since Pilch admits that he expected such an outcome. But at that crucial moment he yearned for a minimal solidarity from a Catholic fellow Pole in the sense of at least not having to explain where Polish Lutherans worship, and mourn.

Although, as shall be seen, there are negative feelings on the part of some Polish Catholics toward several minorities, a more widespread and quotidian problem is the above-mentioned general ignorance concerning Polish citizens of a different faith or of a different ethnic background. Because there are so few of either—ethnic minorities constitute an estimated 2 to 3 percent of the population—the vast majority of Poles tend to think there are even fewer members of minorities than is actually the case and are rather uninterested in their problems.[50] The relative invisibility of these and the often concomitant religious minorities likewise extends to the larger media. The religion editor of the largest national newspaper, a man who personally places great store on ecumenism, once apologized to Polish Lutherans that he almost never covered even major events of their church, since at roughly eighty thousand members the entire church is smaller than the least populous Catholic diocese in the country, and for his superiors numbers count most.

For religious minorities the Catholic majority creates problems, among others, simply by being what it is: virtually omnipresent. This affects various aspects of their sense of identity, sometimes evoking contradictory feelings. For instance, according to one researcher, Tatars identify with Polishness, which reflects on their perception of Catholics. Conducting her research in eastern Poland in a region where a number of faith communities coexist, an anthropologist found that Tatars generally felt more comfortable with Catholics than, say, with Orthodox Christians. "I feel indifference toward others [from different religious communities]. I'm closer to Catholics, because I feel I'm a Pole," rather typically claimed one respondent.[51] However, when she delved more deeply, it was not uncommon for Tatar respondents to complain that Poles did not understand them well as Muslims.

One sensitive field that often brings upon religious minorities a direct confrontation with members of the Catholic majority is the difficulty of finding an appropriate life partner within a small, dispersed community. Rabbi Schudrich relates the lament of a young member of the Jewish community: "Rabbi, I am 23 years old. I know all the boys in the community and don't like any of them. How am I going to get married?"[52] Such anecdotes can be multiplied.

A study conducted within the Lutheran community in Warsaw in the early 1990s enumerated the various problems that mixed marriages with Catholics entail.[53] For one thing, they not infrequently lead to members leaving the Church. In principle the Lutheran Church is not against intermarriage but realizes that it creates problems on various levels. For this reason they try to create situations, such as youth camps, where young Lutherans might meet and perhaps find partners. Another matter is the attitude of the Catholic Church toward mixed marriages. At times, Lutherans know the teaching of the Catholic Church better than most Catholics, such as the respondent of the study who cited the teaching of the Second Vatican Council that intermarriage can be a school in ecumenism, but points out that the declaration is not matched by practice, since "canon law maintains that without the acceptance of the Church, generally imposing a number of concessions, mixed marriages are not allowed.[54] While on account of their awareness of the difficulties involved the attitude toward mixed marriages with Catholics among Lutherans is ambivalent, their attitude toward the Catholic Church as an institution was found to be unequivocally negative. Within the problems the Catholic Church creates for mixed marriages they perceive an effective tactic for gaining new members.

One of the reasons the Catholic Church does not fully recognize Lutheran marriages is the fact that the latter church does not consider marriage a sacrament, while Catholicism does. This creates a number of difficulties for the faithful at the institutional level, but a modus vivendi is being sought. An agreement is being worked out by the Polish Ecumenical Council, which includes seven Christian denominations, together with the Catholic Church in Poland, concerning mixed marriages. If the document is accepted by all concerned, some aspects of these marriages will be clarified. For instance, it will effectively be up to the parents how the prospective children's religious education will be conducted. This was an issue that caused much heartache. If the Polish bishops accept the document, it will still have to be accepted by the pope. Chances are fairly good, since the document as it stands was largely modeled after an agreement between the Italian Catholic Episcopate and Lutherans, which was accepted by John Paul II.[55]

Obviously how the churches and faith communities relate to one another, whether through ecumenical or interfaith dialogue, has an impact on how the faithful interrelate. The above example holds promise for a key area affecting believers at a fundamental level. To get to this point, however, a rocky road was traversed that stems back from the period of martial law in 1981.

It was noted earlier that in contradistinction to some individual members, the attitude of the leadership of various non–Catholic faith communities to Solidarity was often ambivalent on account of its prominent Catholic character. An exception would be the Polish Reformed Church that was generally supportive and recognized the potential for dialogue. An official delegation from the Reformed Church even participated in the funeral of the Rev. Jerzy Popiełuszko to demonstrate solidarity with the victim's family and the Roman Catholic Church after the bestial murder of the priest.[56] However, during martial law the Polish Ecumenical Council and the leadership of its member churches supported the Communist authorities. On account of his fairly vocal support of the regime under these circumstances, the Lutheran bishop Janusz Narzyński—with the support of the authorities—became the head of the council in 1982. Even after the fall of Communism this stance was defended by a prominent Lutheran, who claimed:

> Churches that could garner the support of broad masses could in spite of everything protest without consequences and demand their rights, while others, less numerous, like our [Lutheran] Church, had to restrict themselves to elucidating biblical truths, which also played a crucial role, because they helped our minds and souls resist antireligious propaganda. Were we to respond differently we could be easily eliminated with even a small degree of force.[57]

A background of cooperation with the Communist authorities initially decreased the moral authority of the Protestant churches involved in the eyes of the Polish public. It must be remembered, however, that although the heroism of the Catholic Church in the face of the totalitarian regime is beyond question, collaboration had existed at various levels, and this fact was rarely reflected upon in the heady period shortly after 1989.

At any rate, the speed with which the Catholic Church regained many of its former rights in independent Poland, for example, religious education in public schools, also worried the smaller denominations. Concerns about Poland turning into a confessional state were voiced. Even the previously supportive Polish Reformed Church was alarmed. The sense of threat led these denominations to urge their members to support the post–Communist political parties, although in the first decade after the collapse of Communism even these seemed to defer to the Church. Attempts at dialogue did not allay the fears of the Protestants, such as when a professor of the Catholic University of Lublin attended a symposium on church–state relations at the Christian Theological Academy in 1993 in an attempt to calm the mainstream denominations. Nor did the state manage to assuage the fears of Protestants upon completion of its negotiations of the concordat with the Catholic Church with the promise that it would extend similar rights to other churches.

Although the negotiation of agreements with separate churches assuaged some fears, a breakthrough year in allaying the fears of Protestant churches concerning the evolution of a confessional state in Poland was 1997. This was the year that the country's constitution was passed, significantly before the formal validation of the concordat between the Polish state and the Roman Catholic Church, meaning the latter would not be incorporated into the constitution. More importantly, much to the surprise of the Protestants, the post–Solidarity Christian Democratic Party that formed the government, although dominated by Catholics, chose a Protestant politician, Jerzy Buzek, as the prime minister. Although prominently Catholic, nonetheless from that time on the civil religion of Poland usually created places for members of the Polish Ecumenical Council. Symbolic of this, in the year 2000 when ceremonies were held in Gniezno to celebrate the millennium of the Holy Roman Emperor's visit during which the metropolitan diocese was established, the mass that opened the ceremonies was ecumenical, concelebrated by the primate of the Catholic Church, Cardinal Glemp, Archbishop Sawa, the head of the Polish Orthodox Church, and Bishop Jan Szarek of the Lutheran Church of Poland.

A number of ecumenical activities took place between the Protestant, Orthodox and Catholic churches at different levels, right up to John Paul II's visits to their different churches during his pilgrimages to Poland in 1991 and 1997. Another factor that slowly changed the minority churches' attitude toward the Catholic Church was the general changes in Polish society during successive years. Neither the Catholic nor the mainstream Protestant churches were happy with the appearance of new religious movements in the country; moreover the media were more frequently presenting antireligious values: in sum, the country was undergoing a degree of secularization. There were evidently common concerns emerging.

However, there are also problems connected with maintaining dialogue with the Catholic Church on the one hand, so vital in Polish society, and developing Protestant identity as each denomination understood it on the other, especially since, to put it mildly, their partner churches beyond the Polish borders developed in radically different ways. Women clergy in most denominations are among the least of the changes. On the other hand, those churches have not resisted secularization well, according to some theories, in part because in "keeping with the times" they have little of their own to offer. In other words, in accommodating the liberal European temper, these churches are not criticized like the Catholic Church often is by the liberal press, but neither are they attended. Here the model of the Catholic Church, not without its risks, has been proved to maintain greater religious vitality, even outside of Poland in Europe. In Poland this cannot but give its ecumenical partners reason for thought. The historical mainstream Polish Protestant churches have resolved the issue individually. The Lutheran Church is more conservative than Lutheran churches abroad, a stance that keeps it a partner in dialogue with the Catholic Church on crucial issues. The agreement on marriage that is being worked out hinges on a common agreement to the meaning of marriage, which can no longer be taken as a given among all Christian groups. Perhaps because its role was less conformist during the Communist period, the Polish Reformed Church goes its own way to a larger extent, pace women ordained as ministers.

Ecumenism and its complications are one matter; faith communities living together in contemporary Poland is another. The Rev. Janusz Sikora, pastor of the largest Lutheran parish in Cieszyn and one of the largest in the country, talks about the relationship of his faithful with Catholics, where the young attend school together, while attending separate religion classes: "The religion of the teachers and the students does not play a greater role. Here in Silesian Cieszyn, where since the Reformation people of different denominations have lived together, it surprises no one and doesn't create special problems.[58] Of course Silesia is different on account of the visibility of the Protestants and their long history of coexistence with Polish Catholics. Nevertheless, in some Poles the Protestants generate an interest just because they are what they are: an exception to the Catholic rule. As one Lutheran priest puts it, "People belonging to the Church of the majority, especially in Poland, where the statistical disproportions are so great, often look at members of minority Churches with curiosity, at times with a dose of healthy envy.[59] This refers to the monotony that being a member of a majority sometimes generates, and minorities relieve this feeling, whatever their actual doctrine might be. Such fascination at times even leads to the rare instances of members of the majority church converting to a minority Christian denomination or a non–Christian faith. However, living among a predominantly Catholic population does have an effect on a number of aspects of life. At the beginning of Chapter 3, it was mentioned that Jerzy Pilch stressed that lighting candles at cemeteries is not a Lutheran tradition; he nonetheless added that, regretfully in his opinion, Lutherans are beginning to accept that tradition as well.

One of the churches that simultaneously attracts some Poles but also evokes negative feelings in others is the Polish Orthodox Church. At one level the reasons for the latter are similar to the mainstream Protestants. The Orthodox community was also a member of the Polish Ecumenical Council that cooperated with the Communist authorities, which in the initial years of independence cast the odium of suspicion on it. Shortly after the collapse of Communism, some arson attempts occurred on Orthodox edifices, which may have been inspired by Catholic chauvinism. What is more, at approximately half a million members[60] the Church possibly has well over twice as many members as all Protestant churches together in Poland, and it generally arouses different feelings on the part of Polish Catholics than members of the latter, both positive and negative. Not to mention that ethnic factors play a role as well; although different national and ethnic groups make up the bulk of the Orthodox faithful, what unites the majority is that they are not ethnically Polish.

A factor influencing the faith community's attitude toward Poles, in turn, stems from the fact that the Polish Orthodox Church suffered at the hands of Polish Catholics in the interwar period, and further from the Polish Communist regime, particularly in the infamous "Operation Vistula," in which during the course of battles with the Ukrainian Insurgent Army in southeastern Poland in 1947 140,000 civilians were transferred to different parts of the country in order to assimilate them into the Polish population. In independent Poland there is some awareness of this, but primarily among an elite. Whereas the actions of the Communist regime were fairly easy to condemn, in 2008 the Orthodox community has finally found support from the Polish authorities in their unequivocal condemnation of the Polish interwar authorities' destruction of Orthodox churches in the Chełm district.[61] Moreover, after 1997 the Polish Orthodox Church has been largely included in the country's civil religion.

Negative feelings on the part of Polish Catholics toward Orthodox Christians are stronger in eastern Poland, where the population of the latter is higher. This has little effect on the rural population where the Orthodox live in larger communities and support each other. A problem occurs when the Orthodox leave their indigenous communities to move to urban areas, such as in Białystok, whether to seek employment or to study at institutes of higher education. On such occasions a significant number of them feel they must either hide their Orthodox identity or abandon it altogether.[62] On a somewhat lighter side, living among a predominantly Catholic population likewise affects some practices of the Orthodox faithful; for instance they have now started commemorating their deceased at the cemeteries on November 1 alongside the majority of the Polish population.

Since 2001 a Bilateral Catholic-Orthodox Committee has been active, working on various problems between the churches at the institutional level, such as the document on mixed marriages mentioned earlier. Moreover, it was the Polish Orthodox Church that officially invited Kirill I, the current patri-arch of Moscow to Poland, when the latter signed a document with the Catholic Church in Poland on August 17, 2012, which appeals for unity between the two churches and nations. Polish nationalists criticized the Catholic Church for coauthoring such an agreement at a time when there were a number of outstanding issues between Poles and Russians, such as unan-swered questions concerning the Smoleńsk disaster. In turn Archbishop Michalik, the head of the Polish Conference of Bishops at the time, albeit known for his traditionalism, criticized nationalist politicians who spread var-ious conspiracy theories concerning the tragedy. Despite the highly diplomatic tone of the document, symbolically it constitutes a major step forward for dia-logue between the churches.

Generally, however, the livelier relations between the Orthodox Church and its sister churches outside of Poland have also made an impression on Catholic Poles at various levels. When an Orthodox delegation from Mount Sinai visited Poland in 2007 with relics of St. Catherine, Catholic bishops were invited to a number of ceremonies. Archbishop Damian, the head of the visiting delegation, favorably commented his reception: "A pleasant surprise for us has been the fact that apart from Orthodox faithful we also meet Catholic faithful everywhere. It is a sort of return to the single Apostolic Church before the [eleventh century] schism.[63]

What the visiting church dignitary expressed at one level, the simple Orthodox faithful, according to a study carried out in southeast Poland, have expressed in their own way. An elderly Orthodox respondent from the village of Gładyszów proclaims, fairly typically according to the interviewer, "God is one. And there is one God, and that's that. Naturally, there is one God, and everyone should worship Him according to their own faith.[64] For this small community, language and culture rather than doctrine are the primary deter-minants of the different denominations: the Catholics pray in Polish, while the Orthodox in Ukrainian. For another middle-aged woman the main reli-gious distinction is between those who believe in God and those who do not believe: "If someone has no faith, they have no goal. It's a road to nowhere in my opinion.[65]

At this point in such villages it is likely still not that easy to find someone who claims no belief in God; in the cities, where the children of believers might go to better their lot, however, Poland is changing. In general terms, as one historian puts it, "the same processes are occurring in the Orthodox com-munity in Poland as in the rest of society—encroaching secularization, moral relativism, with a part of the younger generation losing interest in traditional religion. An additional factor is the process of assimilation that affects the Orthodox community as a religious minority.[66] Despite these factors, some of which, as the author correctly asserts, pertain to religion as such in the country, the Polish Orthodox Church is likely to remain an important figure on the religious scene in Poland for the foreseeable future.

The Christian denomination that possibly stirs the strongest feelings in Poland is the Ukrainian Greek Catholic Church, largely because of its close association with Ukrainian nationalism. As mentioned, on account of Operation Vistula, the indigenous Ukrainian population from southeast Poland that had not been earlier deported, that is, "repatriated" to Ukraine, was dispersed throughout the country—mainly to the so-called Recovered Territories in western and northern Poland. This included many Polish Orthodox faithful but heavily affected Ukrainian Greek Catholics. After the Stalinist period, a number of the Ukrainians and Lemkos returned to the southeast of Poland, although to a greater extent to cities like Przemyśl rather than to the villages they had been expelled from. In the latter there was often nothing to return to, while the cities also had the advantage of greater anonymity, where their identity was not so obvious. Perhaps a third of Ukrainian Greek Catholics now live in the southeast of Poland.

It was in the city of Przemyśl, however, that one of the most intense confrontations between Ukrainian Greek and Roman Catholics occurred shortly after the collapse of the Communist regime. It is also a place where a significant, largely positive, change in attitude has occurred. Starting with the confrontation, the Carmelite church controversy of 1991 requires knowledge of the historical background. In the seventeenth century a church was built by an aristocratic family for the Carmelite order of monks. During the Partitions, however, the church was turned over to the "Greek Catholics," as the Uniates were called by the Austrians, which—ominously enough—set a pattern for the future. For the time being it became the cathedral of the Eastern Rite denomination. This state of affairs was confirmed in the independent Polish Republic in the Concordat of 1925. However, the Communists gave the church back to the Carmelite order after liquidating the Greek Catholic Church.

In newly independent Poland the Roman Catholic Church decided to return the church to the Ukrainian Greek Catholic Church for several years before they could build a new cathedral for themselves, and the transfer was supposed to take place before John Paul II's visit to Przemyśl on June 2, 1991. However, a radical nationalist group occupied the church with the support of devout elderly Catholic women who picketed the Roman Catholic bishop's palace, with banners supporting slogans such as, "We will not give up the Polish Church." The protest was also joined by a number of lower clergy. With a great deal of pressure the protestors were finally removed, but on account of the situation the pope decided to give the Ukrainian Greek Catholic Church the Jesuit church in which they had held semiofficial services since the mid–

1950s. This did not really satisfy either side. The Greek Catholics lost the church they felt rightfully belonged to them, not to mention that the Jesuit church was not really suitable for a cathedral at the time. Meanwhile, to add insult to injury, the Catholic nationalists went on to campaign for the removal of the copula that had been added to the Carmelite church in the nineteenth century by the Greek Catholics, and achieved their aim in 1996.

The whole incident shows how strong nationalistic religious feelings ran at the time, when at one point even the authority of the Polish pope was insufficient for a fully satisfactory agreement. Nationalism clearly trumped religion. As one anthropologist summarized the complex issue, "It is intensely paradoxical that the secular identity which poses such problems of recognition should be tied to a religious identity uniquely close to that of the majority—a sister Catholic Church.[67] But nationalistic feelings existed on both sides. The religious national Day of All Saints has been appropriated by nationalistic Ukrainian feelings when the dead of military efforts are also honored. Most controversially, this includes the dead from the Ukrainian Insurgent Army, who are heroes for Ukrainians, but on account of the massacres of Polish civilians during World War II are treated as war criminals by Poles.

Fortunately, significant changes have taken place since 1991. As Juraj Buzalka puts it fairly accurately in his study of the Przemyśl area, "Religion, although it is the primary source of division between the Polish and Ukrainian nations, also creates the basis for a new public sphere in which the emphasis is placed on tolerance.[68] In 2001 John Paul II made his memorable pilgrimage to the Ukraine. During the mass celebrated in Lviv, attended by many Poles, he addressed the historical grievances that had accumulated over the centuries between Roman and Greek Catholics: "Today, in praising God for the indomitable fidelity to the Gospel of these his servants [the beatified martyrs], let us feel gently nudged to recognize the infidelities to the Gospel of not a few Christians of both Polish and Ukrainian origin living in these parts. It is time to leave behind the sorrowful past.[69] The last sentence has been quoted quite often. Naturally the Orange Revolution several years later also played a role in changing the attitude of Poles to Ukrainians, which in turn had an effect on the relations between Roman and Ukrainian Greek Catholics.

On the one hand, clergy of both rites have been involved at different levels in a number of initiatives aimed at reconciliation between their faithful; similarly, a number of local NGOs working on the same goal are run by religiously committed people. Drawing on Buzalka's study in which a number of such initiatives have been documented, we can bring attention to several such cases. For instance, since early in the millennium the Ukrainian Greek Catholic Sister Servants of the Holiest Virgin Mary have been awarding an annual Polish-Ukrainian Prize for Reconciliation, selecting both a Pole and a Ukrainian for the honor. In some cases annual rituals are exploited to acknowledge the existence of the minority and promote tolerance. Furthermore, Buzalka reports, "It is common in south-east Poland nowadays for representatives of one rite to attend the annual religious rituals of the other," a practice that has roots at least as far back as the interwar period.[70] A prominent example is the Ukrainian Greek Catholic Jordan ceremony in Przemyśl. A ceremony that closes the Christmas celebrations and that the denomination used to conduct within the walls of their church in Communist years now has entered the public sphere. "Today, interest in Jordan blessings [of water] is growing among both Ukrainians and Poles who are enchanted by the eastern 'spirituality' the ritual enacts.[71] Naturally, years of enmity are not "washed away" by a few rituals. One respondent from Buzalka's study gives a skeptical opinion of the current ecumenism: "Roman Catholic tolerance appears because it has to, because such times have come, not because the church wanted them to come."[72] Since nationalist elements have not disappeared from Polish Catholicism, to some extent such an opinion is not unwarranted.

A former parish priest of nearby Krasiczyn, among others, has been instrumental in reviving the prewar custom of Poles and Ukrainians singing Christmas carols together in his community. The Rev. Stanisław Bartmiński even went as far as renovating a Ukrainian Greek Catholic church that had lapsed into ruin after the Ukrainians had been expelled in Operation Vistula. During the ceremony held after the renovations were complete in May 2004, which included murals inside painted in the Byzantine style, the priest dedicated the church informally to Polish-Ukrainian reconciliation.

Significantly, at the above ceremony some of the former parishioners came from Ukraine for the occasion at the invitation of the Reverend Bartmiński.[73] A few years later, after Poland had entered the EU and introduced all the requisite border restrictions this entailed, such a visit would not be so easy on the part of Ukrainian visitors. Relations between the two nations are to some extent hampered by the fact that it is far more difficult for Ukrainian citizens to visit Poland, and the vital element of human contact is reduced. The Rev. Stefan Batruch, a Ukrainian Greek Catholic priest from Lublin has initiated a festival at the border of the two countries that addresses this problem. Although the Reverend Batruch founded the Foundation of Borderlands Spiritual Culture, the festival is not religious as such. Nevertheless, anything that brings Poles and Ukrainians together simultaneously builds the relations between the two religious communities the groups so strongly identify with. Moreover, a festival on the theme of "good neighborly relations" is important because it aims to go beyond reconciliation and strives for normalcy in formerly highly troubled waters.

However, a problem remains, the source of which stems from beyond the faith communities themselves. Despite the centuries that have passed since it was called into existence and all that Uniate Catholics—of whom the Ukrainian Greek Catholics are the remnant heirs—have suffered at the hands of Russian Orthodox during the Partitions of the nineteenth century and the Soviets in the twentieth century, the Polish Orthodox Church still considers the existence of the Catholic Eastern Rite Church an offence. Thus, in order to maintain good relations between the two largest churches in Poland, the Roman Catholic Church excludes the Ukrainian Greek Catholic Church from any ecumenical event it holds where the Orthodox have been invited. While hurt by this treatment, the Reverend Batruch continues to carry out conciliatory missions: the Polish-Ukrainian border towns directly east of Lublin where he holds the festival are dominated by Orthodox Ukrainians, rather than Greek Catholic ones. Such efforts might alleviate the problem, but it will likely not disappear soon.

If Ukrainian Greek Catholic–Roman Catholic relations are impossible to disentangle from Polish–Ukrainian relations, a similar case holds true with Polish Catholic–Polish Jewish relations. As we have seen, in today's Poland religion is a key to Polish Jewish identity, despite the fact that only a portion of Polish Jews are religiously observant. Nevertheless, they are the most significant bearers of Jewish identity after the destruction of Jewish culture. However, it is a mark of the improved Polish–Jewish relations that even though many Jews still prefer not to reveal their identity in public, there exists a substantial group of Jews who, while claiming no interest in Judaism, for various reasons are still proud of their roots. For instance, Adam Michnik, while accepting the Jew of the Year Award from New York Central Synagogue in 1991, stressed the fact that his main Jewish solidarity was with the tragic fate of his ancestors and with their suffering, but not with Jewish religion or tradition.[74] In fact, at this point, Michnik's main contribution in Poland is to various aspects of Polish culture. Polish culture, on the other hand, while still manifesting anti–Semitic attitudes on the part of a portion of the population, has made notable strides in accepting both Jewish traditions and religion as an integral part.

When the future chief rabbi of Poland, an American, came to Poland to attend a summer program in Kraków shortly after Karol Wojtyła became John Paul II, he was surprised to see a portrait of the pope in the home of a Jewish friend in Warsaw.[75] Since Rabbi Schudrich offers no explanation for this fact, it is quite possible that at that juncture it was more of a patriotic gesture on the part of a rather assimilated Jew who was pleased that a Pole had reached such a high position in the world. But the election of the Polish pontiff, with his demonstrative interest in Jews and Judaism, was to exert a significant change in the attitude of Catholic Poles toward their Jewish fellow citizens.

Shortly after the Solidarity movement ensued, Jewish topics were finally prominently discussed in Catholic periodicals. Not to mention this was the peak period of the Jewish Flying University. Various meetings between religious Jews and Catholics took place, among others at the Catholic University of Lublin.[76] Even post–martial law Poland did not bring an end to the interest, but it was to take a different turn.

One of the complications in the Christian-Jewish dialogue that emerged was the fact that, albeit disproportionately, both Poles and Jews suffered in World War II. With their own background as victims, at times Polish Christians exaggerated the commonality of this fact. As Stanisław Krajewski puts it, "Thinking about World War II, Poles see rather a bond of suffering with Jews than the bond of common Christianity with Germans.[77] An essay published in January 1987 in *Tygodnik Powszechny*, a weekly in which Karol Wojtyła had frequently published, set a whole new tone to the discussion, introducing more serious, and painful, soul-searching on the part of Polish Catholics. In his "Biedni Polacy patrzą na getto" (The Poor Poles Look at the Ghetto), literary critic Jan Błoński used the poem by Czesław Miłosz referred to at the beginning of the chapter to reflect on the sins of omission that Christian Poles had committed in their relations with Polish Jews, especially in their time of need during the Holocaust, for which Poles had consequently too often indicated their own dilemma as an excuse for inaction:

> Eventually, when we lost our home [i.e., Poland was occupied by Nazis], and when, within that home, the invaders set to murdering Jews, did we show solidarity toward them? How many of us decided that it was none of our business? There were also those (and I leave out of account common criminals) who were secretly pleased that Hitler had solved for us "the Jewish problem." We could not even welcome and honor the survivors, even if they were embittered, disoriented and perhaps sometimes tiresome.[78]

These were strong words for the time. Even though the confessional mode was well within the Christian tradition, this was too much for a good deal of the Catholic readership. The essay also received attention far beyond the confessional press. Yet in 1991, shortly after the collapse of Communism, the Polish episcopate issued a letter to commemorate the fortieth anniversary of the Vatican Council's letter that lifted the historic charge of deicide from the Jews containing the following statement: "We are especially disheartened by those among Catholics who in some way were the cause of the death of Jews."[79]

With regard to the response to Błoński's essay, "What was rejected above all," observes an American scholar, "was the notion that Poles need forgiveness from the Jews."[80] By admitting obliquely that Poles did indeed need forgiveness likewise for sins of commission, in the quoted passage the Polish bishops' letter of several years later already goes farther than that ground-breaking essay, which only went as far as to state that the indifference of the majority to the fate of the Jews was their main sin. Evidence that the Poles needed forgiveness was also to be supplied in much stronger terms in due course.

In March 2001 a bomb exploded in Polish–Jewish relations in the form of the publication in Polish translation of a book by Jan Tomasz Gross, a Polish-American historian and sociologist, titled *Neighbors: The Destruction of the Jewish Community in Jedwabne, Poland*. The book described the massacre of the Jewish inhabitants of a German-occupied town by Poles after the Soviets had been expelled in 1941. In fact, such pogroms took place in a number of villages in that region of Poland at that time, but by focusing on one well-documented instance and with its vivid prose, the book made a devastating impact on Poles.

Summarizing the initial response in Poland, Istvan Deak reported, "The reception of Gross's book in Poland has been nothing short of astonishing: it seems to have evoked more favorable responses than negative ones."[81] The book had the effect of initiating a much-needed debate on the darker side of the behavior of Poles during the war. Subsequent books by Gross have broadened the debate, including the period right after the war, but have not had the impact of *Neighbors*. On account of these books, together with the studies of historians working in Poland, the conviction that those involved in such crimes were from the margins of society had to be put aside,[82] although significant portions of contemporary society remain in denial.[83] After a number of years Adam Michnik added that the debate over Polish participation in the Holocaust had no equivalent in any of the neighboring countries in East Central Europe, even though comparable atrocities occurred.

The response within the Catholic Church itself at the time, however, was mixed, with the balance tipping toward a defensive posture.[84] At one extreme there were the strong attacks on the part of the nationalist Catholics. The primate of the Catholic Church at the time also issued a counterattack, pointing out the complicity of Polish Jews in cooperating with the Soviets during the war and other Polish Communist agencies shortly afterward. Fortunately a couple of bishops acted in a manner befitting their role as spiritual leaders. Among others, acknowledging Polish suffering during the war, Archbishop Życiński nonetheless made the horror of what had happened quite clear: "The victims of barbarous aggression can easily grow accustomed to it and end up applying new aggression against the innocent." He concluded,

> Today, we need to pray for the victims of the massacre, displaying the spiritual solidarity that was missing at the hour they left the land of their fathers. In the name of those who looked upon their death with indifference, we need to repeat David's words, "I have sinned against the Lord," [a reference to his responsibility for the death of Uriah] regardless of whether any protest from the onlookers might have been efficacious in that situation.[85]

On May 17, 2001, at the Church of All Saints in Warsaw a prayer service was held for the Jewish victims of Jedwabne. Unfortunately, a number of misunderstandings arose concerning the event. Among others, since it was a Saturday—the Sabbath—there was no Jewish delegation in attendance. Despite everything, it was a moving ceremony, generally well received, attended by most of the Polish bishops. Speaking on behalf of the Church, Bishop Stanisław Gądecki, the head of the Polish Conference of Bishops Commission for Dialogue with Judaism, stated, "We are deeply disturbed by the actions of those who caused Jews to suffer and even murdered them in Jedwabne and in other places over the ages."[86]

One of the shortcomings of such initiatives by the Church directed at Polish Jewish reconciliation and dialogue has been the fact that most events connected with it have taken place in the larger cities. A rare exception was an initiative undertaken by Archbishop Życiński, who went out into the small towns of his Lublin diocese in order to commemorate and mourn the murdered Jews of the towns during the Holocaust,[87] towns in which the Jewish population had in some cases comprised the majority of the inhabitants. At each of the towns a mass was conducted, while after its conclusion a procession would lead from the church to the local Jewish cemetery, at which Kaddish would be recited by a member of the Lublin Jewish community. The masses, quite moving for the participants, were also a venue for the archbishop to put forward difficult questions concerning the failings of the Catholic Church in relation to the Jews right up until the present, for instance the presence of anti–Semitic literature in some Catholic bookstores (in fact, there was such a bookstore at the church where the bishops held the prayer service described above). Most dramatically, at the town of Izbica the archbishop invited Thomas Blatt, a Polish Jew who was a survivor of the nearby Sobibór concentration camp and had managed to escape together with a group of fellow Jewish inmates, some of whom were murdered by Polish villagers. The survivor came from the United States especially for the event. Needless to say, nationalist Catholics attacked the archbishop for this and others of his initiatives.

Soul-searching has also taken place on the Jewish side. Most notably articulated by Stanisław Krajewski, who is the cofounder of the Polish Council of Christians and Jews (founded in 1989). Bemoaning the fact that Jewish involvement with Communism has not been seriously studied, he nevertheless asserts, "For some Jews, communism even became a quasi-religion, and because of the communist government the mid–twentieth century could witness members of one of the world's most clearly persecuted social groups not only as victims, but also as oppressors. This is a cause for self-criticism and shame."[88] As of yet, Krajewski is rather isolated in his attitude within the Jewish community, but notably during an interview given during the Jedwabne debate in solidarity with Polish Catholic soul searching, Rabbi Schudrich declared, "Humans must apologize for every committed wrong. That is also the duty of Jews. We must recognize that we were not only victims, but that we had among us people who wronged others. The Jews currently must open their eyes wider regarding their own history in the last few decades."[89] In that same interview he had clearly rejected the concept of collective guilt in relation to the murders committed by Poles. On account of the very limited number of Jewish scholars in the country, the issue of Jewish complicity in Communist crimes must of necessity be dealt with by Christian Polish scholars, but it will require great sensitivity.[90] At any rate, it is easy to see why such an issue would be brought up on various occasions by nationalist Catholics, which is why Krajewski is likely correct in insisting that more thorough scholarly historical study is necessary.

As we mentioned earlier, John Paul II has had an impact on how Polish Christians view Polish Jews. For instance, when the pope visited Israel during the millennium celebrations in 2000 and apologized for the wrongs Christians had done to Jews, a survey conducted in Poland reported that 55 percent of Poles accepted his statement. His stance has at least formally been followed within the Polish Catholic Church. For instance, a special committee within the Polish episcopate is responsible for dialogue with Judaism. Since 1998 it has organized an annual nationwide Day of Judaism on January 17, celebrated in conjunction with the Week of Prayers for Christian Unity. Over the years the activities featured in celebrating the day have become enriched. One of the acute problems connected with the initiative is that, as Krajewski reports, "there is just a handful of Jews educated enough and willing to participate in the events."[91] In other words, the initiative came when the Polish Jewish community is simply so small. Members of the Polish Council of Christians and Jews often participate in the events.

In various forms, from academic to religious to cultural, dialogue between Polish Christians and Polish Jews is continually conducted. Since they form a much larger group, the Christian participants express various stances. Naturally dialogue requires openness, but Rabbi Jonathan Magonet, who is involved in Jewish-Christian dialogue in Europe, has warned that "respect for the 'other' should be accompanied by a similar respect for one's own."[92] Indeed, there are participants in the dialogue who have become so immersed that they have seemingly lost a sense of their own identity. During a conference on Abraham Joshua Heschel in Warsaw in 2007, a former Jesuit became so accommodating in his dialogic fervor that another Christian participant felt it necessary to remind him of the centrality of Jesus Christ for Christian identity.[93] On the other hand, some participants in Poland forget that dialogue requires any self-criticism. During a discussion in the Polish Council of Christians and Jews, among others, of anti–Semitic statements by the Rev. Henryk Jankowski of Gdańsk, one of the members ended up having to resign following protests that he effectively defended the statements of the chauvinistic prelate.[94]

Sometimes crises lead to creative initiatives. For instance, the one concerning the convent at Auschwitz related in Chapter 2 prompted Cardinal Franciszek Macharski in 1992 to establish what is now known as the Center for Dialogue and Prayer in the city of Oświęcim, where the Auschwitz concentration and death camp existed during the Nazi occupation. The educational program is assisted by Fr. Manfred Deselaers, a German priest who has learned Polish and is involved in reconciliation between Poles, Germans and Jews. The center is built in the neighborhood of the former concentration and death camp, now a museum, and creates a space for reflection, education and prayer. Other initiatives might take place at the parish level, such as the campaign of a solitary priest in a small village near Warsaw to raise the level of awareness among his parishioners about the Jewish past. In an interview the priest demonstrates his deep empathy for Polish Jews participating in events such as the Day of Judaism: "One must understand, that the Jews remember what we do not know or do not want to know. Those wounds given during and after the war, but also in our times are so many, that I am filled with awe that they want to meet us and talk. Were I in their shoes I don't know if I'd be up to it."[95]

At the ecclesiastical level, one can largely agree with Porter-Szücs's summary of the situation: "The boundaries of Polish Catholicism may have expanded well beyond anti–Semitic militancy, but they have not contracted enough—yet—to push such views outside the Church."[96] Where does this leave the largely Catholic public? Catholic Poles have a very emotional attitude toward Jewish Poles. In Poland, as sociologist Alina Cała has put it, "Jews can be liked or hated; it is hard to be indifferent to them."[97] On the one hand, if not outright anti–Semitism, negative feelings for Jews persist. Although anti–Semitism does not take on a violent form and acts of vandalism rarely occur, negative feelings might be displayed through simple matters. For instance, a group of residents in Biłgoraj for years blocked an initiative to have a street named after Isaac Bashevis Singer, the Yiddish writer and Nobel laureate who had spent a number of years of his youth in the town. Occasionally, as during the *Neighbors* debate, because some Poles felt threatened, negative feelings increased for a time—anti-Semitic graffiti was seemingly ubiquitous then. It is difficult to say what the solution is for such a state of affairs. One Polish researcher of anti–Semitism in Poland claims, "For my part, I feel that in Poland only the Church can deal with anti–Semitism and hatred, I don't see any other force that could undertake the task."[98] While the Church could no doubt do more—some within it are even a part of the problem—this would unlikely make a great difference at this point. Even when its social authority was at a peak, the Church had no magic wand for removing problems in Polish society.[99] The bishops might issue a statement, like in the case of the document of 2003 entitled *Dialog—zadanie na nowy wiek* (Dialogue: A Task for the New Century), in which they bemoan anti–Semitic graffiti and the like,[100] but the overall social effect would be minimal.

But there is nonetheless hope: in 2008 a survey indicated that more Poles like Jews (34 percent) than dislike them (32 percent), the remainder being indifferent. Moreover, the same trend of a better attitude toward generally disliked national and ethnic groups—Ukrainians, Romani, etc.—was also noticeable.[101] Although unpleasant incidents still occur—for instance, in 2011 vandals painted a swastika on the monument at Jedwabne, more recent surveys suggest that this generally positive tendency maintains.

Moreover, there is a strong current of fascination with almost everything Jewish within Polish society. A number of festivals concentrate on Jewish culture, a major one in Kraków, and several more where it plays a prominent part. According to a report published in *Jewish Policy Research Report* in 2002, despite their small number in the country, there was a comparatively high number of events per thousand Jews: thirty-eight in Poland, whereas in Belgium, Sweden, Italy there were only two or three events.[102] On one level there is a fascination with Polish Jewish popular culture, like klezmer music; on the other hand, a number of university programs now exist that provide more in-depth knowledge. Regarding all of this activity and attention, one Catholic journalist has stated, "Polish Jews—rather on account of their determination than numbers—still have a contribution to make in our Polish reality."[103] Others are more sober in their assessment of all this attention and have mixed feelings that this interest has occurred when the Jewish community has practically disappeared, creating a "virtual culture."

Among the holiest of places for the Jewish community are its cemeteries. There are so many of them in Poland that they are beyond the resources of the remaining Jewish community to maintain; in some places, although not very many, the local Christian community makes an effort at their maintenance; many more are in a state of extreme neglect. During the celebration of the Day of Judaism in 2001, Bishop Stanisław Gądecki addressed the participants at the Synagogue in Łódź. The celebrations had been initiated by visiting the Jewish cemetery in the city, the largest in Europe. Referring to that event, the bishop reflected further on the presence of Jews in Poland:

> There, it is easier to discover that our present identity is rooted in the lives of those who lived before us in this land, and that our current faith is marked by the faith of our forefathers. So many Jews lived for so many centuries in Poland and here they died in a normal fashion, and their graves are all over the country.... But we

also cannot forget and must commemorate those whose death was neither quiet nor calm.... Let the testimony of the life and death of these millions of people be for us—Christians and Jews—not so much a means, as an obligation for building mutual brotherly relations, and through this a discovery of God's love, who works through people when they do not turn away from Him.... Preparing for our human paths at the beginning of the new millennium in Poland, let us go forward with hope![104]

Owing to the both rich and tangled past, as well as the seminal relationship of one religion to the other for various reasons, for the foreseeable future Polish Christian and Polish Jewish relations will be a major concern for both parties, and hope is certainly needed. However, in his book *The Future Church* John Allen puts it bluntly: for the Catholic Church due to the urgent issues that have ensued after 9/11 relations with Jews will take a back step to relations and dialogue with Islam.[105]

In Poland, however one counts it, the Muslim population already numbers at least several times that of the Jewish one, not that it is likely to increase too quickly. Selim Chazbijewicz, for one, does not see a dramatic rise in the Muslim population as probable for a number of reasons: for example, Poles had no colonies with a Muslim population; consequently, there are few of them that know Polish the way many Muslims know the languages of former colonial powers, which made it easier for them to immigrate to those countries.[106] Nevertheless, as a member of the European Union, the prospects for a relatively steady if modest growth of the Muslim population in the country are fairly high, which means the problem of dialogue with Islam will become more pressing for Polish Christians.

The Muslims of Poland are engaged in some initiatives to familiarize Poles with their religion. The oldest Muslim community in Poland also has the longest tradition of an outreach to the country's Christians. The Muslim Religious Association invites Christians to pray for peace to Kruszyniany, the site of the oldest Tatar community with a continuous presence within Poland's current borders, dating back to the seventeenth century. The Tatars invite Poles to take part in a number of their holidays; they also organize Days of Tatar Culture.

It was during an interfaith meeting that took place in the Days of Tatar Culture in Warsaw in 1997 that the Joint Council of Catholics and Muslims was founded. The initiative was organized by an NGO that, among other things, had been active in offering aid to Chechen war victims. The council soon gained the acknowledgment of the Vatican and the Polish Conference of Bishops and was instrumental in the getting the Polish bishops to initiate an annual Day of Islam on the model of the Day of Judaism. Their tenth-anniversary declaration in 2008 ends with a note of urgency:

After September 11, 2001, the cooperation of the two religions took on a completely different dimension. Understanding between Christians and Muslims is no longer a matter that concerns only philosophers and theologians, but each and every one of us. Extremism and terrorism arise among others from rejection and misunderstanding. This is why interreligious dialogue is a problem of world security.[107]

More or less at the time of this declaration, Chazbijewicz reported in an interview that as far as Poland was concerned, the WTC attacks did not seriously affect the situation of Muslims in the country; rather than hatred, some Polish Muslims or Muslim groups at most experienced dislike on the part of some Poles.[108] As a prominent member of the Tatar community he could command more respect than Muslims without such deep roots in Polish history. Nevertheless, in an interview with a conservative Catholic periodical he went beyond the common assurances of the pacific nature of genuine Islam and admitted that a number of currents of Islam were in need of reform to be able to cope with the modern world, especially those strains connected with the Wahabbi movement. He contrasted this with the ability which the Tatars exhibited for centuries to enter into close relations with the Christian majority and develop internally. As a leading member of the Joint Council of Catholics and Muslims he also summarized his experience in interfaith dialogue with Christians: "It is easiest to conduct dialogue with the Catholic Church. Protestants, similarly to us [Muslims], are too dispersed.... The Catholic Church has historical experience with Muslims that other Christians lack. The Catholic Church simply knows how to talk with us."[109] He bemoans the fall of the institution of the caliphate in Islam at the beginning of the twentieth century, which in his view gave some order to Islamic thought and reigned in extremism.

Over the past several years the Polish Church has indeed demonstrated a fair degree of sensitivity toward Islam in the country. The Church hierarchy condemned a Polish periodical for publishing a caricature of Mohammed in February 2006,[110] thus defending the religious sensibilities of Polish Muslims. Moreover, the themes of the Day of Islam are often practical. The theme of the ninth one was, "United on behalf of the dignity of marriage and the family." Besides the problem of peace and tolerance, the quality of life in Poland is a problem that concerns both parties and most religions in general.

One current issue that has affected both the Jewish and Muslim communities—at least their more orthodox members—concerns the kosher slaughter of animals. Following the example of several other EU parliaments and under the pressure of animal rights groups in the country, in July 2013 the Polish parliament passed a bill banning kosher slaughter. At present the extent of the ban is unclear: in order to appease the affected religious groups government officials claim that the bill only affects commercial slaughter—which was quite lucrative in Poland on account of export demand—without affecting the practice for the needs of the country's religious minorities, while some members of parliament claimed the ban has no exceptions. A number of Catholics have expressed the opinion that the ban limits religious freedom; others claimed it was necessary on account of animal rights. The chief rabbi of Poland has strongly protested the ban.

This hardly ends the list of faith communities and their relations with Catholic Poles. In more general terms, however, the Catholic Church has been involved in the ecumenical movement since the Second Vatican Council. In Poland the situation was complicated as mentioned on account of Communism and its politics of attempting to use the non–Catholic churches against the dominant Catholic Church. Nevertheless Catholic involvement in ecumenical matters in the country started in 1974, when relations with the Polish Ecumenical Council were established. These were markedly extended in 1998 and shortly afterward resulted in a document where the baptism of several separate churches was mutually accepted, setting the pattern for the document on mixed marriages discussed earlier. Currently, most visibly, the Catholic Church participates in the Week of Prayer for Christian Unity together with the member churches of the Polish Ecumenical Council. Although there are no statistics available, this is likely the period when more Catholics attend services in non–Catholic Churches than at any other time. Otherwise, they might attend funerals or marriage ceremonies, sometimes discovering their friends' different religious affiliation in this manner. As mentioned above, to these ecumenical efforts have been added the interfaith initiatives such as the Day of Judaism and Day of Islam, which precede and follow the Week of Prayer, and which are fairly unusual in Europe.

Such ecumenical and interfaith initiatives have been criticized as being typically top-down efforts, with the bishops in control.[111] This may have been largely the case a number of years back—although the efforts of the bishops are by no means to be knocked[112]—but it is less so at present. To reiterate, the greatest problem is the near invisibility of the minority religions, which makes ecumenism and interfaith dialogue a nonissue for perhaps the majority of Catholics. But while a conservative stream also exists that is covertly against ecumenicism—open criticism in the face of the official position of the Church is rare—Polish Catholics are likely far more aware of ecumenical and interfaith issues than in the past. Not to mention they are treated seriously by the partners in dialogue. During a meeting at a Dominican church in Lublin in September 2011, Selim Chazbijewicz stressed the unique nature on a European scale of the Day of Islam that the Catholic Church in Poland celebrates, and claimed that such efforts are influencing the attitude of much of the Muslim community toward Christian Poles.

At one level, since the 1970s there have always been a group of "Open

Catholics"—centered around the *Znak* and *Więź* monthlies—that have been influenced by John Paul II and his attitude toward such issues. A similar approach was evident in the programming of religia.tv, a religious cable television station that often included information on different faith communities, but is now limiting its programming on account of financial difficulties. Another group, while not against ecumenicism per se, takes what can be called an evangelical stance. This more conservative group supports dialogue with churches that maintain a firmer evangelical approach to Christian doctrine. For instance, in his article "Śmierć anglikanismu" (The Death of Anglicanism) in an issue of *Fronda*, Tomasz Terlikowski reports on the near schism within the Anglican Church, stressing the positive evangelical nature of the African Church on the one hand, with a critique of the departure of the liberal British Church from Christian doctrine on the other hand, due to which in his view it no longer fully qualifies as a partner for ecumenical dialogue.[113] There exists a gamut of stances in between.

At a more general level, one might add resources like the web page Ekumenizm.pl—Ekumeniczna Agencja Informacyjna (Ecumenical Information Agency), established in 2004 by young Christians of various denominations, although predominantly from the Polish Christian mainstream denominations. Catholic venues are more likely to make a greater impact through distribution; so, for instance, Christians from other denominations often enough have books published by Catholic publishers, like some books by Krzysztof Dorosz, for instance. Moreover, information about different Christian denominations is more frequently published, like the book *W drodze za Chrystusem. Kościoły chrześcijańskie w Polsce mówią o sobie* (Following Christ: Christian Churches in Poland Speak about Themselves) published by a Jesuit publishing house in 2009, and distributed, among other places, in the religion section of the largest bookstore chain in Poland.

Multiculturalism has generally become quite fashionable in Polish society, which also influences attitudes toward minority religions, informally strengthening "open Catholicism." There are numerous festivals on this theme, such as the Festival of Three Cultures in the late summer in Włodawa, a town in eastern Poland in which historically Jews, Catholics and Orthodox Christians coexisted. In these festivals the religious element of the minority cultures is highlighted to a greater or lesser extent, but is rarely absent. These events are fairly numerous, with the caveat that they usually only last a short period, frequently a weekend at most. An example of a more systematic grassroots project is the establishment of the Dzielnica Wzajmnego Szacunku Czterech Wyznań (Four Faiths' Quarter of Mutual Respect) in the center of Wrocław. The project takes advantage of the close proximity of four different places of worship: a Lutheran church, a Polish Orthodox church, a Roman Catholic church and a synagogue.

The initiative came in 1995 from Jerzy Kichler, who was the vice president of the Jewish religious congregation in the city then. After witnessing acts of vandalism on Christian churches close to the synagogue at that time, he decided something constructive should be done. He met with encouragement from his Christian counterparts, and before any formal project was established, the group met in a less organized fashion for several years. One of the cofounders recalls, "We invited one another to our name-day parties, we even organized a common Christmas carol get-together.... We knew that this would be a strange situation for the Jews, but after a while even they joined in the singing!"[114] In 2005 the quarter was established. As it has been reported, "the founders of the Quarter continue their original work, in which they are assisted by the official representatives of all four faiths ... as well as by lay people and young volunteers, who put into practice the ideals of intercultural and inter-religious dialogue."[115] The various projects include working with children and teaching them about different religions through hands-on work. There are also plans to extend the initiative to other groups.

Such events and projects are likely to multiply for a time, but their overall impact depends on a number factors. For one, what will be the response of different groups within the Catholic Church? As mentioned earlier and will be examined more closely in the next chapter, the Church is divided—among other things, there is a more open current and a more closed one. However, another issue, probably more weighty in the long run, is the question of what will be the actual role of religion in Polish society in the coming years.

Even for non–Christians, Polish religiosity and relatively high family values—anecdotal evidence suggests—can be appealing to immigrants from countries with a high level of religiosity that wish to avoid more secularized European countries.[116] The question is whether Poles will be able to fully reconnect with their Jagiellonian tradition in a contemporary way, where, as John Paul II has put it in a related context, "tolerance is not enough." Possibly the religiosity of Poles has another pertinent effect. It is difficult to state with certainty, but it seems that currently a phenomenon more similar to that of the United States than Europe holds true for Polish society: the general religiosity of Polish society has an effect on the minority religions as well. For instance, the Lutherans of Poland are likely more religious than their coreligionists in neighboring Germany,[117] among other things, because religion is important for Polish society in a way that it is not for German society. For instance, at the peak of his ski-jumping career when attempting a jump, the Lutheran Adam Małysz, several-times world champion, would first make the sign of the cross. But Polish society is dynamic and undergoing transformation, and this affects each of the religious traditions as well. Toward the end of his career, overt religious signs were not present when Małysz jumped.[118]

At the other geographical end of the European Union, Rabbi Jonathan Sacks writes about the importance of religious values from the dominant Abrahamic religious traditions for British society in a tone that implies he cannot count on a general consensus. "When the Catholic Church defends heterosexual marriage, when Muslim women speak of their embrace of the veil as a protest against overt sexual display, when Orthodox Jews speak of modesty as a value and parenthood as a sacred responsibility, they are saying things we need to hear," insists Sacks. In what now sounds like an understatement, he further reports that these crucial values have difficulty gaining a fair hearing within certain, quite prominent, spheres in his highly secularized society: "Moral relativism has an imperialism of its own, and political correctness is one of its cruder weapons."[119] At this juncture his message would hardly be necessary for Poles to hear, but will this be the case a few years down the road? European multiculturalism, while supportive of various cultures, does not always respect the deeper values held by the different faith communities.[120] The forces that could tip the scale toward the situation in Britain, and in a number of other European states, are essentially in place in Poland, while a growing number of Poles are similar to those Sacks implies are not respectful of the Catholic, Muslim or Jewish voices, or at least not to the values they hold. In other words, the situation of minority religions is not only dependent on the attitude of Polish Catholics toward them, but also on what position religion will hold in Polish society in the coming years. This, among other things, will be the subject of the final chapter. And it this state of affairs, as we will see, that results in some of the internal divisions—and diversity—of the Catholic Church in Poland.

5

Poland and the European Union

Toward Secularization or Postsecularization?

An incident witnessed by the author in the winter months of 2003 may help illustrate Poland's position straddling a highly secularized Europe on the one hand, where even in "conservative" mainstream denominations such as Catholicism boundaries are continually stretched by some, and, on the other hand, a number of re-evangelized parts of former Communist countries where Christianity is making a comeback. Fr. Tadeusz Bartoś, a member of the Dominican order at the time, had written an article about the nature of the conscience for the religion page of *Gazeta Wyborcza*, a national newspaper with liberal leanings. His interpretation of the theology of conscience raised a few hackles among a number of respondents. Later the editor of the religion page took the theologian on a tour of several Polish cities where he would discuss the issue with all comers. When the pair came to Lublin, several seminarians attended the talk at a local university. Situated as it is close to Ukraine, the diocese's seminary helps prepare a number of Eastern Rite Catholic seminarians from former socialist bloc countries for priesthood. One of these, a young Catholic from Armenia, could hardly contain himself after the discussion was over, complaining to the author of what he considered the near heretical nature of such a theological proposal.

The young man's emotions were understandable. Doubtlessly he had come to Poland on account of John Paul II and wished to be strengthened spiritually and intellectually in the pope's homeland Church before carrying out his vocation in a country where "scientific atheism" had been the order of the day for decades, spiritually devastating his own homeland. Here the seminarian came across a challenge to his possibly neophyte orthodoxy from an unexpected quarter: a member of the Polish clergy. The comparatively volatile religious situation in Poland at present is demonstrated in what might be an epilogue to the incident. Several years later Fr. Bartoś decided to give up his vocation and left the Dominican order, additionally writing *Jan Paweł II: Analiza krytyczna* (John Paul II: A Critical Analysis) in 2008,[1] a critical book about John Paul II, no less, the first of its kind in the country by someone who declared himself a Catholic. Although no Hans Küng, this was enough for the former Dominican to become a darling of the liberal Catholics, and for some time his opinion was readily sought in their press venues.

The faithful, increasingly educated, are often enough beginning to ask more questions of their church. Unsurprisingly, even at present it is hardly rare for some such Poles, unhappy with the answers they gain for their questions, to lapse in their practice, if not to leave the Church altogether. And not a few of those who stay are tending to look westward rather than worrying about their sisters and brethren to the east, if they had ever really thought about them and their quite different needs. If one were to ask why they should even bother with the latter, it is worth recalling that with the ongoing shift of Catholicism—and Christianity in general—to the global south, in the foreseeable future the dominant Catholic discourse might resemble the young seminarian's neo-orthodoxy even more forcefully, which will become less palatable for a significant portion of Polish Catholics.[2]

Not that the young seminarian would have had trouble finding like-minded Polish Catholics. As will be seen below, a similar division is also developing within the Polish Church as exists in the Church globally: one of the reasons religion in Poland is so interesting to observe. But before we go into greater detail on this post–European Union Church and religion in Poland from the perspective of its spectrum of stances to modernity, we will very briefly examine the situation of religion in the greater polity of the EU and Europe itself, from whence the prevailing external winds flow.

Religion and Modernity in Europe and Poland

By now it should be plain that when Poland and several other East Central European countries joined the European Union in 2004, subsequently followed by Romania and Bulgaria, they were separated from Western Europe by considerably more than the economic backwardness that the devastation of two successive totalitarian systems had wrought in the area. In the third chapter, the lack of social trust that affected Poland, and obviously the entire region to a greater or lesser extent, was partly examined. Moreover, as historian Timothy Snyder put it, the two regions possess radically differing historical narratives that have at times underpinned political misunderstanding, and which require suturing if any type of deeper social cohesion is to develop in the European Union.

> The future of European solidarity ... depends on a rethinking of the immediate European past. Without historical knowledge of the East, European mass publics will be swayed by simple arguments flowing from national prejudice.... Moreover, it will be very hard for east Europeans to believe that they are full partners in Europe so long as their experiences in the second half of the twentieth century are not part of a larger European story.[3]

Part of that past and its specificity in the Polish context has been outlined in the first two chapters. One might add that a similar problem arises from the radically differing narratives—or discourses—that the two parts of Europe follow with regard to religion. One can speculate that among the obstacles for the acceptance of the earlier Polish experience on the part of Western Europe has been its strong religious nature. Worth repeating at this point is Brian Porter-Szücs's observation quoted in the introduction about the stereotype of "a unique, atavistic, not quite European form of public religiosity in Poland." How this broader European discourse currently works in Poland will be one of the questions dealt with in this chapter.

To begin with what is fairly evident, one of the dominant processes religion has undergone in Europe is secularization, which among its several definitions is the name given to the process of the receding role of religion in some parts of the world. In the past, in academic spheres at least, it has been attributed the force of fate accompanying modernity; while many scholars still feel that way, to others it seems more of an aberration that affects certain parts of the world more forcefully than others, among them Europe. Secularization in the above sense has two facets that often closely interact but are not identical: one is declining religious vitality, that is, decreasing religious practices of the various faith communities; the other is the increasingly strident secular discourse that at best seeks to privatize religion, creating a "naked public square," and at its most vehement attempts to discredit religion altogether.[4] This part of the chapter will look at each of these aspects successively, both in Europe briefly and in Poland in more detail, before studying the response of religion to the challenge.

As the seeming exception in the world, in which if anything religion is currently resurgent,[5] religion in Europe, especially its culturally and economically prominent western part where religious vitality has fallen so low, has been the focus of a number of sociological studies. The author of one of these, Andrew Greeley, prudently starts his book-length study from early in the millennium with a comment warning the reader of how difficult it is to gauge something as complex and dynamic as religion with a blunt tool such as a sociological questionnaire: "When one is asked whether one believes in God, one might answer with a number of counter-questions such as when and what kind of God and with what kind of confidence and with what sort of relationship, if any."[6] Despite the generally low level of religious practice on the Continent, belief in God remains fairly high, except in some places such as East Germany or the Czech Republic. And, Greeley adds, when respondents are allowed to admit to their uncertainties of belief, "in all but the top three countries [of his reported study], they are more likely to admit some kind of faith in God than when they were asked the more simple question about believing in God."[7] The editors of a more recent study of religion on the Continent, cataloguing some of the of characteristics of religion in Europe, point to evidence for a number of seeming paradoxes, such as "religion is still in decline," yet simultaneously "phenomena of religious vitality ask for explanation"; "religion is weak," they add, but nevertheless religion attracts the attention of "national and international politics, media and cultural institutions who reflect on the inhomogenous presence of religion"; the list goes on.[8]

The question of religious practice is the aspect of the story that has perhaps gained the most attention. Although religious practice is generally low, it is somewhat higher in Catholic or even mixed Catholic-Protestant countries than in more solidly Protestant countries, such as the Scandinavian north. But there are no hard-and-fast rules. In formerly Catholic—now largely secularized—France, for instance, there are only 5 percent of Catholics practicing their religion, and while statistics are higher in Germany, they are also losing their faithful. The greatest recent implosion has been in Ireland, a country where in the 1970s, 85 to 90 percent of Catholics attended mass every week, but by the first decade of the new millennium only about half were doing so—still a high percentage for Europe, but a substantial drop in a short period of time. The drop in religious vocations has paralleled and even exceeded that of the practices of the faithful. By the year 2000, in France the number of priests had fallen to half the figure of a mere three decades earlier: a number of dioceses were able to survive on account of priests brought over from the global south, frequently from Francophone West Africa.[9] Nevertheless, if we extend the boundaries to the east, there have been significant reversals, especially in countries with a predominantly Orthodox Christian culture. In Russia and Latvia, for instance, strong increases in belief in God have been registered, accompanied by increases in religious affiliation.[10] Generally, the initial period after the downfall of Communism witnessed a modest religious revival in most of the Eastern European countries, obviously excluding former East Germany and the Czech Republic.[11] To complicate the overall issue, in pluralist societies it is difficult to generalize about religious vitality. As sociologist David Martin puts it on the example of the United Kingdom, "Nearly three out of four Britons describe themselves as Christian, and three out of a hundred as Muslim, even though religious practice in Birmingham is probably more Muslim than anything else, with Catholicism ranking perhaps second."[12] Generally, Greeley summarizes a vast array of data on the majority of European countries as follows: "Catholics, Orthodox, and Muslims are more likely than Protestants to believe in God, to be theists, to accept that God is personally concerned with humans and endorse the possibility of religious miracles."[13]

Nevertheless, crude measurements of religious belief and practice fail to tell the whole story of religious vitality in Europe. In Sweden, for instance, despite the low level of church attendance, the Church of Sweden plays a significant role in the lives of most Swedes: 76 percent maintain their affiliation with the Church even if only 10 percent of the population attend services, as a rule a meager once a month. In most cases attachment to the Church is manifested through occasions such as children's baptisms or relatives' burials; however, at times the social role of the Church comes to the fore. One such occasion was in September 1994 after the greatest maritime disaster in recent history, when the MS *Estonia* had sunk in the Baltic Sea and 580 Swedes drowned (out of the 900 victims). As Per Petterson reports, "Many forms of religious reactions appeared, and the majority church, The Church of Sweden, immediately took on a central role in comforting the close relatives and coping with the feelings of grief in general."[14] A follow-up study showed that 85 percent of Swedes fully or in part agreed with the statement, "The Estonia-disaster shows that people have religious feelings that are not shown under normal circumstances."[15] What the above demonstrates in part is the superficial nature of the division between "existentially secure" secular countries, such as those in Europe, and the "existentially insecure" religious countries of the developing world. One scholar asks in this regard, "Why do Scandinavians, with such high levels of human development, have such notoriously high suicide rates?" To this and other questions he adds, "There are a variety of ways people living in various cultures and countries and at different levels of income, can feel at risk in our global era."[16] This observation seems increasingly true in a Europe simultaneously undergoing a financial and an identity crisis.

In earlier chapters some of the statistics concerning religion in Poland have already been provided. Figures of anywhere from the low nineties to mid-nineties are given for the percentage of declared Roman Catholics in Poland. Since contemporarily there has been no religion category in the national census, these figures come primarily from surveys, meaning they are largely self-reported. A somewhat different picture emerges through a statistic provided by the U.S. embassy in the country, which reports that in 2003 there were just a little over thirty-four million Poles baptized in the Catholic Church. Taking into account that at that time Poland had a population of close to thirty-nine million, this gives a figure of closer to 88 percent of the population as at least nominal members of the Church, without taking into account lapsed Catholics.[17] The same is the case with regard to church attendance. According to surveys for a number of years, the figure hovered around 50 to 55 percent weekly attendance. At the time of writing it occasionally falls below the 50 percent mark—down from the 60 plus percent figure at the end of the 1990s[18]—whereas Church sources, which actually count the number of people attending mass once a year, give a lower figure, in the vicinity of 40 percent.[19] During a conference he attended in Poland, sociologist Jose Casanova speculated on whether Poles do not overreport their religiosity—in a similar manner to Americans and in contradistinction to most Europeans.[20] This is undoubtedly the case, but, as the sociologist himself indicated, this also makes a strong statement about the meaning of religion in the country.

Within the overall picture of belief and practice lies a great deal of variation. The incremental decline in religious practice in Poland has been linked by some to the increasing urbanization of the country. In Warsaw, for instance, where religious practices hover around the 20 percent mark, the first outreach program has been announced in 2012 along the lines of the French Church in an attempt to attract more people to the Church. However, this tendency does not always hold true, since—despite cities such as Warsaw and Łódź having a low level of practice—some cities like Katowice, an area of Poland that has been urbanized for longer than other parts of the country, remain highly religious. A factor that plays a role here seems to be the regional differences in religious practices. When the first national survey of church attendance was conducted in the early 1980s, the difference between the most observant and the least observant dioceses in Poland was 40 percent; roughly a quarter of a century later, results have been very similar. What is astounding is that mapping these differences seems to indicate that they have roots extending all the way back to the Partitions. As historian James Bjork puts it, "As Polish social scientists have recently come to note with fascination, when one attempts to map various indices of religious behavior and experience, the cartographic image that emerges is not a monochromatic block of ethnoreligious uniformity."[21]

Another category, or rather group, that stands out regarding religious practice is that of Polish youth. As noted earlier, their reported level of religious practices is about 10 percent lower than Polish society as a whole. If anything, the distance is increasing. In this context it is interesting to look at another European trend. In the middle of the first decade of the new millennium, research suggests an overall growth in religious belief among the young, except in Ireland, which remains in the throes of a crisis, but the phenomenon varies from country to country: for instance, the author of the study notes, "Christian renewal prevails in Portugal or Denmark, increased believing without belonging in France and Great Britain, growth in those who 'never belonged' in the

Netherlands."[22] The phenomenon might in part explain the popularity of the World Youth Days in Europe. Moreover, since Polish youth are better educated than any previous generation, Greeley's findings that—although it previously was the case—university education no longer signifies a drop in religious belief in Europe,[23] which to some extent explains the above findings, are quite relevant in speculating on the long-term outcome of the above trend. Nonetheless, from the context of Polish youth, European youth are generally less religious. How this dynamic with its different vectors will play out is quite hard to predict: for instance, whether the downward Polish trend will stop before it reaches the inching-upward European trend. Furthermore, as Greeley points out, there is a lack of longitudinal research in Europe as such to determine whether young people who leave the Church do not return to it later in life, as has proved to be the case for a significant number in the United States. As mentioned earlier, this information is lacking in Poland as well.

A factor possibly affecting the religious practices of the young in the country is the high rate of unemployment among this age group. At the time of writing, connected with the partial recession in Europe, unemployment is increasing among Poland's youth—following a similar trend in the Continent—affecting approximately a quarter of the country's population in that cohort, and with university education hardly a guarantee for finding a position upon graduation. In the case of those for whom the experience lasts longer, it can be quite demoralizing, and religious practices are generally quite low among the chronically unemployed.

For the time being, one of the predicators of declining religious vitality apparently has bypassed Poland. Studies find that there seems to be a strong correlation between "empty pews and empty cradles." Yet, as Philip Jenkins notes in this regard, "though Catholic loyalties still thrive in Poland and Slovakia ... these countries are marked by characteristically low European birth rates."[24] In fact, Poland's birth rate is close to the bottom end of the European scale,[25] which itself is quite low. Nonetheless, there would seem to be a noticeable internal correlation between religion and demography within the Catholic population. Demographer Eric Kaufmann has noted that conservative religious groups tend to have higher birthrates in Europe than in the surrounding, more secular, society.[26] Anyone who stays in Poland longer will likely notice that Catholics who belong to renewal groups—who are more engaged religiously—likewise show a similar tendency, but this has not been studied as such. Currently, bringing up larger families in the country requires tremendous sacrifices, since a greater number of children is one of the most certain predictors of poverty.

However, if religious practice in Poland seems to be largely unaffected by the demographic downturn, it is too early to claim with certainty that the latter will not have an effect in the long run. According to demographer Mary Eberstadt, the vitality of the natural family—among other things, attested to by its fertility—affects the vitality of religion in a society. Eberstadt asks the question of why this relationship holds, suggesting that

> there is the phenomenological fact of what birth does to many fathers and just about every mother. That moment ... is routinely experienced by a great many people as an event transcendental as no other.... The sequence of events culminating in birth is nearly universally interpreted as a moment of communion with something larger than oneself, larger even than oneself and the infant.[27]

In historical terms, she observes, the decline of the natural family in Europe occurred earlier in France than elsewhere, as did the decline in religiosity. Furthermore, the effect of the declining birthrate on religious practice takes time. Eberstadt points out that the drop in religiosity in Ireland was preceded by a decline in the birthrate for a full generation. The decline in religious practices was precipitous, it might be added—as was the preceding decline in fertility.[28] A similar decline took place in the Netherlands before the marked decline in religiosity. If Eberstadt is correct, then the effects of Poland's demographic downturn on religiosity are still to come.

A possible effect of the lower birthrate on religiosity in Poland might be the fact that women are becoming noticeably less religious in Poland. Eberstadt argues that the act of childbirth is one of the factors contributing to the almost universal higher level of religiosity of women over men.[29] Significantly, as has been reported, over the past two decades the percentage of urban women attending mass has shrunk to the point that—even though there remain more of them in the churches than men—whereas shortly after the collapse of Communism the disproportion was 26 percent, currently there are only 8 percent more of them than men. Meanwhile the attendance of men has remained fairly stable.[30] A number of factors are involved in this statistical change, many of them generating disagreement, as does the question what can result from the phenomenon—for instance the probable long-term negative impact of a key group within the Church regarding the transmission of religious values leaving the pews. If it were the case that it is singletons—as elsewhere, an increasing percentage of the female population,[31] that is, those women who do not transmit tradition—who are largely not attending mass, while once women have children they return to the pews, then the phenomenon would not as such dramatically affect the transmission of religious values. Of more significance is the obvious fact that there are successively fewer Poles to transmit the tradition to. The statistical breakdown of which women are attending and which are not is unknown at present.

One more question regarding secularization concerns its effects upon religious minorities in Polish society. Similar processes take place within minority communities to those affecting the largely Catholic majority of society, but the dynamic varies considerably. Historian Grzegorz Kuprianowicz, who belongs to the Orthodox Church, feels that membership in a minority that is connected to a non–Catholic religious tradition can slow down the process of secularization to some extent, since religion is a stronger marker of identity for such a group than for the majority. On the other hand, however, secularization within the Catholic community affects minorities as such in that members who assimilate to the majority are no longer faced with the same degree of earlier social pressure toward becoming Catholic.[32]

Religious vitality and its role in secularization is quite complex. One element to be borne in mind is aptly expressed by Martin: "Counting matters, but one needs some account of religion as a mode of social consciousness and identity rooted in history and geography, time and place."[33] Such an account, however, can be rendered in a number of ways depending on the type of discourse that is used. We will start with what can be called secular discourse and end with the responses of religion to the times, especially on the part of its more conscious and articulate groups.

The persistence of substantial religious belief, if not practice, in much of Europe surprises some on account of the seemingly ubiquitous secular nature of the Continent's culture. This latter phenomenon, which will be briefly examined now, can in part be accounted for by Peter Berger's observation that "there exists an international subculture composed of people with Western-type education, especially in the humanities and social sciences, that is indeed secularized."[34] The "subculture," however, has a significant impact on European mainstream culture and how it perceives religion.

The secular worldview can be neutral toward religion, but often enough it takes the form of "secularism," which does not simply pertain to the decline of practices or privatization of religious belief, but also to the conviction of the negative nature of religion. Thus disbelief or lapsed practice is not necessarily the same as secularism. Gauging how predominant the negative secularist attitude toward religion is presents great difficulties, but the phenomenon is certainly widespread and varied. Its inherent suspicion of religion takes on a number of forms, largely symbolic and attitudinal at present. Professor of law Steven Smith describes the motivation behind one that is particularly common: "One of the most familiar rationales for attempting to separate religious arguments and symbols from the public sphere is that religion is dangerously divisive."[35] The author may be writing about elite opinion in America, but this matches a deep-rooted European mode of elitist thinking. While possessing some basis in reality, such prejudices often ignore positive and integrating consequences of religion. The elites have effectively managed to impart their attitude to a substantial portion of the European population. According to the results for the European countries participating in the 1998 International Social Survey Program, 61 percent of the respondents agreed that religion causes conflict and 65 percent that religion is intolerant. One of the authors of the survey, however, claims that against his protests the questions were decidedly loaded: on the one hand through their abstraction, and on the other hand through the questions that were omitted: "There [were] no positive items suggesting that sometimes religion brings peace, not conflict, and that sometimes men and women with strong religious beliefs are not intolerant."[36]

A negative attitude toward religion is the first step toward negative actions. Indeed, there is a marked rise in hostility toward religion in a number of European countries. According to Pew Research Center reports conducted in 2009 and 2011 measuring government restrictions as well as social hostilities toward religion worldwide, Europe is considered a part of the world where the attitude toward religion has undergone significant deterioration. As the authors of the report put it, "Europe had the largest proportion of countries in which social hostilities related to religion were on the rise from mid–2006 to mid–2009. Indeed, five of the 10 countries in the world that had a substantial increase in social hostilities were in Europe: Bulgaria, Denmark, Russia, Sweden and the United Kingdom."[37]

In part the hostile attitude may be generated by the fear that has been stirred up by the activities of radical Islamist groups and to some extent, albeit unfairly, generalized to the larger Muslim population in Europe. However exaggerated, these attitudes have some basis in real events, such as terrorist bombings. More surprising is the anti–Christian animus evoked in a number of other circumstances, for instance in response to the modest growth of Christianity within some European countries on account of immigrants from developing countries, notably of African origin. Paradoxically, many of these countries gained Christianity from European missions. "To a remarkable extent," observes historian Jenkins regarding the situation early in the millennium, "recent controversies suggest real suspicion of the immigrant churches, which media and policy makers regard almost as an alien cult."[38] A symbol of the new spiritual energy derived from outside Europe is the current archbishop of York, John Sentamu from Nigeria, whose religiosity combines a Cambridge education with an evangelical temperament. In an opinion piece for the *Daily Mail* on February 13, 2009, relating stories of affronts Christians have received in the country and castigating those responsible, he finally turns to Christians themselves: "My challenge, then, to the 72 percent of this nation who marked themselves as 'Christian' in response to the census of 2001 is that if they wish to safeguard that same Christian tradition, they must renew their faith and become actively involved in their local church."

To be sure there exists a tension within opposing ideals. Religious freedom is enshrined in all the European constitutions and is considered a universal right. Nevertheless, as Jose Casanova adds regarding this fact, "secular assumptions still linger in the dominant contra-supposition of human autonomy versus religious heteronomy as a form of subjection to external authority and therefore as a traditional form of self that is not yet emancipated."[39]

Worth noting, on the other hand, is that some major individual departures from secularism's fold have occurred in the last several years. For instance, in Germany a major voice that has conceded the positive role religion can play in the public sphere belongs to Jürgen Habermas. Initially quite critical of religion, Habermas's position has evolved considerably. Already in his public debate with the then Cardinal Ratzinger, subsequently Pope Benedict XVI, he admitted to Christianity's role in underpinning Europe's values of human rights, tolerance, and democracy. "Everything else is postmodern chatter," he averred.[40] Others have joined him in similar statements. These individuals and others like them hardly constitute a trend, nor can they match the New Atheists for media attention; however, such public intellectuals might constitute a new body of bipartisan mediators between religion and modernity.

On a similar tenor, it has been observed that "the poetics of a spiritual Eastern Europe do have a Western audience—and Western patrons."[41] Among the contributors to this "poetics," the late Czech intellectual and politician Vaclav Havel ranked high. Among them can also be included a number of Polish artists and intellectuals. This interest has been explained by the existence of nostalgia for a "cosmic-sacred" enchantment that is missing in Western Europe, the lack of which has deprived much of its cultural activity of deeper meaning.[42] Such a phenomenon may not account for much in public attitudes toward religion, but it signifies the existence of a crack in what has been called the "iron cage" of disenchantment.

Yet if spirituality has some positive connotations, institutional religion seems to bear the brunt of negative attitudes. For instance, in an analysis of British newspapers of various readerships conducted by Polish scholars, albeit the Church in Poland has been given credit for leading the nation's struggle against Communism and for its support in the last phase of the referendum for entry into the EU, more frequently it is accused of spreading "anti-European values," such as "nationalism, anti–Semitism, xenophobia, homophobia, as well as blocking the right of women to abortion."[43] The results of the Pew study cited above suggest that such an image is as much a reflection of media bias as a description of the actual institution in Poland.

An unwitting but tenacious Polish student clashed against the powerful Western European secularist narrative when he participated in an Erasmus exchange program at a Belgian university in 2008. Polish students who participate in such exchanges have been a rather select group and usually do quite

well. In this case, for his term paper, which was on the topic of European identity, the student decided to focus on the Christian input in that identity, especially as it pertained to Poland. The paper was rejected, and even after an
extensive and well-documented rebuttal of the critique the paper was not
accepted.[44] In Europe the secular mind-set has an undoubted foothold in academia, and in some cases a student must be quite bold to challenge it. But
things are changing quickly in Poland. Although less likely at present than in
Western Europe, similar treatment of a student expressing strong religious
views in his or her work is not inconceivable at a Polish university.

At the conclusion of the historical section in Chapter 2, I reported an
anticlerical event from the summer of 2010 that Krzysztof Michalski related
to the tradition of Poland's prewar anticlericalism. Though anticlericalism
may not be identical to secularism, it is in part influenced by it, since with its
impact on the modern social imaginary the secular worldview also partially
shapes expectations toward religion, even among some of the religious. This
issue will be examined now, but I will start from a general look at religion and
the elite in Poland.

Although in the interwar period anticlericalism was not rare among the
elite—in other words, the elite at that time were rather typically European in
their outlook on religion—it was mentioned earlier that during the Communist period a number of artists and intellectuals became more supportive of
religion, if not actually religious. This did not end with the collapse of Communism, even though some, like Czesław Miłosz and Adam Michnik, were
critical of public actions taken by the Catholic Church itself in the country
in the early years subsequent to the event. During an interview toward the
end of his life, for instance, eminent philosopher Leszek Kołakowski was asked
his opinion about Christianity, and he responded quite favorably about its
tradition and institutions, but added that he did not practice the faith. When
pushed further he added, "I feel that [Christianity] is the foundation of our
culture. But more than that, I have the feeling that it is very important for me
personally. And so in a loose sense I can claim to be a Christian."[45] Others
have gone further to a full religious stance, while some have not gone so far
but nonetheless maintained respect for religion.

A number of the major cultural achievements in Poland during the past
several decades have had significant elements of religious inspiration, for
instance some of the poetry of Miłosz,[46] Anna Kamieńska or Adam Zagajew-
ski; the music of Krzysztof Penderecki and Henryk Górecki—a conductor
remarked of the latter's *Third Symphony*, "It is like listening to angels"[47]—or
the films of Krzysztof Zanussi, to name a few. Even though not personally religious, Krzysztof Kieślowski likewise pondered metaphysical themes in his
films. There have been a number of exceptions to this pantheon, for instance

the Nobel Prize–winning poet laureate Wisława Szymborska, to mention just one, whose worldview and poetry had little to do with religion, but such artists were rarely anticlerical. These outstanding representatives of Polish culture have been followed by a number of epigones that are hardly beacons of faith, but, on the other hand, neither are they its enemy.

Continuing with the field of the arts, however, some of the most talented artists at present continue the tradition of their predecessors to the best of their abilities. The filmmaker Jan Jakub Kolski in his own fashion continues the tradition, exploring themes of popular religion in a creative manner. Some artists use religious symbolism in a provocative fashion to make valid points, for instance in his film *Dzień świra* (Day of the Wacko) from 2002, Marek Koterski parodies a bedtime prayer to show how Poles often despise their neighbors. Such artistic devices have a long tradition in Polish art. However, another group of artists—both in the "high arts" and in popular culture— have discovered the "culture of transgression," which not infrequently includes affronting religious sensibilities, to no small degree for publicity. The seminal case in this regard was Dorota Nieznalska's *Passion* exhibition of 2001–2, in which a photograph of male genitalia was affixed to a cross-shaped frame.[48] The subsequent indignant reaction was to be expected, and the artist was tried and sentenced for "offending religious feelings." She was soon exonerated by a higher court. The whole affair gave the artist a great deal of publicity. If Nieznalska's exhibition was ersatz Andres Serrano and his *Piss Christ*, her work spawned numerous ersatz works in its own stead, each generating further ill will and often enough much publicity. Popular culture thrives on transgression to a greater degree than high art, so affronts occur often enough in that field, such as the instance of tearing up the Bible by a heavy metal artist posing as a Satanist that was the subject of another trial. Even the mainstream media, especially after the Smoleńsk tragedy and the subsequent War of the Crosses, started to use any visual means possible to offend the Church regarding issues it held against secular liberal opinion—for instance the cover of a nationwide weekly displayed a single-sex Holy Family in support of gay unions, and so on.

Those more familiar with the Solidarity period might ask in this context what remains from the dialogue between the Church and the Left, carried on most notably by Adam Michnik on one side, with his groundbreaking *The Church and the Left* of 1977, and the Rev. Józef Tischner on the other. If Michnik complains that the Church is not the same after 1989, the same can be said about the Left in Poland, which has accepted much of European secularism at present, together with its anti–Catholic bent. The situation has degenerated from dialogue to one dominated by cultural wars with trenches dug out on both sides. Any chance at dialogue, in one journalist's sober assessment, is limited to "the grassroots level, in various particular social problems.... I have in mind, for instance, local initiatives for easing poverty, of giving the poor a better chance."[49] Aleksander Hall, a moderate Catholic social thinker, agrees, adding that among the top figures of the Left commonly presented in the media, he sees little desire for dialogue with the Church, "only a tendency for uttering monologues from a stance of moral superiority, which comes from presenting the only correct opinion" (*Rzeczpospolita*, March 20, 2013). Although not denying the Church has handled some situations poorly, he does not feel this is at the bottom of such attitudes. Thus, as the memory of John Paul II fades in Poland, some currents are certainly moving into or are awakening in the country that are hardly neutral toward religion. Anticlericalism is high on the list among these.

The sociologist Mirosława Grabowska, the head of a major opinion poll organization in Poland, points out that surveys do not ask questions that enable her to gauge anticlericalism accurately in the country, but she offers a few suggestions as to how it might operate. One of its modes is accentuating stereotypes about the Church or priests, for instance the alleged greediness of the latter. Stereotypes often thrive on secondhand information. Grabowska differentiates between the anticlericalism of those who identify themselves as Catholics and those who do not: "For practicing Catholics the cause of anticlericalism is personal experience, for non-practicing Catholics, it's caused by the media."[50] The stereotype of the greedy cleric, for instance, is potent in the countryside and villages and is to some extent based on experience. Significantly, in the national election of 2011, one-third of the supporters of the most vocal anticlerical party were from among that group.[51]

However, as Grabowska suggests, external anticlericalism is strengthened not just by the mistakes those identified with the Church make or when they allegedly or genuinely interfere with politics. The Rev. Andrzej Draguła brings up an aspect of the new anticlericalism important in this context, especially within its media representations in the growing culture of transgression, that is, its faux-blasphemous facade: "Instead of blasphemy we have cultural and media players in blasphemy, who wave their fists at a God they don't believe in."[52] When external anticlericalism is connected to genuine convictions, currents of secularism or at least strong disagreement on various stands the Catholic Church represents can feed it. This can take a mild form. Some groups are simply prone to forward the unadulterated secularist worldview. The editor of the website Racjonalista.pl proclaims, "We are against any sort of influence of the Church on the political or public life, we aim to remove religion, if not into non-being, then at least into the private sphere."[53]

In his book *American Jesus* of 2003, an expert on religion in America astutely observes, "American culture has long been both Christian and plural, both secular and religious, and much of the dynamism of U.S. religious history derives from that paradox."[54] A good deal of the same dynamic of various competing vectors is currently taking place in Poland. Anticlericalism is certainly one dynamic factor. If, as Michalski insists, anticlericalism can serve the hygienic function of keeping religion in its place in a secular state, to some extent the current anticlericalism plays a necessary function in today's Poland. Writing several months after the Smoleńsk tragedy, Catholic journalists Maciej Müller and Tomasz Ponikło noted that anticlericalism had become trendy in Poland, in part because of the imbroglio around the crosses in 2010 (which will be discussed in detail below). They suggested, however, that while many of the attacks on the Church were unwarranted, they did create the opportunity for soul-searching: "For the Church to survive the attacks with dignity, and also to preempt some of its adversaries, it can attempt to accept them as a challenge to perfection—both for its organization and for the virtue of humility."[55] This challenge is not frequently taken up at higher levels of the Church. One of the rare bishops unafraid of engaging in soul-searching is Bishop Czaja of the Opole diocese. Referring to internal criticism of the Church, he confesses, "The troubles Catholics have with the Church hierarchy are an expression of the fact that currently there are things that are scandalous, various unseemly matters, that people have a right to be upset. Sometimes deeply faithful people are lost on account of this."[56] After the entry into the Polish Sejm in 2011 of an openly anticlerical movement, the Rev. Henryk Zieliński is more specific: "The election results reveal that the scale of anticlericalism is greater in Poland than that of atheism.... Perhaps there would not be the success of Palikot [the leader of the party] if some prelate, bishop, or even cardinal went to remove the cross from in front of the presidential palace."[57] At this point, it is too late for a few such gestures to turn the trend; whether they would have actually helped is a matter of pure conjecture.

From the above it might seem that there is little ground between a certain type of religious discourse in Poland and its anticlerical opposite, which is to some extent the case. There is a middle ground, but it does not have a high profile. Nor is it a comfortable place to be. The situation of Zbigniew Lew-Starowicz, head of the Polish Sexuological Association, is indicative of this problem. Although he agrees adults cannot be instructed as to how they conduct their sex lives, he nonetheless is convinced that marriage increases the chances for an ideal sexual relationship, and this is clear from his academic work. Yet he complains that liberal journalists are quite selective during their interviews with him, thus distorting his views, while, conversely, the Catholic media avoids interviewing him, since they believe the constructed image of him in the public media.[58] A Catholic journalist taking the bull by the horns, Marek Zając pleas for an end to partisanship on both sides of the barricades, which members of the Church should take upon themselves to initiate: "In recurring polemics Catholics should take on the role not of defenders of the interests of the Church, but as propagators of commonsense. Let us demonstrate that we are not after privileges, but the common good of all citizens."[59] More on moderate Catholics—the affirmative orthodox—will be written below.

Although the question of anticlericalism has hardly been exhausted, we will now look at the different reactions and strategies within Polish Catholicism that have developed in the face of secular culture and secularism as such. As is fairly evident from the above discussion of secularism, although some Polish variations exist, in one degree or another many of the problems facing religion in Poland are similar to those elsewhere in Europe and much of the developed world. To what extent can the same be said about the solutions attempted by Polish Catholics in this regard? Since the religious members of Polish society are primarily Catholics, we will briefly examine some of the major currents in Catholicism today across the globe before comparing how these currents are present in Poland.

According to Catholic journalist John Allen in his *The Future Church* of 2009, contemporary Catholicism has largely responded to the challenges of modernity in a similar manner to that of Protestants, and so the same broad divisions representing specific responses are present within the Catholic Church. These roughly include a liberal current, along with an evangelical and Pentecostal one. Allen describes these divisions succinctly in a sound bite: "Mainline liberals want to reach a détente with modernity; Evangelicals want to convert it; Pentecostals want to set it on fire."[60] He argues that currently liberalism, quite strong in Europe and North America shortly after the Second Vatican Council, has largely run out of steam. Moreover, if liberalism embraced pluralism, that same pluralism has created the problem of defining oneself. This has opened the way for the evangelical response that dominates in much of the Church today. Catholic Evangelicals are not afraid of proclaiming their identity to the world. Their response is also shaped by that world. As Allen puts it, "The key point of evangelical Catholics, especially the younger breed, is not that they're politically liberal or conservative. It's that their formative experience wasn't growing up in a rigid, stifling Church, but rather a rootless secular culture. Their hunger for identity is better understood in terms of generational dynamics, not ideology."[61] From this perspective John Paul II helped usher in that response, but it would seem he did not create it so much as he mediated a genuine need. Pentecostalism, in this context of a response to modernity, is a major force in global Catholicism—to a lesser extent in Europe—and it is bound to grow. Allen's is not a strictly academic work, and when he writes of the relative strength of the currents his statements are rather impressionistic, although they are the impressions of a highly informed observer. What will be of particular interest in this discussion are the patterns of discourse that result from the three trends described by the author.

Regarding Poland, although the current situation of Catholicism in the country is too complicated to be reduced to three currents, nonetheless the same currents Allen delineates are detectable within the Catholic Church, and two of them indeed play a formative role in elite religious discourse, where the above challenges are treated more reflectively. However, there are difficulties in looking at religion in Poland from such a perspective. For one thing, the nomenclature Polish Catholics generally use is more conventional—the division between liberal and conservative or traditionalist Catholics is commonly stressed—thus placing various groups within the currents Allen outlines will be a preliminary attempt on my part to do so. For another thing, despite some similarities—a postmodern secular culture is indeed present—the dynamics at play in Poland are substantially different. For a start, some Polish Catholics do see the "Church triumphant," as it was dubbed by critics after the fall of Communism, as "rigid and stifling." That is how it was and often has been presented in the media, and evidence can be found to support the claim. Adding to that impression has been the renewed connection of part of the Church with nationalism. Together with the rise of anticlericalism, a liberal current has emerged within Polish Catholicism; while an overlap exists, the former is likely stronger than the latter. Moreover, an evangelical current is quite powerful, even dominant, yet on account of this, the question Allen poses in his report on World Youth Day in Madrid in 2011 also pertains to the evangelical current in Polish Catholicism: "The contest for the Catholic future is ... inside the Evangelical movement, between an open and optimistic wing committed to 'Affirmative Orthodoxy,' i.e., emphasizing what the church affirms rather than what it condemns, and a more defensive cohort committed to waging cultural war" (August 19, 2011, *National Catholic Reporter*). Furthermore, a Pentecostal movement certainly exists within Polish Catholicism. And at approximately thirty thousand members at present and over ten times that number of sympathizers, Odnowa w Duchu Świętym (Renewal in the Holy Spirit), the dominant Pentecostal group in the Church, is one of the more dynamic renewal movements in the country.[62] Most important in terms of the present discussion, however, representatives of the movement do not significantly participate in the debate on the place of the Church in Polish society. Thus the movement is not nearly as salient as the other two movements in formulating which direction Polish Catholicism will take, and for that reason my subsequent discussion will focus on the first two currents.

During the Communist regime under the strong leadership of Cardinal Wyszyński from within the Church and Pope John Paul II's powerful influence, liberal Catholicism did not develop as such in Poland. Once the regime collapsed it was to be expected that a liberal Catholicism would emerge, as indeed it has. Undoubtedly the influence of secular trends from Europe has had an impact on liberal Catholicism in the country. But it is also a reaction to the perceived narrow-mindedness of the part of the hierarchical Church as suggested above, and it typically includes opening up to liberal currents observed in many Catholic communities in Europe and America. The liberal trend has especially gained momentum after the death of the Polish pope.

Liberal Catholicism naturally has its representatives in academia. In Poland the ranks of liberal Catholic scholars have been strengthened by a number of high-profile academic clergy, like the above-mentioned Tadeusz Bartoś, who left the priesthood or religious life but remained in the Church, offering a liberal interpretation of Catholic doctrine. Perhaps the closest to a Hans Küng among them would be ex–Jesuit Stanisław Obirek, who in his most recent book *Umysł wyzwolony: W poszukiwaniu dojrzałego katolicyzmu* (The Liberated Mind: In Search of a Mature Catholicism) of 2011 outlines a program for a nondogmatic, largely cultural Catholicism.

A striking feature of the liberal wing of Polish Catholicism is its dearth of organized effort. None of its members have established any organizations or even periodicals of any note of their own. A rare exception would be the journal *Kontakt* published by a younger group at the Warsaw Club of Catholic Intelligentsia, who also run a blog. What gives liberal Catholicism a relatively high profile nonetheless is the willingness of a fairly powerful media to provide these Catholics with a venue in which to voice their views. Most notably in this regard is the weekend-edition religion page in *Gazeta Wyborcza*. Although members of the open Evangelical Catholicism contribute to the page on occasion, in recent years the religion reporter of the paper, the ex-nun Katarzyna Wiśniewska, sympathizes with more liberal Catholic causes, and she also dominates the reporting on religion. Thus, for instance, Wiśniewska will report on the decreasing religiosity of women mentioned above and blame it almost fully on the "male-dominated" patriarchal Church in Poland for not changing its attitude toward women.[63] Whatever truth there is to such a criticism, it is unlikely the major reason why women are attending masses less frequently, as is evident from the fact that Christian denominations in European countries where women have been ordained have been unable to keep women, or anyone else, in the pews either: in fact they have had far more difficulty than the Church in Poland.

One might add, however, that there are indeed a significant number of women Catholics who simply want greater recognition and input of women in the Polish Church. This is a complex issue; for our purposes a simple example can give some insight. In Poland girls are not allowed to serve at the altar, as in many Catholic churches in other European countries and in North America, which is a possibility well within canon law. In the critique of women's role in the Polish Church, the more radical liberal Catholics are joined by many moderate Catholics. For instance, in a survey of what bothers women in the Church, Sr. Barbara Chyrowicz, a supporter of John Paul II's "new feminism," admits that she is "annoyed by the feeling of superiority even quite young priests express with regards to women." Furthermore, she continues, "I have no idea what needs to be done to get it through to some bishops that they can learn something from women."[64]

The position of liberal Catholics is rather ambivalent. Their demands for reform within the Church have little chance of making headway in the foreseeable future. The liberal wing of the Polish Church is largely impotent, despite being quite shrill at times. Their most sensible criticisms of the Church, on the other hand, are also conveyed by the affirmative Evangelical Catholics. One pertinent question is likewise why the liberal Catholic wing is not stronger in the country. Perhaps, since liberal Christianity in both the Protestant and Catholic versions has not infrequently been a stepping stone to secularization, in Poland a number of potential liberal Catholics have simply done away with the intermediate stage and embraced such an end quite early on, reinforcing the anticlerical movement rather than attempting constructive criticism.

At least pertaining to the liberal current in Poland, Kaufmann's provocative assessment of religion in Western Europe likewise seems to hold: "The mushy middle between fundamentalist religion and irreligion seems to be hemorrhaging as people either choose unalloyed secularism or full-orbed faith." He adds pessimistically, "Even if moderate religion can hang on, its atheist detractors are as determined as religious fundamentalists to kick it in its teeth."[65] The statement of the editor in chief of the Polish edition of *Newsweek* when a moderate Catholic columnist left the journal in protest of a spate of anti–Church articles in mid–2012 articulates this aggressive mode, evidencing its presence in Poland: "I myself prefer the Ayatollah [Tomasz] Terlikowski [see below—C.G.] to the pseudo-liberal, pseudo-doctrinal, sucking two-breasts simultaneously liberal Catholics. With Terlikowski I have nothing in common; however, at least he is not a bizarre hypocrite, one that has moderate views, which allows him to pose as an *arbiter elegantiarum*. In times of sharp division and sharp conflict being in the middle is rather a sign of non-commitment and opportunism than rationality."[66] Nonetheless, for the time being at any rate a moderate middle does exist, but with more vigor on the side of the affirmative orthodox than with the liberals. And such strident anticlericalism is not so strong.

The European lifestyle trends that attract the liberal Catholics are largely supportive of an expressive individualism. The latter, albeit less powerful a cultural mode than in North America, is nonetheless quite strong in much of

Europe as well, especially among the elite and popular culture. One might ask whether the current modest resurgence of orthodox faiths in Europe,[67] from Judaism to various denominations of Christianity, not to mention the growing presence of Islam, in part indicates a turn to communitarianism in response to some of the negative effects of expressive individualism on society. Such a turn has developed in the United States, more or less coincident with the rise of Protestant evangelical Christianity[68]; although largely unheralded, it would be surprising if it did not exist in Europe as well, even if in a weaker form. Certainly the most articulate spokesman of Orthodox Judaism in Europe, Rabbi Jonathan Sacks, sees morality in communitarian terms.

Poland under Communism had largely been shielded from the onslaught of expressive individualism,[69] especially in its most radical forms; thus it still holds a high attraction for parts of society that have little awareness of its drawbacks. In no small degree liberal Catholicism in the country rides this current. Certainly the presence of a measure of expressive individualism helps a society be creative. A moderate liberal voice in Polish Catholicism is healthy, and it would be an exaggeration to call the existing one particularly radical. The liberal critique of nationalistic tendencies in the Church, for instance, cannot be ignored. A significant problem, however, lies in the fact that the phenomenon is one thing in countries that have not experienced the social devastation of a totalitarian system and have a high degree of initial social trust, and another in Poland, which, as Chapter 3 shows, is sorely lacking in this virtue at this outset. It has been argued, for instance, that expressive individualism does little to build social trust,[70] and it erodes institutions such as the family—human capital in the jargon of social scientists. Far more sensitive to both of these issues than liberal Catholics in Poland are the Evangelical Catholics, who—at least those from the "affirmative orthodoxy" wing—are more interested in aspects of their faith that contribute to building social capital.

Qualifying the different groups within Polish Catholicism for the evangelical current is somewhat difficult, since it is the current that has no correlation in Polish discourse on Catholicism in the country. Some instantiations are more spontaneous. For instance, the diminishing of religious practice in some cities has motivated religious Poles to be more active. This is the case in Łódź, where religious practice is the lowest in Poland, with a mere 20 percent of the city dwellers attending mass with any regularity, and alternative lifestyles are the most common (almost 30 percent of children are born out of wedlock, a very high percentage for Poland). It is in this city and context that lay Catholics are most active in various evangelical efforts at bringing their faith out into the public.[71]

Yet how Evangelical Catholicism functions in religious discourse in Poland is a more complex question, which I will attempt by giving a historical perspective. If John Paul II gave an impetus to the affirmative wing of Evangelical Catholicism in global Catholicism, then it can be said to have started earlier in Poland with Karol Wojtyła, together with his milieu in the Kraków diocese—the clerical and lay contributors of *Tygodnik Powszechny* weekly and *Znak* monthly, which influenced groups of Catholics in Warsaw and elsewhere. Their promotion of human dignity and a Catholicism influenced by a philosophy of personalism, for instance, even affected the rhetoric of those in the Polish Church who were not willing to take the concepts quite so far.[72] In the nomenclature of Polish Catholics, this group was known as an exemplar of "open Catholicism," which was ready for dialogue with various milieus in Poland and was quite supportive of the original Solidarity. Its members included the legendary the Rev. Józef Tischner. Currently, however, the situation is more complicated. The *Tygodnik Powszechny* and *Znak* group has evolved toward a cross-over milieu between Evangelical Catholicism and the liberal current, although the latter is not nearly as strong within the group as its conservative critics insist. Nevertheless, it must be mentioned that in whatever way one describes Karol Wojtyła's former milieu, it is the class act of Polish Catholicism, and few groups can speak as graciously about those who criticize it as its members.[73] The members of the Warsaw group centered round *Więź* quarterly seem to be the most intellectually vital group of affirmative orthodoxy. Among others they have created the think tank "Laboratorium Więzi," which has the most highly developed program in the country for reflection upon and education toward the place of religion in civil society. Besides publishing the monthly and conducting pointed surveys, the group organizes numerous public meetings on pertinent topics in Warsaw. It is from the affirmative orthodox wing of the Church that the most fruitful efforts for dialogue with other religious groups usually emerge or its members are engaged in its various enterprises, some of which were described earlier.

The division between the open wing of Evangelical Catholicism in Poland and its combative counterpart is largely a generational one. Paradoxically it is the younger group that tends toward the more defensive stance, together with a more traditionalist approach to their Catholicism. This can partially be comprehended along the line of trends in Europe described by Kaufmann: "Younger Christians tend to be more traditionalist in their faith—why else buck the trend set by one's secular peers?"[74] In Poland "secular peers" are hardly ubiquitous, so the issue is better understood as distinguishing oneself from lukewarm religious peers, as well as anticlerical voices. Evidence of the former attitude is the provocative cover illustration of *Pressje*, one of the current's periodicals, where the "M" for Mary in John Paul's coat of arms was replaced by McDonald's golden arches, ostensibly symbolizing a protest against the McDonaldization of the cult of the former pope in Poland.[75] But in relation

to the older affirmative orthodox, the combative stance might also be comprehended along the lines of Chesterton's adage: "Children are innocent and
love justice, while most adults are wicked and prefer mercy." Since the older
milieu of Evangelical Catholics was originally active during the Communist
regime, it was also to some extent infiltrated by the secret service.[76] Their openness at present at least in part stems from the bitter knowledge of how complicated human affairs can be.

These younger Evangelical Catholics are a far-ranging group. They publish a number of periodicals like *Fronda* and *Christianitas* and several others, or
contribute to older diocese periodicals such as *Gość Niedzielny* (Sunday Visitor).
On the one hand, one of their members is also editor in chief of the ecumenical
website Ekumenizm.pl. They revere the late Richard John Neuhaus and have
published a book of interviews the founding editor of *First Things* gave to
Polish Catholic periodicals along with translations of a number of his articles.
Paradoxically, almost in unconscious opposition to his Polish publishers, in
one of the above interviews Neuhaus praises Catholicism for its inclusiveness,
stating that while he himself holds orthodox Catholic views, he disagrees with
conservative Catholics who would gladly exclude critical liberal Catholics
from the Church.[77] This magnanimous attitude is not quite in line with the
acerbic tone that emanates from some of his Polish publishers' polemics. These
Evangelicals are more demonstratively patriotic. Moreover, like the Protestant
Evangelical tradition, one could say these Catholics have their version of the
jeremiad—although, as Porter-Szücs describes it, Polish Catholics had something of a jeremiad tradition of their own in the interwar period, which focused
on the alleged historical decline and stagnation of the country.[78]

The combative stance of the young Evangelical Catholics is part of the
reason for their relatively limited support in the community at large, or even—
albeit not absent—among the Polish episcopate. Bishops could well be wary,
since among the members of this group of Catholics was a journalist active
among a group in 2007 involved in uncovering the alleged past collaboration
of one of the prominent bishops with the secret service, effectively blocking
his promotion to the head of the diocese of Warsaw.[79] In fact, a trait that connects younger Evangelical Catholics with their liberal coreligionists is their
often irreverent stance toward the Church hierarchy. For instance, both
Tomasz Terlikowski of the first group and Katarzyna Wiśniewska of the other
group are quite eager to call bishops to order, although they will be different
bishops for different reasons.

Allen stresses that the "perceived animosity of secular elites has reinforced
the drive toward evangelical Catholicism."[80] As described above, this perception is growing in Poland as well. These younger Evangelical Catholics also
have a fairly good sense of where they stand in society and how difficult it will

be to promote Catholic values in the future. Political support is on the wane. In an interview, Terlikowski observed that the younger members of the major Christian Democratic parties, currently the strongest in the Sejm, are going secular and will not support Christian moral issues once the older members retire ("Duży Format," magazine insert in *Gazeta Wyborcza*, February 14, 2011). This observation was made even before the new anticlerical party entered the Sejm in 2011.

Pertinent in this respect, Allen points out that with the political climate turning against orthodox religion in the West, legal persecution of Catholics is a possibility.[81] If anything, the climate for orthodox religion has further degenerated in a number of Western countries since Allen penned his words; in Europe, Bishop Philip Tartaglia of Paisley in Scotland has gone as far as to predict that one day he could be tried on account of his public defense of Catholic teachings.[82] However, such a danger is not likely in Poland in the foreseeable future. But if one were to look for similar resolve in Poland, it would be among the young Evangelicals, who are also unafraid of facing the consequences for taking on tougher issues.[83] Certainly they are not afraid of antireligion litigation, which already rears its head. Joanna Najfeld, one of the few pro-life feminists in the country, belongs to the group. For instance, she has gone as far as accusing one of the pro-choice activists of connections with the pharmaceutical industry, and she had enough evidence that she was acquitted at court when she was accused of slander.[84] There have also been Catholics on the losing end of such encounters.[85]

Another general descriptor of the Evangelicals according to Allen is their attitude toward secularization. Actually they welcome it, because of the necessity "for religion to become a conscious choice."[86] Among the Evangelical Catholic thinkers (of the affirmative orthodox trend) who have studied secularization most closely is the Rev. Andrzej Draguła, a member of Laboratorium Więzi, and a resident of Zielona Góra, one of the more secularized dioceses in Poland. He has examined the collapse of the mass church in Quebec in the 1960s and does not exclude the possibility of something similar happening in Poland. The Reverend Draguła sees the possibility of a cleansing process of the Polish Church through secularization. "Instead of pronouncing negative judgments on the present, we should learn to maintain a distance toward it and liberate ourselves from overly close attachments to historical forms [of Catholicism], seeking new roads for evangelization in a secularized world."[87] Evangelical Catholics are indeed foremost among those who look for new forms of bringing the Gospel to Poles. For instance, there is Szymon Hołownia, a popular writer on religion, and also a TV talent and talk show host. Someone wrote to him calling him "the Woody Allen of Polish Catholicism," which he admitted described his mission aptly.[88] For a time he had a column in the

Polish edition of *Newsweek*, and he has no qualms about reaching any audience, such as the readers of women's magazines. Nor is he averse to engaging in a dialogue about faith with those for whom religion seems to be little more than worn out wives' tales, like with his fellow talk show host Marcin Prokop in their popular co-authored book *Bóg, kasa i rock'n'roll* (God, Cash, and Rock'n'Roll) of 2011. Based in Warsaw with its low level of religious practice, he certainly has a realistic view of the difficulties of communicating the religious message to today's young.

One might add that initiatives like Lednica 2000 and numerous others certainly come under the category of innovative means to evangelize Poles: the summer is awash with numerous religious festivals, but they compete with the more numerous secular festivals and events. Nonetheless, the Reverend Draguła's pronouncement brings us to one of the primary differences between Evangelical Catholicism in Poland and its counterpart abroad. Allen characterizes one important aspect of the latter: "Historically speaking, Evangelical Catholicism isn't really 'conservative,' because there's precious little cultural Catholicism these days left to conserve" (*National Catholic Reporter*, August 19, 2011). This might be a sweeping claim, but in many Western countries it has greater or lesser substance behind it. Regarding Poland, however, where clearly a strong Catholic culture exists, any sensible program for action requires a judicious blend of continuity and change. Terlikowski is one of the commentators—at least conceptually—promoting such an approach. Quite critical of what he describes as the crisis of the moral fiber within the post–1989 Church, Terlikowski nevertheless insists that reform must stay true to Polish Catholic identity. He reminds Polish Catholics that attempts at reform in other European Churches that failed to take into account native traditions were disastrous. He suggests that reforms must "on the one hand be founded on a profound engagement with the social and moral life, on the other hand they require building a strong religiosity based on Polish identity."[89] The problem is which traditions in Polish Catholicism are to be drawn upon: some are illustrious by any standards; others, the less said the better. Another question is which "Polish identity" is selected: also quite a problematic issue, to which we will return.

In their own way, if not equally powerful, the liberal and evangelical currents in Polish Catholicism are among the most important voices in the elite religious discourse of the country. We will return to them in the context of religion in the public sphere, where they play an important role among other Catholic voices, but first we will consider their attitudinal relationship with each other. The liberal and evangelical currents in Polish Catholicism obviously differ in their vision of the Church, at times even contradicting each other. These differences are an expression of pluralism within Polish Catholicism, and even of a measure of vitality. A pertinent question, however, is to what extent they communicate. Attempts have been made to get members of different groups to engage in conversation. For instance in the January 2010 issue of *Więź*, Zbigniew Nosowski, who founded Laboratorium Więzi, gathered together a number of Catholic thinkers from quite diverse camps to discuss his think piece "Polskie katolicyzmy" (Polish Catholicisms) concerning the state and divisions of Catholicism in Poland. Allen writes of the drift of contemporary Catholicism toward "tribalism," that is, "Catholics of differing temperaments and perspectives often are engaged in completely separate conversations, with few points of reference."[90] In Poland, attempts at dialogue like Nosowski's are rather few among divergent Catholic groups; conversely, strains of "tribalism" seem more evident, at least at the level of Catholic discourse.

During his last visit to Poland in 2002, John Paul II consecrated the new Basilica of Divine Mercy at Łagiewniki near Kraków. The Jesuit priest Fr. Wacław Oszajca was asked to comment on the visit on public television. He expressed his hope that the theme of divine mercy inspiring the visit would help bring the divided Catholics of the country closer together. More or less a decade after that historic visit, Polish Catholics are, in some ways at least, farther apart than closer together. It would not be much of an exaggeration to claim that more than dialogue with other religious groups, an intra–Catholic dialogue is called for in Poland—and one that goes beyond the parties to the divisions just discussed, but also including the assertive nationalist Catholics. As one of the program directors of the most recent Gniezno Convention in 2012 has put it concerning this issue, "Regarding this problem, can we Catholics be credible in building ecumenical bridges with Christians or members of other religions if we cannot overcome the divisions in our own community?"[91]

Moreover, the separate narratives for Europe and East Central Europe concerning religion mentioned at the beginning of this section have now become internalized, and the division also exists within Poland itself. Unsurprisingly, there are few signs of Western Europe having absorbed any of the religious narrative that Poles are partly giving up, although here and there the situation of religion in the Continent is changing and is no longer unequivocally secular; a number of scholars even speak with some qualifications of a "postsecular Europe."

The Public Sphere: The Catholic Church, Cultural Wars, Civil Religion, and the Common Good

When religion is discussed in the context of democratic society, those voices that confer a positive role to religion in the public sphere speak in terms of its role in civil society.[92] This perspective separates the role of religion from the state and politics and, with regard to its institutional representatives— churches and synagogues—relegates its influence to one of persuasion. In Poland, one of the difficulties with such an understanding of the public sphere and discussing the Catholic Church's role within it is the fact that civil society remains underdeveloped. As mentioned in Chapter 3, although NGOs are developing rapidly enough in the country, the public as of yet does not set much store with them. No doubt this will change, but Poles are still largely preoccupied with top-down solutions to problems. Thus the relationship of the Church with the state, although not our primary concern in this context, must in part be examined. Before discussing this more fully, we will begin by outlining the broader European context.

At the outset it is worth stressing that if the Church in Poland played a major role in the democratization of the country and more or less indirectly in the region during the Communist era not so very long ago, this was hardly exceptional. According to a study conducted by the authors of *God's Century: Resurgent Religion and Global Politics* (2011), religion has played a leading or significant role in the democratization process in over 70 percent of the seventy-eight cases of "substantial democratization" documented by Freedom House in the period between 1972 and 2009. The "religious actors" in this wave come from every major religious body; however, the Catholic Church has clearly led the field—making a contribution in thirty-six out of forty-eight countries where religion played a leading role. Although this religious activism was rarely decisive, the authors cautiously conclude, "In the absence of this robust Catholic activism, it is likely that fewer countries would have enjoyed substantial, sustained, and stable democratic progress."[93] To no small extent this activism was the result of the change in attitude toward human rights of the post–Vatican Second Church and subsequently the involvement of John Paul II.

Despite the above, the Catholic Church has been the object of much rancor in Europe. Although anti–Catholicism has not been the subject of study to the extent it has in the United States,[94] watchdog organizations like Observatory on Intolerance and Discrimination against Christians in Europe have plenty to report on the subject.[95] In part anti–Catholicism can be explained as resulting from the surprisingly negligible awareness of the sub- stantial contribution of religion in general and Catholicism in particular in the recent process of democratization in the world over the last several decades, while, conversely, extensive media coverage of the internal sexual abuse scan- dals—obviously a genuine problem—renders the latter quite familiar to the public at large. Moreover, the role that secularism plays among the political and cultural elite is augmented by the related problem of the divergent vision of human rights that the same political and cultural elites frequently hold. Among others, the latter stems from a different view on human dignity. The secular view—largely based on expressive individualism—is fairly well known, so we will briefly rehearse what might broadly be called the Catholic view that remains rather superficially understood.

Although at the time it only had observer status as a candidate for the EU, the Polish government campaigned for the *Invocatio Dei* in the preamble to the constitution that was being negotiated in 2003.[96] The attempt failed, and the constitution itself was aborted; however, it brought the attention of some upon the invocation that was incorporated into the Polish constitution, which harkens back to the Jagiellonian spirit in updated language:

> Having regard for the existence and future of our homeland, which recovered the possibility of a sovereign and democratic determination of its fate in 1989, we, the Polish nation—all citizens of the Republic, both those who believe in God as the source of truth, justice, good and beauty, as well as those not sharing such faith but respecting those universal values as arising from other sources, equal in rights and obligations toward the common good—Poland, beholden to our ancestors for their labors, their struggle for independence achieved at great sacrifice, for our culture rooted in the Christian heritage of the Nation and universal human values.[97]

In this portion of the document—praised, among others, by Jürgen Habermas and constitutional law professor Joseph Weiler—a particular concept of human dignity is implicit. It is a concept that parallels John Paul II's recognition of human dignity being rooted in the communal experience of human beings: "The community is the vehicle through which we experience our own dignity and the dignity of others, and the connectedness of persons and the value of persons are discovered through their interdependence."[98] Such an understanding of human dignity stems from the Church's own tradition as well as its response to the contemporary development of human rights.

The development of human rights after World War II, in turn, gained a major impetus from the concerted international response to the inconceivable atrocities of the war in the UN Charter of 1945, which harkened to "the dignity of the human person."[99] The principle soon became incorporated in the Universal Declaration of Human Rights. However, the caveat behind this landmark declaration was the fact that the claim concerning the unique worth of the human person was primarily a political statement without a firm axiological basis in the diverse cultures of the signatories—including, to an increasing degree, Western culture itself. Czesław Miłosz, among others, was aware of the difficulties posed by the lack of a firmer foundation for the concept of human dignity:

> I wonder at this phenomenon because maybe underneath there is an abyss. After all, these ideas had their foundation in religion, and I am not over-optimistic as to

the survival of religion in a scientific-technological civilization. Notions that seemed buried forever have suddenly been resurrected. But how long will they stay afloat if the bottom has been taken out?[100]

Miłosz's concerns remain quite valid: as legal scholar Steven Smith puts it, "in the cage of modern secular discourse—'dignity' cannot be redeemed in [a] religious sense."[101] Harvard philosopher of law Mary Ann Glendon notes how this lack of a solid foundation for the concept of human dignity has led to considerable controversy in various fields over its definition in the several decades after the UN charter had been drawn up, particularly in Western countries. As the Vatican representative to the international 1995 Beijing Conference on Women sponsored by the United Nations, Glendon was also in the position to report that the dignity-based vision of human rights was attacked at the gathering on account of new priorities. A European-led coalition even felt that the word "dignity" was essentially averse to their stance on gender equality.[102]

The rest of the story, one might say, is history. It can be added that, as is relatively well known, at the time of the Universal Declaration, the Catholic Church did not place much store in the basic right of the freedom of religion, but as we have seen, once it did, quite soon it became a bulwark in its support of democratization processes later in the century. Nevertheless, in the foreseeable future it is hard to imagine that any viable compromise can be attained between the Catholic Church with its interpretation of human dignity and rights and that held by a substantial portion of the elite in the West. As director of the Religious Freedom Project at Georgetown University, Thomas Farr, puts it, "religion in Europe is no longer seen as intrinsic to human dignity and social flourishing. It is generally understood as merely an opinion and, as a species, a dangerous opinion at that: While it is fine to practice your religion in churches, synagogues, mosques and temples, democracy requires that you keep it there."[103]

Thus in a Europe where identification with the EU is currently declining, potentially constructive forces either are on the defensive or are engaged in blocking a number of the others' initiatives. More significantly from the perspective of this study, most of these currents largely developed while Poles had their own problems with a totalitarian state, but once an independent state came into being the clash was inevitable. Even when its prestige was at a peak soon after its seminal role in attaining the liberty of Poles through the collapse of Communism, the Church in Poland—much to its surprise and consternation—faced substantial resistance to its campaign in 1993 to reinstate the ban on abortion on demand that the Communist regime had lifted in the 1950s,[104] one of the reasons why the pertinent legislation only became law in 1997.[105] And so in Poland as elsewhere in Europe, at a certain level competing views of human dignity at crucial junctures led to the sterile confrontation of forces in an ongoing cultural war.

Another important context for the public role of religion in Poland is the nature of the state. A likely obstacle to a fuller development of civil society in Poland lies in the fact that the Polish state remains quite centralized, partly by default due to its having evolved from the Communist state, but also because of current interests. During the so-called Round Table Talks of 1988 that were a major stage in the ending of Communism, the Solidarity negotiators astutely picked up on the importance of local government, which was then almost completely subordinated to the central government throughout the Soviet bloc, and negotiated what concessions were possible from the Communist regime at the time. However, things have not advanced much since. Local and even voivodeship governments have little ability to raise their own funds through taxes, and their weakness is reflected in the fact that their politicians—possibly aside from some mayors—have a relatively low profile in society, not to mention that participation in municipal elections remains quite low. An opportunity for introducing a federal system was missed during the course of the rationalization of the administrative system in the country in 1999, which had been modeled on a version of the French *department* system. The country's forty-nine voivodeships were reduced to sixteen (later one more was added), and the amount of self-governing powers was debated. Ironically, it was the dominant Solidarity-backed party, Solidarity Electoral Action, ostensibly a proponent of the Church's social teaching, that forced a statist solution quite distant from the Catholic principle of subsidiarity. For the latter a federalist solution would be more appropriate, enhancing the further development of a grassroots civil society. Subsidiarity supports the latter, since as an American legal scholar puts it, "[the] preference for the local puts individuals and their relationships at the center of the social order, ensuring the efficacy of their conscience-driven efforts."[106]

One might add that if some anticlerical Zapatero-like politician were to govern Poland in the future, such a centralized state makes it much easier to damage the Church, for instance through affecting hiring policies at many state-subsidized Catholic institutions, or by cutting off their funding altogether. What few observers take into consideration is that any amplified secularist campaign would also have an adverse effect on minority religious communities: although Catholicism would be the main target, all religious communities would suffer in the long run. However that may be, the statist political stance of major Christian Democratic parties that have their roots in the no-longer existing Solidarity Electoral Action must be understood in relation to the influential nationalist wing of Catholicism, whose ideologues pine for a strong state and in this respect have little regard for Catholic social teaching above and beyond its more overt moral imperatives. Thus, as we have seen earlier, the Catholic Church in Poland is replete with vertical structures, while in its own manner the Polish state has much the same structures.

The attitude of the political parties to the Church varies depending on their historical background and, more importantly, their electorate. While the phenomenon of a party that campaigned so blatantly on anticlerical sentiments as happened in 2011 is new, the Palikot movement basically took a large portion of the vote away from older, less overtly anticlerical parties, so the electorate did not grow radically, although its base is changing now that the Communist roots of the sentiment are becoming less significant.[107]

The Christian Democratic parties are also adapting to a changing electorate. At present there are two major parties with roots in the Solidarity tradition which can be called Christian Democratic, albeit in a fairly loose sense. Between them they have formed consecutive governments since the period after John Paul II's death, most significantly in opposition to each other. Where moral issues are involved, both parties generally have not upheld party discipline, allowing their members in the Sejm to vote according to the dictates of their consciences, which, might be added, is a stance supported by public opinion.

The currently ruling Civic Platform Party likewise has the largest Polish representation in the European parliament after the elections of 2009, and it belongs to the Christian Democratic grouping of that body. Despite this, it has more critics in Church circles at home.[108] This is not altogether surprising, since—several years after the death of John Paul II—in various ways the party presently seems to be positioning itself for future cooperation with anticlerical parties, which would have been unthinkable earlier. The Law and Justice Party, on the other hand, an heir to the statist sentiments of Solidarity Electoral Action, tends to openly support parts of Catholic moral teaching, such as in its stance on in vitro, and has been rewarded by broader support from various Church circles. A number of its members are associated with Radio Maryja and have received plenty of air time during election campaigns, and they have responded by supporting a number of the radio station's issues afterward, most energetically the bid for Telewizja Trwam to receive a concession in the modern digital broadcasting platform. After the victorious 2005 elections, for several years the party both formed the government and had its own president as head of state. Nevertheless, in 2011 after the secession of several hard-core members following an election failure, for a time the party proclaimed it would support the reinstatement of the death penalty, which goes against John Paul II and Benedict XVI's teachings. At that point most bishops tellingly expressed critical opinions about the death penalty.[109] Moreover, the bishops have made it fairly clear that their actions in no way take into account the interests of the Law and Justice Party,[110] although these may coincide at times.

Despite two nominally Christian Democratic parties controlling most of the seats in the Polish Sejm, in the years following John Paul's death, the Church's influence on politics has been waning—significantly, it is the Hungarians who in April 2011 passed a constitution that defends the human being from conception and not the Poles. Validating the Evangelical Catholics' fears expressed above if he is correct, a liberal journalist predicts that any pretense on the part of politicians paying lip service to the Church's values will not last: "The trial of strength will come soon enough—if not during this Sejm's tenure, in the nearest years."[111] Both parties' attitude toward the Church is rather opportunistic, picking and choosing what they wish to support from its teaching, with their treatment of the Church depending on political circumstance. In this, of course, they are not all that different from various Christian Democratic parties in Europe that have largely lost their initial ideals somewhere along the political way. Thus it has been observed by various commentators that currently there is less likelihood of the Church influencing the state than politicians manipulating the Church for their own ends. Not that the problem has not been perceived by some bishops: former primate Archbishop Henryk Muszyński, one of the more moderate bishops, declared in 2012, "Unfortunately, the instrumental treatment of the Church is getting more obvious. There is a willingness of politicians to drag the Church into their disputes, hiding behind [its authority] and using it for their goals."[112]

Additionally, both parties appeal to different Catholics, with one attracting more educated urban ones, the other rather traditional or even nationalistic Catholics. For this reason, among others, one party is more attractive to minorities in Poland than the other. On account of the two major Christian Democratic parties, Catholic discourse in the national media is also largely divided politically, with the liberal and affirmative orthodox Catholics largely supportive of the Civic Platform—one reason why some hardly distinguish the groups—while the defensive Evangelical Catholics together with various traditionalist groups rather tending toward the Law and Justice Party, but not without reservations in either case.[113] One might add that for a small but possibly growing number of Catholics neither party satisfactorily reflects their views.

In principle at least, the institutional Church's position toward the state, on the other hand, has not essentially changed since the statement by the Conference of Bishops after the constitution was accepted. In an interview for *Gazeta Wyborcza* on March 1, 2012, the body's general secretary Bishop Wojciech Polak basically reiterated the desire for cooperation and autonomy: "The voice of the Church should be listened to, but whether and in what measure it is taken into consideration ultimately depends on the legislators. Legislation will never exclusively take into account the views of Catholics. Nevertheless the quality of the state's legislation will depend on the moral awareness to which Catholics also contribute." In a major pastoral letter of 2012 the Conference of Bishops has also expressed well-warranted concern that the level of political discourse has declined in Poland, resulting in Poles becoming discouraged from participating in the political process, that is, from contributing to the common good at an essential level.[114]

In the past, however, especially in the early years of independence, various measures of support for particular parties have sporadically occurred on the part of some priests and bishops, sometimes blatantly, sometimes in a more implicit manner. At least during elections this has markedly declined, certainly in any overt sense. A good example is the national election in 2011 to the Sejm, when it was reported that one parish priest openly supported a party from the pulpit. With ten thousand parishes in the country, it was also an indication of how closely the media watch the Church.

Nevertheless, it was also with good reason during a Congress of Christian Culture at the Catholic University of Lublin in September 2012 that the papal nuncio to Poland, Archbishop Celestino Migliore, reminded the Polish Church that it should not be involved in politics the day before a major demonstration organized by the opposition Law and Justice Party in support of Fr. Rydzyk's allegedly suppressed Telewizja Trwam, which—although the cardinal of the archdiocese of Warsaw refrained from conducting a mass for the protestors—had the sympathy of a number of bishops and priests throughout the country. Fr. Maciej Zięba—one of the most astute observers of the Church— sees this support of the station, playing into the hands of a specific political party, as a major mistake on the part of the hierarchical Church.[115]

Despite its lesser sway on the "moral awareness" informing state policy, the Church is nonetheless still quite visible in what might be called the nation's civil religion, which may be one of the reasons many Poles—along with the mainstream media—tend to overestimate its influence. Generally civil religion has a positive influence on Polish society; for now I will describe the position it holds from the perspective of its relationship between the Church and state and society in general. Politicians from the president of the country on down appear at religious events, and at seminal moments of state, representatives of the Church and sometimes other religions are present. At present there seems to be a somewhat cool relationship between the state and Church, which is evidenced at the level of civil religion. For instance, the Church hardly participated in the events connected with the country's presidency in the European Union in 2011. By contrast, political scientist Sławomir Sowiński noted that the Church was more visibly present in Hungary during its presidency that preceded Poland's (*Rzeczpospolita*, December 2, 2011). Indeed, after the ceremony that accompanied the transfer of the presidency, a number of Hungarian delegates undertook a pilgrimage to Częstochowa. To some extent this coolness in Poland is connected with the very fact that a Christian Democratic party holds power but hardly subordinates itself to the wishes of the Church. The Civic Platform's occasional flirtation with anticlerical parties likewise adds to this state of affairs.

One might add that although at some levels or by particular groups civil religion might be resented—a recognized liberal journalist has complained, "After twenty years of independence, no public act in Poland is valid without a Catholic prayer and a priest sprinkling holy water"[116]—more generally it is rather popular in Poland. When an anticlerical party suggested in 2011 that one of civil religion's symbols, the cross that is present in the assembly hall of the Sejm, be removed, according to a survey published in *Gazeta Wyborcza* on October 18, 2011, 71 percent of Poles were either opposed to the idea or were not bothered by the presence of the cross—most surprisingly, the same percentage of youth held this view, despite the fact that their cohort was the most supportive of that party. An even higher percentage of Poles supported the presence of crosses in hospitals, indicating that in some fields civil religion is almost fully accepted.

Civil religion is present in Poland in a more ritualistic manner than in the United States, for instance, excepting when they are sworn in office, politicians rarely make references to God or the Bible.[117] Religious rituals occur at many levels of Polish society, suturing popular religion with civil religion. For instance, a state university might have a religious ceremony at the opening of a newly constructed building, or a hypermarket might have the store blessed when it is opened, even though a number of courses taught in the new university building will have content critical of religion, while the hypermarket will likely be open on Sundays, depriving many of its employees of rest on that day. Not to mention that the cross on the wall of the Sejm, if it remains, will likely witness the passing of a number of laws that go against Church teaching.

One of the sensitive unresolved issues between the Catholic Church and the state concerns the restitution of property confiscated by the Communists during the Stalinist period. The Church lost over a hundred thousand hectares and several thousand buildings. To date it has only received or been compensated for somewhat over one-fifth of this property, according to religion reporter Ewa Czaczkowska (*Rzeczpospolita*, May 6, 2011). Nonetheless, the restitution has concerned an enormous amount of property, and cases of corruption were suspected in some instances. Moreover, related to the issue, shortly after Stalinism ended in 1955, a Church Fund was established that was ostensibly an act of compensation for the confiscated property. Among other things, it was to deal with matters such as covering insurance for priests and nuns. The institution largely remained a dead letter for most of the regime's subsequent rule, being reactivated just before the collapse of Communism. Essentially, the commission running the fund continues to support the Catholic Church as well several other denominations with matters such as insuring clerics—likewise from other denominations. Neither side is too happy with the fund; other financial arrangements are now being considered. In European practice, some sort of subsidy for major churches and religious organizations is practiced in most states, except, naturally, France.

The Church certainly has had a PR problem connected with its finances, largely on account of their lack of transparency. For instance, each parish gives an oral financial report once a year. And so practicing parishioners might have a relatively good idea of the financial state of their parish, but until recently few had any idea of the state of the Church as a whole. As late as 2011 during a public discussion of the topic, Grabowska put it this way: "Transparency in this sphere would greatly benefit the institution."[118] Indeed, in response to controversy over Church finances, a report was finally issued in February 2012.[119] Among other things, readers learned that the bulk of Church expenses are covered by offerings from parishioners, that is, from the less than 40 percent of Catholics who actually attend masses, and the sums are not very high. As one of the more evenhanded commentators summarized the report, the Church in Poland is neither particularly wealthy nor impoverished; moreover, each diocese reflects the economic condition of its parishioners, which varies considerably in different parts of the country.[120]

An overlap between church and state is in the subsidy of Catholic institutes of higher learning. The precedent was set by the Catholic University of Lublin—now renamed John Paul II Catholic University of Lublin—which, understandably, had been funded by the Church and other benefactors during Communism: the only private university in the entire socialist bloc. Under the radically different economic conditions of independent Poland, the university in Lublin could not survive long without a subsidy from the Ministry of Higher Education. Consequently for several years in the 1990s it systematically increased its student enrollment in order to qualify for a full subsidy, which was based on the size of the student body.[121] During the course of this process it faced the problem of maintaining its Catholic specificity, which it can be argued it does to this day, but to a substantial degree it hardly differs from a state university. There are more Catholic institutes of higher learning in Poland today, but the state has a strong grip on a number of them through funding, which at present hardly matters but might be decisive in the future. It should be added that the Polish Orthodox Church also has its seminary (Prawosławne Seminarium Duchowne) recognized and subsidized by the state, granting undergraduate degrees in theology, while the Christian Theological

Academy even offers postgraduate degrees in theology for the denominations that belong to the Polish Ecumenical Council.

Concurrently, faculties of theology were opened at a number of larger state universities. There was some debate among scholars concerning this, but generally the process proceeded without much hindrance. A rector of the University of Silesia during that period commented that the debate at his university finally forced the academic community to focus on something beyond economic and financial matters that absorbed them at that juncture.[122] The theology programs were necessary to prepare teachers for religious education programs that had been returned to the public schools. As we have seen in Chapter 2, religious education in Poland is confessional, with Catholicism being the main provider in public schools throughout the country, and the Christian Orthodox and Lutherans participating in some areas. This is not so unusual in Europe, where most countries provide some manner of religious education, and a confessional version exists in one form or another in over a dozen countries practically throughout the EU. It basically involves the religious communities preparing and confirming the educators as well as the program of studies for the students.[123] An ethics program is the primary alternative for students who opt out in Poland, and, especially in high school, there are an increasing number of such cases. The program is to be provided by the state, which has not been overly effective in carrying out its responsibility.[124]

Parents are generally happy with such a state of affairs, on account of, among other things, its convenience in their often hectic lives. However, almost since its inception, even within Church circles the religious education program has been a subject of criticism, with some of the voices claiming that from the catechetical and pastoral perspective it would be more effective to conduct it at the parishes as was the case during Communist times. At the very least, according to sociologist the Rev. Janusz Mariański, the system requires substantial revision to increase effectiveness (*Gazeta Wyborcza*, September 17–18, 2011). The youth themselves would generally like to see a greater emphasis on a broader knowledge of religion, including non–Catholic or even non–Christian faiths. Likewise worth noting is that the religious studies program augments the sexual education program in Polish schools which stresses sexual abstinence along with family values. Despite going against mainstream media and critics, according to data from surveys, among others, EUROSTAT or HIV/AIDS Surveillance in Europe, this approach has been surprisingly effective on a European scale, as witnessed by a low level of teenage pregnancies and STDs in the country—Poland has among the lowest number of HIV infections and AIDS victims per 100,000 residents in Europe[125]: this despite the fact that the disease has reached near epidemic proportions in some post–Communist countries, such as Ukraine and Russia. No doubt other societal factors play a role—Poles are hardly prudish, or particularly cautious for that matter, so religion likely has some moderating impact.

A major aspect of the Church's presence in the Polish public sphere is through its mission of presenting Catholic teaching and applying it to the best of its abilities to local situations and problems. A major concern in Poland after the collapse of the Communist regime was dealing with the historical memory of the injustice that Polish society had inflicted upon the church. Surprisingly, the Church did not lobby for a truth commission to deal with the Communist past, nor did one come about in Poland. Some critics in the country could consign this to the institutional Church not wishing to bring inordinate attention to fact that there were instances of collaboration with the regime on the part of the hierarchy and priests, but the authors of *God's Century* suggest a different reason in light of the overall stellar engagement of the Church in that period: "During the Cold War, human rights, democracy, and ecclesial autonomy dominated the Polish Catholic Church's thinking, giving it strong conceptual resources to oppose the Communist regime but leaving it with little robust thinking about justice in its aftermath—a political theology of reconciliation, for instance."[126]

When one considers the moral issues facing the contemporary society that Poland has become, for a time a surprising level of inaction characterized the Polish hierarchy. Following entry into the European Union, for instance, the Church in Poland—compared to, say, bishops in the United States—was actually rather lenient with Catholic politicians who presented legislative proposals that were essentially against its teaching; for example, communion was not withheld from such politicians by any of the bishops, nor was the Church particularly supportive of attempts to come up with legislation that attempted to approach Catholic teaching in matters such as in vitro. From mid–2011 on, however, the public voice of the Church has become less passive, at least in moral issues. One matter that the bishops could not ignore in that year was a grassroots petition by lay Catholic groups to increase the restrictions with regard to permitted abortions in the country. Six hundred thousand signatures were gathered, many of them from young Poles. Legally the Sejm then had to consider the petition: it was rejected, but the bishops gave it their support. Despite the failure of the enterprise, a point was made. As it has been put by one pundit, "The pro-abortion groups are against the existing legislation. Thus it is only possible to maintain it by showing that for us [Catholics] it is also a difficult compromise, and that we would really want to go further."[127] The right-to-life movement is growing in the country, with annual marches taking place in ever more cities and with increasing numbers of participants. In this matter Poles lead Europe, claims one social psychologist.[128]

Moral issues inspire Polish Catholics at the grassroots level to a greater extent than other social issues. If the Church also enunciates moral issues more clearly at present, it has yet to attain sufficient force in addressing social issues, which under the guidance of Wyszyński and Wojtyła were largely present, and which are also essential to its teaching on human dignity. Two decades past the fall of Communism, Wiesław Chrzanowski, one of the country's prominent Catholic social and political thinkers, complained, "It is astounding that after so many of John Paul II's documents on the topic of Catholic social thought that the problem has virtually disappeared from the concern of the Polish Church."[129] In his book of 2010, *Recovering Solidarity: Lessons from Poland's Unfinished Revolution*, Gerald Beyer analyzes the problem in depth. Acknowledging the exemplary work of Church agencies such as Caritas, he points out it is Church social documents which constitute an important tool in educating public opinion concerning social problems and they have not been utilized effectively by Polish bishops. Beyer contrasts the "nice generalities" that prevail in the major social documents authored by the Polish bishops after 1989 with the detailed policy analysis that a number of bishops' conferences throughout the world have produced, such as the conferences of the United States, Canada and the Philippines, among others. This, he claims, partially stems from ambivalence about the importance of social justice for evangelization on the part of Polish bishops. The issue is especially pertinent on account of burning issues such as severe child poverty that plague Polish society, which he extensively documents.[130] There are exceptions on the part of individual bishops, such as the case of Archbishop Damian of Silesia, who early in 2001 produced a detailed pastoral letter on unemployment in the region and offered some concrete policy suggestions. Beyer recommends, among other things, that Polish bishops take the role of lay experts and lobbyists seriously, in the manner of the American bishops: "This would fit within the parameters of the 'cooperation for the good of the human person and the common good' called for by the Constitution and the Concordat between the Holy See and the Republic of Poland."[131]

Voices raising issues such as poverty in Polish society and insisting that the Church must be more responsive can be found among the younger generation of Catholics. For instance, editors of the quarterly *Kontakt* acknowledge the institution's engagement in many charities, but add, "The contemporary world expects more systemic solutions on the part of the Church. Charitable work is not enough. Their frequently structural character demands solutions going beyond the often hopeless attempts of healing individual symptoms."[132] Unlike in the case of more easily identifiable moral issues that gain grassroots support, however, these largely isolated Catholic voices are unlikely to stir the hierarchy by themselves. Still, it may be that the Church hierarchy is becoming more sensitive to its social mission. In the three-year pastoral program the bishops announced in November 2010, there is the postulate to create social councils in all the dioceses similar to the ones existing in several of them at present, which would draw upon lay experts.[133] Their latest social pastoral letter *W trosce o człowieka i dobro wspólne* [In Concern for People and the Common Good], published in March 2012, is intended as a summary of the Polish transformation after 1989 and thus touches on so many matters that it is indeed relatively general. Nevertheless, a number of specific social problems afflicting Polish society are laid out, among others the high unemployment among the young, including those with university degrees, or the high number of Poles who feel compelled to work abroad. Some practical solutions are also proffered, such as—in the case of the educated unemployed—adapting post-secondary education to the needs of the employment market.[134] Moreover, it remains to be seen how the newly elected Pope Francis will affect the overall stance of the Church in Poland toward this crucial issue, which for the pontiff is of seminal importance. One clue might be that in the first major diocese vacated through the retirement of an archbishop, the new pope selected a candidate known for his sensitivity toward social issues.

One of the complaints that concerned Catholics of various stripes voice is that there is no outstanding leader in the Church. In contrast, the Rev. Adam Boniecki, former editor in chief of *Tygodnik Powszechny*, avers that under the new circumstances it is fortunately no longer necessary for someone exceptional to be the head of the Church: "We now have normal times, bishops direct their dioceses, each of them is subordinate to the Pope, and there is a Conference of Bishops. We live in an era that values the collegiality of the Church and the Conference is an example of this."[135] However, Fr. Maciej Zięba counters that a great problem among the leadership of the Church is the lack of a clear overarching pastoral vision of how to meet contemporary challenges facing Polish society: "There is no evangelical diagnosis of reality that manages to weld tradition with modernity, as John Paul II provided for years."[136] He argues that the bishops are primarily concerned with strengthening the Church at the institutional level. Among the consequences of this narrow focus is the tendency to reduce the surrounding reality to polarized schemas. In part, Zięba's point might be illustrated by an example of the Church leadership's vision: in an interview discussing the state of the Church, the current president of the Conference of Bishops, Archbishop Michalik, proclaimed in all seriousness, "Folk religion is an expression of respect for every person. It is the future of the Church."[137] For all its undoubted merits, folk religion can hardly offer a solution to the pastoral problems of today's Poland. We can also recall here Bishop Czaja's assessment quoted in Chapter 2, that the Church is hampered by an "apologetic and polemical vision, [which is] not very proactive." The alleged crisis of vision is one of the factors contributing to Fr. Zięba's pessimism about the long-term future of the Church in Poland. The debate on leadership and vision is much needed and ongoing, although it rarely receives greater attention in the media.

To appreciate the challenges the Church faces in developing any effective pastoral vision that extends to its presence in the public sphere it is worth briefly considering who might these Catholics be that it should be attempting to reach? Given their numbers, naturally the faithful do not form a uniform body. To get a better understanding of this matter, we might start with the findings of the respected sociologist Irena Borowik, who divides the roughly 95 percent of Polish society that declares themselves to be Catholic into three groups of believers, and from how she presents it, a different Church resonates for each them. There is a sizeable group of fervent Catholics, constituting roughly 15 to 20 percent, but the majority of believers (from 60 to 70 percent) are nonreflective in their faith, and their religiosity is largely based on tradition. A substantial group also tends toward an indifferent attitude to their faith, not following Church teaching to any particular extent, but nevertheless accepting religious rituals of transition, such as Church marriages. Borowik's categories are not the only ones that have been proposed, but most sociologists agree on the existence of a number of categories of faithful in the country, and hers can serve as a point of departure for discussing what attitudes Catholics hold toward their faith community.

Thus, if for the sake of argument we accept Borowik's categorization, it is for the rather large middle group she further claims that a somewhat lackluster Conference of Bishops is suitable, since its members are actually put off by "religious virtuosity." Such a status quo approach, annoying as it might seem for dedicated Catholics, argues Borowik, is particularly appropriate in a period of transition:

> For centuries the Church in Poland played an essential substitute role in society—at a cultural and political level. It was a guarantor of stability, a mediator, it mobilized civil society. And now, in the conditions of traumatic [social and economic] transformation, it is just as functional [in this role] as in the past. Thus no rapid change will occur overnight.[138]

One might add that on a number of levels a degree of uncertainty is affecting much of the European Union at present, so the "transition period" might be extended beyond optimistic expectations.

Regarding the first group of fervent Catholics, despite its size which impresses sociologists, since the majority of believers have a more casual attitude to their faith, it is understandable why the more involved Catholics not infrequently voice complaints along the lines of, "The greatest danger for the future of Polish Catholicism is the superficiality of many nominal Catholics."[139]

Moreover, one can be struck by its size on the one hand and on the other by its relative lack of participation in the Church renewal groups and organizations that were mentioned earlier. Nevertheless, lay involvement in dynamic campaigns such as the right-to-life movement likely comes predominantly from their ranks and suggests that when issues touch these Catholics deeply, they can be readily mobilized for various causes. One might further ask how they mark their presence in society. At the level of visual culture the fervent Catholics who do not identify with folk religion have few means to demonstrate their faith in the public sphere, although new "signs" have appeared. One of the symbols that Fr. Góra introduced during the Lednica 2000 is a gigantic fish-shaped gate, an obvious Christian symbol, which the participants walk through. More or less at the same time, the Ichthys, or Christian fish symbol, started to appear on the back of cars in the country. If folk religion is demonstrated by drivers with rosaries hanging from rearview mirrors or St. Christopher figures on the dashboard, still common enough in Poland, the fish sticker on the car is a more conscious symbol of a witnessing Christian— significantly, unlike the former, it is on the outside of the car for everyone to see. This even stops some interested Catholics from placing the symbol on their cars, since they feel they might not live up to the good driving practices that should accompany its presence.[140]

Regarding the third group of believers that Borowik categorized, significantly, the interview in which she presented her research—in 2011—took place before the elections which ushered in the anticlerical party. It seems that a considerable number of its supporters likely came from the third "indifferent" group; thus their indifference must be qualified, to say the least, but it is difficult to gauge the importance of such a vote on their part. A possible explanation concerning the attitudes of the third group or its equivalent might be what sociologist the Reverend Mariański calls the individuation of belief taking place within Polish society, especially among the young. This is characterized by a selective approach to the Catholic faith that stresses religious experience over doctrine and has an ambivalent attitude toward the institution of the Church at best, and thus anticlericalism and a degree of Catholic identification are not incompatible.

Like Fr. Zięba, the Reverend Mariański argues that the Church needs an effective pastoral program, especially for such groups as the one above. He admits that developing an effective pastoral program is extremely difficult. If the Church is too rigorous it risks frightening away such adherents and turning Catholicism into a minority religion; conversely, abandoning any demands and forwarding religion primarily as a vague source of deeper meaning in life risks distorting the essence of the Church's message. Some combination of both approaches is necessary, but this means walking a fine line. Mariański recommends a realistic attitude on the part of the Church, which must "accept that it has to deal with [Polish] Catholics as they actually are, and not any others, and concentrate on pastoral work."[141]

Given the combination of the distinct nature of Catholic social teaching, the institution's status in the country, as well a number of groups that wish to manipulate the Church's authority, it is hardly surprising that there have been no lack of complicated and contested issues connected with the public presence of religion in Poland since it entered the European Union, sometimes including outright culture wars. Only a sample of the controversies of religion in the public sphere will be catalogued here, as well as an attempt to pinpoint the factors that govern how the Church is perceived by the faithful.

Few events have marked themselves deeper than developments in Polish society after the Smoleńsk tragedy of 2010. The institutional Church itself had little control over matters that concerned it deeply. This was demonstrated in the War of the Crosses, briefly introduced in the historical outline, that led to the so-called Smoleńsk heresy, which we will now discuss at some length. To reiterate the main events, when a spontaneous group established itself to prevent the cross that had been set up in front of the presidential palace in Warsaw during the initial period of mourning after the tragedy from being moved, the losing presidential candidate from the Law and Justice Party sided with the group. For months he led a march after the evening mass on the tenth of each month—the day of the airline catastrophe—up to the group "defending" the cross. Even presidential negotiations with the archbishop of Warsaw who agreed on the transfer of the cross from in front of the palace to a nearby church did not convince the defenders. The delegation of priests sent by the archbishop to conduct the cross to the site was snubbed by the group and disobeyed. Eventually, on September 16, presidential security forces clandestinely transferred the cross to the church agreed upon earlier.

This was hardly the end of the affair. Contributing to the bad atmosphere, among other things, the government mishandled the matter of the investigation of the causes that lead up to the tragedy, initially allowing the Russians virtually total freedom to investigate the disaster, which ended in an insulting report quite critical of the Polish side. Nor have the results been particularly conclusive when the Polish government took the investigation into its own hands. In the long run this has led to an intermittent series of public protests, not to mention conspiracy theories and much rancor on both sides. In the short term, grassroots support for the protesting group was also evident in many churches, for instance at Easter time, when the traditional tomb of Christ displays would be decorated with a model of the airliner that crashed in Smoleńsk. Thus elements of folk religion with its love of spectacle were incorporated in the protest.

The primary forces in Polish society were divided. As mentioned, a major anticlerical demonstration occurred while the original protest lasted, and eventually an anticlerical party emerged and successfully—almost triumphantly—entered the Polish Sejm. The Solidarity Trade Union sided with the "defenders" and subsequent protestors, among others promising to disrupt the official celebrations of the thirtieth anniversary of the August agreement that led to the legalizing of the original Solidarity Trade Union in 1980. The government decided to hold the main event in Kraków, while the Law and Justice Party led a counter-celebration in Gdańsk. For a period, there effectively existed a parallel civil religion in the country, with the president and the government presiding over official events, while the Law and Justice Party led parallel events. Occasionally this remains the case, for instance during the anniversaries of the disaster. At any rate, for a time the conflict negatively affected the support for the institutional Church, which dropped approximately 10 percent to about half of Polish society.[142]

The Church hierarchy itself was somewhat ambivalent about the War of the Crosses. On the one hand, there was the awareness that the nationalistic cult of the defenders was getting out of control and dividing Polish Catholics; on the other hand, on account of the anticlerical backlash, some bishops sided with the defenders. In the first camp, Cardinal Dziwisz of Kraków at one point in reference to some of the heated rhetoric reminded the defenders that "one can only speak of martyrs [referring to the victims of the airline disaster] with reference to people that died to defend their faith."[143] Toward the end of the affair the Conference of Bishops finally put their foot down, calling on the faithful "to stop treating the cross as a tool in political disputes." Porter-Szücs evaluates their frustrated effort: "After a summer of explicit engagement by so many priests and bishops, the highest Church leadership tried to put the genie of partisan engagement back into the bottle. In part they were motivated by fear of a backlash, in part by a recognition that a line had been crossed."[144]

A year after the event, after the smoke had partially cleared, a journalist who coined the phrase "Smoleńsk heresy" argued that Polish bishops were basically lenient with the excesses of the cult, still in evidence then, because they recognized that genuine religious feeling had been tapped in a part of society. "A hard-handed approach to the Smoleńsk religion would weaken religion in Poland as a whole," claimed Cezary Michalski in the Polish edition of *Newsweek*, concluding, "This is what the bishops think and they are likely right."[145] Although the Church temporarily suffered a substantial loss of public support on account of the crisis, under the circumstances it is difficult to say what the bishops could have actually done to assuage matters for all parties concerned, and they could easily have made them worse. Michalski also felt the bishops were playing a waiting game with the cult, hoping that temperatures would cool down. The "Smoleńsk religion" is a quasi-permanent feature of Polish Catholicism at the time of writing: it goes through cooler periods and then flares up on occasion; after the last general elections the question of anticlericalism has also come to the fore. The overall approach of the bishops outlined by Michalski seems to have been successful enough that public support for the Church has largely rebounded to about 60 percent positive.

The necessity of treading a fine line by the Church in the public sphere is evident in dealings with anticlerical excesses intermittently occurring in Polish society. For instance, the forceful reaction of the Church and some of its members in response to provocative events such as a pop star's ripping up a Bible onstage was considered unnecessarily strong on the part of some and was interpreted as a sign of weakness.[146] Similarly, according to Józef Baniak, a prominent sociologist of religion, anticlericalism in Poland is simply not that strong, and so the Church should not overreact to it.[147] To the extent that the authors have a point, it is also likely the case that no response to such incidents or the trend they represent would be just as inappropriate. The provocative warning of former archbishop of Canterbury Lord Carey of Clifton that if Christians act as doormats they can be expected to be treated as such bears a degree of validity in present-day Poland as well. From this perspective the protest voiced by the Polish Conference of Bishops in the social pastoral letter of 2012 in response to the growing anticlericalism in Polish politics cannot be seen as overly assertive (as some Polish pundits have claimed): "We are ... worried about the accelerating attacks on the Church in order to make political gains. We strongly protest ridiculing the Church, its moral teachings and actions, unfairly accusing these actions of being unethical. The spread of anticlericalism is disturbing and harmful."[148]

At a more banal level but affecting a much larger portion of the population was the question of shopping on Sundays. The Catholic Church confronted the rising consumer society in Poland at this juncture and clearly lost. For its part, the Church argued about the nature of Sunday for Catholics and the exploitation of many workers who lose a day of rest. Polish Catholics were rather unconcerned with politically correct arguments about the fact that not everyone in society is Catholic (although many who are not Catholic are nonetheless Christian), but simply could not refrain from shopping, and the politicians accepted this. For some Poles, with their hectic schedules, Sunday is one of the few days they can do this task. For others, it was simply a pleasant activity. In this regard the Reverend Draguła points out, "It must be accepted [by the Church] that shopping, also on Sunday (or rather—on account of the free time—primarily on Sunday), is a form of entertainment for many people, what is more—a community-building form of entertainment, likewise integrating the family."[149] A small but significant concession the Church gained has been that the shopping malls are now closed on national holidays, a number of which are also religious holidays. Moreover, if the Church is learning that it cannot sway legislature, it is recovering its emphasis on persuasion as a means of educating public opinion. The last Sunday of 2012 the bishops released a pastoral letter devoted to the family, which included the statement positively noted by the media: "Today, when work has become a mere commodity, and the economy seems to reign over all aspects of life, the need to recover the sense of Sunday as a holiday is all the more urgent." Some satisfaction has also been noted in certain Church circles that in contrast to some European countries where cultural Catholicism exists in the form of shopping centers being closed on Sundays but believers rarely attending religious services, in Poland a happy hybrid exists in which Poles usually attend church first and then go to the shopping centers.[150]

On the whole the Church's relations with municipal and other local authorities are good, indeed better than with the central authorities. Nevertheless, glitches also arise in the domain of local politics under certain circumstances and in particular cities. In Kraków, for instance, for a number of years a left-wing mayor did not wish to highlight the religious heritage of the city, and so did not improve the roads to growing pilgrimage centers, such as to the World Center of Veneration of the Image of the Divine Mercy in nearby Łagiewniki. This despite the fact that, as the expert Antoni Jackowski has explained, as a rule religious tourism does not decline in times of economic recession; that is, it would simply be a good investment (*Gazeta Wyborcza*, August 2011). Similar tensions arise in Częstochowa, where after years of electing local politicians that were close to the Church, the citizens of the city felt left out and several years ago finally elected a leftist mayor. Sparks have been flying since.

At the very least, the above situations along with other similar ones indicate two matters. For one thing, how the Church communicates is almost as important as what it communicates; for another, on top of traditional ongoing concerns, the Church in Poland faces a number of new ones it must contend with for its voice in the public sphere to remain effective. Concerning the first matter, a Catholic public relations expert has argued that the role of the Church in Polish society unavoidably exposes it to occasional crises and that it must develop an efficient manner of confronting them.[151] The situation after the Smoleńsk catastrophe bred a number of crises, and it was evident the Church had some way to go in "being prepared" for events. Moreover, after the War of the Crosses, for an extended period the Catholic Church was constantly in the media. Reflecting on the period, a popular television anchorman complained that it was difficult to get more prominent bishops into the television studio, and added, "Church matters are routinely commented upon by five priests or journalists from this or that Catholic journal. Such is the voice of the Church in the Polish media."[152] Indirectly the head of the Catholic Information Agency admitted as much when he advised Catholic leaders to not avoid informing the media on difficult topics and to do so in a clear manner without lofty language: "The fact that the media present the Church in a peculiar manner, often focusing on sensational matters and with a particular bias is no excuse. Perhaps they write the way they do because of the attitudes they meet with when dealing with representatives of the Church?"[153]

In reference to the anchorman's observation, for anyone observing the mainstream media after 2010 it does seem that only a few priests and almost no bishops have been commenting on serious problems pertaining to the Church with any regularity. And the response of the Congregation of Marian Fathers in the late fall of 2011 to their member Fr. Adam Boniecki, a priest who had been asked by John Paul II to be the editor of the first Polish edition of *L'Osservatore Romano*, to refrain from speaking on television, was hardly encouraging for more of them to do so. Among others, Fr. Boniecki had commented on the debate concerning the possible removal of the cross from the walls of the Sejm that year, claiming that both sides had valid arguments. Archbishop Henryk Muszyński was one of the rare bishops who sided with him, suggesting that there is a lack of balance in Church circles between the treatment of the so-called open Catholics and the closed ones, a clear allusion to the freedom with which Fr. Rydzyk of Radio Maryja could say what he pleased without censure by his order.

Nevertheless, the image of the Church the media construct in their presentation of the institution can be selective or even stilted. For instance, Eugeniusz Sakowicz, a lay expert for the Polish Conference of Bishops, notes that in his experience extending over a number of years the media in Poland are virtually uninterested in the Catholic Church's involvement in the crucial field of interreligious dialogue.[154] However, a litmus case is the presentation of Radio Maryja. Sociologist Ireneusz Krzemiński, who points out that the station engenders elements of an unhealthy sect within the Polish Church based on the charisma of its leader, observes that in their charges that Radio Maryja uniformly propagates xenophobia and anti–Semitism, the station's critics tend to exaggerate. "Firstly," argues Krzemiński, "despite a very clear model of religion and the worldview that is presented, which unequivocally connects the Radio and its listeners with particular political actors, it can be proved that the Radio's broadcasts are not limited to these contents and an astute listener can find contents not in accordance with this preferred model."[155] The sociologist notes that despite the invectives that the liberal *Gazeta Wyborcza* and Radio Maryja hurl at each other, "[a] common characteristic [for both media] is a clear black-and-white schema of the reality they present."[156] To what degree or even whether either Radio Maryja or *Gazeta Wyborcza* can be described as Manichean is debatable; nevertheless they can accurately be viewed as the sites where the barricades of Poland's culture war are clearest, and from which the volleys at opponents are mainly issued, although a number of other periodicals and journals participate in the struggle on both sides.

The case of Radio Maryja does not mean that the media only present the negative side of religion. For instance, during John Paul II's last days in April 2005, the media focused all its attention on the event and played an important role in the national mourning, one might say no less than the Church. A Catholic journalist points out that this attention was extended through the creation of the "John Paul II Generation," in no small measure as a media brand.[157] As a media brand, however, it more or less shared the duration of such a product and after a few years largely ceased to exist. One might also add that the media generally participate in the civil religion by presenting the news concerning religious holidays—especially television broadcasts—in a positive to neutral manner. This includes the major holidays of non–Catholics, particularly the largest group, the Orthodox Christians, with their different liturgical calendar.

One additional source of distortion results from the media's penchant for sharp contrasts. Televised debates drawing upon members of assertive evangelical Catholics in opposition to anticlerical voices generate more excitement than those between moderate Catholics and reasonable members of the secular elite, so the latter are less frequently seen together. Summarizing the media picture of religion, University of Warsaw sociologist Tomasz Żukowski claims in an interview with Ewa Czaczkowska that voices critical of the Church are overrepresented (*Rzeczpospolita*, April 6, 2012), which seems an accurate opinion. However, one might argue that in part the distrust that Poles seem to have for the media serves the Church well enough, since the negative image projected of the institution by and large does not affect the trust that the public generally holds toward it. What seems to support this interpretation is that surveys over the past several years indicate that a growing portion of the public feels the media are anticlerical. Thus to no small extent the image presented tends to reinforce negative stereotypes of the Church for those who are already critical of it while increasing the sense of a hostile secular atmosphere encompassing them for many faithful.

It should be mentioned the Catholic Church has its own media: everything from periodicals to popular Internet sites—Opoka.org is among the more popular Internet sites in the country. Research conducted in 2011 found that roughly eight hundred thousand Poles regularly visited the more popular Internet sites dealing with religious topics, while several million visited them intermittently. Moreover, approximately 40 percent of the parishes had their own Internet sites.[158] A number of weekly periodicals are published by dioceses; among them the well-edited *Gość Niedzielny* can compete with the top secular weeklies in terms of the size of its readership. There is currently no official Catholic daily newspaper recognized as such by the Church hierarchy, but Radio Maryja publishes its own daily, *Nasz Dziennik*. The radio station also runs the oldest continuously broadcast national religious television channel, the above-mentioned Telewizja Trwam, which it established in 2003. Engaged Catholics take advantage of opportunities such as Internet television to create low-budget stations, such as Boska.tv. All of these media are not without meaning, but they do not resonate in Polish society to the extent that the secular media do.

The divisions within the Church discussed earlier are likewise evident within its media, especially within the Catholic groups that are not directly connected with the institutional Church. Furthermore, much as with the secular press, religious periodicals and other media must compete for the reader or viewer, whose needs change, and tradition is no guarantee of success. There is the case of the Jesuit *Przegląd Powsechny* (Universal Overview), an elite monthly that had been published for over a century—not counting a hiatus during the war and early Communist period—and was essentially the oldest periodical in Poland when it went bankrupt in 2012; in contrast the Dominican monthly *W Drodze* (The Way) faced the same declining readership over the same period when it relied on intellectual Catholic readers but changed its focus to pastoral issues, where the order's strength lay, and its readership more than tripled in several years.

Returning to the question of public relations brought up at the beginning of this discussion of the media, one important means for diminishing the impact of stereotypes concerning the Church is providing the public with more information on difficult topics. Slowly the institution is becoming aware of the importance of this aspect of PR. The case of the belated report on the financial situation of the Church was mentioned earlier. In a similar vein, toward the end of 2012 the Catholic Information Agency published a collection of mini-reports in the volume *Kościół. Stereotypy, uprzedzenia, manipulacji* (The Church: Stereotypes, Biases, and Manipulations),[159] in which a number of stereotypes concerning the Church are countered with fairly concrete information about the Church in Poland and beyond. These reports include the relationship of the Church to the state, the institution's finances, religious education in schools, pedophilia among priests, and a number of other hot-button issues. The responses are brief but include literature for further study. Such a general response does not solve the issue of information and a number of the answers are open to criticism, but it demonstrates a greater awareness on the part of the Church in its policy on informing the Polish public. Another problem is the resonance of such a document, since it was not widely covered in the press.

From the above—persistent stereotypes on the one hand, fairly high trust on the other—the question also arises of whether the Church hierarchy has been reasonably successful overall in relating to its enormous faith community. One must cautiously answer in the affirmative, but in the context of the dynamic nature of the situation, the Reverend Mariański's warning to the bishops that they must avoid giving Poles excuses to accept anticlerical charges is quite valid. Although respect for the hierarchical Church remains relatively high, the sociologist maintains that an Irish scenario where a major breakdown of trust in the institution takes place is still conceivable.[160]

Turning now to the fundamental problems that continue to concern religion in Poland in the public sphere, few are more constant than that of religion and national identity. It is worth first examining the nonreligious context of "Polishness" in a broader context. To an overwhelming extent contemporary Poland is an ethnic nationalist state and has been one since the conclusion of World War II. Although the historical circumstances for this fact are particular to Poland, and—it must be noted—within this ethnic unity itself there is considerable difference,[161] it is rather a typical state of affairs in contemporary Europe, where, as political philosopher Jerry Muller observes, only a few states are of a different category. Since ethnic nationalist states in Central Europe have had an ambivalent history to say the least, Muller makes a counterintuitive observation based on the overall evidence: "Liberal democracy and ethnic homogeneity are not only compatible; they can be complementary."[162] He concludes his account of the issue claiming that ethnonationalism "corresponds to some enduring propensities of the human spirit that are heightened by the process of modern state creation, it is a crucial source of both solidarity and enmity, and in one form or another, it will remain for many generations to come."[163] Both the "solidarity"—quite striking in the 1980s—and "enmity" that accompany the ethnic nation are evidenced in Poland's past and recent history. The role of religion, so closely intertwined with Polish ethnicity, is likewise ambivalent at times in this process. For instance, Porter-Szücs further observes that "a large majority of Polish Catholics find Radio Maryja distasteful or even repugnant, yet it has at least as much claim on the Catholic tradition as its opponents."[164] The recent War of the Crosses of 2010 which can be mapped on this divide provides an obvious example of the enmity that arises when an "us" and "them" situation is created, with both sides contributing to the resultant ill will.

Albeit divisive events occur, the situation is nevertheless fluid, and changes of attitude are possible for different groups over time or under new circumstances. For instance, with the comparatively more widespread support that Radio Maryja has gained from the struggle to attain better airwave access for Telewizja Trwam in 2012, reportedly the tone of the broadcasts has mellowed somewhat to accommodate the new broader base of listeners. If the trend is genuine and continues, it would not be the first instance of a relatively radical group softening somewhat over time.

In his meticulously researched and evenhanded treatment of religion and national identity, Porter-Szücs observes that, although extremists exist, "fewer and fewer people would say today that someone must be Catholic in order to be Polish, or that Poles must rally round the Church in order to preserve their national existence. Nonetheless, the legacy of the Polak-Katolik [Catholic equals Pole] lingers on."[165] One might add that the fervor of the nationalistic group garners such a disproportionate share of attention that it gives the impression of a much larger group than on closer examination seems to be the case: by one estimate perhaps one and a half to two million members of the roughly thirty million Catholics in the country fall into this category[166]—not a negligible number, but hardly a dominant group. One can add that according to Grzegorz Ryś, the auxiliary bishop of Kraków, the core of the Catholic Church in the country quietly forwards an evangelical religious humanism, with roots in the Second Vatican Council and Karol Wojtyła's teaching,[167] in other words by an affirmative orthodoxy.

From this evangelical perspective, both Polishness and Christian identity pose a challenge rather simply being an unreflective marker of identity, and this opens them to Poles of different worldviews. Bishop Ryś sees the formative questions posed to each and every Pole under the new circumstances: "What kind of people does our 'Polishness' make of us? What kind of people does our Christianity make of us? Our different faith community? Our atheism? All other 'factors?' ... Which of these factors is of ultimate importance for us? ... What transformations do they undergo in us through their mutual interactions: in us and in the world we create around ourselves?"[168] From this perspective both Polishness and Catholicism are open-ended projects that contribute to the common good at different levels and accept contributions from various parties. It is likely from this perspective focused on the person and his or her development that religion in Poland contributes to the different aspects of civil society we examined in Chapter 3.

A rather substantial sphere where perhaps a greater degree of agreement exists in Polish society, also with qualifications, is in what might broadly be termed the civil religion in the country. Observing the demoralization of post–Communist countries, an American political observer argued that civil religion can play a substantial role in creating the values that keep a culture together in East Central Europe: "These shared values can contribute to shaping national identity rather than having national identity shaped by ethnicity and nationality."[169] Evident here is the common academic prejudice against ethnicity and nationality that Muller contests, but the opinion that civil religion can largely transcend these elements when it is necessary to create a common good bears a good deal of validity in the Polish context.

In a free and democratic country as Poland is now, civil religion is not a proposal but a fact, although not clearly defined and rather polyvalent. Much as in the United States where the term originated, in Poland the phenomenon is rather one derived from custom—albeit of fairly recent pedigree—and practice as opposed to being formally institutionalized. It is one of the junctures at which religion connects to national identity in the broadest possible public sphere. We can repeat Hosking's opinion again where he argues that religion involves trust because it "expresses in symbolic and ritual form the norms and values to which members of the society attribute the highest importance." Civil religion builds public trust in Poland because it tacitly acknowledges the Catholic Church as the primary repository of symbols and values in the country's society.

Some of the forms of civil religion were described earlier. Other forms exist, although it is difficult to gauge the actual impact of any of the forms on society, since it does not work in isolation from other factors. For instance, often enough schools send children to attend masses, for instance, at the opening and closing of the school year, during which time the priests stress the importance of education. It can be added in this context that morale at Polish schools is rather high, as evidenced by the fact that the country has one of the lowest high school dropout rates in Europe. At least to some extent this can be attributed to the support that the most important agents in society attribute to education, such as the Church and other faith communities.

Poland is a pluralistic society, and if the symbols and values of civil religion seem to be supported by a fairly broad consensus, it naturally does not mean they are no longer uncontested. More frequently still, as evidence given above suggests, similarly with other parts of Europe, "[g]eneralized Catholic symbols provide a collective memory but are no longer directly linked to predictable social actions."[170] Civil religion can also be manipulated, or become ambivalent at times, like when a competing civil religion arises, which was described earlier, and in Poland is not all that rare. And, obviously, some Poles do feel excluded by its largely Catholic nature. One might add that sufficient venues exist where they can vent their disapproval, and there are those groups that certainly do. What is perhaps most important, however, civil religion is largely organic and has evolved in a natural manner from the role that the Church has played and continues to play in Polish civil society. To claim that it could be constructed, as suggested above, without recourse to existent religions so that all the different groups in society can feel included is—at least in Poland—unrealistic[171]: such a civil religion would have the faux universality of an artificial language and likely the same usefulness. For instance, one could not imagine the construction of a "National Cathedral" in Poland as one has in the United States. Although, in its present state, confusion might occur over where state funerals should be held, as was the case with the tragically deceased President Kaczyński, when a national prayer service for the president and the victims of the airline disaster was held in Warsaw, and a separate funeral for the president and his wife was held at Wawel Cathedral in Kraków—the latter actually quite a divisive event.

To state the obvious, civil religion is not the same as a historic transcendental religion and is no substitute for it. The Reverend Draguła captures the threat of reductionism at times implicit in the attitude toward symbols of civil religion in the case of parallel legal decisions in 2011 allowing crosses to remain on classroom walls in Italy and the cross in the Polish Sejm, where cultural arguments largely took the fore: "Should we express our joy ... that the cross hangs in these places in reality as a cultural sign? Should we be satisfied with this state of affairs? Perhaps instead of our victory it is our defeat?"[172] Put in theological terms, one can say civil religion has no salvific value. On the other hand, some recognize that transcendental religion has a place in civil religion, since the faithful themselves have a valid place in the public sphere. One of the constitutional experts consulted by the government in the case of the cross on the wall of the Sejm raised the point that "there exists a collective freedom of religion, which includes the right of every religious community on a given territory to determine what place its religion and symbols will occupy in public life."[173] In the context of the controversy he was arguing against the reduction of religious symbols in public buildings to mere cultural artifacts when in fact they have religious meaning for most Poles. Whatever public statements are issued, at the level of lived religion this reality cannot be denied.

The relationship between genuine religion and civil religion might better be seen as, in the best instances, dialogic. At one level, when civil religion is in dialogue with a lived religion it adds to social trust by implicitly acknowledging that the values undergirding a community's culture do not spring out of a vacuum—that is, they are not a construct. It can be added that in Poland, at least, transcendental religion hardly needs the civil religion, but the reverse is not the case. Moreover, although for obvious reasons the Catholic Church has a virtual monopoly as a source of civil religion and some of its rituals in the country, civil religion in Poland is flexible enough to include other denominations and religions when the situation warrants it, as in the case of the public prayer service for the ninety-six victims of the Smoleńsk catastrophe, which involved the Orthodox and Lutheran churches alongside the Roman Catholic Church. Conversely, public officials sometimes appear at non–Catholic celebrations; for example, the late President Kaczyński publicly lit a Hanukkah candle to honor the Jewish community. At the municipal level, the participation of civic authorities in Przemyśl in the Jordan ceremonies of the Ukrainian Greek Catholics described earlier is an example of such openness. It might be appropriate to talk of civil religion as a covenant—in the best traditions of the term[174]—joining the constructive forces in Polish civil society, both religious and secular. The covenant in Poland has been formulated in the part of the preamble cited earlier in this section pertaining to "all citizens of the Republic, both those who believe in God as the source of truth, justice, good and beauty, as well as those not sharing such faith but respecting those universal values as arising from other sources, equal in rights and obligations towards the common good."

Jerry Muller further makes the observation that the success of ethnonationalism in Europe has largely sapped it of its own emotional power. "Many Europeans are now prepared, and even eager," he notes, "to partici-pate in transnational frameworks such as the EU, in part because they perceived that the need for collective self-determination has largely been satisfied."[175] All things considered, it is remarkable how quickly Poles have reached this stage after having regained self-determination upon the collapse of the Communist regime for an extremely brief historical period. Concerns about relinquishing a certain degree of sovereignty to a political institution with doubtful democratic procedures were not unfounded, but they are not a matter for this analysis.[176] Moreover, Europe's faltering in the wake of the recent wave of crises has surprised some. At any rate the question marks concerning the European project as the recession of the past several years continues at the time of writing in both Poland and the remaining countries of the Continent do not undermine the magnitude of the sea change of attitudes that went into undertaking the project in the first place. In a 2012 issue of *The American Interest*, Paweł Świeboda evaluates the current stance: "Poland is not daunted by its partners' moment of weakness. It still believes strongly in the continued relevance of the West, but it does so without waxing romantic about it and without neglecting to hedge its risks and look after its own interest."[177]

As for the Polish Church itself, as a transnational institution it is involved with other European churches through bodies such the Commission of the Bishops' Conferences of the European Community that is engaged in monitoring European policy. At the time of writing, Bishop Piotr Jarecki of Warsaw is even one of the vice directors of the organization. The Rev. Piotr Mazurkiewicz, the general secretary of COMECE, notes the difficulties that

Christian communities face in Europe and that some of them seem involved in a salvaging operation, but comparing them to the difficulties that Polish Catholics withstood under Communism gives a much needed perspective, and he remains optimistic. Among other things he notes that Christians were surprised by the assault aimed at them by secular culture and elites over the past few decades, but they are slowly wakening from the state of shock: "There are an increasing number of NGOs that appeal to Christian values.... There are a number of initiatives that in a few years or more will bear fruit."[178] The delegate from the Polish Conference of Bishops to COMECE is Archbishop Muszyński of Gniezno. In Poland he is involved in efforts to integrate religious communities in East Central Europe and preparing them for the challenges that face them. This is a major motivation behind the Gniezno Conventions, a semiannual forum with a broad ecumenical and interreligious character. Just as important is the effort to consolidate the Church in Poland: it is one of the few forums that gathers thinkers and activists from the entire spectrum of the body to discuss various issues—excepting, that is, the Radio Maryja community, which to date has isolated itself from the initiative.[179]

Leaving aside such macro issues, an issue at the opposite end of the scale is worth examining. As mentioned earlier, the position of the parish is recognized by sociologists as the element of the Church that Catholics in Poland identify with the closest. In an era of the growing influence of transnational political organizations and para-states, some Catholic thinkers argue that the latter by no means trump the local, that is, the historically much disparaged "parochial." Nicholas Boyle, a Catholic professor at Cambridge University, for instance, suggests that "the Church of the future will need to draw its moral strength not from its international presence but from its claim to represent people as they are locally and distinct from the worldwide ramifications of their existence as participants in the global market."[180] If such a hypothesis has substance—it resembles arguments for the importance of the "glocal" in the era of globalization—it means the days of the parish and its significance for the Polish neighborhood broadly understood are hardly over. Other secular local institutions play important roles, such as schools, but they concern people of a certain age, or particular orientations, while in Polish circumstances parish churches are open in principle to everyone. Rural parishes generate closer ties with the local population than those in urban areas: among other things, urban elites are more mobile and selective in the parishes they attend. However, as it has been observed, "urban parishes, which on account of their specific circumstances are confronted with social-cultural pluralism to an incomparably greater degree than rural parishes, are places of a much richer parish life, a growing number of religious groups and associations."[181]

Besides urban and rural parishes, an important division is the historical and recent parish. One of the noticeable differences between the two is found in the churches at their center, not just from the perspective of their architecture, but also the narratives they project from accumulated detail. A writer for a Polish American periodical describes the impression a visitor might receive in a rather common church: "One is struck upon entering a Roman Catholic church in Poland by the clutter of symbols and the abundance of imagery.... It might appear to a visitor that the Polish churches are houses for the local religious artifacts of the ages."[182] The author is primarily describing a historical church, with its layers of narrative having accrued through the centuries. These churches are found close to the centers of older cities and towns, occasionally in rural areas. One might call them testaments to the analogical imagination, and Poles are quite comfortable with them.

Contemporary churches attempt to catch up with their own clutter, but some of the discourses they evidence are different and clash with traditional ones. For instance, in the Church of Divine Providence in Wesoła, a district of Warsaw, the parish priest commissioned a marvelous mural by the Orthodox painter Jerzy Nowosielski that fills the entire altar section of the church. On the one hand, this modernist interpretation of Orthodox art in which high art combined with an ascetic Eastern Christian religious aesthetic has a home in a Catholic church. On the other hand, the Polish Catholic religious sensibility with its emotionalism demands and supplies a clashing parallel outlet. One critic comments upon the resulting juxtaposition:

> Should one be surprised that on the wall to the left side of the altar a large painting of "Jesus, I trust in You" has been hung together with a portrait of St. Faustina, while on the right side [a copy of] Our Lady of Częstochowa and a realistic portrait of John Paul II. These spoil the artistic effect of Jerzy Nowosielski's work. But the people need something which helps them pray.[183]

The above example is also the case of an ambitious parish priest imposing his vision on his parishioners. In recent years parish councils have finally been established in approximately half of Polish parishes, and they will at least have an advisory voice in the artwork within churches, among other things.

Parishes remain major focal points in the local community, although to a greater extent than in the past participation in them is a matter of choice. An interesting question, then, is considering the fact that the increased mobility of Poles has somewhat decreased ties to particular parishes, whether or not parishes in the general sense will paradoxically gain some of that loyalty, since they remain constant points of reference in the various communities that Poles end up in. Certainly the Polish Church could encourage such a partial public "haven in a heartless world."

Thanks to the continuing construction of new churches, a number of crafts continue to survive, often traditional ones, such as stained-glass window ateliers. Moreover, the liturgy in the Polish Church is constantly developing, with new hymns sung alongside traditional ones, some of them quite moving. There is a rich body of Christmas carols that range in style from the majestic to the intimate. Usually one or more churches in larger urban centers act as cultural centers, where parishioners or those interested can attend concerts or various events, most often for free; not to mention they can be located where the district community provides few other significant cultural resources. According to Andrew Greeley, while attending church regularly, a liturgical imagination develops that stimulates sensitivity toward art at a number of levels extending well beyond religion.[184] If there is indeed something like the liturgical imagination that Greeley speaks of as a by-product of the analogical imagination—obviously quite a bold suggestion on his part—all this has an impact on Polish society. At any rate it is virtually indisputable that religion in Poland is part of the very fiber of society, and many of its interconnections work at a level indiscernible to the naked eye.

* * *

What might be among the major challenges facing the Church and other religions in Poland in the upcoming years? In a society in flux at so many levels, that is a very difficult question. How the Church deals with problems connected with Polish identity under changing circumstances is important, but the sensitivity it shows toward social problems is also crucial. One new problem seems practically inevitable. John Allen points out that dealing with an aging population will be a major challenge for the Church throughout much of the world in the coming years, but it also creates an opportunity, since the elderly are generally more religious than the young.[185] Whether or not one can speak of opportunities in Poland, the challenge of the aged will certainly confront the Church in a most acute manner. First, however, it is worth examining the background of the problem.

Although on a European scale religion seems to positively affect the stability of marriages in Poland,[186] in the face of a number of potent trends it generally has little influence over the size of families. The average number of children per woman in Poland was approximately 1.4 in 2010, well under the demographic replacement level and one of the lowest in the world. Workplaces are hardly family friendly, while husbands typically lag behind their share of household chores in families where both parents work, which is typically the case. Housing is a serious problem for young families: there is very little inexpensive rental housing or apartments, and so they are forced to save for down payments for mortgages, which require a stable income. These and other factors are a strong deterrent to having more than one child; even two-child families are hardly common—despite the fact that surveys suggest Poles would love to have more children.[187] For its part, the Polish government is attempting to implement different child-support programs to alleviate the situation, but these are in their infancy and are still not up to the European norm—the government spends roughly one-third of the amount per capita that the government in France does. On top of this, while it has not hit Poland quite as hard as a number of EU states, the economic recession of recent years—most noticeable with heightened unemployment that disproportionately affects the young—increasingly adds to the sense of uncertainty, which is certainly a disincentive to raising children, despite the alarum raised both in the media and, much earlier, by the Church. Immigration is only a partial solution to demographic problems, since Poland is not that attractive to immigrants as of yet; moreover, lack of experience in this field would likely mean a good deal of social tensions arising were the number of immigrants to radically increase, at least for a time[188]—currently more Poles are actually leaving the country looking for employment abroad in the EU than there are immigrants to replace them.

Logically, a major pending problem resulting from the sharp demographic decline is the aging of Polish society. At the time of writing due to a small baby boom in the 1980s, Poland has a relatively young population by European standards, but the demographic trend will reverse this situation. What is increasingly obvious, this constitutes a threat to the economic development of the country, not to mention the welfare state, which—in Poland with a rapidly rising public debt—despite a low initial point of departure will nevertheless probably experience sharper restrictions in the foreseeable future. It is hard to imagine all the social consequences of such a development at present. Regarding the aged, intergenerational tensions will most certainly increase on account of the political struggle for limited public resources, while the question of euthanasia, barely discussed at present, will likely arise in much greater force under such circumstances, despite the protests of the Church.

And all this will affect religion in Poland. As mentioned at present the religious life of the elderly is closely connected with their parish in a manner that has not changed significantly over the years. For instance, the elderly participate in a number of religious groups, such as the Live Rosary, and they frequently travel on pilgrimages arranged by the parish, which are less expensive as trips than those from commercial travel agencies. The aged are among the most avid listeners of Radio Maryja, which provides ongoing religious programming including reciting the rosary and broadcasting masses, needless to say a boon for the homebound.[189]

Underpinning this lifestyle, however, at least in the case of the less self-sufficient among the aged, are the efforts of various family members that either help their parents live in their own homes or together with their adult children. Poles are willing to make considerable sacrifices to avoid placing elder family members into homes for the aged, which they consider a failure in their responsibility toward them.[190] However, with the shrinking of families, the rise in the number of divorces, and the necessity of moving on account of the job market, this state of affairs is already changing, and quite soon a significantly larger portion of the elderly population will most certainly be placed in such facilities. The Church will be faced with having to make more of an outreach effort even at the basic level of pastoral care. Currently the Church runs shelters for the homeless, soup kitchens and hospices for the terminally ill in Polish society at a very low cost; no doubt it will similarly participate heavily in any expansion of facilities for the aged, or—if these are developed—in programs aimed at increasing the self-sufficiency of the group. In the event, this will no doubt be done quietly, without much fanfare, and accepted as a matter of course.

In other words, there will be considerably more for the Church and various religious bodies Catholic and otherwise to do in such a prospective Poland. However, at this point it is naturally very difficult to say what the actual contribution of the Church—not to mention other religious groups, from all the faith communities—will be in such matters and in many other problems that will likely arise as well, since to no small extent it will depend on the resources available to it and how these are managed. For instance, will the declining number of religious callings—most radically in the case of women religious—shake up the vertical structures that Polish Catholics have become accustomed to? Will lay Catholics step in and take up a more active role in many of the initiatives the Church is involved in? The answer to these and numerous other questions will shape how the Church and religion in general will be present in the public sphere in Poland, as well as its civil society, in the coming years. What that public sphere will look like is another question: will it be amiable, neutral or hostile to the presence of religion—the answer is likely all three of the above, but in varying and unpredictable degrees.

At present it is difficult not to agree with the Solomonic judgment of the Rev. Janusz Mariański, among the most knowledgeable sociologists of religion in the country, that the Church in Poland is neither as weak as its opponents think, nor as influential as some of its supporters feel. Toward the end of his latest book on religion in Poland, the Reverend Mariański expresses the following qualification before offering his proposals concerning the future of religion in Poland: "Determining the future religious condition of societies is much easier in conditions of social stability than in periods of radical transformation, in which nearly all elements of social reality undergo reevaluation, redefinition, clarification, etc."[191] When pressed in interviews he suggests that a number of processes can take place in the Polish Church and society at the same time: "In my opinion the Church of the future will be multicolored," he claims. Which is an optimistic way of saying, as he puts it, "We cannot assume that we will be dealing with uniform attitudes."[192] The balancing act the Church must often perform at present will become even more pronounced.

Several years after John Paul II died, in an attempt to shore themselves and fellow Christian leaders up for future challenges, members of Laboratorium Więzi wrote a manifesto entitled "Toward a Community of Witnesses." Among others the authors recommend, "Don't turn away from the world, even if much within it troubles you. It is your world: its pain should be your pain. Be a prophet of hope, and not a prophet of sorrow. Sometimes you must fight—but fight for 'something,' not against 'someone.' Every person is a challenge for the Church. Learn from others through dialogue."[193] Such postulates naturally reflect a number of the current problems within the Church; not a few of its people fight against "someone," and the advice will not be easy for many to follow. Nevertheless it might inspire a creative minority, as Benedict XVI put it. And if a significant "Community of Witnesses" did exist, Poles would be fortunate indeed: prophets of hope always serve a nation well. It is doubtful times will be so untroubled that the future will be different.

Epilogue

John Paul II's Polish and European Legacy

No event in the past several decades has affected Poland to the extent that John Paul II's nine-day visit to his homeland in 1979 did, which paved the way for the birth of Solidarity and, eventually, a free and independent country. Since this course of events played more than a nominal role in bringing down the Soviet Empire, it is likely what future historians will claim as the greatest legacy of the Polish pope. More generally, the whole chain of events was a seminal contribution to what Samuel Huntington noted as the Third Wave of Democratization between 1974 and 1991 where dozens of countries were variously affected, and which he observed was "overwhelmingly a Catholic Wave."[1] Yet in Lamin Sanneh's *Disciples of All Nations: Pillars of World Christianity* of 2008, a book initiating a major series at Oxford University Press describing the global resurgence of Christianity after World War II, a seemingly less spectacular event involving John Paul is highlighted: his apostolic leadership in the first African Synod that took place initially in Rome in 1994, then concluded in Cameroon a year later. The synod was a major step for the Catholic Church to come to practical and theological terms with the religious resurgence taking place on the continent.[2]

In terms of the papacy's impact on religious growth, Sanneh's choice is quite valid. On the one hand, Poland has gained a chance at normalcy and entered the European Union, but currently religion is—if not quite on the decline—hardly holding its own; on the other hand, there is an expanding Catholic Church on a neighboring continent. At the onset of the new millennium Poland ranked in the top ten Catholic countries in the world with not a single African country on the list; by 2050 it is projected that three African countries will be on the list, and Poland will no longer rank[3]: that's even optimistically assuming that the process of secularization goes no further than it has. Religious demography, however, is hardly the whole story in the comparison.

As in Poland, the Church in Africa has also actively participated in the democratization of a number of countries on the continent.[4] But some African Churches are currently more active than the Polish one; among others, as Gerald Beyer has noted, several Conferences of Bishops in Africa—for instance, Cameroon and Congo—have been able to come up with astute policy analysis in their pastoral letters on social issues, something which the Church in Poland has yet to do with any level of relevancy,[5] while Sanneh describes a vibrant African Church capable of drawing lessons from other Christian denominations.

The pope from Poland, of course, belonged to the entire Catholic Church in all its diversity. One of John Paul's legacies for Poles that is most difficult to gauge is the effect of their watching a pope they identified with so closely visiting almost every major Catholic and many Christian communities around the globe. Certainly it has not eliminated a more narrowly focused current in Polish Catholicism, but for more than a few faithful these pilgrimages undoubtedly brought home both the variety and the universality of the Church. Many young Poles themselves experienced this unity and diversity through participation in World Youth Days, meeting Catholics from around the world. The experience no doubt helped them see their own church from a different perspective. Szymon Hołownia, an engaged Catholic clearly aware of the magnitude of the difficulties facing believers in Poland, does not refer to John Paul, but it is likely under the former pontiff's influence that he has averred to his countrymen, "I am convinced, that the thing which can help us withstand the oncoming storm, is opening up to the universal nature of the Church."[6] Almost in imitation of John Paul he himself went on a tour of Christianity around the world, meeting with Catholics, Protestants and Orthodox Christians. A keen observer and good listener, he reported home: "Everywhere I traveled, I became convinced they await us Poles with open arms. They need us, just like we need them."[7] Pope Francis seems to agree and has planned another WYD in Poland for 2014.

Hołownia is fully aware that the position of the Polish Church on the map of Christianity is waning. He explains to a journalist from a Polish women's magazine that Poles have too high an opinion regarding their Catholicism, and that the "heart of the Church" is now rather in Asia: "Please go to Manila, in the Philippines, and visit the Minor Basilica of the Black Nazarene, look at a procession in which several million faithful participate.... Such images help us gain a real image of the Church. We have learned a lot, but I get the impression that sometimes we still behave as if we were God's beloved child. But that's not so. God loves all of us [around the world] equally."[8] Hołownia pierces the romantic image of their own religiosity that some Poles hold, but it is undeniable that despite his qualification, there is something special about the Polish religious experience. And Poles have had an exceptional teacher in John Paul II to remind them about this.

Among other matters, at the time of writing the Polish pope plays a major role in the Poles' sense of national identity: in their historical memory, for instance, surveys demonstrate that the dates of his election as pope and demise are deemed the most important dates, surpassing even the Independence Day holiday. Concerning this "teacher," few aspects of Polish religion have been examined to the extent that the impact of John Paul's pontificate on society has, and from quite a variety of perspectives. As we have seen, the majority of Poles accepted the pontiff's efforts on behalf of ecumenism or interfaith dialogue: indirectly validating his claim about the internalizing of the Jagiellonian experience by Poles—at least in the case of the statistical Pole. After reviewing a vast body of statistics in his recent book *Katolicyzm polski* (Polish Catholicism) of 2011, the Rev. Janusz Mariański cautiously argues, "It can be hypothetically claimed that John Paul II's charisma—at least on the symbolic level—slowed down the increasing tendency in Polish society toward permissive attitudes and moral relativism in daily life." Mariański admits that at many levels the influence has not stayed the secular and consumer society tides affecting Polish society, but he concludes:

> Despite all the limitations related to the influence of John Paul II on their religiosity and morality he continues to be an important factor supporting the vitality of Polish Catholicism, an important religious and national symbol not only for those who feel a strong tie with the Roman Catholic Church, but also for those who to a greater or lesser degree have moved away from it.[9]

In contemporary Europe, this is actually saying something, yet it might seem unimpressive when reflecting upon the stature of John Paul II, now Blessed, soon to be canonized. Regarding the latter, for many Poles there can be little doubt as to the late pontiff's sanctity. Since his beatification on May 1, 2011, a formal cult has been initiated and segued with the existent popular one. In this vein, a number of new parishes in the country are seeking and will seek permission to have John Paul as their patron.

At another level, some Polish Catholics have examined and reflected upon the Pope's message to his countrymen, a message that was carefully crafted and delivered over the years, and plumbed it for its profundity and continuing relevance. It remains to be seen, for instance, to what extent John Paul's "new feminism" will be developed in Poland. Catholic feminist Małgorzata Bilska, for instance, connects the concept with the necessity of true community:

> The new feminism is not simply a defense of the natural function of the woman as a mother and a wife; it does not see human nature solely through the perspective of gender. It is "new" and constitutes an alternative (it cuts itself off from feminist tradition), but it is also "feminist" (by definition it sees the necessity of change). From the old current it differs through its personalist value system and anthropology.[10]

The Warsaw Catholic think tank Centrum Myśli Jana Pawła II (Centre for the Thought of John Paul II) commissioned two volumes particularly significant in that they are by authors from both sides of the vibrant Evangelical Catholic camp, where the legacy of the pope's teaching seems strongest in Polish society, and can be understood as programs for continued religious activism. In his *Rzeczpospolita papieska: Jan Paweł II o Polsce do Polaków* (The Papal Republic: John Paul II on Poland and to Poles), published in 2009, the assertive Evangelical Catholic Tomasz Terlikowski outlines what he sees as the salient features of the pope's teaching to Poles, concentrating on its development during his major pilgrimages to Poland and their changing context. In Terlikowski's perspective, it is crucial that John Paul simultaneously beseeched Poles to remain true to their Christian tradition and entreated them to give it appropriate new forms: "This, after all, was what Solidarity demonstrated, which—while being a thoroughly modern and universal movement—drew upon the best sources of Catholicism and republicanism."[11] At length, Terlikowski concludes, "John Paul II proposed to Poles participation in a great experiment, which was to include not only building a free Poland (in this he succeeded), but also a state that can be described as a democracy based on values, in contradistinction to the liberal democracy in its western version."[12] The Polish elites have largely rejected participation in such a project, but Terlikowski sees the possibility of bringing it to fruition in civil society if enough dedicated Catholics participate.

From the affirmative orthodox group, in his *Polski rachunek sumienia z Jana Pawła II* (The examination of the Polish Conscience with John Paul II), published a year later, Zbigniew Nosowski describes the pope's message less in terms of the civilization that he proposed Poles should create than the challenge addressed to them through his Christian humanism. What is common for both authors is a focus on a "democracy based on values" implicit in the pope's teaching. This includes the fact that both honoring tradition and facing modernity creatively are important in forging a viable Polish Catholic identity. Nosowski likewise stresses the inclusive nature of a "culture of life." However, beyond legalism he believes it is crucial to persuade Polish society to accept the constitutive values in order for them to become genuinely internalized.

Where Nosowski primarily differs from Terlikowski is that his point of departure is the pope's vision of the person, which was of seminal importance for him. "[John Paul II] led people toward God, and not—as Terlikowski asserts—on the barricades of a cultural war," argues Nosowski.[13] The value that the Polish pontiff saw as fundamental for the person was his or her freedom, which, in turn, meant that even in his role as the head of the Catholic Church John Paul could only persuade people to accept what was good: "The

Pope knew as no one else, that people can be weak. He was also fully aware that people need help in being free. But he felt this meant primarily supporting the process of liberating people from the weaknesses and limitations within themselves."[14] Nosowski also stresses the open nature of Polish identity for John Paul, which stems from his personal experience of minorities in interwar Poland. He quotes a passage from *Memory and Identity* concerning the pope's experience of friendship with Jews from that period: "What struck me was their Polish patriotism. Fundamental to the Polish spirit, then, is multiplicity and pluralism, not limitation and closure."[15] The basis for national identity from this perspective is not ethnicity, but culture, which is more inclusive. Yet, Nosowski points out that according to John Paul this "Jagiellonian" understanding of culture and national identity cannot be reduced to a "post-identity" multiculturalism: it combines a strong sense of one's own identity together with openness—in other words, "an awareness of the role of Christianity, especially Catholicism, for the Polish nation, together with a readiness to meet with and an openness toward other religions, cultures, nationalities."[16]

No book can adequately capture the full magnitude of John Paul's legacy in Poland. The former pope represents the acme of Polish religious moral thought that has roots stemming from Paweł Włodkowic. Yet, both Terlikowski and Nosowski in their own manner—one in more assertive terms, the other more affirmatively—together with a good number of other Poles understand John Paul's message in prophetic terms. Which means, among other things, that it constitutes a task to fulfill that does not lose its relevancy no matter how many or few Poles respond to it. It is rather safe to assume that for some time the legacy of the pope will at the very least stimulate a creative minority, which with time will likely eclipse the residual memory that continues to inspire a significant portion of the society. It should be remembered, however, that strains also exist within Polish Catholicism that radicalize it and undercut the pope's legacy. Few Poles have a better grasp of John Paul's social thought and knowledge of the current state of the Church in Poland than Fr. Maciej Zięba. For him, the question of whether or not it still can be considered a Church guided by John Paul's spirit is an open question, but he personally has serious reservations.[17]

The Polish pope supported his countrymen's decision to enter the European Union in 2004, but despite enormous efforts on John Paul's part his legacy within the latter remains problematic. Charting the relationship between the pontiff and the Continent, in his *The End and Beginning* of 2010, George Weigel summarizes the results of the frustrating struggle: "Without precluding the possibility of dramatic change over the long haul, it must be conceded that John Paul's extensive efforts to re-evangelize Europe and lead it out of the twenty-first century version of John Bunyan's Slough of Despond achieved only modest short-term results."[18] However, the real loser in the struggle according to Weigel is Europe:

> [W]ithin a few years of John Paul's death, Europe's unprecedentedly low birth rates had become an unmistakable empirical fact, as the continent's demographic self-destruction cast a long shadow over its cultural, fiscal, and political future. At least some of those aware of the gravity of the situation understood, with the late Pope, that one of the roots of the crisis was Europe's postmodern insouciance about the human capacity to know the truth of things—an insouciance that John Paul II had bent every effort to shake, but without transformative success.[19]

Not everyone will agree on the depth or the exact nature of the current crisis, or even if there is a genuine crisis in Europe. Nonetheless, the halcyon days inspiring books like Jeremy Rifkin's *European Dream: How Europe's Vision of the Future Is Quietly Eclipsing the American Dream*, published in the same year Poland entered the EU, are largely a thing of the past. To say the least, at a number of levels Europe is no longer a model to be followed by the world. Economic problems concerning the eurozone dominate in the media; however, one can ask whether the lack of an axiological foundation for a common identity is not among the more weighty—largely unrecognized—problems facing the Continent today. Nor has John Paul's admonition for European leaders to concentrate on culture over economics lost any of its currency. In this vein Fr. Maciej Zięba, among his other roles former head of the European Solidarity Center in Gdańsk, reiterates the need to build a European identity based on solidarity and pointedly adds, "If, while honoring pluralism, we do not make order in the European cultural edifice, we will continue to construct terrible political projects and have enormous economic difficulties."[20]

Fr. Zięba realistically sees this as a long-term project, but the most important matter is to start at all. He is a great believer in a genuinely open society and provocatively argues that its lack in Europe is partially responsible for the diminishing role of religion on the continent. One might add that at times religion persists in a stilted fashion. Noting the continued presence of what has been called "vicarious religion" on the continent—that is, religion, as in Scandinavian countries, as a kind of insurance policy—Peter Berger has suggested, "It is conceivable that a renewed public role of the churches would emerge if Europe were subjected to a more lasting crisis."[21] At present it seems more of a malaise gripping the continent than a profound crisis, and it is likely a long way from a growing sense of uncertainty to any impetus for "dramatic change" that Weigel implies could conceivably contribute to Europe's moral regeneration. Nonetheless, a greater number of people would no doubt accept John Paul's diagnosis that there is a moral dimension to the torpid European state of affairs than in the past, and some would follow him even further.

In the middle of the first decade of the new millennium, sociologist

Christie Davies analyzed the decline of morality in Great Britain and concluded resignedly, "People do not have to be good for their societies to be viable."[22] In the summer of 2011 the riots in England and accompanying freefor-all looting indicated that a "good enough" morality underpinned by impersonal technological safeguards and social engineering might not suffice. A prophetic voice from outside the Catholic fold responded to this event, yet oddly resonant to John Paul's earlier admonitions. It belonged to Jonathan Sacks, at the time Chief Rabbi of the Orthodox Jewish community in England. Sacks is likewise deeply concerned about Western civilization; for him the lootings of 2011 were a symptom of a far deeper malaise. In his essay that year for the September issue of *Standpoint* magazine bluntly entitled "How to Reverse the West's Decline," he posed the challenge facing Europe and the West in terms no less cutting than John Paul II: "The question is not radical Islam but, does the West believe in itself anymore? Is it capable of renewing itself as it did two centuries ago? Or will it crumble as did the Soviet Union from internal decay.... That is the challenge of 9/11. It's about time we came together to meet it." Prophets are never at a loss for powerful statements: whether the medium is an encyclical or monthly magazine is of minor importance. Like John Paul, Sacks is also a cautious optimist, a "prophet of hope," and at the moral level his solution bears echoes of the re-evangelization proposed by the pope:

> There is, to my mind, only one sane alternative. That is to do what England and America did in the 1820s. Those two societies, deeply secularised after the rationalist 18th century, scarred and fractured by the problems of industrialisation, calmly set about remoralising themselves, thereby renewing themselves.[23]

One of the allies Sacks sees in this mission of remoralizing the West is the Catholic Church. In a lecture delivered at Gregorium University in Rome in 2011 shortly after the above essay was published, he proclaimed, "For half a century Jews and Christians have focused on the way of dialogue that I call face-to-face. The time has come to move on to a new phase, the way of partnership that I call side-by-side."[24] Thus, he continued, "the task ahead of us is not between Jews and Catholics, or even Jews and Christians in general, but between Jews and Christians on the one hand, and the increasingly, even aggressively secularizing forces at work in Europe today on the other, challenging and even ridiculing our faith." His incisive presentation of the Judeo-Christian ethic is worth quoting at length, since it describes how that ethic underpins civil society:

> [The Judeo-Christian] ethic, based on justice, compassion and respect for human dignity, took moral restraint from "out there" to "in here." Good conduct was not dependent on governments, laws, police, inspectorates, regulatory bodies, civil

courts and legal penalties. It was dependent on the still, small voice of God within the human heart. It became part of character, virtue and an internalised sense of obligation. Jews and Christians devoted immense energies to training the young in the ways of goodness and righteousness. A moral vision, a clear sense of right and wrong, was present in the stories they told, the texts they read, the rituals they performed, the prayers they said and the standards the community expected of its members.[25]

It is clear that for Sacks the morally cultivated conscience is seminal to this ethic, as it was for John Paul II. In his book, Nosowski goes to some length to stress how important the conscience is in the teaching of the pope, but it is—it must be stressed—a conscience that is not subjective, that is, the focal point of radical individualism. John Paul makes this clear in his encyclical of 1993 *Veritatis splendor*: "Moral conscience does not close man within an insurmountable and impenetrable solitude, but opens him to the call, to the voice of God."[26] Robert Vischer, a professor of law, further explains this relationship of the conscience to the common good: "Much of the conscience's real-world bite is made possible through the specific knowledge we gain of the human condition, and one primary conduit for this knowledge is our relationships."[27] Even if the situation is not as dire as Sacks presents it, any degree of remoralization would certainly strengthen Europe at a number of levels, not the least in believing in itself, and—just maybe—could move it a little closer to that "great European Community of the Spirit" John Paul envisioned.

Sacks referred to Benedict XVI's call for Catholics to be a "creative minority" in Europe, wryly reminding the pope that the Jews have been a creative minority for millennia: all the more reason for Christians and Jews to work together. On account of the volatile nature of present conditions, although it is still conceivable that despite a noticeable decline Poles will maintain a relatively robust religiosity, it is also not inconceivable that Catholics will eventually be a "creative minority" in Poland; some Catholic thinkers have even considered this possibility already. Addressing a congress of lay Catholics in 2011, the Reverend Draguła extended the concept to include that of a "critical minority," by which he means religion "does not oppose postmodern consumer society, but becomes an alternative to it."[28] In other words, Catholics must set a positive example for others to emulate; they must become more fully a "community of witnesses." Certainly, the role of Polish Catholics in their society would be transformed under such circumstances, but it might create opportunities as well. Moreover, if some of the trends sociologists have described are discouraging concerning the future of religious vitality in the country, history demonstrates that religion in Poland has proved to have remarkable regenerative powers when the need arises. It might be the task of a creative minority to keep the flame going until such a time.

As for now, the call for Christians and Jews to engage in dialogue "side by side" is finally being tentatively undertaken in Poland. Since the Bible is common to both traditions, its defamation during a heavy metal concert referred to earlier has evoked a response from the Council of Christians and Jews. The act was not just offensive to religious sensibilities, however, but also a symptom of a dangerous underlying nihilism that should be countered:

> There should be no place in Polish public life for those who propagate an ideology of hatred based on nationalism, ethnicity, religion or culture. We appeal to the media, the world of culture and academia or the opinion-making elite, not to elevate people who consciously flaunt the fundamental principles of decency and social life.[29]

Quite evident in this statement, core issues such as the family which unite most religions[30] are not the only ones. And doubtless there will be many opportunities to continue such cooperation in Poland, cooperation that extends to the various faith communities in the country. Moreover, building mutual trust between different religious groups is largely commensurate with building the social trust in general that Polish society sorely needs, and which is a precondition for a more positive role for Poland in Europe where the virtue of trust also seems on the decline. The role Poles will play in Europe is likewise related to their part in Sacks's prophetic question above: Do they really believe in themselves?

It is, of course, the prerogative of religious leaders such as John Paul II or Jonathan Sacks to formulate questions that cannot in essence be answered but are nonetheless quite vital for Europe and the individual nations like Poland within it—the role of the prophet has hardly expired. If it were possible to provide a sensible answer to the above question, given how important the vigor of their religious identity has been for any major elevation of the Polish national spirit, religious vigor and genuine faith in themselves seem intimately connected for Poles, and it is difficult to imagine one existing without the other. Hardly anything in secular European experience demonstrates that some alternative is particularly inspiring, especially in times of difficulty. In this context it becomes clear that by encouraging Poles to make their contribution to a "European Community of the Spirit," in his prophetic discourse John Paul II was in essence challenging his countrymen to be themselves to the fullest degree possible.

* * *

Terlikowski paraphrases John Paul II who insisted that the deep Christian roots of Polish culture are necessary for comprehending Polish identity and its spiritual landscape: "Poland cannot be understood without Christ, the

Marian cult, the wayside chapels or the Stations of the Cross."[31] Nevertheless, both Terlikowski and Nosowski stress the importance of building new forms that add to this tradition.

There is one new tradition, only budding at present, which symbolically honors the old and builds the new: the revived Feast of the Three Kings. As a strictly religious holiday it has an old tradition in the Catholic liturgical calendar known as the Feast of the Epiphany, but as a renewed national holiday—it was likewise a national holiday in prewar Poland—it is quickly becoming transformed without apparently losing its roots, not to mention bolstering civil religion in the country. The holiday is connected with the venerable European tradition of the Twelve Days of Christmas, which it concludes. To some extent the holiday's close relationship to Christmas obscures the fact that the biblical narrative on which it is based refers to different dimensions of religious experience than those associated with the dominant traditional holiday. In Christmas, through the Incarnation the transcendent is personalized, and quite naturally the family is at its center. The narrative at the heart of the revived holiday focuses on the journey toward the Truth, despite the dangers and sacrifices involved. A popular Polish carol treating the theme has the lines: *Nic Monarchów nie odstrasza, do Betlejem spieszą* (the Monarchs are dauntless in their journey, they hurry on to Bethlehem).[32] In the Poland of today the dangers and distractions that challenge one's faith are certainly present and range from the trivial to the substantial. Not to mention it is ironic that such a festive religious holiday has grown in the face of a public sphere that likewise supports a substantial anticlerical culture.

The public face of Christmas in Poland is the Crèche, evoking joyful and communal contemplation; for the Feast of the Three Kings it is the parade—a symbol of a community in motion. In the case of Poles who have been undergoing a period of transformation with no early end in sight, they themselves are a people in motion. In this they now resemble their mentor John Paul II, constantly on the move in his numerous pilgrimages; thus, in many ways they have a fitting holiday to symbolize his heritage.

Moreover, the parade is inclusive. Everyone can join in—become part of the retinue—and be both audience and performer in the public ritual. One of the organizers in Kraków in 2012 reported, "At the start there were about a thousand participants. The rest joined in, on the streets."[33] In 2013 the fourth such parade in Warsaw attracted fifty thousand participants. And, in a similar fashion, each year more and more cities organize the event, while its organization remains largely grassroots, supported by the Church. The parade emanates from the folk religion tradition of the procession, but is far more festive. It includes elements of street theater and develops numerous local embellishments. Festivity is a much needed element in Poland's public sphere.

There can be little doubt that times of celebration—a key element of a culture of leisure—are important for fostering social trust. Moreover, a robust culture of leisure has an important implicit religious dimension: "Culture and leisure mean that we accomplish the highest purpose in creation not in necessity, but in delight and freedom," stresses an American Catholic philosopher.[34]

Along with the festivity, however, a lesson may be learned. An apocryphal element of the narrative relates that the eponymous three kings represent the three races of humanity. Already in the larger cities immigrants from Africa and Asia play the parts of the pertinent kings in the parade: likely the highest profile that immigrants receive in Poland's civil religion. For the time being, this can be counted as tokenism, but only because there are few immigrants to join the parade. Such a context would be natural to extend immigrants a welcome, and it would be quite fitting—and hardly surprising—for some faith-based NGOs to take advantage of this element to initiate a program connected with the holiday to educate the public to further accept them in Polish society. More generally, with a creative interpretation the holiday can symbolize openness to variety within, now more frequently in the form of immigrants, and a celebration of the difference that Poles add to Europe by bringing their own traditions to that larger public sphere.

The Feast of the Three Kings can be seen in part as a fresh symbol of religious unity in diversity in the country. If the coat of many colors of old has become somewhat monochrome in the last period of the country's history, not to mention having gained some nationalist stains, the open nature of this new holiday, at least symbolically, is oriented toward restoring luster to its hues. Admittedly, it is a long step from the event's symbolism evoking openness to actual readiness on the part of society for such a reality in whatever form it might arise, but it bolsters the cultural festivals that already celebrate pluralism and diversity in Poland and takes another step in the right direction— perhaps a little step, but little steps are necessary to build solid foundations.

Chapter Notes

Introduction

1. Cf. Philip Jenkins, *The Next Christendom: The Coming of Global Christianity* (Oxford: Oxford University Press, 2002); Lamin Sanneh, *Disciples of All Nations: Pillars of World Christianity* (Oxford and New York: Oxford University Press, 2008).

2. Philip Jenkins, *God's Continent: Christianity, Islam and Europe's Religious Crisis* (Oxford: Oxford University Press, 2007), 87–102.

3. They were, respectively, (in 2001) sportsman of the year Adam Małysz, the recipient of the country's top literary prize Jerzy Pilch, the prime minister Jerzy Buzek (all Lutherans); Poland's minister of foreign affairs, Bronisław Gieremek, was of Jewish descent.

4. John Paul II, *Memory and Identity: Conversations at the Dawn of a Millennium* (New York: Rizzoli, 2005), 87.

5. Quoted in Jonathan Luxmoore and Jolanta Babiuch, *Rethinking Christendom: Europe's Struggle for Christianity* (Herefordshire, UK: Gracewing, 2005), 179.

6. Jonathan Sacks, *The Dignity of Difference: How to Avoid the Clash of Civilizations* (London: Continuum, 2002), 21.

7. Quoted in Maryjane Osa, "Creating Solidarity: The Religious Foundations of the Polish Social Movement," *East European Politics and Societies* 11, 2 (1997): 326.

8. See Stéphane Courtois, et al. (eds.), *The Black Book of Communism: Crimes, Terror, Repression*, trans. Jonathan Murphy and Mark Kramer (Cambridge, MA: Harvard University Press, 1999).

9. Geoffrey Hosking, "Why We Need a History of Trust," review no. 287, *Reviews in History* (July 2002), http://history.ac.uk/reviews/287a (accessed 30 March 2010).

10. Sacks, *The Dignity of Difference*, 11.

11. Brian Porter-Szücs, *Faith and Fatherland: Catholicism, Modernity, and Poland* (Oxford: Oxford University Press, 2011), 15.

Chapter 1

1. Rodney Stark, *One True God: Historical Consequences of Monotheism* (Princeton, NJ: Princeton University Press, 2001), 17.

2. Anita J. Prażmowska, *A History of Poland* (Hampshire, UK: Palgrave Macmillan, 2004), 8.

3. Jerzy Kłoczowski, *A History of Polish Christianity* (Cambridge, UK: Cambridge University Press, 2000), 8.

4. Maria Janion, *Niesamowita słowiańszczyzna. Fantazmaty literatury* (Kraków: Wydawnictwo Literackie, 2006), 12–16.

5. Kłoczowski, *A History of Polish Christianity*, 5.

6. Anna Czekanowska, *Polish Folk Music: Slavonic Heritage, Polish Tradition, Contemporary Trends* (Cambridge, UK: Cambridge University Press, 1990), 10.

7. Kłoczowski, *A History of Polish Christianity*, 36.

8. Charles Taylor, *A Secular Age* (Cambridge, MA: Harvard University Press, 2007), 68.

9. Stark, *One True God*, 220.

10. Andrzej Walicki, "Traditions of Polish Nationalism in Comparative Perspective," *Dialogue and Universalism*, no. 4 (2001): 12.

11. Stanislas V. Belch, *The Contribution of Poland to the Development of the Doctrine of International Law (Paulus Vladimiri, decretorum doctor, 1409–1432)* (London: Veritas Foundation, 1965), 21.

12. Quoted in ibid., 22.

13. Adam Zamoyski, *Poland: A History* (London: Harper Press, 2009), 65.

14. Quoted by Walicki, "Traditions of Polish Nationalism," 16.

15. Zamoyski, *Poland*, 74.

16. Zamoyski, *Poland*, 66.

17. Adam Zamoyski gives the example of a Calvinist writer who scrupulously documented the executions and sectarian killings for the seventeenth century up to 1650. At a juncture when during the same time span over five hundred people were legally executed in England as well as

nearly nine hundred in the Netherlands, the total in Poland was no more than a dozen people (*Poland*, 77).

18. Peter J. Klassen, *Mennonites in Early Modern Poland and Prussia* (Baltimore, MD: Johns Hopkins University Press, 2009), 6.

19. Zamoyski, *Poland*, 75.

20. Benjamin Kaplan calls the Confederation of Warsaw, as well as several other such documents, "Protestant victories," and certainly to some extent this cannot be denied. See his *Divided by Faith: Religious Conflict and the Practice of Toleration in Early Modern Europe* (Cambridge, MA: Belknap Press of Harvard University Press, 2007), 220.

21. Norman Davies, *God's Playground: A History of Poland*, 2 vols., rev. ed. (Oxford and New York: Oxford University Press, 2005), 126.

22. Jonathan Sacks, *The Home We Build Together: Recreating Society* (London: Continuum, 2009), 118–22.

23. Kłoczowski, *A History of Polish Christianity*, 123.

24. Magda Teter, *Jews and Heretics in Catholic Poland: A Beleaguered Church in the Post-Reformation Era* (Cambridge, UK: Cambridge University Press, 2006), 58.

25. Kaplan, *Divided by Faith*, 113.

26. Ihor Sevcenko, "The Many Worlds of Piotr Mohyla," *Harvard Ukrainian Studies* 8, 1/2 (1985): 39.

27. Kłoczowski, *A History of Polish Christianity*, 118.

28. Walicki, "Traditions of Polish Nationalism," 18.

29. The participation in the funeral prayer service was limited to representatives of the religious backgrounds of the passengers that had died in the tragedy. The chief rabbi of Poland had been invited on the catastrophic flight, but since it was to take place on the Sabbath, he did not attend, and thus his life was, so to speak, spared. Although he did not participate in the funeral prayer service, he was given a prominent place among those who attended.

30. A major work on just about every aspect of Jewish presence in Polish lands is Antony Polonsky's three-volume work *The Jews in Poland and Russia*, vol. 1, *1350–1881* (Oxford: Littman Library, 2010); vol. 2, *1881–1914* (Oxford: Littman Library, 2010); vol. 3, *1914–2008* (Oxford: Littman Library, 2012). It is worth recalling in the context of this work that there was a negligible presence of Jews in the Russian Empire before it incorporated a major portion of the Polish-Lithuanian Commonwealth during the Partitions of the late eighteenth century and the subsequent Napoleonic Wars.

31. Luxmoore and Babiuch, *Rethinking Christendom*, 40.

32. Teter, *Jews and Heretics in Catholic Poland*, 70.

33. David Roskies, introduction to Chapter 7, "The Golden Age of Polish Jewry," in *The Literature of Destruction: Jewish Responses to Catastrophe*, ed. David Roskies (New York: Jewish Publication Society, 1988), 107.

34. From the collection by Isaac Bashevis Singer: *The Spinoza of Market Street* (New York: Fawcett Crest, 1980), 165–76.

35. Norman Lamm, *The Religious Thought of Hasidism: Text and Commentary* (New York: Michael Scharf Publication Trust of Yeshiva University, 1999), xxix–xxx passim.

36. Moshe Rosman, *Founder of Hasidism: A Quest for the Historical Ba'al Shem Tov* (Berkeley: University of California Press, 1996), 159–70.

37. Gershon David Hundert, *Jews in Poland-Lithuania in the Eighteenth Century: A Genealogy of Modernity* (Berkeley: University of California Press, 2004), 166.

38. Kaplan, *Divided by Faith*, 307–8.

39. Janusz Kamocki, "Przeniesienie 'małej ojczyzny' Tatarów polskich w kresów na Podlasie," in *Ich małe ojczyzny: Lokalność, korzenie i tożsamość w warunkach przemian*, ed. Mieczysław Trojan (Wrocław: Katedra Etnologii i Antropologii Kulturowej, Uniwersytet Wrocławski, 2003), 64.

40. Davies, *God's Playground*, 1:148.

41. Anna Zielińska, "Tatarzy—polscy muzułmanie," *Przegląd Powszechny* 11 (November 2009): 64–66.

42. Katarzyna Górak-Sosnowska, "Muzułmanie w Polsce," in *Socjologia życia religijne w Polsce*, ed. Sławomir H. Zaręba (Warszawa: Wyd. Uniwersytetu Kardynała Stefana Wyszyńskiego, 2009), 482–97.

43. Tadeusz Isakowicz-Zaleski, "Emigranci spod Araratu," *Przegląd Powszechny* 11 (November 2009): 36.

44. Grzegorz Pelica, "Prawosławie w Polsce—szkic dla studentów socjologii," in *Socjologia życia religijne w Polsce*, ed. Sławomir H. Zaręba (Warszawa: Wyd. Uniwersytetu Kardynała Stefana Wyszyńskiego, 2009), 426.

45. Kłoczowski, *A History of Polish Christianity*, 104.

46. Kaplan, *Divided by Faith*, 139.

47. Brian Porter-Szücs, *Faith and Fatherland: Catholicism, Modernity, and Poland* (Oxford: Oxford University Press, 2011), 6–7.

48. Kłoczowski, *A History of Polish Christianity*, 188.

49. Kłoczowski, *A History of Polish Christianity*, 190.

50. Davies, *God's Playground*, 1:386.

51. Richard Butterwick points out that the reforms would actually have exceeded those of the Habsburgs commonly known as Josephinism. See his *The Polish Revolution and the Catholic Church, 1788–1792* (Oxford: Oxford University Press, 2012), 7.

52. Walicki, "Traditions of Polish Nationalism," 24.

53. Ibid.
54. Kłoczowski, *A History of Polish Christianity*, 217.
55. Ibid., 198.
56. Walicki, "Traditions of Polish Nationalism," 28.
57. Magdalena Opalski and Israel Bartal, *Poles and Jews: A Failed Brotherhood* (Hanover and London: University Press of New England, 1992), 44–47.
58. Porter-Szücs, *Faith and Fatherland*, 87.
59. Kłoczowski, *A History of Polish Christianity*, 231.
60. Keely Stauter-Halstead, *The Nation and the Village: The Genesis of Peasant National Identity in Austrian Poland, 1848–1914* (Ithaca, NY: Cornell University Press, 2004), 153.
61. Kłoczowski, *A History of Polish Christianity*, 222.
62. Walicki, "Traditions of Polish Nationalism," 29.
63. Theodore R. Weeks, "Assimilation, Nationalism, Modernization, Antisemitism: Notes on Polish-Jewish Relations, 1855–1905," in *Antisemitism and Its Opponents in Modern Poland*, ed. Robert Blobaum (Ithaca, NY: Cornell University Press, 2005), 50.
64. Walicki, "Traditions of Polish Nationalism," 36.
65. Quoted in Rafał Łęchota, "Laski—przykład formacji katolickiej lat Drugiej Rzeczpospolitej," *Zeszyty Naukowe Uniwersytetu Jagiellońskiego: Studia Religiologica*, no. 34 (2001): 131.
66. Joseph Rothschild and Christopher Garbowski, "Europa środkowowschodnia: spojrzenie z zewnątrz" (interview), *Akcent*, nos. 1–2 (1990): 331.
67. Edward Wynot, "Poland's Christian Minorities 1919–1939," *Nationalities Papers* 13, 2 (1985): 209.
68. Occasionally nationality would trump religion, as was the case of the Germans in Upper Silesia, who represented two Protestant denominations and a Catholic community but, as Edward Wynot observes, "despite considerable divergence of opinion on theology, liturgical practice and other matters, the three leading church bodies all combined their efforts to support German political as well as cultural demands upon the Polish state" ("Poland's Christian Minorities," 240).
69. Porter-Szücs, *Faith and Fatherland*, 328.
70. Jarosław Gowin, *Kościół w czasach wolności 1989–1999* (Kraków: Znak, 1999), 17.
71. Katarzyna Jarkiewicz, "Bez gwałtu i rewolucji, 1918–1939," in *Dzieje Kościoła w Polsce*, ed. Andrzej Wienck (Warszawa: Wyd. Szkolne PWN, 2008), 401.
72. *Tygodnik Powszechny* obviously had to submit its texts to state censorship, but its editorial policy was independent.
73. Neal Pease, *Rome's Most Faithful Daughter:*

The Catholic Church and Independent Poland, 1914–1939 (Athens: Ohio University Press, 2009), 124.
74. Gowin, *Kościół w czasach wolności*, 17.
75. Konrad Sadkowski, "Roman Catholic Clergy, the Byzantine Slavonic Rite and Polish National Identity: The Case of Grabowiec, 1931–34," *Religion, State & Society* 28, 2 (2000): 176.
76. The complexity of the relationship between the Polish state and the Polish Catholic Church and their antagonism toward the Vatican's attempt to promote the neounion as a means to win over the Orthodox of Poland back to the Catholic fold is lucidly presented by Neal Pease (see his *Rome's Most Faithful Daughter*, 149–72).
77. Konrad Sadkowski, "Clerical Nationalism and Antisemitism: Catholic Priests, Jews, and Orthodox Christians in the Lublin Region, 1918–1939," in *Antisemitism and Its Opponents in Modern Poland*, ed. Robert Blobaum (Ithaca and London: Cornell University Press, 2005), 183.
78. Kłoczowski, *A History of Polish Christianity*, 279.
79. Jarkiewicz, "Bez gwałtu i rewolucji, 1918–1939," 399.
80. Edward Wynot, "Prisoner of History: The Eastern Orthodox Church in Poland in the Twentieth Century," *Journal of Church and State* 39, 2 (1997): 319–39.
81. Pelica, "Prawosławie w Polsce," 432.
82. Wynot, "Prisoner of History," 329.
83. Kłoczowski, *A History of Polish Christianity*, 271.
84. Ronald Modras, *The Catholic Church and Antisemitism: Poland, 1933–1939* (Jerusalem: Harwood Academic Publishers, 1994), 361.
85. In his memoir Tadeusz Petrowicz recalls that in the interwar period only old families still spoke Armenian (*Od Czarnohory do Lublina*, 2nd ed. [Lublin: Wydawnictwo UMCS, 2002], 38). In fact, the community in Kuty that he describes was one of the few places in Poland where Armenian had survived at all.
86. Petrowicz, *Od Czarnohory do Lublina*, 38.
87. Selim Chazbijewicz, "In Search of the Lost Commonwealth: Mono- or Multicultural Poland?" in *W stronę nowej wielokulturowości / Towards a New Multiculturalism*, ed. Robert Kusek and Joanna Sanetra Szeliga (Kraków: Międzynarodowe Centrum Kultury, 2010), 23.
88. Stark, *One True God*, 209.
89. Stanisław Vincenz, *Tematy żydowskie* (London: Oficyna Poetów i Malarzy, 1977), 65. The piece from which the quoted passage by Vincenz is extracted was also published in the Kołomyja memorial book, one of the rare Polish authors who was published in the Jewish memorial books after the Holocaust.
90. Stanisław Vincenz, "Leśny Żyd," in *Tematy żydowskie*, 110. The chapter "Lesny Żyd" is not included in H. C. Stevens's translation of Vin-

cenz's *On the High Uplands: Sagas, Songs, Tales and Legends of the Carpathians*. However, another Hasidic character is described in the chapter "Bałaguła," which has been included in Harold B. Segel's anthology, *Stranger in Our Midst: Images of the Jew in Polish Literature* (Ithaca, NY: Cornell University Press, 1996), 302–19.

91. Glen Dynner, "Merchant Princes and Tsadikim: The Patronage of Polish Hasidim," *Jewish Social Studies: History, Culture, Society* 12, 1 (2005): 64–91.

92. Lamm, *The Religious Thought of Hasidism*, xxxix.

93. Stark, *One True God*, 209.

94. Adina Cimet, *Jewish Lublin: A Cultural Monograph* (Lublin: Maria Curie-Skłodowska University Press, 2009), 192.

95. Istvan Deak, "Heroes and Victims," in *The Neighbors Respond: The Controversy over the Jedwabne Massacre in Poland*, ed. Antony Polonsky and Joanna B. Michlic (Princeton, NJ: Princeton University Press, 2003), 425.

96. See Robert Alvis's description of the process on the example of the German Lutherans of Poznań, in his *Religion and the Rise of Nationalism: A Profile of an East-Central European City* (Syracuse, NY: Syracuse University Press, 2005), 112–44.

97. Taylor, *A Secular Age*, 472.

Chapter 2

1. Timothy Snyder, *Bloodlands: Europe between Hitler and Stalin* (New York: Basic Books, 2010), 392.

2. The actual numbers are unknown, but Jan T. Gross estimates that approximately one and a half million Polish citizens—predominantly ethnically Polish, but just barely—were transported into the depths of the Soviet Union under various auspices (see Gross, *Revolution from Abroad: The Soviet Conquest of Poland's Western Ukraine and Western Belorussia* [Princeton, NJ: Princeton University Press, 1988], 187–202). Gross goes on to claim that before the systematic murder of the Jews initiated in 1942, the Soviets were responsible for three to four times more deaths of Polish citizens than the Nazis, despite the fact that their zone was considerably smaller and less populated[229].

3. Halik Kochanski, *The Eagle Unbowed: Poland and the Poles in the Second World War* (Cambridge, MA: Harvard University Press, 2012), 124.

4. Ibid., 122.

5. Rene Girard, *Violence and the Sacred*, trans. Patrick Gregory (London: Continuum, 1995), 49.

6. George Weigel, *Witness to Hope: The Biography of Pope John Paul II* (New York: Harper-Collins, 2001), 52.

7. Timothy Snyder, *The Reconstruction of Nations: Poland, Ukraine, Lithuania, Belarus, 1596–1999* (New Haven, CT: Yale University Press, 2003), 165.

8. Kłoczowski, *A History of Polish Christianity*, 300.

9. Snyder, *Reconstruction of Nations*, 165.

10. Professor Robert Bubczyk of Maria Skłodowska University, who read my historical chapters in manuscript, points to research that claims the proportions Snyder alludes to are unlikely, but the fratricidal conflicts among the Ukrainian groups are a fact.

11. Weigel, *Witness to Hope*, 74.

12. Kochanski, *The Eagle Unbowed*, 133–40.

13. Kłoczowski, *A History of Polish Christianity*, 308.

14. For an analysis of the Catholic Church's stance toward Jews in the interwar period, see Damian Pałka, *Kościół katolicki wobec Żydów w Polsce międzywojennej* (Kraków: Nomos, 2006), especially from pages 111 on.

15. Nehama Tec, *When Light Pierced the Darkness: Christian Rescue of Jews in Nazi-Occupied Poland* (Oxford: Oxford University Press, 1986), 138–39.

16. Ibid., 137.

17. Dierdre Burke, "Attitudes to Death during the Holocaust: Writings from the Ghettos," *Journal of Beliefs & Values* 20, 2 (1999): 126.

18. Jewish memorial books were written by Holocaust survivors or members of a given community who had emigrated before the war and were edited according to memoirs of life before the Holocaust, during its course, and in the postwar period.

19. "Życie religijne w getcie," in *Tam był kiedyś mój dom ... Księgi pamięci gmin żydowskich*, ed. Monika Adamczyk-Garbowska, Adam Kopciowski, and Andrzej Trzciński (Lublin: Wydawnictwo Marii Curii-Skłodowskiej, 2009), 401–3.

20. Burke, "Attitudes to Death during the Holocaust," 176.

21. Burke, "Attitudes to Death during the Holocaust," 179.

22. Wynot, "Prisoner of History," 330.

23. Aleksandra Sękowska, "Zbór Ewangelicko-Reformowany w Warszawie w latach drugiej wojny światowej," in *Ewangielicy warszawscy w walce o niepodległość Polski, 1939–45*, ed. Alina Janowska (Warszawa: Parafia Ewangelicko-Augsburska Świętej Trójcy, 1997), 33.

24. See Andrzej Paczkowski, "Poland, the 'Enemy Nation,'" in *The Black Book of Communism: Crimes, Terror, Repression*, ed. Stéphane Courtois et al., trans. Jonathan Murphy and Mark Kramer (Cambridge, MA: Harvard University Press, 1999), 363–93.

25. James Bjork, "Bulwark or Patchwork: Religious Exceptionalism and Regional Diversity in

Postwar Poland," in *Christianity and Modernity in Eastern Europe*, ed. Bruce Berglund and Brian Porter-Szücs (Budapest: Central European University, 2010), 129.

26. Stanisław Krajewski, *Poland and the Jews: Reflections of a Polish Polish Jew* (Kraków: Austeria, 2005), 128.

27. Daniel Blatman, "Strangers in their Own Land: Polish Jews from Lublin to Kielce," *Polin: Studies in Polish Jewry* 15 (2002): 357.

28. Marek Lasota, "Czasy PRL-u i odzyskana wolność," in *Dzieje Kościoła w Polsce*, ed. Andrzej Wiencek (Warszawa: Wydawnictwo Szkolne PWN, 2008), 421–22.

29. Ibid., 423.

30. Krystyna Kersten, *The Establishment of Communist Rule in Poland, 1943–1948* (New York: Columbia University Press, 1992), 386–90.

31. For a description of the legal status of the Catholic Church in Poland under the Communists regarding its various fields of activity, see Marian Mazgaj, *Church and State in Communist Poland: A History, 1944–1989* (Jefferson, NC: McFarland, 2010), 20–114.

32. George Weigel, *The Final Revolution: The Resistance Church and the Collapse of Communism* (Oxford: Oxford University Press, 1992), 107.

33. Cardina Stefan Wyszyński, *A Freedom Within: The Prison Notes of Stefan, Cardinal Wyszyński*, 2nd ed., trans. Barbara Krzywicki-Herburt (Surrey, UK: Aid to the Church in Need, 1986), 238.

34. They were called "regained territories" since some of them at least had some historical connections to the Polish crown, albeit back in the Middle Ages.

35. In his prison notes published as *A Freedom Within*, Wyszyński laments, "Your Apostles deserted You as the bishops have abandoned me." In the same entry he adds, "There remains a handful of the laity with me, not at all the strong ones, who have the courage not to disavow me".[261] He is referring to the editors of *Tygodnik Powszechny* who, among others, had the courage not to publish Stalin's death notice, for which the weekly was confiscated by the Communists and published by a group loyal to the regime until Wyszyński's release.

36. Krystyna Gorniak-Kocikowska, "A New Challenge: Poland and Its Church in the Global Society of the Post-Communist Era," in *Quo Vadis Eastern Europe? Religion, State and Society after Communism*, ed. Angeli Murzaku (Ravenna: Longo, 2009), 134.

37. Osa, "Creating Solidarity," 351.

38. Weigel, *Witness to Hope*, 230.

39. For a more detailed comparison of the two Church leaders, see Anne Applebaum, *Iron Curtain: The Crushing of Eastern Europe, 1944–1956* (London: Allen Lane, 2012), 280–86.

40. Tadeusz Dzwonkowski, "Wydarzenia zielonogórskie w 1960 roku. Anatomia konfliktu," in *Wydarzenia zielonogórskie w 1960 roku*, ed. Tadeusz Dzwonkowski (Warszawa: PAX, 2010), 7–139.

41. Kłoczowski, *A History of Polish Christianity*, 319.

42. Quoted in Vincent C. Chrypinski, "The Catholic Church in Poland, 1944–1989," in *Catholicism and Politics in Communist Societies*, ed. Pedro Ramet (Durham, NC: Duke University Press, 1990), 123.

43. Ibid.

44. Porter-Szücs, *Faith and Fatherland*, 151.

45. Weigel, *Final Revolution*, 114.

46. Chrypinski, "Catholic Church in Poland," 122.

47. Weigel, *Final Revolution*, 117.

48. Cathelijne de Busser and Anna Niedźwiedź, "Mary in Poland: A Polish Master Symbol," in *Moved by Mary: The Power of Pilgrimage in the Modern World*, ed. Anna-Karina Hermkens, Willy Jansen, and Catrien Notermans (Farnham, UK: Ashgate, 2009), 91.

49. Taylor, *A Secular Age*, 516–17.

50. Hanna Krall, "Briefly Now," trans. Christopher Garbowski, in *Contemporary Jewish Writing in Poland: An Anthology*, ed. Antony Polonsky and Monika Garbowska (Lincoln: University of Nebraska Press, 2001), 311.

51. Helena Datner and Małgorata Melchior, "Absence and Return: Jews in Contemporary Poland," in *From Homogeneity to Multiculturalism: Minorities Old and New in Poland*, ed. F. E. Ian Hamilton and Krystyna Iglicka (London: School of Slavonic and East European Studies, 2000), 101.

52. August Grabski and Albert Stankowski, "Życie religijne społeczności żydowskiej," in *Następstwo zagłady Żydów. Polska 1944–2010*, ed. Feliks Tych and Monika Adamczyk-Garbowska (Lublin: Wydawnictwo Uniwersytetu Marii Curie-Skłodowskiej, 2011), 220.

53. Blatman, "Strangers in their Own Land," 351.

54. Grabski and Stankowski, "Życie religijne społeczności żydowskiej," 221.

55. Datner and Melchior, "Absence and Return," 104.

56. See, e.g., Grzegorz Babinski, "Ukrainians in Poland after the Second World War," in *From Homogeneity to Multiculturalism: Minorities Old and New in Poland*, ed. F. E. Ian Hamilton and Krystyna Iglicka (London: School of Slavonic and East European Studies, 2000), 114–34.

57. Babinski states, "The exact religious diversity of religious faiths among the Ukrainian minorities in Poland is not known" ("Ukrainians in Poland," 121).

58. Quoted in Wynot, "Prisoner of History," 332.

59. Ibid., 333.

60. Zbigniew Wojewoda, *Zarys historii Kościoła greckokatolickiego w Polsce w latach 1944–1989* (Kraków: Nomos, 1994), 23.

61. Tadeusz Zychiewicz quoted in Wojewoda, ibid., 38.

62. Janusz Komocki, "Przeniesienie 'małej ojczyzny' Tatarów polskich w kresów na Podlasie," in *Ich małe ojczyzny: Lokalność, korzenie i tożsamość w warunkach przemian*, ed. Mieczysław Trojan (Wrocław: Katedra Etnologii i Antropologii Kulturowej, Uniwersytet Wrocławski, 2003), 65.

63. Gerd Nonneman, Tim Niblock, and Bogdan Szajkowski, "Islam and Ethnicity in Eastern Europe," in *Muslim Communities in the New Europe*, ed. Gerd Nonneman, Tim Niblock, and Bogdan Szajkowski (Reading: Ithaca Press, 1996), 38.

64. Bjork, "Bulwark or Patchwork," 149.

65. Weigel, *Witness to Hope*, 232.

66. Ibid.

67. Jonathan Luxmoore and Jolanta Babiuch, *The Vatican and the Red Flag* (London: Geoffrey Chapman, 2000), 206.

68. George Weigel, *The End and the Beginning: Pope John Paul II—the Victory of Freedom, the Last Years, the Legacy* (New York: Doubleday, 2010), 101.

69. Luxmoore and Babiuch, *Vatican and the Red Flag*, 211.

70. Ibid., 212.

71. George Weigel, *Final Revolution*, 129–30.

72. Quoted from Luxmoore and Babiuch, *Rethinking Christendom*, 138.

73. Weigel, *Final Revolution*, 132.

74. Quoted in ibid., 134.

75. Quoted in ibid., 136.

76. Ibid., 135.

77. Quoted in Luxmoore and Babiuch, *Rethinking Christendom*, 140.

78. Quoted in ibid., 143.

79. Porter-Szücs, *Faith and Fatherland*, 259.

80. Weigel, *Final Revolution*, 138.

81. David Ost, *Solidarity and the Politics of Anti-Politics: Opposition and Reform in Poland since 1968* (Philadelphia: Temple University Press, 1991), 31.

82. Ibid., 9.

83. Quoted in Christopher Beem, *The Necessity of Politics: Reclaiming American Public Life* (Chicago: University of Chicago Press, 1999), 127.

84. Weigel, *Witness to Hope*, 424.

85. Davies, *God's Playground*, 2:498.

86. Ibid., 499.

87. Chrypinski, "Catholic Church in Poland," 131–32.

88. Luxmoore and Babiuch, *Rethinking Christendom*, 149.

89. "Why," in Czesław Miłosz, *New and Collected Poems, 1931–2001* (New York: Ecco, 2001), 383.

90. Miłosz's poem was originally published in *Tygodnik Powszechny* in the summer of 1991 (August). I am recalling the homily from memory.

91. Jonathan Luxmoore, "Poland's Identity Crisis," *Commonweal*, 23 November 2007, 11.

92. Piotr Zientara, *New Europe's Old Regions* (London: Institute of Economic Affairs, 2009), 115.

93. The problem is also more complicated: as noted by one scholar, Solidarity's decline "[is] parallel to the decline of the position of the urban working class in the country" (Górniak-Kocikowska, "A New Challenge," 135).

94. Sabrina Ramet, "Thy Will be Done: The Catholic Church and Politics in Poland since 1989," in *Religion in an Expanding Europe*, ed. Timothy A Byrnes and Peter J. Katzenstein (Cambridge, UK: Cambridge University Press, 2006), 123.

95. Jarosław Gowin, *Kościół w czasach wolności 1989–1999* (Kraków: Wydawnictwo Znak, 1999), 258–59.

96. Luxmoore and Babiuch, *Rethinking Christendom*, 161.

97. The editor in chief of the Catholic monthly *Więź* related to the author the opinion of a Lutheran priest that the legal situation of the Lutheran Church in Poland is among the best in Europe on account of the pioneering agreement of the Catholic Church with the Polish State (Zbigniew Nosowski, private interview).

98. Luxmoore and Babiuch, *Vatican and the Red Flag*, 188.

99. Gowin, *Kościół w czasach wolności*, 26.

100. Weigel, *Witness to Hope*, 803.

101. Tomasz Terlikowski, *Grzechy Kościoła. Teraz w Polsce* (Warszawa: Delmart, 2010), 79–84.

102. Ireneusz Krzemiński, *Czego nas uczy Radio Maryja? Socjologia treści i recepcji rozgłośni* (Warszawa: Wydawnictwo Akademickie i Profesjonalne, 2009), 131.

103. Marcin Przeciszewski, "Kościół bez przywódcy i dalekosiężnej strategii?," in *Kościół. Stereotypy, uprzedzenia, manipulacji*, ed. Marcin Przeciszewski (Warszawa, Lublin: Katolicka Agencja Informacyjna and Gaudium, 2012), 69.

104. Quoted in Ramet, "Thy Will Be Done," 129.

105. Genevieve Zubrzycki, *The Crosses of Auschwitz: Nationalism and Religion in Post-Communist Poland* (Chicago: University of Chicago Press, 2006), 199.

106. For a balanced preliminary account of Christians collaborating with the Communist secret service, see Andrzej Grajewski, *Kompleks Judasza. Kościół zraniony. Chrześcijanie w Europie Środkowo-Wschodniej między oporem a kolaboracją* (Poznań: W drodze, 1999), 177–242. Of course such collaboration was not only a Catholic prob-

lem; every religious group in Poland had its collaborators and must currently deal with the issue (e.g., Ryszard Michalak, "Środowiska protestanckie wobec kwestii współpracy duchownych ze służbą bezpieczeństwa PRL," in *Kościoły, polityka, historia. Ze studiów nad problemami mniejszości wyznaniowych w Polsce w XX i XXI wieku*, ed. Stefan Dudra and Olgierd Kiec [Warszawa: Semper, 2009], 161–75).

107. Michael Szporer, "Managing Religion in Communist-Era Poland: Catholic Priests versus the Secret Police," *Journal of Cold War Studies* 12, 3 (2010): 116.

108. Paweł Bieliński, "Pedofilia rozpowszechniona wśród duchownych?," in *Kościół. Stereotypy, uprzedzenia, manipulacji*, ed. Marcin Przeciszewski (Warszawa, Lublin: Katolicka Agencja Informacyjna and Gaudium, 2012), 44.

109. Cf. Jonathan Luxmoore, "Clerical Power Thwarts Victims in Poland," *National Catholic Reporter*, 3 February 2012, 17.

110. Ramet, "Thy Will be Done," 124.

111. Luxmoore, "Poland's Identity Crisis," 11.

112. Cf. Stanisław Zasada, *Generał w habicie. Opowieść o siostrze Małgorzacie Chmielewskiej i Wspólnocie Chleb i Życie* (Kraków: Znak, 2010).

113. Józef Majewski, *Religia, media, mitologia* (Gdańsk: Słowo, Obraz, Teoria, 2010), 23.

114. Cf. Majewski, ibid., 101–3; Terlikowski, *Grzechy Kościoła*, 177.

115. Quoted in Antonio Carioti, "Respecting Others," *IMWPost*, no. 104 (April–August 2010): 7.

116. Bishop Andrzej Czaja, "Kościół nie jest sam dla siebie" (interview), *Więź*, no. 10 (October 2010): 14.

117. Peter Berger, "Poland between Rome and Brussels," Peter Berger's blog, American Interest Online, 31 August 2010, http://blogs.the-american-interest.com/berger/2010/08/31/poland-between-rome-and-brussels.

118. Luxmoore and Babiuch, *Rethinking Christendom*, 174.

119. Ibid., 160.

120. Jose Casanova, "Religion, European Secular Identities, and European Integration," in *Religion in an Expanding Europe*, ed. Timothy A. Byrnes and Peter J. Katzenstein (Cambridge, UK: Cambridge University Press, 2006), 69–70.

121. Berger, "Poland between Rome and Brussels."

Chapter 3

1. Andrew Greeley, *The Catholic Imagination* (Berkeley: University of California Press, 2000), 5–9.

2. Greeley, *Catholic Imagination*, 5.

3. For an analytical description of the Poles' spontaneous "sites of commemoration" with regard to John Paul's death, see Ewa Klekot, "Mourning John Paul II in the streets of Warsaw," *Anthropology Today* 23, 4 (2007): 3–6.

4. "Jerzy Pilch o Adamie," 14–5, in the introduction to Adam Pilch, *Byłem przechodniem. Wybór Kazań* (Warszawa: Świat Książki, 2011).

5. This is to be distinguished from the crisis of the crosses that followed, which was largely goaded on by political concerns of the different parties.

6. While Tracy and Greeley actually use the term "religious imagination," it is clear they intend the term to refer to theistic religions.

7. Lamm, *The Religious Thought of Hasidism*, 5.

8. Greeley, *Catholic Imagination*, 10.

9. Aryeh Wineman, "Parables and *Tsimtsum*," *Prooftexts* 16, 3 (1996): 296.

10. Meredith McQuire, *Lived Religion: Faith and Practice in Everyday Life* (Oxford: Oxford University Press, 2008), 25.

11. Greeley, *Catholic Imagination*, 11. Greeley's claim is rather sweeping, and would require qualification if he included Orthodox Christianity.

12. Roman Jusiak, OFM, *Kościół katolicki wobec wybranych kwestii społecznych i religijnych w Polsce* (Lublin: Wydawnictwo KUL, 2009), 124.

13. Ibid., 127.

14. Kłoczowski, *History of Polish Christianity*, 237.

15. Ibid.

16. Daniel Olszewski, *Polska kultura religijna na przełomie XIX i XX wieku* (Warszawa: Pax, 1996), 92–134.

17. Cf. Olszewski, etc.

18. McQuire, *Lived Religion*, 28.

19. Cf. Henryk Gapski, "Krzyż w kulturze polskiej," *Ateneum Kapłańskiej* 109, 1 (1987): 104.

20. Jan Adamowski, "Motywacje stawianie krzyży i kapliczek przydrożnych," in *Krzyże i kapliczki przydrożne jako znaki społecznej, kulturowej i religijnej pamięci*, ed. Jan Adamowski and Marta Wójcicka (Lublin: Wydawnictwo Uniwersytetu Marii Curie-Skłodowska, 2011), 17–42 .

21. Marian Kornecki, untitled introduction to *Kapliczki, figury i krzyże przydrożne na terenie diecezji tarnowskiej*, vol. 2, ed. Jan Rzepa (Tarnów: Kuria Diecezjalna, 1983), vii.

22. The most thorough catalogue of wayside shrines to date was carried out in the diocese of Tarnów: Jan Rzepa, *Kapliczki, figury i krzyże przydrożne na terenie diecezji tarnowskiej*, 2 vols. (Tarnów: Kuria Diecezjalna, 1983). To give one example, 3,538 crosses were counted in the diocese, and thousands of other Christ figures and images in shrines. In a seminar the author attended in the spring of 1987 at the Catholic University of Lublin, associate professor Henry Gapski claimed that according to his unpublished

study of the catalogues, he determined that there was a greater number of the crosses and shrines in the proximity of the historically oldest parishes; that is, they were an expression of an internal need generated by generation upon generation of churchgoing.

23. Aleksander Jackowski, "Wayside Shrines and Crosses," trans. Anna Grodecka, Andrzej Różycki, and Piotr Szczegłów, in *Pejzaż frasobliwy: Kapliczki i krzyże przydrożne* (Warszawa: Wyd. Krupski i S-ka, 2000), 10.

24. Cf. Anna Szymoszyn, *Bohater religijny w świętej przestrzeni. Kult św. Wojciecha na przełomie XX i XXI wieku* (Poznań: Wydawnictwo Poznańskie, 2010).

25. David Morgan, *Visual Piety: A History and Theory of Popular Religious Images* (Berkeley: University of California Press, 1999), 24.

26. The Rev. Edmund Ilcewicz, *Święta Otylia, patronka Urzędowa* (Urzędów: Towarzystwo Ziemi Urzędowskiej, 1999), 11–12.

27. Krzysztof Garbacz, *Na szlaku biłgorajskich kapliczek i krzyży przydrożnych* (Zielona Góra: Agencja Wydawnicza PDN, 2009) 15.

28. McQuire, *Lived Religion*, 26.

29. Magdalena Zowczak, "Między tradycja a komercją," *Znak* 3 (March 2008): 35.

30. Stanisław Vincenz, *Zwada. Na wysokiej połoninie:* Pasmo 2, Księga Pierwsza (Warszawa: PAX, 1981), 168.

31. Quoted in Izabella Bukraba-Rylska, "Religijność ludowa i jej niemuzykalni krytycy," *Znak*, no. 3 (March 2008): 14.

32. Olszewski, *Polska kultura religijna*, 153.

33. For a thorough study of one community regarding its care of the crosses and shrines within its bounds, see Marta Jechna and Aleksandar Ćirlić, "Kapliczka jako miejsce 'odwieczne.' Społeczne egzystencja kaplicy i krzyży przydrożnych w okolicy wsi Ostałówek," in *Krzyże i kapliczki przydrożne jako znaki społecznej, kulturowej i religijnej pamięci*, ed. Jan Adamowski and Marta Wójcicka (Lublin: Wyd. Uniwersytetu Marii Curie-Skłodowska, 2011), 257–64.

34. Piotr Wojciechowski, "Czego zawdzięczam religijności ludowej," *Znak* 3 (March 2008): 125.

35. Related in Andrzej Kaczmarzewski, "Kościół i klasztor oo. Bernardynów. Dzieje kultu cudownego wizerunku Matki Bożej Rzeszowskiej," in *Kościoły, klasztory i parafie dawnego Rzeszowa*, ed. Małgorzata Jarosińska (Rzeszów: Mitel, 2001), 93–101.

36. Ibid., 96.

37. Ibid., 97.

38. Aleksandra Witkowska, "Uroczyste koronacje wizerunków maryjnych na ziemiach polskich w latach 1717–1992," in *Przestrzeń i sacrum. Geografia kultury religijnej w Polsce i jej przemiany w okresie od XVII do XX wieku na przykładzie ośrodków kultu i migracji pielgrzymkowych*, ed. A.

Jackowski, Z. Jabłoński , I. Sołjan , E. Bilska (Kraków: Instytut Geografii Uniwersytetu Jagiellońskiego, 1996), 89.

39. Antoni Jackowski, "Rozwój pielgrzymek w Polsce," in *Przestrzeń i sacrum. Geografia kultury religijnej w Polsce i jej przemiany w okresie od XVII do XX wieku na przykładzie ośrodków kultu i migracji pielgrzymkowych*, ed. A. Jackowski, Z. Jabłoński, I. Sołjan, and E. Bilska (Kraków: Instytut Geografii Uniwersytetu Jagiellońskiego, 1996), 24.

40. Olszewski , *Polska kultura religijna*, 180–81.

41. Witkowska, "Uroczyste koronacje wizerunków maryjnych," 87–90.

42. A pioneering account of the history of Polish spirituality that treats the religiosity of the upper classes is found in Karol Górski, *Zarys dziejów duchowości w Polsce* (Kraków: Znak, 1986).

43. Kornecki, untitled introduction, vii.

44. Maria Bogucka, *The Lost World of the "Sarmatians"* (Warszawa: Polish Academy of Sciences, Institute of History, 1996), 185.

45. The economic decline had a particularly acute effect on the condition of the peasants since it was dominated by agriculture. The Polish and Lithuanian landowners tried to cut their losses in the seventeenth century by demanding, among other things, exorbitant servitudes from peasants.

46. Olszewski, *Polska kultura religijna*, 207.

47. Cf. Jusiak, *Kościół katolicki*, 135.

48. Ilcewicz, *Święta Otylia*, 9–10.

49. Bogucka, *The Lost World of the "Sarmatians,"* 184.

50. Historically there was a Carthusian monastery in the Polish-Lithuanian Commonwealth, not to mention several Camaldonese monasteries, where the rule was just as severe.

51. Polish women have a greater toleration—or vocation—toward contemplation. Currently there is one men's contemplative monastery in the country, while for women there are four.

52. Michał Buczkowski, *Gorzkie żale. Między rozumem a uczuciem* (Kraków: WAM, 2010), 56.

53. Ibid., 6.

54. Kalwaria Zebrzydowska, known additionally as the Mannerist Architectural and Park Landscape and Pilgrimage Park, was added to the UNESCO list of World Heritage Sites in 1999.

55. Dariusz Kosiński, *Teatra polskie. Historie* (Warszawa: PWN i Instytut Teatralny, 2010), 100.

56. Olszewski, *Polska kultura religijna*, 149–50.

57. Kosiński, *Teatra polskie*, 94.

58. Olszewski, *Polska kultura religijna*, 152.

59. Quoted in Violeta Szostak, "Koledzy, którzy mnie krzyżują," Duży Format insert of *Gazeta Wyborcza*, no 13 (1 April 2010): 4.

60. Magdalena Zowczak, *Biblia ludowa. Interpretacje wątków biblijnych w kulturze ludowej*,

Monografie Fundacji na rzecz Nauki Polskiej series (Wrocław: Funna, 2000), 484–85.

61. Barbara Ogrodowska, *Radość wszelkiego stworzenia. Rzecz o Adwencie i Bożym Narodzeniu* (Warszawa: Verbinum, 2008), 107–8.

62. Ladislaus Reymont, *The Peasants: A Tale of Our Own Time*, vol. "Winter," 2nd ed., trans. Michael Dziewicki (New York: Knopf, 1928), 79.

63. Zowczak, *Biblia ludowa*, 485.

64. Jerzy Kopeć quoted in Zowczak, *Biblia ludowa*, 34.

65. Lech Wałęsa even donated his Nobel Peace Prize to the monastery museum at Jasna Góra as a votive offering.

66. Jaroslav Pelikan, *Mary Through the Ages: Her Place in the History of Culture* (New Haven, CT: Yale University Press, 1996), 125–28.

67. Buczkowski, *Gorzkie żale*, 48.

68. See the discussion in Adrian Thomas, *Górecki*, Oxford Studies of Composers (Oxford: Clarendon Press, 1997), 81–94.

69. Anna Maria Harley, "Górecki and the Paradigm of the 'Maternal,'" *Musical Quarterly* 82, 1 (1998): 105.

70. I am relating the version provided in Anna Niedźwiedź, *The Image and the Figure: Our Lady of Częstochowa in Polish Culture and Popular Religion*, trans. Anna Niedźwiedź and Guy Torr (Kraków: Jagiellonian University Press, 2010), 47.

71. de Busser and Niedźwiedź, "Mary in Poland," 87.

72. Jackowski, "Rozwój pielgrzymek w Polsce," 24.

73. Ibid., 17.

74. de Busser and Niedźwiedź, "Mary in Poland," 90.

75. David Gitlitz and Linda Kay Davidson, *Pilgrimage and the Jews* (Westport, CT: Praeger, 2006), 106.

76. Ibid., 110.

77. Janusz Kamocki, "Przeniesienie 'małej ojczyzny' Tatarów polskich w kresów na Podlasie," in *Ich małe ojczyzny: Lokalność, korzenie i tożsamość w warunkach przemian*, ed. Mieczysław Trojan (Wrocław: Katedra Etnologii i Antropologii Kulturowej, Uniwersytet Wrocławski, 2003), 64.

78. Jackowski, "Rozwój pielgrzymek w Polsce," 43.

79. Antoni Jackowski, "Współczesne migracje pielgrzymkowe w Polsce," in *Przestrzeń i sacrum. Geografia kultury religijnej w Polsce i jej przemiany w okresie od XVII do XX wieku na przykładzie ośrodków kultu i migracji pielgrzymkowych*, ed. A. Jackowski, Z. Jabłoński, I. Sołjan and E. Bilska (Kraków: Instytut Geografii Uniwersytetu Jagiellońskiego, 1996), 66–67.

80. Licheń is an extraordinary Marian site that developed on account of its resistance to the Russian partitioners in the nineteenth century, but after 1989 a huge basilica was erected there. Cf. de Busser and Niedźwiedź, "Mary in Poland," 99.

81. de Busser and Niedźwiedź, "Mary in Poland," 99.

82. Ibid., 100.

83. Peter Gomes, *The Good Life: Truths That Last in Times of Need* (New York: HarperCollins, 2003), 137.

84. Szymon Hołownia, *Kościół dla średnio zaawansowanych*, 2nd. ed. (Kraków: Wyd. Znak, 2010), 200.

85. Jackowski, "Współczesne migracje pielgrzymkowe w Polsce," 79–82.

86. Kosiński, *Teatra polskie*, 76–86.

87. Peter Berger, "In Defense of a Commercialized Christmas," Peter Berger's blog, 28 December 2010, http://blogs.the-american-interest.com/berger/2010/12/28/in-defense-of-a-commercialized-christmas.

88. Katarzyna Smyk, *Choinka w kulturze polskiej. Symbolika drzewka i ozdób* (Kraków: Universitas, 2009), 30–41.

89. Karal Ann Marling, *Merry Christmas! Celebrating America's Greatest Holiday* (Cambridge, MA: Harvard University Press, 2000), 175.

90. Once-common religious esthetic practices like painting Easter eggs continue to take place but are not nearly as prevalent as decorating Christmas trees.

91. Cf. Kosiński, *Teatra polskie*, 107.

92. Taylor, *A Secular Age*, 468.

93. Józef Baniak, *Deskralizacja kultu religijnego i świąt religijnych w Polsce* (Kraków: Nomos, 2007), 514.

94. Cf. Kosiński, *Teatra polskie*.

95. Weigel, *Witness to Hope*, 493–94.

96. Kosiński, *Teatra polskie*, 104.

97. Marta Bierca, "Mistyka typu ludowego. Kobieca pobożność maryjna w świetle teologii feministycznej," in *Kobiety i religie*, ed. Katarzyna Leszczyńska and Agnieszka Kościańska (Kraków: Nomos, 2006), 131–37. Anna Niedźwiedź studies the question of Marian devotion in popular religion and offers a rich typology of different focuses along with Church outreach programs. See especially her *The Image and the Figure*, 139–77.

98. Bukraba-Rylska, "Religijność ludowa i jej niemuzykalni krytycy," 26.

99. Cf. Erika Doss, "Spontaneous Memorials and Contemporary Modes of Mourning in America," *Material Religion* 2, 3 (2006): 294–318.

100. Cf. Izabella Bukraba-Rylska, "Społeczeństwo polskie wobec wartości rustykalnych," in *Jak się dzielimy i co nas łączy?*, ed. Małgorzata Głowacka-Grajper and Ewa Nowicka (Kraków: Nomos, 2007), 244.

101. During World War II Warsaw tragically lost its Jewish population, which had constituted approximately one-third of its prewar total, and much of the remaining civilian population as a consequence of the Nazi reprisals after the failure of the Warsaw Uprising in 1944.

102. Jan Gryciuk, "Religijność ludowa w środowisku wielkomiejskim," in *Religijność ludowa. Ciągłość i zmiana*, ed. The Rev. Władysław Piwowarski (Wrocław: Wydawnictwo Wrocławskiej Księgarni Archidiecezjalnej, 1983), 222.

103. A good example of this ambivalence toward the folk roots of a significant portion of Poland's urban culture is witnessed from the paradox that in a plebiscite to choose the rallying song for the Polish national soccer team during the Euro 2012 soccer championships, which the country hosted, a folk ensemble won, but immediately afterward, Internet forums were filled with alarmed voices concerning the folk kitsch the song allegedly represented.

104. Bukraba-Rylska, "Religijność ludowa," 26.

105. Ibid., 29.

106. Anna Niedźwiedź, interviewed by Michał Kuźmiński and Piotr Mucharski, "Wszyscy jesteśmy kalwariami," *Tygodnik Powszechny*, no. 34 (20 August 2006): 8.

107. Quoted in Jusiak, *Kościół katolicki*, 147.

108. Bukraba-Rylska, "Społeczeństwo polskie," 255–56.

109. Cf. Jonathan Luxmoore, "Clerical Power Thwarts Victims in Poland," *National Catholic Reporter*, 3 February 2012, 17.

110. Michael Slackman, "Poland, Bastion of Religion, Sees Rise in Secularism," *New York Times*, 12 December 2011, http://www.nytimes.com/2010/12/12/world/europe/12poland.html (accessed April 16, 2012).

111. Thomas, *Górecki*, 82.

112. Czesław Miłosz, "Nowoczesność idylliczna?" *Znak*, no. 12 (December 2003): 52–53.

113. Peter Dews, "Disenchantment and the Persistence of Evil: Habermas, Jonas, Badiou," in *Modernity and the Problem of Evil*, ed. Alan D. Schrift (Bloomington: Indiana University Press, 2005), 51.

114. David Roskies, ed., *The Literature of Destruction: Jewish Responses to Catastrophe* (New York: Jewish Publication Society, 1988), 108.

115. Norman Solomon, "Czy Shoa wymaga radykalnie nowej teologii?" in *Żydzi i chrześcijanie w dialogu*, ed. Waldemar Chrostowski (Warszawa: Akademia Teologii Katolickiej, 1992), 136.

116. Roskies, *Literature of Destruction*, 504–5.

117. Yaffa Eliach, *Hassidic Tales of the Holocaust* (New York: Vintage, 1988), 130.

118. Ibid., 217–20.

119. Grabski and Stankowski, "Życie religijne społeczności żydowskiej," 221.

120. Kłoczowski, *History of Polish Christianity*, 307.

121. Magdalena Stopa, "W poszukiwanie świadków," in *Kapliczki warszawskie*, ed. Anna Beata Bohdziewicz and Magdalena Stopa (Warsaw: Dom Spotkań z Historią, 2009), 9.

122. Hanna Kulczycka cited in Anna Beata Bohdziewicz and Magdalena Stopa, *Kapliczki warszawskie* (Warsaw: Dom Spotkań z Historią, 2009), 59.

123. Andrzej Morka, *Doświadczenie Boga w Gułagu* (Sandomierz: Wydawnictwo Diecezjalne w Sandomierzu, 2007), 107.

124. Ibid., 128.

125. Ibid., 177.

126. Ibid., 371.

127. Leszek Kolakowski, *Modernity on Endless Trial* (Chicago: University of Chicago Press, 1990), 73.

128. Quoted in Michał Łuczewski, "Polskie odrodzenie religijne i doświadczenie totalitaryzmu. Analiza fenomenologiczna," *Teologia Polityczna*, no. 5 (2009/2010): 322.

129. Ibid.

130. Peter Hitchens, *Rage against God* (London: Continuum, 2010), 111.

131. Mirosława Grabowska, "Zjawiska religijne i kłopoty z ich badaniem," in *Religijność społeczeństwa polskiego lat 80. Od pytań filozoficznych do problemów empirycznych*, ed. Mirosława Grabowska and Tadeusz Szawiel (Warszawa: Wydział Filozofii i Socjologii Uniwersytetu Warszawskiego, 2005), 105.

132. Janusz Głowacki, interviewed by Katarzyna Kubiszyn, "Wałęsa robi różnice," *Tygodnik Powszechny*, no. 12 (20 March 2011): 30.

133. Quoted in Łuczewski, "Polskie odrodzenie religijne i doświadczenie totalitaryzmu," 330.

134. As is well known, for publishing *Captive Mind* in 1953 Czesław Miłosz became a virtual pariah in France, which in large measure led to his departure for the United States. For a well-documented account of the influential French intellectuals fascination with the Soviet Union and Communism, see Tony Judt, *Past Imperfect: French Intellectuals, 1944–1956* (Berkeley: University of California Press, 1992).

135. Łuczewski, "Polskie odrodzenie religijne," 323.

136. Kay Hymowitz, "The New Girl Order," *City Journal*, Autumn 2007, http://www.city-journal.org/html/17_4_new_girl_order.html.

137. Gerald Beyer, *Recovering Solidarity: Lessons from Poland's Unfinished Revolution* (Notre Dame, IN: University of Notre Dame Press, 2010), 69.

138. According to a European Social Survey of 2006, Poland was at the bottom of the twenty-three European countries surveyed in social trust. See Maria Rogaczewska, "Czy 'pokolenie JP2' zbuduje w Polsce społeczeństwo obywatelskie," in *Pokolenie JP2. Przeszłość i przyszłość zjawiska religijnego*, ed. Tadeusz Szawiel (Warszawa: Wydawnictwo Naukowe Scholar, 2008), 149.

139. David Herbert, "Faith, Trust, and Civil Society," in *Trust and Civil Society*, ed. Frank

Tonkiss et al. (Hampshire: Macmillan, 2000), 66–67.

140. For instance, the Catholic University of Lublin almost automatically received a Fulbright Fellowship, while other universities had to compete for the fellowship. What is significant, however, is that Polish universities used all such available opportunities. Conversely, it could happen, for instance, that a Soviet scholar would qualify for a fellowship but would not receive permission from the authorities to use it.

141. Osa, "Creating Solidarity," 353.

142. Barbara Fedyszak-Radziejowska, "Family, Children, Work and Friends, or the Things That We Consider the Most Important," in *Values of Poles and the Heritage of John Paul II*, ed. Tomasz Żukowski (Warszawa: Centre for the Thought of John Paul II, 2009), 80.

143. Bartłomiej Gapiński, *Sacrum i codzienność. Prośby o modlitwę nadsyłane do Kalwarii Zebrzydowskiej w latach 1965–1979* (Warszawa: Wydawnictwo TRO, 2008), 107–8.

144. Hitchens, *Rage against God*, 59–60.

145. This seems to be one of the great lacunae in examining societies of the countries under Communist regimes: the attack on the family and its effects.

146. Cf. Gerald Beyer, "A Theoretical Appreciation of the Ethic of Solidarity in Poland Twenty Five Years After," *Journal of Religious Ethics* 35, 2 (2007): 211.

147. Christopher Beem, *The Necessity of Politics: Reclaiming American Public Life* (Chicago: University of Chicago Press, 1999), 112.

148. Gapiński, *Sacrum i codzienność*, 107–31.

149. Osa, "Creating Solidarity," 355.

150. Maryjane Osa, *Solidarity and Contention: Networks of Polish Opposition* (Minneapolis: University of Minnesota Press, 2003), 141–42.

151. Osa, "Creating Solidarity," 355.

152. Beem, *The Necessity of Politics*, 125.

153. Zbigniew Stawrowski quoted in Beyer, "A Theoretical Appreciation of the Ethic of Solidarity," 209.

154. Józef Tischner, *The Spirit of Solidarity*, trans. Marek Zaleski and B. Fiore (San Francisco: Harper & Row, 1984), 97–98.

155. Zbigniew Stawrowski, "Doświadczenie *Solidarności* jako o wspólnoty etycznej," in *Lekcja sierpnia: Solidarność w oczach następnego pokolenia*, ed. Dariusz Gawin (Warszawa: Wyd. Instytutu Filozofii i Socjologii PAN, 2002), 115.

156. Beyer, "A Theoretical Appreciation of the Ethic of Solidarity," 211.

157. Samuel H. Barnes, "The Mobilization of Political Identity in New Democracies," in *The Postcommunist Citizen*, ed. Samuel H. Barnes and Janos Simon (Budapest: Erasmus Foundation and Institute for Political Science of the Hungarian Academy of Sciences, 1998), 127.

158. Osa, "Creating Solidarity," 347.

159. Edmund Wnuk-Lipiński, "Vicissitudes of Ethical Civil Society in Central and Eastern Europe," *Studies in Christian Ethics* 20, 1 (2007): 30–43.

160. As Robert Putnam puts it, "civic community has deep historic roots" (in his *Making Democracy Work: Civic Tradition in Modern Italy* [Princeton, NJ: Princeton University Press, 1992], 183). Putnam warns former Communist countries that institutional changes can foster the growth of social capital but that it will take considerable time for this to occur.

161. Cf. Beyer, "A Theoretical Appreciation of the Ethic of Solidarity"; Beem, *Necessity of Politics*, 120–22.

162. Quoted in Tomasz Terlikowski, *Rzeczpospolita papieska. Jan Paweł II o Polsce do Polaków* (Warszawa: Centrum Myśli Jana Pawła II, 2009), 74.

163. Cf, e.g., Zientara, *New Europe's Old Regions*, 120.

164. Marc Morje Howard, *The Weakness of Civil Society in Post-Communist Europe* (Cambridge, UK: Cambridge University Press, 2003), 30.

165. Piotr Sztompka, "Trust and Emerging Democracy: Lessons from Poland," *International Sociology* 11, 1 (1996): 53–56.

166. Artur Włodarczyk, "Ile mrówki jest w Polaku," *Gazeta Wyborcza*, no. 301 (27 December 2010): 22–23.

167. Barnes, "The Mobilization of Political Identity in New Democracies," 127.

168. Wojciech Sadłoń, "Polski Kościół wobec laicyzacji: Ilość," *Tygodnik Powszechny*, no. 49 (2010): 17.

169. Archbishop Nycz, interviewed by Zbigniew Nosowski and Marek Rymsza, "Kościół obywatelski," *Więź*, no. 3 (2009): 71.

170. See the Rev. Jan Drob, interviewed by Rafal Sztejka SJ and Czesław Wasilewski SJ, "Kościół—nie przedsiębiorstwo," *Przegląd Powszechny*, nos. 7–8 (2009): 15–23.

171. Jenkins, *God's Continent*, 70–78.

172. Francis Fukuyama, "The Great Disruption: Human Nature and the Reconstitution of Social Order," *Atlantic Monthly* 283, 5 (1999): 55–80.

173. Nosowski, *Polskie*, 10.

174. The Rev. Janusz Mariański, *Kościół katolicki w Polsce a życie społeczne* (Lublin: Wyd. Gaudium, 2005), 90.

175. Mirosława Grabowska, "Przeobrażenia polskiej religijności," *Znak*, no. 6 (2011): 48.

176. Tomasz Żukowski, "Ale nam się wydarzyło, czyli przegląd cudów polskich," *Teologia Polityczna* 5 (2009/2010): 131.

177. Ibid., 138.

178. Sadłoń, "Polski Kościół wobec laicyzacji," 17.

179. Ewa Czaczkowska, "Wiara częścią tożsamości," *Kościół w Polsce* insert in *Rzeczpospolita*, no. 287 (9 December 2010): 2.

180. Fedyszak-Radziejowska, "Family, Children, Work and Friends," 72–73.

181. Ibid., 76.

182. Czaczkowska, "Wiara częścią tożsamości," 2.

183. Tomasz Szlendak, *Supermarketyzacja. Religia i obyczaje seksualne młodzieży w kulturze konsumpcyjnej* (Wrocław: Wydawnictwo Uniwersytetu Wrocławskiego, 2004), 116–17.

184. Paweł Gierech, "Kilka uwag o polskiej młodzieży początku XXI wieku," *Teologia Polityczna* 5 (2009/2010): 230.

185. Szlendak, *Supermarketyzacja*, 128 passim.

186. Cf. Gierech, "Kilka uwag o polskiej młodzieży," 228.

187. Sociologist Krzysztof Koseła expressed this opinion in an e-mail to the author, 4 January 2011.

188. Gierech, "Kilka uwag o polskiej młodzieży," 233.

189. Grabowska, "Przeobrażenia," 52.

190. Marcin Jakimowicz, "Rekolekcje pokolenia ADHD," *Gość Niedzielny*, 19 June 2011, 20–23.

191. The Rev. Andrzej Draguła, interviewed by Marek Zając, "Przystanek Jezus gra dalej," *Tygodnik Powszechny*, no. 48 (30 November 2003): 10.

192. Rogaczewska, "Czy 'pokolenie JP2' zbuduje w Polsce społeczeństwo obywatelskie," 164.

193. Gierech, "Kilka uwag o polskiej młodzieży," 237.

194. This does not change the fact that the parish is the primary institution where the elderly feel a sense of belonging. See Rogaczewska, "Polska parafia w obrębie społeczeństwo obywatelskiego," *Trzeci Sektor*, no. 15 (2008): 35.

195. Stanisław Burdziej, "Religia jako źródło kapitału społecznego," *Trzeci Sektor*, no. 15 (2008): 25.

196. Tadeusz Kamiński, "Kościół i trzeci sektor w Polsce," *Trzeci Sektor*, no. 15 (2008): 22.

197. Barbara Fedyszak-Radziejowska, "The Social Capital of Poles: A Difficult Revitalization Process," in *Values of Poles and the Heritage of John Paul II*, ed. Tomasz Żukowski (Warszawa: Centre for the Thought of John Paul II, 2009), 115.

198. Rogaczewska, "Czy 'pokolenie JP2' zbuduje w Polsce społeczeństwo obywatelskie," 158–59.

199. As far as the Great Orchestra of Christmas Charity is concerned, another aspect worth pointing out is that on account of the media attention the event garners, volunteering for it follows the pattern pertaining to modern volunteering suggested by Robert Wuthnow, wherein volunteers are interested in gaining skills or participating in a project associated with success (cf. Robert Wuthnow, "Civil Society: Changing from Tight to Loose Connections," in *Unfinished Work: Building Equality and Democracy in the Era of Working Families*, ed. Jody Heyman and Christopher Beem [New York: New Press, 2005], 70). The "Great Orchestra" charity drive is an event with much media attention, and which is always touted as a great "success."

200. Herbert, "Faith, Trust, and Civil Society," 70.

201. Fedyszak-Radziejowska, "The Social Capital of Poles," 113.1

202. Gregorz Górny, *Między Matriksem a krucyfiksem* (Poznań: W drodze, 2010), 100.2

203. *Better Together*, report of the Saguaro Seminar on Civic Engagement (Cambridge, MA: John F. School of Government. Harvard University, 2000), 63, http://bettertogether.org/thereport.htm.

204. Ibid.

205. Cf. Marek Rymsza, "Nie pod korcem. O społecznym wymiarze praktykowanie wiary," *Więź*, no. 7 (July 2010): 71.

206. Zbigniew Nosowski, "Profesjonalizm jako droga duchowości," *Więź*, no. 7 (2010): 83–84.

207. Rogaczewska, "Czy 'pokolenie JP2' zbuduje w Polsce społeczeństwo obywatelskie," 166.

208. Quoted in Porter-Szücs, *Faith and Fatherland*, 53.

209. Kuba Wygański and Adam Puchejda, "Od zaufania do zaangażowania" (interview), *Znak*, no. 1 (2011): 32.

210. Władysław Piwowarski, "Religijność narodu a religijność życia codziennego," in *Religijność społeczeństwa polskiego lat 80. Od pytań filozoficznych do problemów empirycznych*, ed. Mirosława Grabowska and Tadeusz Szawiel (Warszawa: Wydział Filozofii i Socjologii Uniwersytetu Warszawskiego, 2005), 198.

211. Rogaczewska, "Polska parafia," 29.

212. Burdziej, "Religia jako źródło kapitału społecznego," 26.

213. Mariański, "Parafia szansa przemian polskiego katolicyzmu," 202.

214. Wojciech Sadłoń, "Jak wiara łączy i mobilizuje. Stosowany wymiar religii w świetle badań ISKK," *Więź*, no. 7 (July 2010): 15.

215. Cf. Sadłoń, "Jak wiara łączy i mobilizuje," 19–20. However, while the total membership of the groups is known, what is not is how many parishioners participate in more than one group. Qualitative studies show that this is likely not infrequently the case.

216. Ibid., 19–21.

217. Hołownia, *Kościół dla średnio zaawansowanych*, 144.

218. Stanisław Bartmiński, *Krasiczyn. Dzieje parafii i społeczności*, vol. 2, *Duchowieństwo i*

parafianie, aktywność społeczna wiernych (Krasiczyn, Przemyśl: [Wieści Krasiczyńskie Tygodnik Parafialny], 2010), 226–32.

219. The Reverend Bartmiński actually became the model and also consultant for *Plebania*, a long-running television serial that centered around the life of a parish in a small community.

220. Cf. Jakimowicz, "Rekolekcje pokolenia ADHD."

221. Cf. Krystyna Ewa Siellawa-Kolbowska, "Oaza jako przestrzeń doświadczenia mistycznego i społecznego," in *Pokolenie JP2. Przeszłość i przyszłość zjawiska religijnego*, ed. Tadeusz Szawiel (Warszawa: Wydawnictwo Naukowe Scholar, 2008), 62.

222. Quoted in Ewa Karabin, "Już nie kuźnia? Duszpasterstwa akademicka dzisiaj," *Więź*, no. 7 (2010): 37.

223. Quoted in ibid.

224. Karolina Kitzman-Czarnecka, "Kalejdoskop obywatelskich organizacji religijnych," *Trzeci Sektor*, no. 15 (2008): 52.

225. Beyer, *Recovering Solidarity*, 192.

226. Kitzman-Czarnecka, "Kalejdoskop obywatelskich organizacji religijnych," 49.

227. Rogaczewska, "Czy 'pokolenie JP2' zbuduje w Polsce społeczeństwo obywatelskie," 160.

228. Marcin Choduń, "Podwórko pod dachem," *Tygodnik Powszechny*, no. 26 (26 June 2011): 6–7.

229. In 2001 the Rev. Arkadiusz Nowak received the United Nations' Poverty Award for his work on behalf of AIDS victims. The same year the Polish Episcopate wholeheartedly supported one of Marek Kotański's initiatives, Ruch Czystych Serc (the Pure Hearts Movement). See "Życie bogate i twórcze. Biografia Marka Kotańskiego," Otwarty Portal Monaru, n.d., http://monar.info.pl/PagEd-index-topic_id-4-page_id-17.html.

230. Andrew Curry, "Poland's New Ambitions," *Wilson Quarterly* 34, 2 (Spring 2010): 38.

231. Jan Herbst, "Drugi trzeci sektor, czyli o aktywności społecznej wokół Kościoła katolickiego w Polsce," *Teologia Polityczna*, no. 5 (Summer 2009/Fall 2010): 184.

232. Zientara, *New Europe's Old Regions*, 96.

233. Janusz Mariański, *Społeczeństwo i moralność. Studia z katolickiej nauki społecznej i socjologii moralności* (Tarnów: Biblos, 2008), 206.

234. Alicia Chesser, "Neuhaus Invades Poland," *First Things: A Monthly Journal of Religion & Public Life*, no. 192 (April 2009): 25–26.

235. Piotr Włoczyk, "Masz talent," *Tygodnik Powszechny*, no. 11 (11 March 2012): 13–15.

236. Rafał Dutkiewicz, *Nowe horyzonty* (Warszawa: Rosner & Wspólnicy, 2006), 117.

237. Ibid., 122.

238. Kamiński, "Kościół i trzeci sektor w Polsce," 21.

Chapter 4

1. John Paul II, *Memory and Identity*, 87.

2. Isakowicz-Zaleski, "Emigranci spod Araratu," 38.

3. Grzegorz Pełczyński, "Ormianie," in *Mniejszości narodowe i etniczne w Polsce po II wojnie światowej*, ed. Stefan Dudra and Bernadette Nitsche (Krakow: Nomos, 2010), 207.

4. Selim Chazbijewicz, "Tatarzy," in *Mniejszości narodowe i etniczne w Polsce po II wojnie światowej*, ed. Stefan Dudra and Bernadette Nitsche (Krakow: Nomos, 2010), 299–302.

5. Katarzyna Warmińska, *Tatarzy Polscy. Tożsamość religijna i etniczna* (Kraków: Universitas, 1999), 220–21.

6. Tomasz Imran Stefaniuk, "Islam and Muslims in Poland," in *W stronę nowej wielokulturowości / Towards a New Multiculturalism*, ed. Robert Kusek and Joanna Sanetra Szeliga (Kraków: Międzynarodowe Centrum Kultury, 2010), 176–79.

7. From the last official statistics of 2008, the Tatar Muslim Religious Association has approximately one thousand members while the Muslim League has approximately one thousand five hundred members. See Grzegorz Gudaszewski and Mariusz Chmieliweski (eds.), *Wyznania religijne, stowarzyszenia narodowościowe i etniczne w Polsce 2006–2008* (Warszawa: Główny Urząd Statystyczny, 2010), 106, 110.

8. Konstanty Gebert, "Our Identities—New, Old, Imagined," in *Poland: A Jewish Matter. Proceedings of a Symposium Exploring Contemporary Jewish Life in Poland, Marking the End of Jewish Programming for Polska! Year*, ed. Kate Caddy, Mike Levy, and Jakub Nowakowski (Warsaw: Adam Mickiewicz Institute, 2010), 47.

9. Ibid., 48.

10. Grabski and Stankowski, "Życie religijne społeczności żydowskiej," 232–34.

11. Ibid., 238.

12. Ibid., 239.

13. Feliks Tych, "Attempts to Rebuild Jewish Life in Post-War Poland," in *Memory: The History of Polish Jews Before, During, and After the Holocaust*, ed. Feliks Tych (Warszawa: Shalom Foundation, 2008), 201.

14. Grabski and Stankowski, "Życie religijne społeczności żydowskiej," 244.

15. For a description of the trilingual culture of the Jews in interwar Poland, see Chone Shmeruk, "Hebrew-Yiddish-Polish: A Trilingual Culture," in *The Jews of Poland between Two World Wars*, ed. Yisrael Gutman, Ezra Mendelsohn, Jehuda Reinharz, and Chone Shmeruk (Hanover: University Press of New England, 1989), 285–311.

16. Michael Schudrich, "Giving Back the Jewish Past," in *Poland: A Jewish Matter; Proceedings of a Symposium Exploring Contemporary Jewish*

Life in Poland, ed. Kate Caddy, Mike Levy, and Jakub Nowakowski (Warsaw: Adam Mickiewicz Institute, 2010), 60. For an assessment of what is left of the material culture of the Jewish community (much was destroyed by the Nazis or fell into ruin after the war), see Elenora Bergman and Jan Jagielski, "Ślady obecności. Synagogi i cmentarze," in *Następstwa zagłady Żydów. Polska 1944–2010*, ed. Feliks Tych and Monika Adamczyk-Garbowska (Lublin: Wydawnictwo Uniwersytetu Marii Curie-Skłodowskiej, 2011), 471–92.

17. Jonathan Sacks, "Judaism and Politics in the Modern World," in *The Desecularization of the World: Resurgent Religion and World Politics*, ed. Peter Berger (Washington, DC: Ethics and Public Policy Center, 1999), 60.

18. Krajewski, *Poland and the Jews*, 34.

19. Wynot, "Prisoner of History," 334.

20. Ibid., 335.

21. Grzegorz Kuprianowicz, "Prawosławie w Polsce od 1919 roku do współczesności," in *Prawosławie. Światło ze wschodu*, ed. Krzysztof Leśniewski (Lublin: Prawosławna Diecezja Lubelsko-Chełmska, 2009), 805–6.

22. Ibid., 826.

23. Ibid., 821.

24. Lech Nijakowski, "Tworzenie, odtwarzanie, niszczenie i zanikanie granic między grupami etnicznymi," in *Etniczność, pamięć, asymilacja. Wokół problemów zachowania tożsamości narodowych i etnicznych w Polsce*, ed. Lech Nijakowski (Warszawa: Wydawnictwo Sejmowe, 2009), 71–72.

25. Cf., e.g., Olga Sitkiewicz, "Oblicza magii w opowieściach i praktykach mieszkańców pogranicza polsko-ukraińskiego," in *Religijność chrześcijan obrządku wschodniego na pograniczu polsko-ukraińskim*, ed. Magdalena Lubańska (Warszawa: Wyd. DiG, 2007), 111–28.

26. Zbigniew Podgórzec, *Rozmowy z Jerzym Nowosielskim: Wokół ikony—Mój Chrystus—Mój Judasz*, ed. Krystyna Czerni (Kraków: Znak, 2009), 302–9.

27. Sacks, *Home We Build Together*, 81.

28. Stefan Dudra and Sylwester Woźniak, "Kościół greckokatolicki na Ziemi Lubuskiej," in *Kościoły, polityka, historia. Ze studiów nad problemami mniejszości wyznaniowych w Polsce w XX i XXI wieku*, ed. Stefan Dudra and Olgierd Kiec (Warszawa: Semper, 2009), 61–63.

29. Stanisław Stępień, "Developments since 1989: Poland," in *Churches In-between: Greek Catholic Churches in Postsocialist Europe*, ed. Stéphanie Mahieu and Vlad Naumescu (Berlin: Lit, 2008), 94–95.

30. Juraj Buzalka, "Syncretism among the Greek Catholic Ukrainians in Southeast Poland," in *Churches In-between: Greek Catholic Churches in Postsocialist Europe*, ed. Stéphanie Mahieu and Vlad Naumescu (Berlin: Lit, 2008), 201.

31. Bohdan Halczak, "Ukraińcy (po 1989 r.)," in *Mniejszości narodowe i etniczne w Polsce po II wojnie światowej*, ed. Stefan Dudra and Bernadette Nitsche (Krakow: Nomos, 2010), 125.

32. Bp Jan Szarek and the Rev. Jan Gross, "Struktura oraz życie współczesne Kościoła," in *Świadectwo wiary i życia. Kościół luterański w Polsce wczoraj i dziś*, ed. The Rev. Jerzy Below and Magdalena Legendź (Bielsko-Biała: "Augustana," 2004), 7–31.

33. Krzysztof Dorosz, *Bóg i terror historii* (Warszawa: Semper, 2010), 16.

34. Lech Tranda, "... nie ważne skąd przychodzisz, ważne co cię boli," in *Drogi chrześcijaństwa*, ed. Bohdan Sławiński (Warszawa: Jacek Santorski, 2008), 126.

35. Krzysztof Brzechczyn, "Kościół Baptystyczny w Polsce w latach 1858–2008. Stan badań i postulaty badawcze," in *Kościoły, polityka, historia. Ze studiów nad problemami mniejszości wyznaniowych w Polsce w XX i XXI wieku*, ed. Stefan Dudra and Olgierd Kiec (Warszawa: Semper, 2009), 37–50.

36. Renata Czyż, "Zróżnicowanie wyznaniowe Śląska Cieszyńskiego. Geneza—historia—stan obecny," in *Kościoły, polityka, historia. Ze studiów nad problemami mniejszości wyznaniowych w Polsce w XX i XXI wieku*, ed. Stefan Dudra and Olgierd Kiec (Warszawa: Semper, 2009), 93–104.

37. Grzegorz Pełczyński, "Wspólnoty ewangelickie w Polsce. Problem tożsamości," in *Tożsamości religijne w społeczeństwie polskim. Socjologiczne studium przypadków*, ed. Maria Libiszowska-Żółtkowska (Warszawa: Difin, 2009), 182–83.

38. Roland Recht, *Believing and Seeing: The Art of Gothic Cathedrals*, trans. Mary Whittall (Chicago: University of Chicago Press, 2008), 219.

39. Bjork, "Bulwark or Patchwork," 146.

40. Krzysztof Tarka, "Litwini," in *Mniejszości narodowe i etniczne w Polsce po II wojnie światowej*, ed. Stefan Dudra and Bernadette Nitsche (Krakow: Nomos, 2010), 154–55.

41. Arkadiusz Staniszewski, "Dzieje, obyczaje i obrzędy religijne Romów w odniesieniu do kultury katolickiej," *Socjologia Religii* 1 (2003): 260–66.

42. An example is proffered by the United States. Even from among the large influx of post–1965 Asian immigrants, as R. Stephen Warner puts it, "many immigrants come disproportionately from Christian segments of religiously mixed countries." See his "The De-Europeanization of American Christianity," in *A Nation of Religions: The Politics of Pluralism in Multireligious America*, ed. Stephen Prothero (Chapel Hill: University of North Carolina Press, 2006), 234.

43. Jacek Dziedzina, "Jestem z Ba Lan," *Gość Niedzielny*, no. 8 (27 February 2011): 47.

44. Damian Cichy, SVD, and Marta Szymczyk, "Dzisiaj misje przyjechali do nas," *Przegląd Powszechny*, no. 12 (2010): 47–49.

45. Archbishop Józef Życiński died in March 2011.

46. Chazbijewicz, "In Search of the Lost Commonwealth," 25.

47. Stefan Dudra, "Łemkowie," in *Mniejszości narodowe i etniczne w Polsce po II wojnie światowej*, ed. Stefan Dudra and Bernadette Nitsche (Krakow: Nomos, 2010), 275.

48. Sławomir Kursa, "Prawna ochrona religijnej tożsamości narodowych i etnicznych w Polsce," in *Prawa mniejszości narodowych*, ed. Teresa Gardocka and Jacek Sobczak (Toruń: Adam Marszałek, 2010), 394.

49. Jerzy Pilch, "Jerzy Pilch o Adamie Pilchu," in Adam Pilch, *Byłem przechodniem. Wybór Kazań* (Warszawa: Świat Książki, 2011), 11.

50. Slawomir Lodzinski, "National Minorities and the 'Conservative' Politics of Multiculturalism in Poland," in *From Homogeneity to Multiculturalism: Minorities Old and New in Poland*, ed. F. E. Ian Hamilton and Krystyna Iglicka (London: School of Slavonic and East European Studies, 2000), 40.

51. Warmińska, *Tatarzy Polscy*, 133.

52. Schudrich, "Giving Back the Jewish Past," 63.

53. Ewa Nowicka and Magda Majewska, *Obcy u siebie. Luteranie warszawscy* (Warszawa: Oficyna Naukowa, 1993), 68–88.

54. Ibid., 73.

55. Joanna Bątkiewicz-Brożek, "Mieszani, ale święci," *Gość Niedzielny*, no. 27 (10 July 2011): 26–27.

56. Olgierd Kiec, "Kościoły ewangelickie w Polsce w latach 1980–2008," in *Kościoły, polityka, historia. Ze studiów nad problemami mniejszości wyznaniowych w Polsce w XX i XXI wieku*, ed. Stefan Dudra and Olgierd Kiec (Warszawa: Semper, 2009), 133–34.

57. Quoted in ibid., 130.

58. The Rev. Janusz Sikora, personal e-mail communication with author, 8 September 2010.

59. Bogusław Milerski, "Droga luterańska," in *Drogi chrześcijaństwa*, ed. Bohdan Sławiński (Warszawa: Jacek Santorski, 2008), 109.

60. The Central Statistical Office estimates that there are just over five hundred thousand Orthodox in Poland as of 2008 (cf. Gudaszewski and Chmieliweski, *Wyznania religijne*, 49).

61. Kuprianowicz, "Prawosławie w Polsce," 822.

62. Nijakowski, "Tworzenie, odtwarzanie, niszczenie i zanikanie granic między grupami etnicznymi," 71–72.

63. Marcin Bielesz, "Dzień Kościoła apostolskiego," *Gazeta Lublin*, regional insert to *Gazeta Wyborcza*, 22 August 2007, 3.

64. Anna Chlebicka, "Wizje chrześcijańskiej wspólnoty w oczach mieszkańców Gładyszowa," in *Religijność chrześcijan obrządku wschodniego na pograniczu polsko-ukraińskim*, ed. Magdalena Lubańska (Warszawa: Wyd. DiG, 2007), 144.

65. Ibid., 155.

66. Kuprianowicz, "Prawosławie w Polsce," 832. For a sociological examination of Orthodox youth and their attitudes toward religion, see Wiesław Romanowicz, "Tradycja religijna w świadomości młodzieży prawosławnej," in *Socjologia życia religijnego. Tradycje badawcze wobec zmiany kulturowej*, ed. Sławomir Zaręba (Warszawa: Wydawnictwo Uniwersytetu KSW, 2010), 334–47.

67. Christopher Hann, "The Development of Polish Civil Society and the Experience of the Greek Catholic Minority in Eastern Europe," *Protecting the Human Rights of Religious Minorities in Eastern Europe*, ed. Peter G. Daunchin and Elizabeth A. Cole (New York: Columbia University Press, 2000), 251.

68. Juraj Buzalka, *Nation and Religion: The Politics of Commemoration in South-East Poland* (Berlin: Lit, Verlag, 2007), 133.

69. Weigel, *The End and the Beginning*, 277.

70. Buzalka, *Nation and Religion*, 135.

71. Ibid.

72. Ibid., 138.

73. Ibid., 141.

74. Gebert, "Our Identities—New, Old, Imagined," 49.

75. Rabbi Michael Schudrich, "Czego nauczyłem się od Jana Pawła II," *Więź* no.1 (2010): 106.

76. Bożena Szaynok, "Kościół katolicki w Polsce wobec problematyki żydowskiej (1944–1989)," in *Następstwa zagłady Żydów. Polska 1944–2010*, ed. Feliks Tych and Monika Adamczyk-Garbowska (Lublin: Wydawnictwo Uniwersytetu Marii Curie-Skłodowskiej, 2011), 579.

77. Krajewski, *Poland and the Jews*, 213.

78. Quoted in Michael Steinlauf, *Bondage to the Dead: Poland and the Memory of the Holocaust* (Syracuse, NY: Syracuse University Press, 2006), 114.

79. Ibid., 132.

80. Ibid., 114.

81. Deak, "Heroes and Victims," 425.

82. Among the Polish historians who have augmented the accounts of Jan Gross concerning the collaboration of segments of Polish society with the Nazis in the Holocaust are Jan Grabowski and Barbara Engelking. The debate will no doubt be a long-term one as more research is conducted.

83. An example of denial might be the response to the first work of popular culture that deals with the issue, Władysław Pasikowski's film of 2012, *Pokłosie* [Gleanings], where a member of a rural community in northwest Poland, the same region as Jedwabne, literally and figuratively unearths remains of a massacre of the Jewish neighbors during the time of the war and is rewarded by being murdered. The actor who played the inquisitive protagonist was mobbed by hate mail on his Facebook account.

84. Dariusz Libionka, "Debata wokół Jedwabnego," in *Następstwa zagłady Żydów. Polska 1944–2010*, ed. Feliks Tych and Monika Adamczyk-Garbowska (Lublin: Wydawnictwo Uniwersytetu Marii Curie-Skłodowskiej, 2011), 758–65.

85. Antony Polonsky and Joanna B. Michlic, introduction to part 4, "Debate on Church," in *The Neighbors Respond: The Controversy over the Jedwabne Massacre in Poland*, ed. Antony Polonsky and Joanna B. Michlic (Princeton, NJ: Princeton University Press, 2004), 149.

86. Ibid., 153.

87. Christopher Garbowski, "Opłakiwanie Żydów w miasteczkach Lubelszczyzny," *Przegląd Powszechny*, no. 2 (February 2003): 240–43.

88. Krajewski, *Poland and the Jews*, 107.

89. Quoted in Polonsky and Michlic, introduction, 150–51.

90. One effort at bringing together all the current scholarship on Jewish involvement in Communism in postwar Poland has been by Paweł Śpiewak (see his *Żydokomuna. Interpretacje historyczne* [Warszawa: Wydawnictwo Czerwone i Czarne, 2012]). The book is more of a scholarly essay, however, and has been variously criticized by historians for inaccuracies, but praised by some far a balanced discussion.

91. Krajewski, *Poland and the Jews*, 229.

92. Jonathan Magonet, "Jewish Attitudes to Interfaith Dialogue," in *How to Conquer the Barriers to Interfaith Dialogue: Christianity, Islam and Judaism*, ed. Christiane Timmeerman and Barbara Segaert (Brussels: Peter Lang, 2007), 64. Regarding the assertion that all sides in religious dialogue must be firmly rooted in their faith traditions, Joseph Weiler goes even farther, stating that a Christian who tries to enter into dialogue by denigrating his or her own deeply held beliefs might evoke suspicion, resentment or contempt: "suspicion due to the lack of good faith inherent in this way of entering relations; resentment due to the paternalistic attitude of someone who believes that uncomfortable truths have to be hidden from an inferior interlocutor, as if from a child; and contempt toward someone who is afraid to affirm the very foundations of his credo: 'If he does not respect his own identity, how can he respect mine?'" See his "A Christian Europe? Europe and Christianity: rules of commitment," *European View* 6 (2007): 147.

93. Edward K. Kaplan, "Healing Wounds: Reflections on Abraham Joshua Heschel and Interfaith Partnership in Poland," *Religion and the Arts* 12 (2008): 414–15.

94. Krajewski, *Poland and the Jews*, 230.

95. Zuzanna Radzik, "Żydzi z mojej parafii," *Tygodnik Powszechny*, no. 5 (29 January 2012): 20–1.

96. Porter-Szücs, *Faith and Fatherland*, 327.

97. Steinlauf, *Bondage to the Dead*, 124.

98. Joanna Tokarska-Bakir quoted in Jolanta

Ambrosewicz-Jacobs, "Świadomość Holokaustu wśród młodzieży polskiej po zmianach systemowych 1989 roku," in *Następstwa zagłady Żydów. Polska 1944–2010*, ed. Feliks Tych and Monika Adamczyk-Garbowska (Lublin: Wydawnictwo Uniwersytetu Marii Curie-Skłodowskiej, 2011), 657.

99. Even at its peak the Catholic Church's authority in Poland was most effective when it coincided with the needs and desires of the Polish population. For instance, while few question the role of the Church during the Solidarity movement, at the same time it was hardly effective in stemming the problem of alcoholism rampant in the country, despite its concerted effort.

100. Cf. Eugeniusz Sakowicz, "Dialog międzyreligijny w Polsce," in *Dialog chrześcijan z wyznawcami innych religii za wzorem św. Franciszka z Asyżu*, ed. Salezy Brzyszek and Zenon Styś (Warszawa: Franciszkański Centrum dla Europy Wschodniej i Azji Północnej, 2006), 217–18.

101. Antoni Sułek, "Zwykli Polacy patrzą na Żydów. Postawy społeczeństwa polskiego wobec Żydów w świetle badań sondażowych," in *Następstwa zagłady Żydów. Polska 1944–2010*, ed. Feliks Tych and Monika Adamczyk-Garbowska (Lublin: Wydawnictwo Uniwersytetu Marii Curie-Skłodowskiej, 2011), 862.

102. Monika Adamczyk-Garbowska and Magdalena Ruta, "Od kultury żydowskiej do kultury o Żydach," in *Następstwo zagłady Żydów. Polska 1944–2010*, ed. Feliks Tych and Monika Adamczyk-Garbowska (Lublin: Wydawnictwo Uniwersytetu Marii Curie-Skłodowskiej, 2011), 724.

103. Agnieszka Sabor in ibid., 728.

104. Bishop Stanisław Gądecki, *Kto spotyka Jezusa, spotyka judaizm. Dialog chrześcijańsko-żydowski w Polsce* (Gniezno: Gaudentinum, 2002), 165–66.

105. John L. Allen, *The Future Church: How Ten Trends Are Revolutionizing the Catholic Church* (New York: Doubleday, 2009), 96.

106. Selim Chazbijewicz, interviewed by Łukasz Adamski, "Islam musi się zmienić," *Fronda* 53 (2009): 245.

107. Zdzisław Bielecki, "Jubileusz 10 lecie RWKM," RWKM—Rada Wspólna Katolików i Muzułmanów, n.d., http://www.rwkm.pl/index.php?option=com_content&task=view&id=1&Itemid=15 (accessed 11 August 2011).

108. Adamski and Chazbijewicz, "Islam musi się zmienić," 241–42.

109. Ibid., 246.

110. Stefaniuk, "Islam and Muslims in Poland," 184.

111. Górniak-Kocikowska, "A New Challenge," 136–37.

112. See, for instance, the catalogue of the interfaith initiatives of the Polish Conference of Bishops in Eugeniusz Sakowicz's report "Dialog międzyreligijny w Polsce" cited above.

113. Tomasz P. Terlikowski, "Śmierć anglikanizmu," *Fronda* 53 (2009): 129–43.

114. Quoted in Maria Jasińska, "The Quarter of Mutual Respect in Wrocław," in *W stronę nowej wielokulturowości / Towards a New Multiculturalism*, ed. Robert Kusek and Joanna Sanetra-Szeliga (Kraków: Międzynarodowe Centrum Kultury, 2010), 191.

115. Ibid., 192.

116. See the Rev. Piotr Mazurkiewicz, interviewed by Dominika Cosić, "Europa musi mieć swoją twarz," *Znak*, no. 7 (October 2011): 85.

117. For Lutheran practice in Germany, for instance, see Jenkins, *God's Continent*, 28–9.

118. However, in interviews Adam Małysz always confirmed the importance of faith in his life. One could add that making the sign of the cross the way he did, many Polish viewers were under the impression that the ski jumper was Catholic.

119. Sacks, *Home We Build Together*, 215.

120. Jenkins, *God's Continent*, 98; Tariq Madood, "Muslims and European Multiculturalism," in *Religion in the New Europe*, ed. Krzysztof Michalski (Budapest: Central European Press, 2006), 98–101.

Chapter 5

1. Tadeusz Bartoś, *Jan Paweł II. Analiza krytyczna* (Warszawa: Sic!, 2008).

2. The situation in Catholicism is analogous to but not as dramatic as in the world Anglican community that is nearing schism between the liberal West and Evangelical global south community. Lamin Sanneh looks at the different global churches' agendas virtually in terms of a neocolonialism of the Western churches over the emerging churches in the global south: "Can the wealth of the Western church purchase the agreement or acquiescence of the Third World Christian Leaders in the West's radical social agenda?," he asks. See his *Disciples of All Nations*, 227.

3. Tymothy Snyder, "United Europe, Divided History," in *What Holds Europe Together?*, vol. 1, *Conditions of European Solidarity*, ed. Krzysztof Michalski (Budapest: Central European Press, 2006), 188.

4. Cf., e.g., David Herbert, *Religion and Civil Society: Rethinking Public Religion and Civil Society* (Farnham, UK: Ashgate, 2003), 57.

5. Monica Duffy Toft, Daniel Philpott, and Timothy Samuel Shah, *God's Century: Resurgent Religion and Global Politics* (New York: Norton, 2011).

6. Andrew Greeley, *Religion in Europe at the End of the Second Millennium* (New Brunswick, NJ: Transaction, 2004), 1.

7. Ibid., 5.

8. Hans-Georg Ziebertz and Ulrich Riegel, "Post-secular Europe—a Concept Questioned," in *Europe: Secular or Post-Secular?* ed. Hans-Georg Ziebertz and Ulrich Riegel (Berlin: LIT Verlag, 2009), 10.

9. Jenkins, *God's Continent*, 32–33.

10. Greeley, *Religion in Europe*, 9 passim.

11. Ibid., 123–30.

12. David Martin, "Integration and Fragmentation: Patterns of Religion in Europe," in *Religion in the New Europe*, ed. Krzysztof Michalski (Budapest: Central European Press, 2006), 79.

13. Greeley, *Religion in Europe*, 15.

14. Per Petterson, "The Nordic Paradox—Simultaneously Most Secularised and Most Religious," in *Europe: Secular or Post-Secular?* ed. Hans-Georg Ziebertz and Ulrich Riegel (Berlin: LIT Verlag, 2009), 82.

15. Ibid., 83.

16. Scott M. Thomas, "Outwitting the Developed Countries? Existential Insecurity and the Global Resurgence of Religion," *Journal of International Affairs* 61, 1 (2007): 35, 36.

17. Cf. Górniak-Kocikowska, "A New Challenge," 140–41.

18. Greeley, *Religion in Europe*, 126.

19. Porter-Szücs gives a chart of attendance according to church statistics for the years 1980–2008. See his *Faith and Fatherland*, 12.

20. Jose Casanova, "Religion and the Dynamics of Freedom: Poland, Europe, and the World," in *Values of Poles and the Heritage of John Paul II*, ed. Tomasz Żukowski (Warszawa: Centre for the Thought of John Paul II, 2009), 11.

21. Bjork, "Bulwark or Patchwork," 152. Detailed regional studies of Polish religious practices and attitudes are currently under way. See, e.g., Witold Zdaniewicz and Sławomir Zaręba, eds., *Postawy społeczno-religijne mieszkańców Archidiecezji Szczecińsko-Kamieńskiej* (Szczecin: Ottonianum, 2006).

22. Yves Lambert, "A Turning Point in Religious Evolution in Europe," *Journal of Contemporary Religion* 19, 1 (2004): 34.

23. Greeley, *Religion in Europe*, 17–18.

24. Jenkins, *God's Continent*, 46.

25. Ewa Fratczak, "Population Aging in Poland," in *Population Ageing in Central and Eastern Europe: Societal and Policy Implications*, ed. Andreas Hoff (Surrey, UK: Ashgate, 2011), 11–31.

26. Eric Kaufmann, *Shall the Religious Inherit the Earth? Demography and Politics in the Twenty-First Century* (London: Profile Books, 2010), 158–63.

27. Mary Eberstadt, "How the West Really Lost God," *Policy Review*, no. 143 (June–July 2007): 12–13.

28. Ibid., 9.

29. Ibid., 14–15.

30. Katarzyna Wiśniewska, "Kobiety wychodzą z kościoła," *Gazeta Wyborcza*, 13–15 August 2011.

31. The singletons among women are growing

in numbers in Poland for much the same reasons as in other countries: more women concentrating on their careers coincide with the decrease in marriageable men. The latter are less likely to have a higher education and delay taking on marital responsibilities longer than previously.

32. Personal communication with the author on 8 March 2012.

33. Martin, "Integration and Fragmentation," 68.

34. Quoted in Steven D. Smith, *The Disenchantment of Secular Discourse* (Cambridge, MA: Harvard University Press, 2010), 23.

35. Smith, *Disenchantment of Secular Discourse*, 139.

36. Greeley, *Religion in Europe*, 77.

37. Brian Grim et al., *Rising Restrictions on Religion* (Washington, DC: Pew Research Center's Forum on Religion & Public Life, 2011), 10.

38. Jenkins, *God's Continent*, 98.

39. Casanova, "Religion and the Dynamics of Freedom," 8.

40. Quoted in Toft, Philpott, and Shah, *God's Century*, 7.

41. Bruce Berglund, "Drafting a Historical Geography of Eastern European Christianity," in *Christianity and Modernity in Eastern Europe*, ed. Bruce Berglund and Brian Porter-Szücs (Budapest: Central European University, 2010), 360–61.

42. Berglund, "Drafting a Historical Geography of Eastern European Christianity," 360–61.

43. Irmina Wawrzyczek, Zbigniew Mazur, and Hanna Szewczyk, *Oswajanie Innego. Obraz Polski i Polaków w prasie brytyjskiej w latach 2002–2007* (Lublin: Gaudium, 2010), 234.

44. I am indebted for this information about the Polish student in Belgium to Professor Tomasz Schramm, a historian at Adam Mickiewicz University in Poznań and, among others, the vice director of *Association Internationale d'Histoire Contemporaine de'l Europe* since the year 2000.

45. Leszek Kołakowski, interviewed by Zbigniew Menzel, *Czas ciekawy, czas niespokojny*, part 2 (Kraków: Wyd. Znak, 2008), 177.

46. Cf. Lucy Beckett, *In the Light of Christ: Writings in the Western Tradition* (San Francisco: Ignatius Press, 2006), 579–609.

47. Quoted in Berlund, "Drafting a Historical Geography of Eastern European Christianity," 355.

48. Cf. Genevieve Zubrzycki, "History and the National Sensorium: Making Sense of Polish Mythology," *Qualitative Sociology* 34 (2011): 47–50.

49. Marek Beylin, interviewed by Dominika Kozłowska, "Historia pewnego sojuszu," *Znak*, no. 1 (January 2012): 39.

50. Cited in Maciej Müller and Tomasz Poniklo, "Antyklerykalizm szkodzi Kościołowi.

Ale jest mu niezbędny," *Tygodnik Powszechny*, no. 43 (24 October 2010): 4.

51. Joanna Podgórska, "Msza za świeckie państwo," *Polityka*, no. 45 (2–7 November 2011): 30. Anticlericalism in rural Poland in part stems from the stereotype of the greedy parish priest. According a comparative study, however, the parish priest in the country actually earns less than even the assistant priests in urban parishes (cf. Kazimierz Korab, "Zachłanność proboszczów wiejskich? Glossa do rozważań na temat stereotypu," *Przegląd Powszechny*, no. 7–8 (July–August 2009): 39.

52. The Rev. Andrzej Draguła, *Copyright na Jezusa. Język, znak, rytuał między wiarą a niewiarą* (Warszawa: Biblioteka "Więzi," 2012), 76.

53. Müller and Poniklo, "Antyklerykalizm szkodzi Kościołowi," 4.

54. Stephen Prothero, *American Jesus: How the Son of God Became a National Icon* (New York: Farrar, Strauss & Giroux, 2003), 7.

55. Müller and Poniklo, "Antyklerykalizm szkodzi Kościołowi," 4.

56. Bishop Andrzej Czaja, interviewed by Zbigniew Nosowski, "Kościół nie jest sam dla siebie," *Więź*, no. 10 (October 2010): 6.

57. The Rev. Henryk Zieliński, "Nobilitacja ksenofobii," *Idziemy* 43 (23 October 2011), http://www.idziemy.com.pl/komentarze/nobilitacja-ksenofobii (accessed 3 April 2012).

58. Sylwia Krasnodębska and Lew-Starowicz, "Kochajmy się wiernie" (interview), *Uważam Rze*, no. 15 (16–27 May 2011): 43.

59. Marek Zając, "Archipelag rozsądku," *Tygodnik Powszechny*, no. 44 (30 October 2011), 4.

60. Allen, *Future Church*, 56.

61. Ibid., 57.

62. Ewa Miszczak, *Katolicki ruch odnowy w Duchu Świętym w Polsce* (Lublin: Wydawnictwo Marii Curie-Skłodowskiej, 2011), 53.

63. Wiśniewska, "Kobiety wychodzą z kościoła."

64. Elżbieta Adamiak, Anna Karoń-Ostrowska, and Zbigniew Nosowski, "Być kobietą, być w Kościele," *Więź* 1–2 (January–February 2009): 30. For a discussion on the Church and women there are several articles in the volume *Gender and Religion in Central and Eastern Europe* (edited by Elżbieta Adamiak, Małgorzata Chrząstowska, Charlotte Methuen, and Sonia Sobkowiak, published by the Faculty of Theology in Poznań in 2009). In the same book there are also articles about women and the different religious traditions in Poland.

65. Kaufmann, *Shall the Religious Inherit the Earth*, 30.

66. Tomasz Lis quoted in Marek Zając, "Rok zły," *Tygodnik Powszechny*, no. 45 (4 November 2012), 4.

67. Kaufmann, *Shall the Religious Inherit the Earth*, 158–205.

68. It may seem odd to juxtapose the Evangelical movement with the communitarian movement in the United States, since the religious movement is known for its individualism. However, upon reading the chapter concerning Pastor Rick Warren and Saddleback Church in Robert Putnam and Lewis Feldstein's *Better Together: Restoring the American Community* of 2004, it is evident that part of the success of Evangelicals is in building social capital.

69. This naturally does not mean that Poles were not exposed to Western trends before 1989. For instance, when Joan Baez gave a concert at the Catholic University in Lublin in the mid–1980s she related a humorous anecdote about meeting Franciscan monks in Gdańsk, to whom she bragged about her upcoming meeting with Mark Knopfler of Dire Straits, and the monks "dropped their Rosaries" in surprise; i.e., the monks were quite aware whom she meant.

70. Cf. Robert N. Bellah, "Religion and the Shape of National Culture," *America* 181, 3 (31 July 1999): 9–14.

71. Przemysław Kucharczak, "Się chce," *Gość Niedzielny*, 20 November 2011, 38–41.

72. Porter-Szücs, *Faith and Fatherland*, 147–48.

73. For instance, in the review of a book-length interview with the current president of the Conference of Bishops in Poland, Artur Sporniak indicates his agreement with a number of the stands that the bishop takes and praises his general tone of evangelical concern, even though the bishop is known to be a critic of *Tygodnik Powszechny* and the interview contains a number of slurs on the milieu ("Trzymamy za słowo," *Tygodnik Powszechny*, no. 1 [1 January 2012], 16–17).

74. Kaufmann, *Shall the Religious Inherit the Earth?*, 159.

75. Cf. Draguła, *Copyright na Jezusa*, 73.

76. The most controversial book on this topic is Roman Graczyk's *Cena przetrwania? SB a "Tygodnik Powszechny"* of 2011, which deals with the alleged cooperation of several *Tygodnik Powszechny* authors with the Communist secret service.

77. John Richard Neuhaus, *Prorok z Nowego Jorku* (Warszawa: Fronda, 2010), 57–58.

78. Porter-Szücs, *Faith and Fatherland*, 106–8.

79. Terlikowski gives his account of the Wielgus affair and his role within it in his *Odwaga prawdy. Spór o lustrację w polskim Kościele* (Warszawa: Prószyński I S-ka, 2007), 132–65.

80. Allen, *Future Church*, 65.

81. Quoted in ibid., 87.

82. Thomas Farr, "The Catholic Church and the Global Crisis of Religious Liberty," *National Catholic Register*, 13 June 2012, http://www.ncregister.com/daily-news/the-catholic-church-and-the-global-crisis-of-religious-liberty (accessed 17 June 2012).

83. Among the Polish evangelical Catholics, Terlikowski, for one, has written on the possible need for civil disobedience on the part of Christians in Poland. See his *Rzeczpospolita papieska. Jan Paweł II o Polsce do Polaków* (Warszawa: Centrum Myśli Jana Pawła II, 2009), 148.

84. Przemysław Kucharczak, "Joanna Najfeld uniewinniona," *Gość Niedzielny*, 18 September 2011, 4.

85. For instance, there is the case of Alicja Tysiąc, a Polish woman whom in 2007 the European Court of Human Rights awarded 25,000 euros in damages after she was refused a therapeutic abortion. In the Catholic weekly *Gość Niedzielny*, editor the Reverend Gancarczyk then wrote that Tysiąc received an award because "she wanted to kill her baby" and compared the judges to Nazis. He was then tried and fined for hate speech. While not condoning abortion, a number of Catholic commentators criticized Gancarczyk as well. See Draguła, *Copyright na Jezusa*, 19–24.

86. Allen, *Future Church*, 57.

87. The Rev. Andrzej Draguła, *Ocalić Boga. Szkice z teologii sekularyzacji* (Warszawa: Biblioteka "Więzi," 2010), 35.

88. Szymon Hołownia, interviewed by Barbara Kasprzycka, "Woody Allen naszego katolicyzmu," *Magazyn Dziennika* (27–28 September 2009): 11.

89. Terlikowski, *Grzechy Kościoła*, 166.

90. Allen, *Future Church*, 84.

91. Marek Rymsza, "Warto przegonić Lulka," *Więź*, no. 5–6 (May–June 2012): 66.

92. Cf. David Herbert, *Religion and Civil Society: Rethinking Public Religion and Civil Society* (Farnham, UK: Ashgate, 2003), 95–118.

93. Toft, Philpott, and Shah, *God's Century*, 102.

94. Cf. Philip Jenkins, *The New Anti-Catholicism: The Last Acceptable Prejudice* (Oxford: Oxford University Press, 2003).

95. See, e.g., Gudrun Kugler, ed., *Shadow Report: On Intolerance and Discrimination against Christians in Europe, 2005–2010* (Vienna: Observatory on Intolerance and Discrimination against Christians in Europe, 2010), passim.

96. For an account of the Invocatio Dei debate in the EU constitution and a discussion of its implications, see Luxmoore and Babiuch, *Rethinking Christendom*, 194–216.

97. Quoted in *Faith and Fatherland*, 200. It must be added this preamble was the result of a bitterly contested compromise (ibid., 200–201).

98. Quoted in Mary Ann Glendon, "The Bearable Lightness of Dignity," *First Things: A Monthly Journal of Religion & Public Life* (May 2011): 44.

99. Cf. ibid., 41.

100. Quoted in ibid., 43.

101. Smith, *Disenchantment of Secular Discourse*, 178.

102. Glendon, "The Bearable Lightness of Dignity," 43.

103. Farr, "The Catholic Church and the Global Crisis of Religious Liberty."

104. Weigel, *Final Revolution*, 157.

105. Ramet, "Thy Will Be Done," 135–37.

106. Robert K. Vischer, *Conscience and the Common Good: Reclaiming the Space between Person and Space* (Cambridge, UK: Cambridge University Press, 2010), 106.

107. Zbigniew Nosowski, "Zapateryzm na polskim przedmieściu? Powyborcze wyzwania dawne i nowe," *Więź*, no. 1 (January 2012): 32.

108. The leader of the Civic Platform, Donald Tusk, is quite opportunistic in his stance toward the Church. Before the election that brought his party to power in 2007, he publicly stated that he had a conversion experience when John Paul II died. This was only a couple of years after the death of the pontiff, when sentiment toward him was high. A few years later during the election campaign in 2011, when the party's popularity was weakening and it seemed they might have to form a coalition with a the post–Communist anticlerical party, the prime minister tactlessly stated he would not go down on his knees before priests, alluding to legislation on in vitro that might be introduced after the elections.

109. For a brief analysis of how the two Christian Democratic parties represent different Catholic electorates, see Porter-Szücs, *Faith and Fatherland*, 391–93; see also Terlikowski, *Grzechy Kościoła*, 36–38.

110. For instance, Łukasz Kasper and Marcin Przeciszewski point out that the document signed by the Polish Conference of Bishops and Kyryl I, the Patriarch of the Russian Orthodox Church, referred to in Chapter 4, was signed by all the bishops despite their awareness that the radical right would consider it naïve. See Kasper and Przeciszewski, "Kościół wtrąca się do polityki?," in *Kościół. Stereotypy, uprzedzenia, manipulacji*, ed. Marcin Przeciszewski (Warszawa, Lublin: Katolicka Agencja Informacyjna and Gaudium, 2012), 103.

111. Adam Leszczyński, "Dialog? Ale po co?" *Znak*, no. 1 (January 2012): 33.

112. Archbishop Henryk Muszyński, interviewed by Łukasz Dulęba and Marcin Pera, "Dialog, a nie walka," *Więź*, no. 1 (January 2012): 87.

113. For instance, after the general election in 2011 in an opinion piece by Fr. Jacek Prusak, a journalist from the affirmative Orthodox camp upbraided a liberal Catholic journalist who had claimed that the constitution should direct a Catholic politician's choices, reminding her that "[t]he constitution is not the Bible, and political views should not shape a Catholic's identity, but his faith should shape his political views.... The Church ... has the right to be present in the public sphere" (*Gazeta Wyborcza*, 15–16 October 2011). On the other hand, a younger assertive evangelical Catholic criticized Catholics who place too much faith in either political party: "A sizeable portion of politically active Catholics either follow their idol Jarosław Kaczyński ... believing his messianic narrative about the direct threat to the existence of our state from Russia or the Civic Platform, a threat from which he alone can save us, or they select the peace and quiet of the ruling party, placing 'social peace' above the principle of justice" (see Tomasz Rowiński, "Porzućcie romantyzm!" *Znak*, no. 4 [April 2011]: 21).

114. Konferencja Episkopatu Polski, *W trosce o człowieka i dobro wspólne* (Warszawa: Biblos, 2012), 39.

115. See Fr. Maciej Zięba, interviewed by Zbigniew Nosowski, "Kościół między młotem a kowadłem," *Więź*, no. 10 (2012): 15.

116. Jacek Żakowski quoted in Piotr Kraśko et al., *Bitwa o Kościół* (Kraków: Wydawnictwo Salwator, 2010), 25.

117. An exception would be swearing into office, where a significant portion of politicians add to their oath the optional "So help me God."

118. Mirosława Grabowska, interviewed by Marcin Żyla, "Polak lubi tacę," *Tygodnik Powszechny*, no. 10 (4 March 2012): 5.

119. For a detailed summary of the financial report, see "Raport KAI o finansach Kościoła poniedziałek," Franciszkańska3.pl, 27 February 2012, http://franciszkanska3.pl/Raport-KAI-o-finansach-Kosciola,a,14134 (accessed 25 May 2012).

120. Ewa Czaczkowska and Jarosław Stróżyk, "Ile Kościół ma naprawdę pieniędzy," *Uważam Rze*, no. 13 (26 March, 1 April 2012): 36.

121. During the mid–1990s the author had several conversations with the then press secretary of the Catholic University of Lublin during which this strategy was outlined for him.

122. Tadeusz Sławek, "W obronie wolności myślenie," *Gość Niedzielny*, no. 50 (10 December 2000): 7.

123. Jean Paul Willaime, "Different Models for Religious Education in Europe," in *Religion and Education in Europe: Developments, Contexts and Debates*, ed. Robert Jackson, Siebren Miedema, Wolfram Weisse, and Jean Paul Willaume (Munster: Waxmann Verlag, 2007), 60–61.

124. Liberal religion journalist Katarzyna Wiśniewska defends the Church against its critics in this matter: "One cannot blame the Church on account of the fact that there are no ethics classes in schools; this is a matter for the ministry of education" (Kraśko et al., *Bitwa o Kościół*, 43).

125. Cf. Krystyna Kluzowa, Janina Palus, and Jadwiga Wronicz, "Edukacja seksualna w Polsce

na tle wybranych krajów Unii Europejskiej," *Wychowawca: Miesięcznik nauczycieli i wychowawców katolickich*, no. 6 (2011): 24–27.

126. Toft, Philpott, and Shah, *God's Century*, 205.

127. Tomasz Terlikowski and Robert Mazurek, "Kościół powolutku odzyskuje głos," *Rzeczpospolita*, 1–2 October 2011, P10.

128. Ireneusz Siudem cited in Jarosław Stróżyk, "Cała Polska maszeruje w obronie życia i rodziny," *Rzeczpospolita*, 2–3 June 2012, A5.

129. Wiesław Chrzanowski, interviewed by Cezary Michalski, "Katolicy zapomnieli o społeczeństwie," *Europa. Magazyn idei Dziennika*, no. 4 (26 January 2008): 2.

130. Beyer, *Recovering Solidarity*, 62–64.

131. Ibid., 182.

132. Ignacy Dutkiewicz and Misza Tomaszewski, "Porzucone ideały," *Znak*, no. 1 (January 2012): 16.

133. Among the postulates of the pastoral program of the Polish Conference of Bishops for the years 2010–2013 is establishing a social council in every diocese. See the Rev. Marek Korguł, and the Rev. Szymon Stułkowski, "Kościół naszym domem," in *Kościół naszym domem, Kościół domem i szkołą komunii. Program duszpasterski Kościoła w Polsce na lata 2011–2013* (Poznań: Wyd. Święty Wojciech, 2011), 18; also the Rev. Paweł Deskur, "Rada Społeczna przy biskupie diecezjalnym," in *Kościół naszym domem, Kościół domem i szkołą komunii. Program duszpasterski Kościoła w Polsce na lata 2011–2013*, ed. Szymon Stułkowski (Poznań: Wydawnictwo Święty Wojciech, 2011), 254–60.

134. Konferencja Episkopatu Polski, *W trosce o człowieka*, 49–62.

135. The Rev. Adam Boniecki, "Jeden, święty, powszechny ... polski," *Tygodnik Powszechny*, no. 37 (15 May 2011): 2.

136. Fr. Zięba and Nosowski, "Kościół między młotem a kowadłem," 12.

137. Archbishop Józef Michalik, Grzegorz Górny, and Tomasz Terlikowski, *Raport o stanie wiary* (Radom: Polwen, 2011), 12.

138. Irena Borowik, interviewed by Tomasz Ponikło, "(Nie) warto rozmawiać," *Tygodnik Powszechny*, no. 37 (11 September 2011): 18.

139. Zbigniew Nosowski quoted in Porter-Szücs, *Faith and Fatherland*, 11.

140. Cf. Magdelena Smak-Wójcicka, "Dialog symboli religijnych w przestrzeni miejskiej. Nowe i stare formy ekspresji kultu," in *Miasto i Sacrum*, ed. Maciej Kowalewski and Anna Małgorzata Królikowska (Kraków: Nomos, 2011), 154–56.

141. The Rev. Janusz Mariański, interviewed by Jan Turnau and Katarzyna Wiśniewska, "Kościół? Nie, dziękuję," *Gazeta Wyborcza*, 17–18 September 2011, 36.

142. Mirosława Grabowska, "Przeobrażenia polskiej religijności," *Znak*, no. 6 (2011): 49.

143. Cezary Michalski, "Herezja smoleńska," *Newsweek Polska*, no. 18 (8 May 2011): 19.

144. Porter-Szücs, *Faith and Fatherland*, 202–3.

145. Michalski, "Herezja smoleńska," 19.

146. A popular talent show host comments in this vein: "What are we even talking about? This is 2011, and we in Poland are all excited about a mediocre artistic happening the rest of the world experienced thirty years ago. Major politicians and Catholic bishops dedicate time and attention to an opportunistic entertainer, whose social harm is in my opinion nil, and through the tremendous hubbub raised around his person he is simply gaining free publicity" (Hołownia and Prokop, *Bóg, kasa i rock'n'roll*, 40).

147. Cited in Katarzyna Wiśniewska, "Biskupi przeciwko umowom śmieciowym," *Gazeta Wyborcza*, 30 March 2012.

148. Konferencja Episkopatu Polski, *W trosce o człowieka*, 39.

149. Draguła, *Ocalić Boga*, 203.

150. Tomasz Szlendak, interviewed by Michał Kuźmiński, "Maszyna do życia," *Tygodnik Powszechny*, no. 26 (26 June 2011): 4.

151. Monika Przybysz, *Kościół w kryzysie? Crisis management w Kościele w Polsce* (Tarnów: Biblos, 2008).

152. Kamil Durczok, quoted in Kraśko et al., *Bitwa o Kościół*, 172.

153. Marcin Przeciszewski, "Katolicka Agencja Informacyjna. Zasady relacje z mediami," in *Media i Kościół. Polityka informacyjna Kościoła*, ed. Monika Przybysz and Krzysztof Marcyński, SAC (Warszawa: Elipsa, 2011), 52.

154. Eugeniusz Sakowicz, "Dialog między religijny w Polsce," 210.

155. Krzemiński, *Czego nas uczy Radio Maryja?*, 130.

156. Ibid., 129.

157. Górny, *Między Matriksem a krucyfiksem*, 129–30.

158. Andrzej Garapich, introduction to "Megapanel PBI/Gemius: witryny internetowe o tematyce religijnej," in *Internet i Kościół*, ed. Józef Kloch (Warszawa: Elipsa, 2011), 258–59.

159. Marcin Przeciszewski (ed.), *Kościół. Stereotypy, uprzedzenia, manipulacji* (Warszawa, Lublin: Katolicka Agencja Informacyjna and Gaudium, 2012).

160. The Rev. Janusz Mariańsk, interviewed by Artur Sporniak, "Kościół przyszłości będzie wielobarwny," *Tygodnik Powszechny*, no. 18–19 (29 April–6 May 2012): 7.

161. Cf. Bjork, "Bulwark or Patchwork," 129–40.

162. Jerry Muller, "Us and Them: The Enduring Power of Ethnic Nationalism," in *The Clash of Civilizations: The Debate*, ed. James Hodge, Jr. (New York: Council on Foreign Relations, 2010), 114.

163. Ibid., 119.

164. Porter-Szücs, *Faith and Fatherland*, 393.

165. Porter-Szücs, *Faith and Fatherland*, 359.

166. See Zięba, "Kościól między młotem a kowadłem," 18.

167. Bishop Ryś uses the term personalism to speak of religious humanism, which was the dominant form of religious humanism during the time of the Second Vatican Council. See his "Sed contra ... Kilka pytań do Adama Michnika," in Agata Bielik-Robson et al., *Kim są Polacy* (Warsaw: Agora, 2013), 40–42.

168. Ibid., 43.

169. Leon Miller, "Religion's Role in National Unity," *International Journal on World Peace* 24, 1 (2009): 91.

170. Enzo Pace, "Religion as Communication: The Changing Shape of Catholicism in Europe," in *Everyday Religion*, ed. Nancy T. Ammerman (Oxford: Oxford University Press, 2007), 45.

171. Cf. Miller's discussion of how constructing a civil religion in Estonia would aid in developing social cohesion in an ethnically diverse society that has spent the bulk of the last seven hundred years under one occupying power or another. See his "Religion's Role in Creating National Unity," 102–12.

172. Draguła, *Copyright na Jezusa*, 114.

173. Professor Lech Morawski, quoted in ibid., 131.

174. For a discussion of the biblical roots and contemporary importance of covenant in building civil society, see Sacks, *The Home We Build Together*, 118–22.

175. Muller, "Us and Them," 114.

176. Among the ambivalent democratic tendencies in the European Union, one presented by Francis Fukuyama can serve as an example. Although he basically supports the European Union, he nonetheless observes what many less charitable critics of the EU have long noted: "[T]o be quite honest, the whole European project has been an elite-driven affair. We know that on several occasions when the issue of agreeing to a treaty was put up for popular referendum and when the people gave the wrong answer, the elite would say the people were wrong about that, they are going to have to vote again" ("European Identities Part II," American Interest Online, 12 January 2012, http://blogs.the-american-interest.com/fukuyama/ 2012/01/12/european-identities-part-ii/web [accessed 12 February 2012]). He further makes the point that the common antidemocratic tendency of ignoring popular opinion by the political elite on difficult matters is part of the explanation for populist parties gaining in strength in the last few years.

177. Pawel Swieboda, "This Winter in Warsaw," *American Interest* 7, 1 (January–February 2012): 74.

178. The Rev. Piotr Mazurkiewicz, interviewed by Anna Gruszecka, "Zatrzymać ruchome piaski," *W Drodze*, no. 2 (2011): 70.

179. A block of texts devoted to the most recent Gniezno Convention dedicated to the role of religion in the civil society of today's Europe has been published theme in the May–June 2012 edition of the Catholic monthly *Więź*.

180. Nicholas Boyle, *Who Are We Now: Christian Humanism and the Global Market from Hegel to Heaney* (London: Continuum, 2000), 91–92.

181. Andrzej Kasperek, "Znaczenie locum w czasach globalizacji na przykładzie stosunku Polaków do parafii," in *Religia i religijność w warunkach globalizacji*, ed. Maria Libiszowska-Żółtkowska (Kraków: Nomos, 2007), 237.

182. Kevin Hannan, "Polish Catholicism: A Historical Outline," *Sarmation Review*, January 2004, http://www.ruf.rice.edu/~sarmatia/104/241hannan.html (accessed 18 January 2012).

183. Andrzej Horubała, "Kłopot z Nowosielskim," *PlusMinus: Tygodnik "Rzeczpospolitej"* (12–13 March 2011): P14.

184. Greeley, *Catholic Imagination*, 44–46.

185. Allen, *Future Church*, 153–61.

186. The family is highly valued among Poles. Hardly surprising, then, Poles have a high rate of marriage and a relatively low rate of cohabitation on a European scale. The divorce rate, while up from that of a couple of decades ago, is also on the lower end of the continental scale. See W. Bradford Wilcox and Carlos Cavallé, *The Sustainable Demographic Dividend* (Barcelona: Social Trends Institute, 2011), 28–30.

187. Indeed, at the time of writing in contrast to their sisters at home, Polish women that have settled in the United Kingdom have the highest number of births of all immigrant women.

188. Now it is becoming apparent that even experienced societies in Europe have difficulties absorbing immigrant minorities. See, e.g., Paul M. Sniderman and Louk Hagendoorn, *When Ways of Life Collide: Multiculturalism and Its Discontents in the Netherlands* (Princeton, NJ: Princeton University Press, 2009).

189. Stella Grotowska, "Religia w świecie wyobrażonym starego człowieka," in *Religia i religijność w warunkach globalizacji*, ed. Maria Libiszowska-Żółtkowska (Kraków: Nomos, 2007), 314–23.

190. Tomek Kaczor, "Wszyscy jesteśmy seniorami," *Kontakt*, Winter 2011, 19.

191. Mariański, *Katolicyzm polski*, 375.

192. Mariański and Sporniak, "Kościół przyszłości będzie wielobarwny," 7.

193. Zbigniew Nosowski, Michał Paluch, and Piotr Jordan Śliwiński, "Ku wspólnocie świadków," *Więź*, no. 1 (September 2008): 79.

Epilogue

1. Toft, Philpott, and Shah, *God's Century*, 111.
2. Sanneh, *Disciples of All Nations*, 277–78.
3. Allen, *Future Church*, 18.
4. Toft, Philpott, and Shah, *God's Century*, 113.
5. Beyer, *Recovering Solidarity*, 182.
6. Szymon Hołownia, *Last Minute. 24h chrześcijaństwa na świecie* (Kraków: Znak, 2012), 5.
7. Ibid., 7.
8. Szymon Hołownia, interviewed by Maciej Kędziak, "Szymon Hołownia. Jego prywatny Dekalog," *Gala*, no. 50 (13–25 December 2010): 44.
9. Mariański, *Katolicyzm polski*, 363, 64.
10. Małgorzata Bilska, "Wspólnota," in *Chrześcijaństwo przed nami*, ed. Jarosław Makowski and Janusz Salamon (Kraków: Wydawnictwo WAM, 2008), 97–98.
11. Terlikowski, *Rzeczpospolita papieska*, 176.
12. Ibid., 194.
13. Zbigniew Nosowski, *Polski rachunek sumienia z Jana Pawła II* (Warszawa: Centrum Myśli Jana Pawła II, 2010), 12.
14. Ibid., 21.
15. John Paul II, *Memory and Identity*, 87.
16. Nosowski, *Polski rachunek sumienia*, 116.
17. Maciej Zięba, *Ale nam się wydarzyło. O papieżu i Polsce, Kościele i świecie* (Poznań: W drodze, 2013), 182–88.
18. Weigel, *End and the Beginning*, 488.
19. Ibid.
20. Maciej Zięba, OP, interviewed by Marek Zając, "Kiedy rozum ociemniał," *Tygodnik Powszechny*, no. 11, 11 March 2012, 17.
21. Peter Berger, "Observations from America," in *Religion in the New Europe*, ed. Krzysztof Michalski (Budapest: Central European Press, 2006), 92.

22. Christie Davies, *The Strange Death of Moral Britain*, 2nd ed. (New Brunswick, NJ: Transaction Publishers, 2007), 216.
23. Jonathan Sacks, "How to Reverse the West's Decline," *Standpoint*, September 2011, n.p., http://www.standpointmag.co.uk/node/4049/full (accessed 2 February 2012).
24. Jonathan Sacks, "Address to the Pontifical Gregorian University in Rome," Office of the Chief Rabbi, speeches, 12 December 2011, http://www.chiefrabbi.org/ReadArtical.aspx?id=1854 (accessed 2 February 2012).
25. Ibid.
26. Quoted in Vischer, *Conscience and the Common Good*, 55.
27. Ibid.
28. The Rev. Andrzej Draguła, "Świecki w świecie świeckim," Symposium Świeckich Instytutów Życia Konsekrowanego, 5 November 2011, Warszawa, manuscript courtesy of author.
29. Nosowski, "Zapateryzm na polskim przedmieściu?" 36.
30. In Europe this unity on behalf of the family was evidenced during the massive demonstration in Paris, 13 January 2013, where French Jews and Muslims supported the Catholics protesting the changes regarding the family proposed by the president of France.
31. Terlikowski, *Rzeczpospolita papieska*, 195.
32. The carol, entitled "Mędrcy świata" (Wisemen of the World), alternates from mining the biblical narrative to the apocryphal one, beginning as it does by addressing the protagonists, "*Mędrcy świata, Monarchowie*" (O wisemen of the world, O monarchs).
33. Jacek Dziedzina, "Orszak polski," *Gość Niedzielny*, 8 January 2012, 20.
34. James V. Schall, *The Sum Total of Human Happiness* (South Bend, IL: St. Augustine's Press, 2006), 150–51.

Bibliography

Adamczyk-Garbowska, Monika, and Magdalena Ruta. "Od kultury żydowskiej do kultury o Żydach." In *Następstwo zagłady Żydów. Polska 1944–2010*, edited by Feliks Tych and Monika Adamczyk-Garbowska, 715–32. Lublin: Wydawnictwo Uniwersytetu Marii Curie-Skłodowskiej, 2011.

Adamiak, Elżbieta, Małgorzata Chrząstowska, Charlotte Methuen, and Sonia Sobkowiak (eds.). *Gender and Religion in Central and Eastern Europe*. Studies and Texts Series. Poznań: Faculty of Theology, 2009.

Adamiak, Elżbieta, Anna Karoń-Ostrowska, and Zbigniew Nosowski. "Być kobietą, być w Kościele." *Więź*, no. 1–2 (January–February 2009): 26–43.

Adamowski, Jan. "Motywacje stawianie krzyży i kapliczek przydrożnych." In *Krzyże i kapliczki przydrożne jako znaki społecznej, kulturowej i religijnej pamięci*, edited by Jan Adamowski and Marta Wójcicka, 17–42. Lublin: Wydawnictwo Uniwersytetu Marii Curie-Skłodowska, 2011.

Allen, John L. *The Future Church: How Ten Trends Are Revolutionizing the Catholic Church*. New York: Doubleday, 2009.

Ambrosewicz-Jacobs, Jolanta. "Świadomość Holokaustu wśród młodzieży polskiej po zmianach systemowych 1989 roku." In *Następstwo zagłady Żydów. Polska 1944–2010*, edited by Feliks Tych and Monika Adamczyk-Garbowska, 625–58. Lublin: Wydawnictwo Uniwersytetu Marii Curie-Skłodowskiej, 2011.

Applebaum, Anne. *Iron Curtain: The Crushing of Eastern Europe, 1944–1956*. London: Allen Lane, 2012.

Babinski, Grzegorz. "Ukrainians in Poland after the Second World War." In *From Homogeneity to Multiculturalism: Minorities Old and New in Poland*, edited by F. E. Ian Hamilton and Krystyna Iglicka, 114–34. London: School of Slavonic and East European Studies, 2000.

Baniak, Józef. *Deskralizacja kultu religijnego i świąt religijnych w Polsce*. Kraków: Nomos, 2007.

Barnes, Samuel H. "The Mobilization of Political Identity in New Democracies." In *The Postcommunist Citizen*, edited by Samuel H. Barnes and Janos Simon, 117–29. Budapest: Erasmus Foundation and Institute for Political Science of the Hungarian Academy of Sciences, 1998.

Bartmiński, Stanisław. *Krasiczyn. Dzieje parafii i społeczności*. Vol. 2, Duchowieństwo i parafianie, aktywność społeczna wiernych. Krasiczyn, Przemyśl: [Wieści Krasiczyńskie Tygodnik Parafialny], 2010.

Bartoś, Tadeusz. *Jan Paweł II. Analiza krytyczna*. Warszawa: Sic! 2008.

Bątkiewicz-Brożek, Joanna. "Mieszani, ale święci." *Gość Niedzielny*, no. 27 (10 July 2011): 26–27.

Beckett, Lucy. *In the Light of Christ: Writings in the Western Tradition*. San Francisco: Ignatius Press, 2006.

Beem, Christopher. *The Necessity of Politics: Reclaiming American Public Life*. Chicago: University of Chicago Press, 1999.

Belch, Stanislaus. *The Contribution of Poland to the Development of the Doctrine of International Law (Paulus Vladimiri, decretorum doctor, 1409–1432)*. London: Veritas Foundation, 1965.

Bellah, Robert N. "Religion and the Shape of National Culture." *America*, no. 3 (31 July 1999): 9–14.

Berger, Peter. "In Defense of a Commercialized Christmas." Peter Berger's blog. 28 December 2010. http://blogs.the-american-interest.com/berger/2010/12/28/in-defense-of-a-commercialized-christmas (accessed March 7, 2012).

_____. "Observations from America." In *Religion in the New Europe*, edited by Krzysztof Michalski, 85–93. Budapest: Central European Press, 2006.

_____. "Poland between Rome and Brussels." Peter Berger's blog, American Interest Online, August 31, 2010. http://blogs.theamerican-interest.com/berger/2010/08/31/poland-between-rome-and-brussels.

Berglund, Bruce R. "Drafting a Historical Geography of Eastern European Christianity." In *Christianity and Modernity in Eastern Europe*, edited by Bruce Berglund and Brian Porter-Szücs, 329–71. Budapest: Central European University, 2010.

Bergman, Elenora, and Jan Jagielski. "Ślady obecności. Synagogi i cmentarze." In *Następstwo zagłady Żydów. Polska 1944–2010*, edited by Feliks Tych and Monika Adamczyk-Garbowska, 471–92. Lublin: Wydawnictwo Uniwersytetu Marii Curie-Skłodowskiej, 2011.

Better Together. Report of the Saguaro Seminar on Civic Engagement. Cambridge, MA: John F. Kennedy School of Government. Harvard University, 2000. http://better together.org/thereport.htm.

Beyer, Gerald J. *Recovering Solidarity: Lessons from Poland's Unfinished Revolution*. Notre Dame, IN: University of Notre Dame Press, 2010.

_____. "A Theoretical Appreciation of the Ethic of Solidarity in Poland Twenty Five Years After." *Journal of Religious Ethics* 35, 2 (2007): 20–32 [AU: Please complete first number of page range.].

Beylin, Marek. "Historia pewnego sojuszu." Interview by Dominika Kozłowska. *Znak*, no. 1 (January 2012): 34–39.

Bielecki, Zdzisław. "Jubileusz 10 lecie RWKM." RWKM—Rada Wspólna Katolików i Muzułmanów, n.d. http://www.rw km.pl/index.php?option=com_content& task=view&id=1&Itemid=15 (accessed 11 August 2011).

Bielesz, Marcin. "Dzień Kościoła apostolskiego." *Gazeta Lublin*. Insert to *Gazeta Wyborcza*, 22 August 2007.

Bieliński, Paweł. "Pedofilia rozpowszechniona wśród duchownych?" In *Kościół. Stereotypy, uprzedzenia, manipulacji*, edited by Marcin Przeciszewski, 43–57. Warszawa, Lublin: Katolicka Agencja Informacyjna and Gaudium, 2012.

Bierca, Marta. "Mistyka typu ludowego. Kobieca pobożność maryjna w świetle teologii feministycznej." In *Kobiety i religie*, edited by Katarzyna Leszczyńska and Agnieszka Kościańska, 117–38. Kraków: Nomos, 2006.

Bilska, Małgorzata. "Wspólnota." In *Chrześcijaństwo przed nami*, edited by Jarosław Makowski and Janusz Salamon, 85–98. Kraków: Wydawnictwo WAM, 2008.

Bjork, James. "Bulwark or Patchwork: Religious Exceptionalism and Regional Diversity in Postwar Poland." In *Christianity and Modernity in Eastern Europe*, edited by Bruce Berglund and Brian Porter-Szücs, 129–58. Budapest: Central European University, 2010.

Blatman, Daniel. "Strangers in Their Own Land: Polish Jews from Lublin to Kielce." *Polin: Studies in Polish Jewry* 15 (2002): 335–58.

Bogucka, Maria. *The Lost World of the "Sarmatians."* Warszawa: Polish Academy of Sciences, Institute of History, 1996.

Bohdziewicz, Anna Beata, and Magdalena Stopa. *Kapliczki warszawskie*. Warsaw: Dom Spotkań z Historią, 2009.

Borowik, Irena. "(Nie) warto rozmawiać." Interview by Tomasz Ponikło. *Tygodnik Powszechny*, no. 37 (11 September 2011): 18–19.

Boyle, Nicholas. *Who Are We Now? Christian Humanism and the Global Market from Hegel to Heaney*. London: Continuum, 2000.

Browning, Don S., et al. *From Culture Wars to Common Ground: Religion and the American Family Debate*. Louisville, KT: Westminster John Knox Press, 1997.

Brzechczyn, Krzysztof. "Kościół Baptystyczny w Polsce w latach 1858–2008. Stan badań i postulaty badawcze." In *Kościoły, polityka, historia. Ze studiów nad problemami mniejszości wyznaniowych w Polsce w XX i XXI wieku*, edited by Stefan Dudra and Olgierd Kiec, 37–50. Warszawa: Semper, 2009.

Buczkowski, Michał. *Gorzkie żale. Między rozumem a uczuciem*. Kraków: WAM, 2010.

Bukraba-Rylska, Izabella. "Religijność ludowa i jej niemuzykalni krytycy." *Znak*, no. 3 (March 2008): 11–30.

_____. "Społeczeństwo polskie wobec wartości rustykalnych." In *Jak się dzielimy i co nas łączy?* edited by Małgorzata Głowacka-Grajper and Ewa Nowicka, 237–56. Kraków: Nomos, 2007.

Burdziej, Stanisław. "Religia jako źródło kapitału społecznego." *Trzeci Sektor*, no. 15 (2008): 23–27.

Burke, Dierdre. "Attitudes to Death during the Holocaust: Writings from the Ghettos." *Journal of Beliefs & Values* 20, 2 (1999): 173–83.

Butterwick, Richard. *The Polish Revolution and the Catholic Church, 1788–1792*. Oxford: Oxford University Press, 2012.

Buzalka, Juraj. *Nation and Religion: The Politics of Commemoration in South-East Poland*. Berlin: Lit, Verlag, 2007.

_____. "Syncretism among the Greek Catholic Ukrainians in Southeast Poland." In *Churches In-between: Greek Catholic Churches in Post-socialist Europe*, edited by Stéphanie Mahieu and Vlad Naumescu, 183–205. Berlin: Lit, 2008.

Carioti, Antonio. "Respecting Others." *IMW-Post*, no. 104 (April–August 2010): 7.

Casanova, Jose. *Public Religions in the Modern World*. Chicago: Chicago University Press, 1994.

_____. "Religion and the Dynamics of Freedom: Poland, Europe, and the World." In *Values of Poles and the Heritage of John Paul II*, edited by Tomasz Żukowski, 7–18. Warszawa: Centre for the Thought of John Paul II, 2009.

_____. "Religion, European Secular Identities, and European Integration." In *Religion in an Expanding Europe*, edited by Timothy A. Byrnes and Peter J. Katzenstein, 65–92. Cambridge, UK: Cambridge University Press, 2006.

Chazbijewicz, Selim. "Islam musi się zmienić." Interview by Łukasz Adamski. *Fronda*, no. 53 (2009): 240–49.

_____. "In Search of the Lost Commonwealth: Mono- or Multicultural Poland?" In *W stronę nowej wielokulturowości / Towards a New Multiculturalism*, edited by Robert Kusek and Joanna Sanetra Szeliga, 17–33. Kraków: Międzynarodowe Centrum Kultury, 2010.

_____. "Tatarzy." In *Mniejszości narodowe i etniczne w Polsce po II wojnie światowej*, edited by Stefan Dudra and Bernadette Nitsche, 298–304. Krakow: Nomos, 2010.

Chesser, Alicia. "Neuhaus Invades Poland." *First Things: A Monthly Journal of Religion & Public Life*, no. 192 (April 2009): 25–26.

Chlebicka, Anna. "Wizje chrześcijańskiej wspólnoty w oczach mieszkańców Gładyszowa." In *Religijność chrześcijan obrządku wschodniego na pograniczu polsko-ukraińskim*,

edited by Magdalena Lubańska, 141–58. Warszawa: DiG, 2007.

Choduń, Marcin. "Podwórko pod dachem." *Tygodnik Powszechny*, no. 26 (26 June 2011): 6–7.

Chrypinski, Vincent C. "The Catholic Church in Poland, 1944–1989." In *Catholicism and Politics in Communist Societies*, edited by Pedro Ramet, 117–41. Durham, NC : Duke University Press, 1990.

Chrzanowski, Wiesław, and Cezary Michalski. "Katolicy zapomnieli o społeczeństwie." (interview) *Europa*. Magazyn idei *Dziennika*, no. 4 (26 January 2008): 2–5.

Cichy, SVD, Damian, and Marta Szymczyk. "Dzisiaj misje przyjechali do nas." *Przegląd Powszechny*, no. 12 (2010): 45–54.

Cimet, Adina. *Jewish Lublin: A Cultural Monograph*. Lublin: Maria Curie-Skłodowska University Press, 2009.

Courtois, Stéphane, et al. (eds.). *The Black Book of Communism: Crimes, Terror, Repression*. Translated by Jonathan Murphy and Mark Kramer. Cambridge, MA: Harvard University Press, 1999.

Curry, Andrew, "Poland's New Ambitions." *Wilson Quarterly* 34, 2 (Spring 2010): 38–42.

Czaczkowska, Ewa, and Jarosław Stróżyk. "Ile Kościół ma naprawdę pieniądzy." *Uważam Rze*, no. 13 (26 March–1 April 2012): 34–36.

_____. "Wiara częścią tożsamości." *Kościół w Polsce* insert in *Rzeczpospolita*, no. 287 (9 December 2010): 1.

Czaja, Bishop Andrzej. "Kościół nie jest sam dla siebie." Interview by Zbigniew Nosowski. *Więź*, no. 10 (October 2010): 5–26.

Czekanowska, Anna. *Polish Folk Music: Slavonic Heritage, Polish Tradition, Contemporary Trends*. Cambridge, UK: Cambridge University Press, 1990.

Czyż, Renata. "Zróżnicowanie wyznaniowe Śląska Cieszyńskiego. Geneza—historia—stan obecny." In *Kościoły, polityka, historia. Ze studiów nad problemami mniejszości wyznaniowych w Polsce w XX i XXI wieku*, edited by Stefan Dudra and Olgierd Kiec, 93–104. Warszawa: Semper, 2009.

Datner, Helena, and Małgorata Melchior, "Absence and Return: Jews in Contemporary Poland." In *From Homogeneity to Multiculturalism: Minorities Old and New in Poland*, edited by F. E. Ian Hamilton and Krystyna Iglicka, 90–111. London: School of Slavonic and East European Studies, 2000.

Davies, Christie. *The Strange Death of Moral Britain*. 2nd ed. New Brunswick, NJ: Transaction Publishers, 2007.

Davies, Norman. *God's Playground: A History of Poland*. 2 vols. Rev. ed. Oxford: Oxford University Press, 2005.

de Busser, Cathelijne, and Anna Niedźwiedź. "Mary in Poland: A Polish Master Symbol." In *Moved by Mary. The Power of Pilgrimage in the Modern World*, edited by Anna-Karina Hermkens, Willy Jansen, and Catrien Notermans, 87–100. Farnham, UK: Ashgate, 2009.

Deak, Istvan. "Heroes and Victims." In *The Neighbors Respond: The Controversy over the Jedwabne Massacre in Poland*, edited by Antony Polonsky and Joanna B. Michlic, 421–29. Princeton, NJ: Princeton University Press, 2003.

Deskur, The Rev. Paweł. "Rada Społeczna przy biskupie diecezjalnym." In *Kościół naszym domem, Kościół domem i szkołą komunii. Program duszpasterski Kościoła w Polsce na lata 2011–2013*, edited by Szymon Stułkowski, 254–60. Poznań: Wydawnictwo Święty Wojciech, 2011.

Dews, Peter. "Disenchantment and the Persistence of Evil: Habermans, Jonas, Badiou." In *Modernity and the Problem of Evil*, edited by Alan D. Schrift, 51–65. Bloomington: Indiana University Press, 2005.

Dorosz, Krzysztof. *Bóg i terror historii*. Warszawa: Semper, 2010.

Doss, Erika. "Spontaneous Memorials and Contemporary Modes of Mourning in America." *Material Religion* 2, 3 (2006): 294–318.

Draguła, Andrzej. *Copyright na Jezusa. Język, znak, rytuał między wiarą a niewiarą*. Warszawa: Biblioteka "Więzi," 2012.

_____. *Ocalić Boga. Szkice z teologii sekularyzacji*. Warszawa: Biblioteka "Więzi," 2010.

_____. "Przystanek Jezus gra dalej." Interview by Marek Zając. *Tygodnik Powszechny*, no. 48 (30 November 2003): 10.

_____. "Świecki w świecie świeckim." Symposium Świeckich Instytutów Życia Konsekrowanego, 5 November 2011, Warszawa. Manuscript courtesy of the author.

Drob, The Rev. Jan. "Kościół—nie przedsiębiorstwo." Interviewed by Rafał Sztejka SJ and Czesław Wasilewski SJ. *Przegląd Powszechny*, no. 7–8 (2009): 15–23.

Dudra, Stefan. "Łemkowie." In *Mniejszości narodowe i etniczne w Polsce po II wojnie światowej*, edited by Stefan Dudra and Bernadette Nitsche, 256–87. Krakow: Nomos, 2010.

Dudra, Stefan, and Sylwester Woźniak. "Kościół greckokatolicki na Ziemi Lubuskiej." In *Kościoły, polityka, historia. Ze studiów nad problemami mniejszości wyznaniowych w Polsce w XX i XXI wieku*, edited by Stefan Dudra and Olgierd Kiec, 51–69. Warszawa: Semper, 2009.

Dutkiewicz, Ignacy, and Misza Tomaszewski. "Porzucone ideały." *Znak*, no. 1 (January 2012): 10–16.

Dutkiewicz, Rafał. *Nowe horyzonty*. Warszawa: Rosner & Wspólnicy, 2006.

Dynner, Glenn. "Merchant Princes and Tsadikim: The Patronage of Polish Hasidim." *Jewish Social Studies: History, Culture, Society* 12, 1 (2005): 64–110.

Dziedzina, Jacek. "Jestem z Ba Lan." *Gość Niedzielny*, no. 8 (27 February 2011): 46–47.

_____. "Orszak polski." *Gość Niedzielny*, no. 1 (8 January 2012): 18–21.

Dzwonkowski, Tadeusz. "Wydarzenia zielonogórskie w 1960 roku. Anatomia konfliktu." In *Wydarzenia zielonogórskie w 1960 roku*, edited by Tadeusz Dzwonkowski, 7–139. Warszawa: PAX, 2010.

Eberstadt, Mary. "How the West Really Lost God." *Policy Review*, no. 143 (June–July 2007): 3–20.

Eliach, Yaffa. *Hassidic Tales of the Holocaust*. New York: Vintage, 1988.

Farr, Thomas. "The Catholic Church and the Global Crisis of Religious Liberty." *National Catholic Register*, 13 June 2012. http://www.ncregister.com/daily-news/the-catholic-church-and-the-global-crisis-of-religious-liberty (accessed 17 June 2012).

Fedyszak-Radziejowska, Barbara. "Family, Children, Work and Friends, or the Things That We Consider the Most Important." In *Values of Poles and the Heritage of John Paul II*, edited by Tomasz Żukowski, 70–91. Warszawa: Centre for the Thought of John Paul II, 2009.

_____. "The Social Capital of Poles: A Difficult Revitalization Process." In *Values of Poles and the Heritage of John Paul II*, edited by Tomasz Żukowski, 106–31. Warszawa: Centre for the Thought of John Paul II, 2009.

Fratczak, Ewa. "Population Aging in Poland." In *Population Ageing in Central and Eastern Europe: Societal and Policy Implications*, edited by Andreas Hoff, 11–31. Surrey, UK: Ashgate, 2011.

Fukuyama, Francis. "European Identities Part II." *American Interest Online*, 12 January 2012. http://blogs.the-american-interest. com/fukuyama/ 2012/01/12/european-id entities-part-ii (accessed 12 February 2012).

_____. "The Great Disruption: Human Nature and the Reconstitution of Social Order." *Atlantic Monthly* 283, 5 (1999): 55–80.

Gądecki, Bishop Stanisław. *Kto spotyka Jezusa, spotyka judaizm. Dialog chrześcijańsko-żydowski w Polsce.* Gniezno: Gaudentinum, 2002.

Gapiński, Bartłomiej. *Sacrum i codzienność. Prośby o modlitwę nadsyłane do Kalwarii Zebrzydowskiej w latach 1965–1979.* Warszawa: Wydawnictwo TRO, 2008.

Gapski, Henryk. "Krzyż w kulturze polskiej." *Ateneum Kapłańskiej* 109, 1 (1987): 98–111.

Garapich, Andrzej. Introduction to "Megapanel PBI/Gemius: witryny internetowe o tematyce religijnej." In *Internet i Kościół*, edited by Józef Kloch, 258–61. Warszawa: Elipsa, 2011.

Garbacz, Krzysztof. *Na szlaku biłgorajskich kapliczek i krzyży przydrożnych.* Zielona Góra: Agencja Wydawnicza PDN, 2009.

Garbowski, Christopher. "Opłakiwanie Żydów w miasteczkach Lubelszczyzny." *Przegląd Powszechny*, no. 2 (February 2003): 240–43.

Gebert, Konstanty. "Our Identities—New, Old, Imagined." In *Poland: A Jewish Matter. Proceedings of a Symposium Exploring Contemporary Jewish Life in Poland, Marking the End of Jewish Programming for Polska! Year*, edited by Kate Caddy, Mike Levy, and Jakub Nowakowski, 43–56. Warsaw: Adam Mickiewicz Institute, 2010.

Gierech, Paweł. "Kilka uwag o polskiej młodzieży początku XXI wieku." *Teologia Polityczna* 5 (2009/2010): 222–38.

Girard, Rene. *Violence and the Sacred.* Translated by Patrick Gregory. London: Continuum, 1995.

Gitlitz, David, and Linda Kay Davidson. *Pilgrimage and the Jews.* Westport, CT: Praeger, 2006.

Glendon, Mary Ann. "The Bearable Lightness of Dignity." *First Things: A Monthly Journal of Religion & Public Life*, May 2011, 41–45.

Głowacki, Janusz. "Wałęsa robi różnice." Interview by Katarzyna Kubiszyn. *Tygodnik Powszechny*, no. 12 (20 March 2011): 30–31.

Gomes, Peter. *The Good Life: Truths that Last in Times of Need.* New York: HarperCollins, 2003.

Górak-Sosnowska, Katarzyna. "Muzulmanie w Polsce." In *Socjologia życia religijne w Polsce*, edited by Sławomir H. Zaręba, 482–97. Warszawa: Wyd. Uniwersytetu Kardynała Stefana Wyszyńskiego, 2009.

Gorniak-Kocikowska, Krystyna. "A New Challenge: Poland and Its Church in the Global Society of the Post-Communist Era." In *Quo Vadis eastern Europe? Religion, State and Society after Communism*, edited by Angeli Murzaku, 133–35. Ravenna: Longo, 2009.

Górny, Gregorz. *Między Matriksem a krucyfiksem.* Poznań: W drodze, 2010.

Górski, Karol. *Zarys dziejów duchowości w Polsce.* Kraków: Znak, 1986.

Gowin, Jarosław. "Kościół a *Solidarność*." In *Lekcja sierpnia: Solidarność w oczach następnego pokolenia*, edited by Dariusz Gawin, 13–38. Warszawa: Wyd. Instytutu Filozofii i Socjologii PAN, 2002.

_____. *Kościół w czasach wolności 1989–1999.* Kraków: Znak, 1999.

Grabowska, Mirosława. "Polak lubi tacę." Interview by Marcin Żyla. *Tygodnik Powszechny*, no. 10 (4 March 2012): 5.

_____. "Przeobrażenia polskiej religijności." *Znak*, no. 6 (2011): 44–52.

_____. "Zjawiska religijne i kłopoty z ich badaniem." In *Religijność społeczeństwa polskiego lat 80. Od pytań filozoficznych do problemów empirycznych*, edited by Mirosława Grabowska and Tadeusz Szawiel, 99–118. Warszawa: Wydział Filozofii i Socjologii Uniwersytetu Warszawskiego, 2005.

Grabski, August, and Albert Stankowski. "Życie religijne społeczności żydowskiej." In *Następstwa zagłady Żydów. Polska 1944–2010*, edited by Feliks Tych and Monika Adamczyk-Garbowska, 215–44. Lublin: Wydawnictwo Uniwersytetu Marii Curie-Skłodowskiej, 2011.

Graczyk, Roman. *Cena przetrwania?: SB a "Tygodnik Powszechny."* Warszawa: Wydawnictwo Czerwone i Czarne, 2011.

Grajewski, Andrzej. *Kompleks Judasza. Kościół zraniony. Chrześcijanie w Europie Środkowo-Wscodniej między oporem a kolaboracją.* Poznań: W drodze, 1999.

Greeley, Andrew. *The Catholic Imagination.* Berkeley: University of California Press, 2000.

_____. *Religion in Europe at the End of the Second Millennium.* New Brunswick, NJ: Transaction, 2004.

Grim, Brian, et al. *Rising Restrictions on Religion.* Pew Research Center's Forum on Religion & Public Life, August 2011. http://www.pewforum.org/uploadedFiles/Topics/Issues/Government/RisingRestrictions-web.pdf (accessed 30 October 2012).

Gross, Jan T. *Revolution from Abroad: The Soviet Conquest of Poland's Western Ukraine and Western Belorussia.* Princeton, NJ: Princeton University Press, 1988.

Grotowska, Stella. "Religia w świecie wyobrażonym starego człowieka." In *Religia i religijność w warunkach globalizacji,* edited by Maria Libiszowska-Żółtkowska, 309–23. Kraków: Nomos, 2007.

Gryciuk, Jan. "Religijność ludowa w środowisku wielkomiejskim." In *Religijność ludowa. Ciągłość i zmiana,* edited by Władysław Piwowarski, 221–40. Wrocław: Wydawnictwo Wrocławskiej Księgarni Archidiecezjalnej, 1983.

Gudaszewski, Grzegorz, and Mariusz Chmieliweski (eds.). *Wyznania religijne, stowarzyszenia narodowościowe i etniczne w Polsce 2006–2008.* Warszawa: Główny Urząd Statystyczny, 2010.

Halczak, Bohdan. "Ukraińcy (po 1989 r.)." In *Mniejszości narodowe i etniczne w Polsce po II wojnie światowej,* edited by Stefan Dudra and Bernadette Nitsche, 113–26. Krakow: Nomos, 2010.

Hann, Christopher. "The Development of Polish Civil Society and the Experience of the Greek Catholic Minority in Eastern Europe." In *Protecting the Human Rights of Religious Minorities in Eastern Europe,* edited by Peter G. Daunchin and Elizabeth A. Cole, 437–53. New York: Columbia, 2002.

Hannan, Kevin. "Polish Catholicism: A Historical Outline," *Sarmation Review,* January 2004. http://www.ruf.rice.edu/~sarmatia/104/241hannan.html (accessed 18 January 2012).

Harley, Anna Maria. "Górecki and the Paradigm of the 'Maternal.'" *Musical Quarterly* 82, 1 (1998): 82–130.

Herbert, David. "Faith, Trust, and Civil Society." In *Trust and Civil Society,* edited by Frank Tonkiss et al., 52–71. Hampshire & London: Macmillan, 2000.

_____. *Religion and Civil Society: Rethinking Public Religion and Civil Society.* Farnham, UK: Ashgate, 2003.

Herbst, Jan. "Drugi trzeci sektor, czyli o aktywności społecznej wokół Kościoła katolickiego w Polsce." *Teologia Polityczna,* no. 5 (Summer 2009/Fall 2010): 175–87.

Hitchens, Peter. *The Rage against God.* London: Continuum, 2010.

Hołownia, Szymon. *Kościół dla średnio zaawansowanych.* 2nd. ed. Kraków: Wyd. Znak, 2010.

_____. *Last Minute. 24h chrześcijaństwa na świecie.* Kraków: Znak, 2012.

_____. "Szymon Hołownia. Jego prywatny Dekalog." Interview by Maciej Kędziak. *Gala,* 13–25 December 2010, 42–46.

_____. "Woody Allen naszego katolicyzmu." Interview by Barbara Kasprzycka. *Magazyn Dziennika,* 27–28 September 2009, 11–12.

Hołownia, Szymon, and Marcin Prokop. *Bóg, kasa i rock'n'roll.* Kraków: Wydawnictwo Znak, 2011.

Horubała, Andrzej. "Kłopot z Nowosielskim." *PlusMinus: Tygodnik "Rzeczpospolitej,"* 12–13 March 2011, P14–15.

Hosking, Geoffrey. "Why We Need a History of Trust." Review no. 287. *Reviews in History,* July 2002. http://history.ac.uk/reviews/287a (accessed 30 March 2010).

Howard, Marc Morje. *The Weakness of Civil Society in Post-Communist Europe.* Cambridge, UK: Cambridge University Press, 2003.

Hundert, Gershon David. *Jews in Poland-Lithuania in the Eighteenth Century: A Genealogy of Modernity.* Berkeley: University of California Press, 2004.

Hymowitz, Kay. "The New Girl Order." *City Journal,* Autumn 2007. http://www.city-journal.org/html/17_4_new_girl_order.html (accessed 1 January 2013).

Ilcewicz, Edmund Ks. Bp. *Święta Otylia, patronka Urzędowa.* Urzędów: Towarzystwo Ziemi Urzędowskiej, 1999.

Isakowicz-Zaleski, Tadeusz. "Emigranci spod Araratu." *Przegląd Powszechny,* no. 11 (2009): 31–40.

Jackowski, Aleksander. "Wayside Shrines and Crosses." Translated by Anna Grodecka, Andrzej Różycki, and Piotr Szczegłów. In *Pejzaż frasobliwy: Kapliczki i krzyże przydrożne,* 10–14. Warszawa: Wydawnictwo Krupski i S-ka, 2000.

Jackowski, Antoni. "Rozwój pielgrzymek w Polsce." In *Przestrzeń i sacrum. Geografia kultury religijnej w Polsce i jej przemiany w okresie od XVII do XX wieku na przykładzie ośrodków kultu i migracji pielgrzymkowych,* edited by A. Jackowski, Z. Jabłoński, I. Sołjan, and E. Bilska, 13–44. Kraków: Instytut Geografii Uniwersytetu Jagiellońskiego, 1996.

_____. "Współczesne migracje pielgrzymkowe w Polsce." In *Przestrzeń i sacrum. Geografia kultury religijnej w Polsce i jej przemiany w okresie od XVII do XX wieku na przykładzie ośrodków kultu i migracji pielgrzymkowych*, edited by A. Jackowski, Z. Jabłoński, I. Sołjan, and E. Bilska, 45–86 (Kraków: Instytut Geografii Uniwersytetu Jagiellońskiego, 1996).

Jakimowicz, Marcin. "Rekolekcje pokolenia ADHD." *Gość Niedzielny*, 19 June 2011, 20–23.

Janion, Maria. *Niesamowita słowiańszczyzna. Fantazmaty literatury*. Kraków: Wydawnictwo Literackie, 2006.

Janowska, Alina. *Ewangelicy warszawscy w walce o niepodległość Polski w latach drugiej wojny światowej. Wspomnienia i relacje*. Warszawa: Parafia Ewangelicko-Augsburgska Świętej Trójcy, 1997.

Jarkiewicz, Katarzyna. "Bez gwałtu i rewolucji, 1918–1939." In *Dzieje Kościoła w Polsce*, edited by Andrzej Wienck, 380–401. Warszawa: Wydawnictwo Szkolne PWN, 2008.

Jasińska, Maria. "The Quarter of Mutual Respect in Wrocław." In *W stronę nowej wielokulturowości / Towards a New Multiculturalism*, edited by Robert Kusek and Joanna Sanetra Szeliga, 188–97. Kraków: Międzynarodowe Centrum Kultury, 2010.

Jechna, Marta, and Aleksandar Ćirlić. "Kapliczka jako miejsce 'odwieczne.' Społeczne egzystencja kaplicy i krzyży przydrożnych w okolicy wsi Ostałówek." In *Krzyże i kapliczki przydrożne jako znaki społecznej, kulturowej i religijnej pamięci*, edited by Jan Adamowski and Marta Wójcicka, 257–64. Lublin: Wydawnictwo Uniwersytetu Marii Curie-Skłodowska, 2011.

Jenkins, Philip. *God's Continent: Christianity, Islam, and Europe's Religious Crisis*. Oxford: Oxford University Press, 2007.

_____. *The New Anti-Catholicism: The Last Acceptable Prejudice*. Oxford: Oxford University Press, 2003.

_____. *The Next Christendom: The Coming of Global Christianity*. Oxford: Oxford University Press, 2002.

John Paul II. *Memory and Identity: Conversations at the Dawn of a Millennium*. New York: Rizzoli, 2005.

Judt, Tony. *Past Imperfect: French Intellectuals, 1944–1956*. Berkeley: University of California Press, 1992.

Jusiak, Roman. *Kościół katolicki wobec wybranych kwestii społecznych i religijnych w Polsce*. Lublin: Wydawnictwo KUL, 2009.

Kaczmarzewski, Andrzej. "Kościół i klasztor oo. Bernardynów. Dzieje kultu cudownego wizerunku Matki Bożej Rzeszowskiej." In *Kościoły, klasztory i parafie dawnego Rzeszowa*, edited by Małgorzata Jarosińska, 93–101. Rzeszów: Mitel, 2001.

Kaczor, Tomek. "Wszyscy jesteśmy seniorami." *Kontakt*, no. 16 (Winter 2011): 16–21.

Kamiński, Tadeusz. "Kościół i trzeci sektor w Polsce." *Trzeci Sektor*, no. 15 (2008): 7–22.

Kamocki, Janusz. "Przeniesienie 'małej ojczyzny' Tatarów polskich w kresów na Podlasie." In *Ich małe ojczyzny: Lokalność, korzenie i tożsamość w warunkach przemian*, edited by Mieczysław Trojan, 63–66. Wrocław: Katedra Etnologii i Antropologii Kulturowej, Uniwersytet Wrocławski, 2003.

Kaplan, Benjamin J. *Divided by Faith: Religious Conflict and the Practice of Toleration in Early Modern Europe*. Cambridge, MA: Belknap Press of Harvard University Press, 2007.

Kaplan, Edward K. "Healing Wounds: Reflections on Abraham Joshua Heschel and Interfaith Partnership in Poland." *Religion and the Arts* 12 (2008): 411–19.

Karabin, Ewa. "Już nie kuźnia? Duszpasterstwa akademicka dzisiaj." *Więź*, no. 7 (2010): 31–37.

Kasper, Łukasz, and Marcin Przeciszewski. "Kościół wtrąca się do polityki?" In *Kościół. Stereotypy, uprzedzenia, manipulacji*, edited by Marcin Przeciszewski, 97–109. Warszawa, Lublin: Katolicka Agencja Informacyjna and Gaudium, 2012.

Kasperek, Andrzej. "Znaczenie locum w czasach globalizacji na przykładzie stosunku Polaków do parafii." In *Religia i religijność w warunkach globalizacji*, edited by Maria Libiszowska-Żółtkowska, 224–37. Kraków: NOMOS, 2007.

Kaufmann, Eric. *Shall the Religious Inherit the Earth? Demography and Politics in the Twenty-First Century*. London: Profile Books, 2010.

Kersten, Krystyna. *The Establishment of Communist Rule in Poland, 1943–1948*. New York: Columbia University Press, 1992.

Kiec, Olgierd. "Kościoły ewangelickie w Polsce w latach 1980–2008." In *Kościoły, polityka, historia. Ze studiów nad problemami mniejszości wyznaniowych w Polsce w XX i XXI wieku*, edited by Stefan Dudra and Olgierd Kiec, 123–59. Warszawa: Semper, 2009.

Kitzman-Czarnecka, Karolina. "Kalejdoskop

obywatelskich organizacji religijnych." *Trzeci Sektor*, no. 15 (2008): 45–53.

Klassen, Peter J. *Mennonites in Early Modern Poland and Prussia*. Baltimore, MD: Johns Hopkins University Press, 2009.

Klekot, Ewa. "Mourning John Paul II in the Streets of Warsaw." *Anthropology Today* 23, 4 (2007): 3–6.

Kłoczowski, Jerzy. *A History of Polish Christianity*. Cambridge, UK: Cambridge University Press, 2000.

Kluzowa, Krystyna, Janina Palus, Jadwiga Wronicz. "Edukacja seksualna w Polsce na tle wybranych krajów Unii Europejskiej." *Wychowawca: Miesięcznik nauczycieli i wychowawców katolickich*, no. 6 (2011): 24–7.

Kochanski, Halik. *The Eagle Unbowed: Poland and the Poles in the Second World War*. Cambridge, MA: Harvard University Press, 2012.

Kolakowski, Leszek. *Czas ciekawy, czas niespokojny*. Part 2. Interview by Zbigniew Menzel. Kraków: Znak, 2008.

_____. *Modernity on Endless Trial*. Chicago: University of Chicago Press, 1990.

Komocki, Janusz. "Przeniesienie 'małej ojczyzny' Tatarów polskich w kresów na Podlasie." In *Ich małe ojczyzny: Lokalność, korzenie i tożsamość w warunkach przemian*, edited by Mieczysław Trojan, 63–66. Wrocław: Katedra Etnologii i Antropologii Kulturowej, Uniwersytet Wrocławski, 2003.

Konferencja Episkopatu Polski. *W trosce o człowieka i dobro wspólne*. Warszawa: Biblos, 2012.

Korab, Kazimerz. "Zachłanność proboszczów wiejskich? Glossa do rozważań na temat stereotypu." *Przegląd Powszechny*, no. 7–8 (July–August 2009): 36–39.

Korguł, The Rev. Marek, and the Rev. Szymon Stułkowski. "Kościół naszym domem." In *Kościół naszym domem, Kościół domem i szkołą komunii. Program duszpasterski Kościoła w Polsce na lata 2012–2013*, 15–33. Poznań: Wyd. Święty Wojciech, 2011.

Kornecki, Marian. Untitled introduction to *Kapliczki, figury i krzyże przydrożne na terenie diecezji tarnowskiej*, vol. 2, edited by Jan Rzepa, v–xx. Tarnów: Kuria Diecezjalna, 1983.

Kosiński, Dariusz. *Teatra polskie. Historie*. Warszawa: PWN i Instytut Teatralny, 2010.

Krajewski, Stanisław. *Poland and the Jews: Reflections of a Polish Polish Jew*. Kraków: Austeria, 2005.

Krall, Hannah. "Briefly Now." Translated by Christopher Garbowski. In *Contemporary Jewish Writing in Poland: An Anthology*, edited by Anthony Polansky and Monika Garbowska, 303–11. Lincoln: University of Nebraska Press, 2001.

Kraśko, Piotr, Kamil Durczok, Katarzyna Wiśniewska, Robert Nęcek, Agnieszka Mrożek, Bartłomiej Król. *Bitwa o Kościół*. Kraków: Sallwator, 2010.

Krasnodębska, Sylwia. "Kochajmy się wiernie." Interview by Lew-Starowicz. *Uważam Rze*, no. 15 (16–27 May 2011): 42–43.

Krasowski, Robert. "Sukces Boga nad Wisłą czy jedynie klęska jego wrogów?" *Europa. Magazyn idei Dziennika* nr 246/51 (20–21 December 2008): 1.

Krzemiński, Ireneusz. *Czego nas uczy Radio Maryja? Socjologia treści i recepcji rozgłośni*. Warszawa: Wydawnictwo Akademickie i Profesjonalne, 2009.

Kucharczak, Przemysław. "Joanna Najfeld uniewinniona." *Gość Niedzielny* (18 September 2011): 4.

_____. "Się chce." *Gość Niedzielny* (20 November 2011): 38–41.

Kugler, Gudrun (ed.). *Shadow Report on Intolerance and Discrimination against Christians in Europe, 2005—2010*. Vienna: Observatory on Intolerance and Discrimination against Christians, 2010.

Kuprianowicz, Grzegorz. "Prawosławie w Polsce od 1919 roku do współczesności." In *Prawosławie. Światło ze wschodu*, edited by Krzysztof Leśniewski, 757–834. Lublin: Prawosławna diecezja lubelsko-chełmska, 2009.

Kursa, Sławomir. "Prawna ochrona religijnej tożsamości narodowych i etnicznych w Polsce." In *Prawa Mniejszości narodowych*, edited by Teresa Gardocka and Jacek Sobczak, 382–94. Toruń: Wyd. Adam Marszałek, 2010.

Lambert, Yves. "A Turning Point in Religious Evolution in Europe." *Journal of Contemporary Religion* 19, 1 (2004): 29–45.

Lamm, Norman. *The Religious Thought of Hasidism: Text and Commentary*. New York: Michael Scharf Publication Trust of Yeshiva University, 1999.

Lasota, Marek. "Czasy PRL-u i odzyskana wolność." In *Dzieje Kościoła w Polsce*, edited by Andrzej Wienck, 420–69. Warszawa: Wydawnictwo Szkolne PWN, 2008.

Łęchota, Rafał. "Laski—przykład formacji katolickiej lat Drugiej Rzeczpospolitej."

Zeszyty Naukowe Uniwersytetu Jagiellońskiego: Studia Religiologica, no. 34 (2001): 129–38.

Leszczyński, Adam. "Dialog? Ale po co?" *Znak*, no. 1 (January 2012): 29–33.

Libionka, Dariusz. "Debata wokół Jedwabnego." In *Następstwa zagłady Żydów. Polska 1944–2010*, edited by Feliks Tych and Monika Adamczyk-Garbowska, 733–74. Lublin: Wyd. Uniwersytetu Marii Curie-Skłodowskiej, 2011.

Lodzinski, Slawomir. "National Minorities and the 'Conservative' Politics of Multiculturalism in Poland." In *From Homogeneity to Multiculturalism: Minorities Old and New in Poland*, edited by F. E. Ian Hamilton and Krystyna Iglicka, 34–63. London: School of Slavonic and East European Studies, 2000.

Łuczewski, Michał. "Polskie odrodzenie religijne i doświadczenie totalitaryzmu. Analiza fenomenologiczna." *Teologia Polityczna* 5 (2009/2010): 313–31.

Luxmoore, Jonathan. "Clerical Power Thwarts Victims in Poland." *National Catholic Reporter*, 3 February 2012.

———. "Poland's Identity Crisis." *Commonweal*, 23 November 2007, 10–11.

Luxmoore, Jonathan, and Jolanta Babiuch. *Rethinking Christendom: Europe's Struggle for Christianity*. Herefordshire: Gracewing, 2005.

———. *The Vatican and the Red Flag*. London: Geoffrey Chapman, 2000.

Madood, Tariq. "Muslims and European Multiculturalism." In *Religion in the New Europe*, edited by Krzysztof Michalski, 97–110. Budapest: Central European Press, 2006.

Magonet, Jonathan. "Jewish Attitudes to Interfaith Dialogue." In *How to Conquer the Barriers to Interfaith Dialogue: Christianity, Islam and Judaism*, edited by Christiane Timmerman and Barbara Segaert, 63–79. Brussels: Peter Lang, 2007.

Majewski, Józef. *Religia, media, mitologia*. Gdańsk: Słowo, Obraz, Teoria, 2010.

Mariański, The Rev. Janusz. *Katolicyzm polski, ciągłość i zmiana. Studium socjologiczne*. Kraków: Wydawnictwo WAM, 2011.

———. *Kościół katolicki w Polsce a życie społeczne*. Lublin: Wyd. Gaudium, 2005.

———. "Kościół? Nie, dziękuje." Interview by Jan Turnau and Katarzyna Wiśniewska. *Gazeta Wyborcza*, 17–18 September 2011.

———. "Kościół przyszłości będzie wielobarwny." Interview by Artur Sporniak. *Tygod-*

nik Powszechny, no. 18–19 (29 April–6 May 2012): 6–7.

———. "Parafia szansa przemian polskiego katolicyzmu." *Socjologia Religii* 1 (2003): 183–205.

———. *Społeczeństwo i moralność. Studia z katolickiej nauki społecznej i socjologii moralności*. Tarnów: Biblos, 2008.

Marling, Karal Ann. *Merry Christmas! Celebrating America's Greatest Holiday*. Cambridge, MA: Harvard University Press, 2000.

Martin, David. "Integration and Fragmentation: Patterns of Religion in Europe." In *Religion in the New Europe*, edited by Krzysztof Micalski, 65–84. Budapest: Central European Press, 2006.

Mazgaj, Marian. *Church and State in Communist Poland: A History, 1944–1989*. Jefferson, NC: McFarland, 2010.

Mazurkiewicz, The Rev. Piotr. "Europa musi mieć swoją twarz." Interview by Dominika Cosić. *Znak*, no. 677 (October 2011): 82–87.

———. "Zatrzymać ruchome piaski." Interview by Anna Gruszecka. *W Drodze*, no. 2 (2011): 67–77.

McQuire, Meredith. *Lived Religion: Faith and Practice in Everyday Life*. Oxford: Oxford University Press, 2008.

Michalak, Ryszard. "Środowiska protestanckie wobec kwestii współpracy duchownych ze służbą bezpieczeństwa PRL." In *Kościoły, polityka, historia. Ze studiów nad problemami mniejszości wyznaniowych w Polsce w XX i XXI wieku*, edited by Stefan Dudra and Olgierd Kiec, 161–75. Warszawa: Semper, 2009.

Michalik, Archbishop Józef. *Raport o stanie wiary*. Interview by Grzegorz Górny and Tomasz Terlikowski. Radom: Polwen, 2011.

Michalski, Cezary. "Herezja smoleńska." *Newsweek Polska*, no. 18 (8 May 2011): 16–19.

Michnik, Adam. *The Church and the Left*. Edited, translated, and with an introduction by David Ost. Chicago: University of Chicago Press, 1993.

Migacz, Dawid. "Przemiany współczesnej rodziny a religijność Polaków." In *Socjologia życia religijnego. Tradycje wobec zmiany kulturowe*, edited by Sławomir Zaręba, 365–77. Warszawa: Wydawnictwo Uniwersytetu Kardynała Stefana Wyszyńskiego, 2010.

Milerski, Bogusław. "Droga luterańska." In *Drogi chrześcijaństwa*, edited by Bohdan

Śławiński, 109–19. Warszawa: Jacek Santorski, 2008.

Miller, Leon. "Religion's Role in National Unity." *International Journal on World Peace* 24, 1 (2009): 91–114.

Miłosz, Czesław. *New and Collected Poems, 1931–2001.* New York: Ecco, 2001.

_____. "Nowoczesność idylliczna?" *Znak*, no. 583 (December 2003): 47–53.

Miszczak, Ewa. *Katolicki ruch odnowy w Duchu Świętym w Polsce.* Lublin: Wydawnictwo Uniwersytetu Marii Curie-Skłodowskiej, 2011.

Modras, Ronald. *The Catholic Church and Antisemitism: Poland, 1933–1939.* Jerusalem: Harwood Academic Publishers, 1994.

Morgan, David. *Visual Piety: A History and Theory of Popular Religious Images.* Berkeley: University of California Press, 1999.

Morka, Andrzej. *Doświadczenie Boga w Gułagu.* Sandomierz: Wydawnictwo Diecezjalne i Drukarnia w Sandomierzu 2007.

Müller, Maciej, and Tomasz Ponikło. "Antyklerikalizm szkodzi Kościołowi. Ale jest mu niezbędny." *Tygodnik Powszechny*, no. 43 (24 October 2010): 3–4.

Muller, Jerry Z. "Us and Them: The Enduring Power of Ethnic Nationalism." In *The Clash of Civilizations: The Debate*, edited by James Hodge, Jr., 100–19. New York: Council on Foreign Relations, 2010.

Muszyński, Abp Henryk. "Dialog, a nie walka." Interview by Łukasz Dulęba and Marcin Pera. *Więź*, no. 1 (January 2012): 81–91.

_____. "Jak modlimy się za Żydow." *Więź*, no. 3 (March 2009): 43–54.

Neuhaus, Richard John. *Prorok z Nowego Jorku.* Warszawa: Fronda, 2010.

Niedźwiedź, Anna. *The Image and the Figure: Our Lady of Częstochowa in Polish Culture and Popular Religion*, translated by Anna Niedźwiedź and Guy Torr. Kraków: Jagiellonian University Press, 2010.

_____. "Wszyscy jesteśmy kalwariami." Interview by Piotr Mucharski. *Tygodnik Powszechny*, no. 34 (20 August 2006): 8.

Nijakowski, Lech. "Tworzenie, odtwarzanie, niszczenie i zanikanie granic między grupami etnicznymi." In *Etniczność, pamięć, asymilacja. Wokół problemów zachowania tożsamości narodowych i etnicznych w Polsce*, edited by Lech Nijakowski, 48–74. Warszawa: Wydawnictwo Sejmowe, 2009.

Nonneman, Gerd, Tim Niblock, and Bogdan Szajkowski. "Islam and Ethnicity in Eastern Europe." In *Muslim Communities in the New Europe*, edited by Gerd Nonneman, Tim Niblock, Bogdan Szajkowski, 27–51. London: Ithaca Press, 1996.

Nosowski, Zbigniew. *Polski rachunek sumienia z Jana Pawła II.* Warszawa: Centrum Myśli Janna Pawła II, 2010.

_____. "Polskie katolicyzmy." *Więź*, no. 1 (2010): 5–26.

_____. Private interview. December 16, 2010.

_____. "Profesjonalizm jako droga duchowości." *Więź*, no. 7 (2010): 74–84.

_____. "Zapateryzm na polskim przedmieściu? Powyborcze wyzwania dawne i nowe." *Więź*, no. 1 (January 2012): 30–44.

Nosowski, Zbigniew, Michał Paluch, and Piotr Jordan Śliwiński. "Ku wspólnocie świadków." *Więź*, no. 1 (September 2008): 78–81.

Nowicka, Ewa, and Magda Majewska. *Obcy u siebie. Luteranie warszawscy.* Warszawa: Oficyna Naukowa, 1993.

Nycz, Archbishop Kazimierz. "Kościół obywatelski." By Zbigniew Nosowski and Marek Rymsza. *Więź*, no. 3 (2009): 58–71.

Ogrodowska, Barbara. *Radość wszelkiego stworzenia. Rzecz o Adwencie i Bożym Narodzeniu.* Warszawa: Verbinum, 2008.

Olszewski, Daniel. *Polska kultura religijna na przełomie XIX i XX wieku.* Warszawa: Pax, 1996.

Opalski, Magdalena, and Israel Bartal. *Poles and Jews: A Failed Brotherhood.* Hanover: University Press of New England, 1992.

Osa, Maryjane. "Creating Solidarity: The Religious Foundations of the Polish Social Movement." *East European Politics and Societies* 11, 2 (1997): 339–65.

_____. *Solidarity and Contention: Networks of Polish Opposition.* Minneapolis: University of Minnesota Press, 2003.

Ost, David. *Solidarity and the Politics of Anti-Politics: Opposition and Reform in Poland since 1968.* Philadelphia: Temple University Press, 1991.

Pace, Enzo. "Religion as Communication: The Changing Shape of Catholicism in Europe." In *Everyday Religion*, edited by Nancy T. Ammerman, 37–49. Oxford: Oxford University Press, 2007.

Paczkowski, Andrzej. "Poland, the 'Enemy Nation.'" In *The Black Book of Communism: Crimes, Terror, Repression*, edited by Stéphane Courtois et al., translated by Jonathan Murphy and Mark Kramer, 363–93. Cambridge, MA: Harvard University Press, 1999.

Pałka, Damian. *Kościół katolicki wobec Żydów w Polsce międzywojennej.* Kraków: Nomos, 2006.

Pease, Neal. *Rome's Most Faithful Daughter: The Catholic Church and Independent Poland, 1914–1939.* Athens: Ohio University Press, 2009.

Pełczyński, Grzegorz. "Ormianie." In *Mniejszości narodowe i etniczne w Polsce po II wojnie światowej*, edited by Stefan Dudra and Bernadette Nitsche, 195–207. Krakow: Nomos, 2010.

_____. "Wspólnoty ewangelickie w Polsce. Problem tożsamości." In *Tożsamości religijne w społeczeństwie polskim. Socjologiczne studium przypadków*, edited by Maria Libiszowska-Żółtkowska, 177–86. Warszawa: Difin, 2009.

Pelica, Grzegorz. "Prawosławie w Polsce—szkic dla studentów socjologii." In *Socjologia życia religijne w Polsce*, edited by Sławomir H. Zaręba, 420–41. Warszawa: Wydawnictwo Uniwersytetu Kardynała Stefana Wyszyńskiego, 2009.

Pelikan, Jaroslav. *Mary through the Centuries: Her Place in the History of Culture.* New Haven, CT: Yale University Press, 1996.

Petrowicz, Tadeusz. *Od Czarnohory do Lublina*, wyd. drugie. Lublin: Wyd. UMCS, 2002.

Petterson, Per. "The Nordic Paradox—Simultaneously Most Secularised and Most Religious." In *Europe: Secular or Post-Secular?* edited by Hans-Georg Ziebertz and Ulrich Riegel, 79–92. Berlin: LIT Verlag, 2009.

Pilch, Jerzy. "Jerzy Pilch o Adamie Pilchu." In Adam Pilch, *Byłem przechodniem. Wybór Kazań*, 5–17. Warszawa: Świat Książki, 2011.

Piwowarski, Władysław. "Religijność narodu a religijność życia codziennego." In *Religijność społeczeństwa polskiego lat 80. Od pytań filozoficznych do problemów empirycznych*, edited by Mirosława Grabowska and Tadeusz Szawiel, 189–201. Warszawa: Wydział Filozofii i Socjologii Uniwersytetu Warszawskiego, 2005.

Podgórska, Joanna. "Msza za świeckie państwo." *Polityka*, no. 45 (2–7 November 2011): 30–32.

Podgórzec, Zbigniew. *Rozmowy z Jerzym Nowosielskim: Wokół ikony—Mój Chrystus—Mój Judasz*, edited by Krystyna Czerni. Kraków: Znak, 2009.

Polonsky, Antony. *The Jews in Poland and Russia.* Vol. 1, *1350–1881.* Oxford: Littman Library, 2010.

_____. *The Jews in Poland and Russia.* Vol. 2, *1881–1914.* Oxford: Littman Library, 2010.

_____. *The Jews in Poland and Russia.* Vol. 3, *1914–2008.* Oxford: Littman Library, 2012.

Polonsky, Antony, and Joanna B. Michlic. Introduction to part 4, "Debate on Church." In *The Neighbors Respond: The Controversy over the Jedwabne Massacre in Poland*, edited by Antony Polonsky and Joanna B. Michlic, 147–54. Princeton, NJ: Princeton University Press, 2004.

Porter, Brian. *When Nationalism Began to Hate: Imagining Modern Politics in Nineteenth Century Poland.* Oxford: Oxford University Press, 2000.

Porter-Szücs, Brian. *Faith and Fatherland: Catholicism, Modernity, and Poland.* Oxford: Oxford University Press, 2011.

Prażmowska, Anita J. *A History of Poland.* Hampshire, UK: Palgrave Macmillan, 2004.

Prothero, Stephen. *American Jesus: How the Son of God Became a National Icon.* New York: Farrar, Strauss & Giroux, 2003.

Przeciszewski, Marcin. "Katolicka Agencja Informacyjna. Zasady relacje z mediami." In *Media i Kościół. Polityka informacyjna Kościoła*, edited by Monika Przybysz and Krzysztof Marcyński, SAC, 47–53. Warszawa: Elipsa, 2011.

_____."Kościół bez przywódcy i dalekosiężnej strategii?" In *Kościół. Stereotypy, uprzedzenia, manipulacji*, edited by Marcin Przeciszewski, 58–71. Warszawa, Lublin: Katolicka Agencja Informacyjna and Gaudium, 2012.

_____ (ed.). *Kościół. Stereotypy, uprzedzenia, manipulacji.* Warszawa, Lublin: Katolicka Agencja Informacyjna and Gaudium, 2012.

Przybysz, Monika. *Kościół w kryzysie? Crisis management w Kościele w Polsce.* Tarnów: Biblos, 2008.

Putnam, Robert. *Making Democracy Work: Civic Tradition in Modern Italy.* Princeton, NJ: Princeton University Press, 1992.

Radzik, Zuzanna. "Żydzi z mojej parafii." *Tygodnik Powszechny*, no. 5 (29 January 2012): 20–21.

Ramet, Sabrina. "Thy Will Be Done: The Catholic Church and Politics in Poland since 1989." In *Religion in an Expanding Europe*, edited by Timothy A Byrnes and Peter J. Katzenstein, 117–46. Cambridge, UK: Cambridge University Press, 2006.

"Raport KAI o finansach Kościoła poniedziałek." Franciszkańska3.pl, 27 February 2012. http://franciszkanska3.pl/Raport-KAI-o-finansach-Kosciola,a,14134 (accessed 25 May 2012).

Recht, Roland. *Believing and Seeing: The Art of Gothic Cathedrals*, translated by Mary Whittall. Chicago: Chicago University Press, 2008.

Reymont, Ladislaus. *The Peasants: A Tale of Our Own Time*. Vols. "Autumn," "Winter," "Summer," "Spring," 2nd ed. Translated by Michael Dziewicki. New York: Knopf, 1928.

Rogaczewska, Maria. "Czy 'pokolenie JP2' zbuduje w Polsce społeczeństwo obywatelskie." In *Pokolenie JP2. Przeszłość i przyszłość zjawiska religijnego*, edited by Tadeusz Szawiel, 142–78. Warszawa: Wydawnictwo Naukowe Scholar, 2008.

_____. "Polska parafia w obrębie społeczeństwo obywatelskiego." *Trzeci Sektor*, no. 15 (2008): 28–36.

Romanowicz, Wiesław. "Tradycja religijna w świadomości młodzieży prawosławnej." In *Socjologia życia religijnego. Tradycje badawcze wobec zmiany kulturowej*, edited by Sławomir Zaręba, 334–47. Warszawa: Wyd. Uniwersytetu KSW, 2010.

Roskies, David (ed.). *The Literature of Destruction: Jewish Responses to Catastrophe*. New York: Jewish Publication Society, 1988.

Rosman, Moshe. *Founder of Hasidism: A Quest for the Historical Ba'al Shem Tov*. Berkeley: University of California Press, 1996.

Rothschild, Joseph. "Europa środkowowschodnia: spojrzenie z zewnątrz." Interview by Christopher Garbowski. *Akcent*, nos. 1–2 (1990): 328–36.

Rowiński, Tomasz. "Porzućcie romantyzm!" *Znak*, no. 4 (April 2011): 14–22.

Rymsza, Marek. "Nie pod korcem. O społecznym wymiarze praktykowanie wiary." *Więź*, no. 7 (July 2010): 62–72.

_____. "Warto przegonić Lulka." *Więź*, no. 5–6 (May–June 2012): 64–66.

Ryś, Grzegorz. "Sed contra ... Kilka pytań do Adama Michnika." In Agata Bielik-Robson et al., *Kim są Polacy*, 37–43. Warsaw: Agora, 2013.

Sacks, Jonathan. "Address to the Pontifical Gregorian University in Rome." Office of the Chief Rabbi. Speeches, 12 December 2011. http://www.chiefrabbi.org/ReadArtical.aspx?id=1854 (accessed 2 February 2012).

_____. *The Dignity of Difference: How to Avoid the Clash of Civilizations*. London: Continuum, 2002.

_____. *The Home We Build Together: Recreating Society*. London: Continuum, 2009.

_____. "How to Reverse the West's Decline." *Standpoint*, September 2011. http://www.

standpointmag.co.uk/node/4049/full (accessed 2 February 2012).

_____. "Judaism and Politics in the Modern World." In *The Desecularization of the World: Resurgent Religion and World Politics*, edited by Peter Berger, 51–63. Washington: Ethics and Public Policy Center, 1999.

Sadkowski, Konrad. "Clerical Nationalism and Antisemitism: Catholic Priests, Jews, and Orthodox Christians in the Lublin Region, 1918–1939." In *Antisemitism and Its Opponents in Modern Poland*, edited by Robert Blobaum, 171–88. Ithaca, NY: Cornell University Press, 2005.

_____. "The Roman Catholic Clergy, the Byzantine Slavonic Rite and Polish National Identity: The Case of Grabowiec, 1931–34." *Religion, State & Society* 28, 2 (2000): 175–84.

Sadłoń, Wojciech. "Jak wiara łączy i mobilizuje. Stosowany wymiar religii w świetle badań ISKK." *Więź*, no. 7 (July 2010): 12–23.

_____. "Polski Kościół wobec laicyzacji: Ilość." *Tygodnik Powszechny*, no. 49 (2010): 16–17.

Sakowicz, Eugeniusz. "Dialog między religijny w Polsce." In *Dialog Chrześcijan z wyznawcami innych religii za wzorem św. Franciszka z Asyżu*, edited by Salezy Brzyszek and Zenon Styś, 209–41. Warszawa: Franciszkański Centrum dla Europy Wschodniej i Azji Północnej, 2006.

Samborska, Anna. "Kościół marzeń." *Duży Format* (insert in *Gazeta Wyborcza*), 13 May 2010, DF6–8.

Sanneh, Lamin. *Disciples of All Nations: Pillars of World Christianity*. Oxford: Oxford University Press, 2008.

Schall, James V. *The Sum Total of Human Happiness*. South Bend: St. Augustine's Press, 2006.

Schudrich, Rabbi Michael. "Czego nauczyłem się od Jana Pawła II." *Więź*, no. 1 (2010): 104–14.

_____. "Giving Back the Jewish Past." In *Poland: A Jewish Matter. Proceedings of a Symposium Exploring Contemporary Jewish Life in Poland*, edited by Kate Caddy, Mike Levy, and Jakub Nowakowski, 57–63. Warsaw: Adam Mickiewicz Institute, 2010.

Sękowska, Aleksandra. "Zbór Ewangelicko-Reformowany w Warszawie w latach drugiej wojny światowej." In *Ewangielicy warszawscy w walce o niepodległość Polski, 1939–45*, edited by Alina Janowska, 31–38. Warszawa: Parafia Ewangelicko-Augsburska Świętej Trójcy, 1997.

Sevcenko, Ihor. "The Many Worlds of Piotr Mohyla." *Harvard Ukrainian Studies* 8, nos. 1–2 (1985): 9–40.

Shmeruk, Chone. "Hebrew-Yiddish-Polish: A Trilingual Culture." In *The Jews of Poland between Two World Wars*, edited by Yisrael Gutman, Ezra Mendelsohn, Jehuda Reinharz, and Chone Shmeruk, 285–311. Hanover: University Press of New England, 1989.

Siellawa-Kolbowska, Krystyna Ewa. "Oaza jako przestrzeń doświadczenia mistycznego i społecznego." In *Pokolenie JP2. Przeszłość i przyszłość zjawiska religijnego*, edited by Tadeusz Szawiel, 50–68. Warszawa: Scholar, 2008.

Sikora, The Rev. Janusz. Personal e-mail communication with author, 8 September 2010.

Singer, Isaac Bashevis. *The Spinoza of Market Street*. New York: Fawcett Crest, 1980.

Sitkiewicz, Olga. "Oblicza magii w opowieściach i praktykach mieszkańców pogranicza polsko-ukraińskiego." In *Religijność chrześcijan obrządku wschodniego na pograniczu polsko-ukraińskim*, edited by Magdalena Lubańska, 111–28. Warszawa: DiG, 2007.

Slackman, Michael. "Poland, Bastion of Religion, Sees Rise in Secularism." *New York Times*, 12 December 2011, http://www.nytimes.com/2010/12/12/world/europe/12poland.html (accessed 16 April 2012).

Sławek, Tadeusz. "W obronie wolności myślenie." *Gość Niedzielny*, no. 50 (10 December 2000): 7.

Smak-Wójcicka, Magdalena. "Dialog symboli religijnych w przestrzeni miejskiej. Nowe i stare formy ekspresji kultu." In *Miasto i Sacrum*, edited by Maciej Kowalewski and Anna Małgorzata Królikowska, 149–58. Kraków: Nomos, 2011.

Smith, Steven D. *The Disenchantment of Secular Discourse*. Cambridge, MA: Harvard University Press, 2010.

Smyk, Katarzyna. *Choinka w kulturze polskiej. Symbolika drzewka i ozdób*. Kraków: Universitas, 2009.

Sniderman, Paul M., and Louk Hagendoorn, *When Ways of Life Collide: Multiculturalism and Its Discontents in the Netherlands*. Princeton, NJ: Princeton University Press, 2009.

Snyder, Timothy. *Bloodlands: Europe between Hitler and Stalin*. New York: Basic Books, 2010.

_____. *The Reconstruction of Nations: Poland, Ukraine, Lithuania, Belarus, 1596–1999*.

New Haven, CT: Yale University Press, 2003.

_____. "United Europe, Divided History." In *What Holds Europe Together?* Vol. 1, "Conditions of European Solidarity," edited by Krzysztof Michalski, 185–88. Budapest and New York: Central European Press, 2006.

Solomon, Norman. "Czy Shoa wymaga radykalnie nowej teologii?" In *Żydzi i chrześcijanie w dialogu*, edited by Waldemar Chrostowski, 128–63. Warszawa: Akademia Teologii Katolickiej, 1992.

Śpiewak, Paweł. *Żydokomuna. Interpretacje historyczne*. Warszawa: Wydawnictwo Czerwone i Czarne, 2012.

Sporniak, Artur. "Trzymamy za słowo." *Tygodnik Powszechny*, no. 1 (1 January 2012): 16–17.

Staniszewski, Akadiusz. "Dzieje, obyczaje i obrzędy religijne Romów w odniesieniu do kultury katolickiej." *Socjologia Religii* 1 (2003): 243–81.

Stark, Rodney. *One True God: Historical Consequences of Monotheism*. Princeton, NJ: Princeton University Press, 2001.

Stauter-Halstead, Keely. *The Nation and the Village: The Genesis of Peasant National Identity in Austrian Poland, 1848–1914*. Ithaca, NY: Cornell University Press, 2004.

Stawroński, Zbigniew. "Doświadczenie Solidarności jak o wspólnoty etycznej." In *Lekcja sierpnia: Solidarność w oczach następnego pokolenia*, edited by Dariusz Gawin, 103–22. Warszawa: Wyd. Instytutu Filozofii i Socjologii PAN, 2002.

Stefaniuk, Tomasz Imran. "Islam and Muslims in Poland." In *W stronę nowej wielokulturowości Towards a New Multiculturalism*, edited by Robert Kusek and Joanna Sanetra Szeliga, 166–86. Kraków: Międzynarodowe Centrum Kultury, 2010.

Steinlauf, Michael. *Bondage to the Dead: Poland and the Memory of the Holocaust*. Syracuse, NY: Syracuse University Press, 2006.

Stępień, Stanisław. "Developments since 1989: Poland." In *Churches In-between: Greek Catholic Churches in Postsocialist Europe*, edited by Stéphanie Mahieu and Vlad Naumescu, 85–97. Berlin: Lit, 2008.

Stopa, Madalena. "W poszukiwanie świadków." In *Kapliczki warszawskie*, edited by Anna Beata Bohdziewicz and Magdalena Stopa, 9–13. Warsaw: Dom Spotkań z Historią, 2009.

Stróżyk, Jarosław. "Cała Polska maszeruje w

obronie życia i rodziny." *Rzeczpospolita*, 2–3 June 2012.

Sułek, Antoni. "Zwykli Polacy patrzą na Żydów. Postawy społeczeństwa polskiego wobec Żydów w świetle badań sondażowych." In *Następstwo zagłady Żydów. Polska 1944–2010*, 853–88.

Swieboda, Pawel. "This Winter in Warsaw." *American Interest* 7, 1 (January–February 2012): 72–76.

Szajkowski, Bogdan, Tim Niblock, and Gerd Nonneman. "Islam and Ethnicity in Eastern Europe." In *Muslim Communities in the New Europe*, edited by Gerd Nonneman, Tim Niblock, and Bogdan Szajkowski, 27–51. Berkshire, UK: Ithaca Press, 1996.

Szarek, Bp Jan, and the Rev. Jan Gross. "Struktura oraz życie współczesne Kościoła." In *Świadectwo wiary i życia. Kościół luterański w Polsce wczoraj i dziś*, edited by the Rev. Jerzy Below and Magdalena Legendź, 7–31. Bielsko-Biała: "Augustana," 2004.

Szaynok, Bożena. "Kościól katolicki w Polsce wobec problematyki żydowskiej (1944–1989)." In *Następstwa zagłady Żydów. Polska 1944–2010*, edited by Feliks Tych and Monika Adamczyk-Garbowska, 553–81. Lublin: Wydawnictwo Uniwersytetu Marii Curie-Skłodowskiej, 2011.

Szlendak, Tomasz. "Maszyna do życia." Interview by Michał Kuźmiński. *Tygodnik Powszechny*, no. 26 (26 June 2011): 3–5.

_____. *Supermarketyzacja. Religia i obyczaje seksualne młodzieży w kulturze konsumpcyjnej*. Wrocław: Wydawnictwo Uniwersytetu Wrocławskiego, 2004.

Szostak, Violeta. "Koledzy, którzy mnie krzyżują." Duży Format of *Gazeta Wyborcza*, 1 April 2010.

Szporer, Michael. "Managing Religion in Communist-Era Poland: Catholic Priests versus the Secret Police." *Journal of Cold War Studies* 12, 3 (2010): 115–20.

Sztompka, Piotr. "Trust and Emerging Democracy: Lessons from Poland." *International Sociology* 11, 1 (1996): 37–62.

Szymoszyn, Anna. *Bohater religijny w świętej przestrzeni. Kult św. Wojciecha na przełomie XX i XXI wieku*. Poznań: Wydawnictwo Poznańskie, 2010.

Tarka, Krzysztof. "Litwini." In *Mniejszości narodowe i etniczne w Polsce po II wojnie światowej*, edited by Stefan Dudra and Bernadette Nitsche, 148–63. Krakow: Nomos, 2010.

Taylor, Charles. *A Secular Age*. Cambridge, MA: Harvard University Press, 2007.

Tec, Nehama. *When Light Pierced the Darkness: Christian Rescue of Jews in Nazi-occupied Poland*. Oxford: Oxford University Press, 1986.

Terlikowski, Tomasz. *Grzechy Kościoła. Teraz w Polsce*. Warszawa: Delmart, 2010.

_____. "Kościół powolutku odzyskuje głos." Interview by Robert Mazurek. *Rzeczpospolita*, 1–2 October 2011, P10–11.

_____. *Odwaga prawdy. Spór o lustrację w polskim Kościele*. Warszawa: Prószyński I S-ka, 2007.

_____. *Rzeczpospolita papieska. Jan Paweł II o Polsce do Polaków*. Warszawa: Centrum Myśli Jana Pawła II, 2009.

_____. "Śmierć anglikanizmu." *Fronda*, no. 53 (2009): 129–43.

Teter, Magda. *Jews and Heretics in Catholic Poland: A Beleaguered Church in the Post-Reformation Era*. Cambridge, UK: Cambridge University Press, 2006.

Thomas, Adrian. *Górecki*, "Oxford Studies of Composers." Oxford: Clarendon Press, 1997.

Thomas, Scott M. "Outwitting the Developed Countries? Existential Insecurity and the Global Resurgence of Religion." *Journal of International Affairs* 61, 1 (2007): 21–45.

Tischner, Józef. *The Spirit of Solidarity*, translated by Marek Zaleski i B. Fiore. San Francisco: Harper & Row, 1984.

Toft, Monica Duffy, Daniel Philpott, and Timothy Samuel Shah. *God's Century: Resurgent Religion and Global Politics*. New York: Norton, 2011.

Tranda, Hanna, and Mirosław Patolon (eds.). *W drodze za Chrystusem. Kościoły chrześcijańskie mówią o sobie*. Kraków: WAM, 2009.

Tranda, Lech. "… nie ważne skąd przychodzisz, ważne co cię boli." In *Drogi chrześcijaństwa*, edited by Bohdan Sławiński, 121–26. Warszawa: Jacek Santorski, 2008.

Tych, Feliks. "Attempts to Rebuild Jewish Life in Post-War Poland." In *Memory: The History of Polish Jews Before, During, and After the Holocaust*, edited by Feliks Tych, 177–214. Warszawa: Shalom Foundation, 2008.

Tych, Feliks and Monika Adamczyk-Garbowska, editors. *Następstwa zagłady Żydów. Polska 1944–2010*. Lublin: Wydawnictwo Uniwersytetu Marii Curie-Skłodowskiej, 2011. Forthcoming in Englis: Feliks Tych an Monika Adamczuk-Garbowska, editors. *Jewish Presence in Absence: Aftermath of the Holocaust in Poland, 1945–2010*, translated by Gregorz Dąbkowski and Jessica Kucia. Jerusalem: Yad Vashem.

Vincenz, Stanisław. "The Bałaguła." Translated by H. C. Stevens. In *Stranger in Our Midst: Images of the Jew in Polish Literature*, edited by Harold B. Segel, 302–19. Ithaca, NY: Cornell University Press, 1996.

———. "Leśny Żyd." In Stanisław Vincenz, *Tematy żydowskie*, 105–12. London: Oficyna Poetów i Malarzy, 1977.

———. *Tematy żydowskie*. London: Oficyna Poetów i Malarzy, 1977.

———. "Wspomnienie o Żydach kołomyjskich." In Vincenz, *Tematy żydowskie*, 60–66.

———. *Zwada. Na wysokiej połoninie:* Pasmo 2, Księga Pierwsza. Warszawa: PAX, 1981.

Vischer, Robert K. *Conscience and the Common Good: Reclaiming the Space between Person and State.* Cambridge, UK: Cambridge University Press, 2010.

Walicki, Andrzej. "Traditions of Polish Nationalism in Comparative Perspective." *Dialogue and Universalism*, no. 4 (2001): 5–50.

Warmińska, Katarzyna. *Tatarzy Polscy. Tożsamość religijna i etniczna.* Kraków: Universitas, 1999.

Warner, R. Stephen. "The De-Europeanization of American Christianity." In *A Nation of Religions: The Politics of Pluralism in Multireligious America*, edited by Stephen Prothero, 233–55. Chapel Hill: University of North Carolina Press, 2006.

Wawrzyczek, Irmina, Zbigniew Mazur, and Hanna Szewczyk. *Oswajanie Innego. Obraz Polski i Polaków prasie brytyjskiej w latach 2002–2007.* Lublin: Gaudium, 2010.

Weeks, Theodore R. "Assimilation, Nationalism, Modernization, Antisemitism: Notes on Polish-Jewish Relations, 1855–1905." In *Antisemitism and Its Opponents in Modern Poland*, edited by Robert Blobaum. Ithaca, NY: Cornell University Press, 2005: 20–38.

Weigel, George. *The End and the Beginning: Pope John Paul II—the Victory of Freedom, the Last Years, the Legacy.* New York: Doubleday, 2010.

———. *The Final Revolution: The Resistance Church and the Collapse of Communism.* Oxford: Oxford University Press, 1992.

———. *Witness to Hope: The Biography of Pope John Paul II.* New York: HarperCollins, 2001.

Weiler, Joseph H. H. "A Christian Europe? Europe and Christianity: Rules of Commitment." *European View* 6 (2007): 143–50.

Wilcox, W. Bradford, and Carlos Cavallé. *The Sustainable Demographic Dividend.* Barcelona: Social Trends Institute, 2011.

Willaume, Jean Paul. "Different Models for Religious Education in Europe." In *Religion and Education in Europe: Developments, Contexts and Debates*, edited by Robert Jackson, Siebren Miedema, Wolfram Weisse and Jean Paul Willaume, 57–66. Munster: Waxmann Verlag, 2007.

Wineman, Aryeh. "Parables and *Tsimtsum*." *Prooftexts* 16, 3 (1996): 293–300.

Wiśniewska, Katarzyna. "Biskupi przeciwko umowom śmieciowym." *Gazeta Wyborcza*, 30 March 2012.

———. "Kobiety wychodzą z kościoła." *Gazeta Wyborcza*, 13–15 August 2011.

Witkowska, Aleksandra. "Uroczyste koronacje wizerunków maryjnych na ziemiach polskich w latach 1717–1992." In *Przestrzeń i sacrum. Geografia kultury religijnej w Polsce i jej przemiany w okresie od XVII do XX wieku na przykładzie ośrodków kultu i migracji pielgrzymkowych*, edited by A. Jackowski, Z Jabłoński, I. Sołjan, and E. Bilska, 87–103. Kraków: Instytut Geografii Uniwersytetu Jagiellońskiego, 1996.

Włoczyk, Piotr. "Masz talent." *Tygodnik Powszechny*, no. 11 (11 March 2012): 13–15.

Włodarczyk, Artur. "Ile mrówki jest w Polaku." *Gazeta Wyborcza*, 27 December 2010.

Wnuk-Lipinski, Edmund. "Vicissitudes of Ethical Civil Society in Central and Eastern Europe." *Studies in Christian Ethics* 20, 1 (2007): 30–43.

Wojciechowski, Piotr. "Czego zawdzięczam religijności ludowej." *Znak*, no. 3 (March 2008): 121–25.

Wojewoda, Zbigniew. *Zarys historii Kościoła greckokatolickiego w Polsce w latach 1944–1989.* Kraków: Nomos, 1994.

Wuthnow, Robert. "Civil Society: Changing from Tight to Loose Connections." In *Unfinished Work: Building Equality and Democracy in the Era of Working Families*, edited by Jody Heyman and Christopher Beem, 63–85. New York: New Press, 2005.

Wygański, Kuba, and Adam Puchejda. "Od zaufania do zaangażowania" (interview). *Znak*, no. 1 (2011): 23–35.

Wynot, Edward. "Poland's Christian Minorities 1919–1939." *Nationalities Papers* 13, 2 (1985): 209–46.

———. "Prisoner of History: The Eastern Orthodox Church in Poland in the Twentieth Century." *Journal of Church and State* 39, 2 (1997): 319–39.

Wyszyński, Cardinal Stefan. *A Freedom*

Within: The Prison Notes of Stefan, Cardinal Wyszyński. 2nd ed. Translated by Barbara Krzywicki-Herburt. Surrey, UK: Aid to the Church in Need, 1986.

Zając, Marek. "Archipelag rozsądku." *Tygodnik Powszechny*, no. 44 (30 October 2011): 4–5.

_____. "Rok zły." *Tygodnik Powszechny*, no. 45 (4 November 2012): 4.

Zamoyski, Adam. *Poland: A History.* London: Harper Press, 2009.

Zasada, Stanisław. *Generał w habicie. Opowieść o siostrze Małgorzacie Chmielewskiej i Wspólnocie Chleb i Życie.* Kraków: Znak, 2010.

Zdaniewicz, Witold, and Sławomir Zaręba (eds.). *Postawy społeczno-religijne mieszkańców Archidiecezji Szczecińsko-Kamieńskiej.* Szczecin: Ottonianum, 2006.

Zięba, Maciej. *Ale nam się wydarzyło. O papieżu i Polsce, Kościele i świecie.* Poznań: W drodze, 2013.

_____. "Kiedy rozum ociemniał." Interview by Marek Zając. *Tygodnik Powszechny* 11 (11 March 2012): 16–7.

_____. "Kościół między młotem a kowadłem." Interview by Zbigniew Nosowski. *Więź*, no. 10 (October 2012): 5–20.

Ziebertz, Hans-Georg, and Ulrich Riegel. "Post-secular Europe—a Concept Questioned." In *Europe: Secular or Post-Secular?* edited by Hans-Georg Ziebertz and Ulrich Riegel, 9–41. Berlin: LIT Verlag, 2009.

Zielińska, Anna. "Tatarzy—polscy muzulmanie." *Przegląd Powszechny*, no. 11 (November 2009): 63–72.

Zieliński, The Rev. Henryk. "Nobilitacja ksenofobii." *Idziemy* 43 (23 October 2011). http://www.idziemy.com.pl/komentarze/nobilitacja-ksenofobii (accessed 3 April 2012).

Zientara, Piotr. *New Europe's Old Regions.* London: Institute of Economic Affairs, 2009.

Zowczak, Magdalena. *Biblia ludowa. Interpretacje wątków biblijnych w kulturze ludowej.* Wrocław: Wydawnictwo FUNNA, 2000.

_____. "Między tradycja a komercją." *Znak*, no. 3 (March 2008): 31–44.

Zubrzycki, Genevieve. *The Crosses of Auschwitz: Nationalism and Religion in Post-Communist Poland.* Chicago: University of Chicago Press, 2006.

_____. "History and the National Sensorium: Making Sense of Polish Mythology." *Qualitative Sociology* 34 (2011): 21–57.

Żukowski, Tomasz. "Ale nam się wydarzyło, czyli przegląd cudów polskich." *Teologia Polityczna* 5 (2009/2010): 129–40.

"Życie religijne w getcie." In *Tam był kiedyś mój dom ... Księgi pamięci gmin żydowskich,* edited by Monika Adamczyk-Garbowska, Adam Kopciowski, and Andrzej Trzciński, 401–3. Lublin: Wydawnictwo Marii Curii-Skłodowskiej, 2009.

Index

293